Paradigms of Clinical Social Work

Volume 3

Emphasis on Diversity

Paradigms of Clinical Social Work

Volume 3

Emphasis on Diversity

Rachelle A. Dorfman · Phil Meyer · Melinda L. Morgan

Brunner-Routledge
Taylor & Francis Group

NEW YORK AND HOVE

Published in 2004 by
Brunner-Routledge
29 West 35th Street
New York, NY 10001
www.brunner-routledge.com

Published in Great Britain by
Brunner-Routledge
27 Church Road
Hove, East Sussex
BN3 2FA
www.brunner-routledge.co.uk

Copyright © 2004 by Taylor & Francis Books, Inc.

Brunner-Routledge is an imprint of the Taylor & Francis Group.
Printed in the United States of America on acid-free paper.

10 9 8 7 6 5 4 3 2 1

Library of Congress Cataloging-in-Publication Data

Paradigms of Clinical Social Work, Volume 3

     Bibliography: p.
     Includes index.
     1. Social case work. 2. Social case work - United States.
 I. Dorfman, Rachelle A. II. Title: Clinical social work.

HV43.P35   1988   361.3'2   88-2879
ISBN 0-415-94406-6 (hbk)

To Shawn Kaplan, who has an extraordinary ability to illuminate, amuse, and surprise with his writing

R.A.D.

To my family, Kenneth Robins, Lily, and Ruben; no man has been more blessed.

P.M.

To Samuel, for all your love and support.

M.L.M.

CONTENTS

FOREWORD

Nancy Boyd Webb, DSW

This book offers a fascinating and informative presentation of 11 different models of clinical social work practice. The philosophy, rationale, and special emphasis of each model come alive in the manner in which each approach undertakes clinical work with the same family case. In this book, we see different viewpoints about assessment and about the focus and the process of treatment. Because there are multiple ways to understand and work with any case, practitioners trained in one specific model may guide the case according to their training and concepts about the appropriate nature of therapeutic work.

The use of the Shore family case as a major recurring theme in each chapter demonstrates to the reader that there are many different ways to Rome. Some approaches emphasize work with the marital dyad, others with the parent–child relationship, and still others with the family as a unit, with all taking their rationale from the principles of their models. One wonders which approach the family would have preferred, and to what extent these seemingly substantive differences matter. All the models emphasize respect for the clients and an understanding of the reciprocal influence of persons and their environments. After all, a systems perspective maintains that a change in any one person will affect others in the family group, and the literature has confirmed that the practitioner's own belief in the efficacy of his or her approach is the essential factor that contributes to therapeutic change in clients.

Appropriate as a text in advanced clinical practice courses, this book combines a three-pronged focus: (a) the 11 models of practice, (b) the in-depth case discussions, and (c) an emphasis on diversity. The contributors follow a similar chapter outline that includes a section about issues on diversity, as these are reflected in their helping perspective and with respect to specific aspects of the case. Although the case involves a Caucasian family, the Shores, many authors chose to hypothetically alter the ethnicity of the family in order to discuss the situation had the family been Russian, African American, Japanese American, Mexican American, or Chinese. This device allows, for example, a discussion of the pressures of immigrant families that must simultaneously deal with adaptation to a new sociocultural environment at the same time they are struggling with personal and family problems. One author chose to discuss diversity in terms of gender and role expectations in this Caucasian family.

Regardless of the model of practice, it is imperative that the therapist thoughtfully examine his or her own cultural biases and beliefs about gender role expectations, child rearing, and appropriate help-seeking behavior. These culturally grounded beliefs inevitably pervade the therapeutic process and apply to the therapist, as well as to the client. It is ironic that many people from non-European cultures consider it shameful to require assistance from a mental health professional, and the practitioner who does not recognize or share these beliefs may misread the client's hesitation as "resistance."

The social work profession is committed to helping people from increasingly diverse backgrounds, and the growing literature provides guidance about culturally competent practice (Fong, in press; Lum, 1999; Webb, 2001). This book makes an important contribution to our understanding of applying concepts about diversity in clinical work with families.

REFERENCES

Fong, R. (Ed.). (in press). *Culturally competent practice with immigrant and refugee children and families.* New York: Guilford Press.

Lum, D. (1999). *Culturally competent practice. A framework for growth and action.* Pacific Grove, CA: Sage.

Webb, N. B. (Ed.). (2001). *Culturally diverse parent–child and family relationships. A guide for social workers and other practitioners.* New York: Columbia University Press.

ACKNOWLEDGMENTS

I am deeply grateful to my co-editors, who performed their editing tasks exquisitely. In the process of editing this book, the three of us learned about each other's shortcomings and strengths—and are better friends and colleagues for it. Thanks also to the many contributors who survived our constant deadlines and changes. Emily Epstein-Loeb, an editor at Brunner-Routledge, deserves special recognition. Her support for the "emphasis on diversity" was immediate and enthusiastic. The Shore family has been the centerpiece in all three volumes of *Paradigms of Clinical Social Work*. I remain indebted to the family members for allowing us a window into their lives. Finally, my heartfelt appreciation goes to my husband, Jay. What can you say about a partner whose greatest joy is seeing you happy?

R. A. D.

Many thanks to our students who, when we are humble enough to ask them, tell us exactly what they need to succeed in the work we all do. Thanks to Rocky for, once again, nudging me into the unknown and making sure I have provisions for the journey—and to Melinda for holding hands along the way. I am especially grateful to members of my family who put up with the smell of midnight oil and the oft-times haggard sight of a sleep-deprived parent.

P. M.

My heartfelt thanks go to the authors who graciously contributed to the book, without whom there would be no book. I would also like to thank the students and the clients who have educated me and enriched my life. I thank my colleagues, who have lent me their guidance. Finally, I would like to express my deepest appreciation for my children, who keep me centered and sane!

M.L.M.

ABOUT THE EDITORS

Rachelle A. Dorfman, PhD, is a Professor Emeritus of Social Welfare at the UCLA Department of Social Welfare and a licensed clinical social worker. She was a visiting professor at the University of Hong Kong and a 1998 recipient of a Fulbright Scholar award to teach gerontology at the National Kaohsiung Normal University in Taiwan. She is the editor of *Paradigms of Clinical Social Work* (Volumes 1 and 2), and author of *Aging Into the 21st Century: The Exploration of Aspirations and Values,* and *Clinical Social Work: Definition, Practice and Vision* and is widely published in professional journals. She received her MSW from Bryn Mawr School of Social Work and her PhD from Temple University.

Phil Meyer, MSW, is a lecturer in the Department of Social Welfare at the University of California, Los Angeles. He serves as a consultant and a supervisor for SPECTRUM Community Services and Research at Charles R. Drew University and the Maternal, Child, and Adolescent Clinic at the University of Southern California, both programs that specialize in treating people living with HIV/AIDS. He is the consumer liaison for the HIV/AIDS Treatment Adherence, Health Outcomes, and Cost Study and has several articles in press about the importance of consumer representation in multi-site HIV, mental health, and substance abuse research. A parent, a poet, and a sometime opera singer, he also maintains an active private practice in Los Angeles.

Melinda L. Morgan, PhD, is an assistant professor of psychiatry and biobehavior sciences at the UCLA Neuropsychiatric Institute and Hospital at the David Geffen School of Medicine, UCLA. She is also a licensed clinical social worker and teaches in the Department of Social Welfare at the UCLA School of Public Policy and Social Research. Dr. Morgan is the principle investigator for a research project on estrogen augmentation in perimenopausal depression and a co-investigator on the research team investigating placebo effects at UCLA. She has been honored as an NCDEU New Investigator and received the NARSAD Young Investigator Award to support her research on estrogen, women, and depression. She is a certified cognitive behavioral therapist with the NIMH multi-site project on treatment-resistant depression. She has spoken nationally and has published research on premenstrual dysphoric disorder, affective disorder in women over the life span, and brain function in depression.

ABOUT THE CONTRIBUTORS

Joseph Anderson, PhD, is a professor and a past director of the Division of Social Work, California State University, Sacramento. He was the MSW program director at Norfolk State University, a visiting professor at National University of Singapore, and the chair of the Department of Social Work, Shippensburg University of Pennsylvania. He is a past member of the CWSE Commission on Accreditation and a past chair of the CSWE Commission on Educational Policy. He was in private practice in Pennsylvania and Virginia and was the clinical director of the Youth Development Center in Loysville, Pennsylvania. His publications include *Diversity Perspectives for Social Work Practice, Social Work With Groups, Social Work Methods and Processes,* and numerous journal articles and book chapters.

Nancy Boyd Webb, DSW, is a distinguished professor of social work and the James R. Dumpson Chair in Child Welfare Studies at Fordham University Graduate School of Social Service, where she has been a faculty member since 1979. Her works include *Play Therapy With Children in Crisis: Individual, Family and Group Treatment; Helping Bereaved Children: A Handbook for Practitioners; Social Work Practice With Children;* and *Culturally Diverse Parent–Child and Family Relationships.* In addition, she has published widely in professional journals and produced a video, *Techniques of Play Therapy.* She is the editor of a book series for Guilford Press on the topic of social work practice with children. In 1985 she founded the post-master's certificate program in child and adolescent therapy at Fordham to meet the need for specialized training with children and families. She consults with agencies and schools around issues of trauma and bereavement and is a frequent keynote speaker at professional conferences and meetings in the United States and abroad. Dr. Webb is a board-certified diplomat in clinical social work and a registered play therapy supervisor with the International Association for Play Therapy.

Elaine P. Congress, DSW, is an associate dean and a professor at Fordham University Graduate School of Social Service in New York City, where she also has served as the director of the doctoral program. Dr. Congress has written extensively in the areas of cultural diversity, social work ethics, social work education, and crisis intervention, including 3 books and over 30 professional journal articles and book chapters. Her book *Multicultural Perspectives in Working With Families* examines assessment, life cycle, and practice issues from a cultural perspective. She developed the *culturagram,* a family assessment tool for assessing and working with culturally diverse families, which was first featured in the November 1994 issue of *Families in Society* and revised in 2000 for *Advances in Social Work.* Another book, *Social Work Values and Ethics: Identifying and Resolving Professional Dilemmas,* presents the ETHIC model of decision making for addressing ethical dilemmas in social work practice.

Ian A. Cook, MD, is associate professor of psychiatry and biobehavioral sciences at the Neuropsychiatric Institute and Hospital at the David Geffen School of Medicine, UCLA. He is a co-investigator of the research team at UCLA investigating the effects of placebo. Dr. Cook is the founding director of the UCLA NPI Academic Information Technology Core. He was honored as an NCDEU New Investigator and received two NARSAD Young Investigator Awards to support his research in depression and neurophysiology. He currently is the recipient of a Career Development Award from the NIMH to study etiologic factors leading to the side effects of psychoactive medications. He has spoken internationally and has published peer-reviewed research on depression and brain function. Dr. Cook is a board-certified psychiatrist, and he is also an examiner for the American Board of Psychiatry and Neurology.

Daniel J. Fischer, MSW, is a clinical assistant professor and an associate director of the Pediatric OCD Program at the University of Michigan, Department of Psychiatry, Child/Adolescent Division. He is also a social work manager and a director of graduate education at the University of Michigan Health Systems Department of Social Work and an adjunct lecturer at the University of Michigan School of Social Work. He completed his MSW at the University of Michigan in 1984. Mr. Fischer is an active clinician, teacher, and researcher in the area of anxiety disorders and cognitive-behavioral therapies.

Kevin J. Fitzsimmons, MSW, is an adjunct professor in the Psychology Department at Antioch University, Los Angeles, and a lecturer in the Graduate Department of Social Work at the University of California, Los Angeles. He is a member of the family therapy faculty at the Southern California Counseling Center. He is currently training clinicians with the Los Angeles County Department of Mental Health in the practices of postmodern psychotherapies. After 20 years of community mental health agency service, he is now in private practice in Los Angeles.

Charles Garvin, PhD, is Professor Emeritus of Social Work at the University of Michigan School of Social Work. He is the author of *Contemporary Group Work* and a coauthor of *Interpersonal Practice in Social Work, Social Work in Contemporary Society,* and *Generalist Practice in Social Work: A Task Centered Approach.* He is co-editor of *The Handbook of Direct Practice in Social Work.* He has written many articles and book chapters on group work, clinical practice, treatment of persons with serious mental illness, treatment of persons in correctional programs, and research in social work. He is a past chair of the Group for the Advancement of Doctoral Education in Social Work (GADE) and the Association for the Advancement of Social Work with Groups (AASWG).

Joseph A. Himle, PhD, is a clinical assistant professor and the director of education, Ambulatory Psychiatry, at the University of Michigan, Department of Psychiatry. He is also the associate director of the University of Michigan Anxiety Disorders Program and an adjunct assistant professor at the University of Michigan School of Social Work. He completed his doctorate in social work and psychology at the University of Michigan in August of 1995. Dr. Himle is an active clinician, a teacher, and a researcher in the area of anxiety disorders and cognitive-behavioral therapies.

Carolyn Jacobs, PhD, is the dean and an Elizabeth Marting Treuhaft Professor at Smith College School for Social Work. She has taught primarily within the research and practice sequences of the Smith College School for Social Work. Her areas of professional interest include religion and spirituality in social work practice, social work research, and statistics. She has written and presented extensively on the topic of spirituality in social work. She is the co-editor of *Ethnicity and Race: Critical Concepts in Social Work.* She is a spiritual director trained at the Shalem Institute for Spiritual Formation. Dr. Jacobs was also elected as a distinguished practitioner in the National Academies of Practice in Social Work in 2001.

Marshall Jung, DSW, is a Professor Emeritus of Social Work, California State University, San Bernardino and a nationally recognized expert in marital and family therapy. He has provided workshops for child welfare and mental health organizations, social and family services agencies, residential treatment facilities, and medical hospitals throughout the United States and in Canada and Hong Kong. He has also presented at many state and national conferences, including the NASW National Conference, the American Association of Marital and Family Therapists, and the National Association of Group Work Annual Conference. Dr. Jung has published in major professional journals, including *Social Work, Families in Contemporary Society,* and *Family Process.* Dr. Jung has coauthored one self-help book and authored two professional ones, the last of which is titled *Chinese American Family Therapy.* He is the father of two children and the grandfather of three. Dr. Jung currently lives with his wife, Rosie, at his retreat and training center in Lake Arrowhead, California.

Jordana R. Muroff, MSW, is a doctoral candidate in the joint doctoral program in social work and psychology at the University of Michigan. She completed her MSW in 1999. She is also a clinical and research fellow at the University of Michigan Department of Psychiatry, Child/Adolescent Outpatient Division, and the Adult Anxiety Disorders Program.

Tammie Ronen, PhD, is a professor at the Bob Shapell School of Social Work, Tel-Aviv University, Israel. She serves as the director of the Child Clinical Program in Graduate Studies and the director of the Research Clinic for Aggressive Children. Dr. Ronen is the author of many papers and books in the area of child therapy and self-control training.

Marga Speicher, PhD, is a Jungian psychotherapist and psychoanalyst in private practice in San Antonio, Texas. She serves as a senior training analyst in the psychoanalytic training program of Inter-Regional Society of Jungian Analysts. She is a clinical associate professor in the Department of Psychiatry, University of Texas Health Sciences Center, San Antonio. Dr. Speicher's professional interests include multitheoretical and multidisciplinary discussion and teaching in psychotherapy, presentation of lectures and workshops on psychological understanding to the general public, and psychological exploration of images in the arts, especially literature and folklore. Her writing has appeared in the *Clinical Social Work Journal* and other publications; her explorations of images in folklore have appeared on audiotape.

Daniel S. Sweeney, PhD, is an associate professor and a clinical director in the Graduate Department of Counseling at George Fox University in Portland, Oregon. He is also the director of the Northwest Center for Play Therapy Studies at GFU and a registered play therapist-supervisor. He has presented at numerous national and international conferences on the topics of play therapy, filial therapy, and sandtray therapy. He has published articles and book chapters on child counseling, play therapy issues, families and parenting, and is an author or a coauthor of several books, including *Play Therapy Interventions With Children's Problems*, *Counseling Children Through the World of Play*, *Sandtray Therapy: A Practical Manual*, and *Handbook of Group Play Therapy*. His books have been translated into Russian, French, and Mandarin.

Marlene F. Watson, PhD, is an associate professor and the director of Graduate Programs in Couple and Family Therapy at Drexel University in Philadelphia. She is also a licensed marriage and family therapist. Dr. Watson is a chair elect on the Commission on Accreditation for Marriage and Family Therapy Education (COAMFTE) and on the editorial review board for the *Journal of Marital and Family Therapy*. She lectures nationally on issues of race, ethnicity, gender, and class. She devotes much of her professional energy to establishing new and innovative therapies. For example, she partnered with the city of

Philadelphia's Coordinating Office for Drug and Alcohol Abuse Programs to provide family therapy services to substance-dependent clients, both behind prison walls and in the community. This work was recognized in the *Utne Reader,* which named her as one of the 10 most innovative therapists in the nation.

Robin Wiggins-Carter, DPA, is the director of the Division of Social Work at California State University, Sacramento, where she has been a faculty member for 12 years. She teaches social work practice and diversity courses. She has published in the area of social work with the African American family and has particular interests in the Afrocentric paradigm, health-care social work, clinical supervision, and gerontological social work. She recently co-edited (with Joseph Anderson) *Diversity Perspectives in Social Work Practice.* She has also contributed several chapters to other edited books. She received her DPA and MPA from the University of Southern California.

Larry M. Zucker, MSW, is an adjunct professor in the Psychology Department at Antioch University, Los Angeles. He is a member of the family therapy faculty at the Southern California Counseling Center. He is a consultant and a supervisor for Clean Slate, Inc., a community-based gang-recovery and tattoo-removal program in Los Angeles. He is also in private practice.

INTRODUCTION

*I*n two previous volumes of *Paradigms of Clinical Social Work*, I invited 32 clinicians and academics to present 25 therapeutic paradigms. All contributors elucidated specific concepts and treatment methods associated with their models by drawing on examples from the in-depth case study of the Shore family found in chapter 1. This simple device, warmly received by students and social work educators, is used again in volume 3 of *Paradigms of Clinical Social Work: Emphasis on Diversity*.

Chapter 2, "Diversity Perspectives for Social Work Practice," launches the book by summarizing the multiple approaches that have evolved within the profession to provide principles and concepts for competence in diversity practice. Chapters 3 through 13 follow a framework similar to the one used in the first two volumes, with the addition of a section called "Application to Diversity," which describes how each model may be applied to a diverse population. The framework for these chapters is reproduced as follows:

- Introduction
- The Concept of the Person and the Human Experience (the underlying philosophical position of the paradigm regarding its view of the person and the human experience)
- Historical Perspective (overview of the origins and the development of the paradigm)
- Key Theoretical Constructs (the explanation of problems, symptoms, and disease and the theory of change identified with this approach)
- Assessment
- The Therapeutic Process (techniques and methods, course of treatment, and therapist–client relationship)
- Application to Diversity (the application of the model to a Shore family that is racially, culturally, or ethnically diverse, with a focus on how treatment may need to be adapted to meet the family's diversity status)
- Limitations of the Model (major problems and issues, failures, underdeveloped areas)

- Research
- Summary
- References

The "Application to Diversity" section arose out of the struggle of the editors (now we are three) to find a way to answer the question, "Are these models relevant for diverse populations?" or, as our students put it, "How do I apply this to the people I work with?" In this book, we present 11 ways that experienced clinicians and educators have grappled with that question. However, the 11 different paradigms in this volume do not hold the definitive answer to the question because at this moment there is no such thing. Rather, they are presented as examples of how clinicians must continually and thoughtfully strive to "start where the client is"—including their client's race, culture, ethnicity, and sexual orientation. The reader is urged to think critically about these paradigms and to develop his or her own approach to working with diversity.

Our efforts faced no shortage of stumbling blocks. First, it was impossible to include all types of diversity in a single volume. Second, we recognized that there are minor and major variations, even within the diverse groups that are presented. For example, not all African Americans share the same socioeconomic status and not all Hispanic groups share similar healing practices. We took great pains to avoid furthering stereotypical characteristics, yet at the same time acknowledged commonalities among specific groups.

We selected paradigms that are often associated with clinical social work, that clinical social workers are interested in, and that support (each in its own way) the person-in-situation principle that is at the core of social work practice. We stretched the meaning of a clinical social work paradigm to include Chapter 12 on psychopharmacology, but we believe it is a stretch that will be forgiven. Although social workers do not prescribe medications, social work practitioners are increasingly employed in medical and psychiatric inpatient and outpatient settings in which clients take psychopharmacological drugs intermittently, regularly, or on a one-time basis. Thus it behooves us to learn about these substances and their role in clinical social work. Chapter 13 focuses on "Spiritually Centered Therapy," a model that is less developed than the other models and may be considered more of a metaparadigm than a well-defined paradigm with specific techniques. Nevertheless, it is gaining popularity, and clinical social workers are intrigued by its potential for helping clients live a more balanced life. Finally, we realized that volumes 1 and 2 paid short shrift to paradigms that focus on children. Therefore, we included three child-oriented chapters, Chapter 4 on cognitive-behavioral therapy for children, Chapter 5 on behavioral child therapy, and Chapter 6 on play therapy. We also decided to emphasize couple and family work in Chapter 9 on constructual marital therapy and Chapter 10 on integrative family therapy.

It is 15 years since we first met the Shore family—Nancy, Charley, Rena, and Michael. They have come a long way since the original case study was written. We have included follow-up reports on the family at 1 year, 10 years, and 15 years. These follow-ups, in the form of epilogues, provide real-life drama to the text; they teach us about the limits and the strengths of social work intervention, and together they remind us that (should we forget) we do not have all the answers.

Rachelle A. Dorfman, PhD

Part I

The Case

1

The Case

❧

Rachelle A. Dorfman, PhD

THE FAMILY

The problems of the Shore family are common ones. Among them are unemployment, illness, and the worrisome behavior of the children. What is uncommon is that the problems never get resolved. Although the family members frequently seek help and are the recipients of various social services, they never seem to function free from symptoms. Individually and collectively, their lives are marked by crisis and emotional distress.

Nancy is 43; her husband, Charley, is 51. The children are Rena, 18, who was adopted as a baby, and Michael, 12. Until recently, the entire family lived in the two-unit duplex they own. Nancy, Charley, and Michael still live in the second-floor apartment. Rena, who occupied the first-floor apartment by herself since she was 13, has moved out; she lives nearby and is "on her own." Charley has been chronically unemployed for 4 years; the family survives largely on the disability checks Nancy has received every month for the last 10 years.

Nancy is a large woman. She calls herself "grossly obese" and makes frequent apologies about her appearance. Her hair is graying and her figure is decidedly matronly, but her flawless skin and the gap between her front teeth give her a youthful quality. The only reservation she has about being interviewed is that "After it's done, I will probably run from social worker to social worker trying to do everything suggested."

For most of her 23-year marriage to Charley, "trying to get everything fixed" has been her full-time job. She is at her best during family crises. "Then," she says, "I take control. I no longer dread the terrible things that might happen because they have already happened. It is the waiting for the crisis to

3

occur that makes me worry." Her anxiety often turns into panic. She becomes nearly immobilized. Unable to leave the house, she chain-smokes and imagines the worst of all possible outcomes. Anxiety attacks occur daily.

There is no shortage of crises. Recurring flare-ups of a back injury that Nancy suffered as a young nurse incapacitate her without warning, confining her to bed for weeks or months. The flare-ups are not the only crises. Three times, doctors predicted that Michael, asthmatic since early infancy, would not survive until morning. Twice Rena ran away from home and was missing for several days.

The small apartment reverberates with the sounds of their crises. One typical scenario began with an argument. Rena, then 16, lunged forward to hit her mother. Charley, in frustration and fury, pulled Rena away from Nancy and beat her, bruising her face badly. It was on that evening, 2 years ago, that Nancy and Charley told Rena she would have to leave when she turned 18.

A new problem with a potential for crisis is emerging. The downstairs apartment—which is now vacant—has never before been occupied by strangers. (Before Rena, Nancy's elderly grandparents lived there.) Because they need the money, Nancy and Charley have decided to rent it to a young couple. Nancy is anxious about being a landlord. She is trying to train Charley and Michael to keep their voices down and their steps light. She wishes that her family lived downstairs and the tenants lived upstairs and says, "I'd rather they walk on me than we walk on them." Again, she fears the crises that are certain to erupt.

Rena has been in her own apartment a few blocks away for 3 months. Nancy worries about that, too. She feels that as an adopted child, Rena is especially sensitive to being "put out." Nonetheless, she still argues with Rena about her "laziness" and failure to finish anything, but there is less explosiveness now that she is on her own.

Despite some relief in the tension at home since Rena left, Nancy is still anxious and often depressed. She has gained 15 pounds, sleeps poorly, cannot concentrate, and is forgetful. Most of the time, she stays inside. Outside, she feels that people make disparaging remarks about her; only at home does she feel safe. Her days are filled with baseball games on TV, soap operas, needlepoint, and worrying about what will happen next.

Charley is blond, tall, and broad-shouldered. It is not difficult to imagine that he was once quite an appealing young man. When he was 27, his dreams and schemes interested and excited Nancy. Occasionally, he still talks of outlandish inventions and "get rich quick" schemes. The difference is that his wife no longer believes in him or his dreams. To her, they are annoying at best and embarrassing at worst.

Charley says, "All I ever wanted was to be somebody. I just want to be known for something, to have someone walk by my house and say, 'That's Mr. Shore's house.'" He boasts about the time he went to California "to become a movie star" and of all the rich and famous people he knew and still knows. He speaks wistfully of "just missed" opportunities for stardom and of inventions that no one took seriously. He likes being interviewed, saying, "It's exciting."

Nancy reminds him that the interview is for a clinical book, not a Broadway play.

Five years ago, Charley performed on amateur night at a downtown comedy club. Nearly every Thursday night since then, he has performed for free in front of a live audience, using the name Joe Penn. His pride is unbounded when he is recognized in public as Joe Penn. Occasionally, someone will even ask for his autograph.

His wife supports this activity because it makes him happy, but her perspective on his act is somewhat different from Charley's. The show embarrasses her. She says that although it is true that the audience laughs, they laugh at Charley, not at his jokes. "He is not funny," she maintains. Charley's defense is that probably the wife of Nancy's favorite comedian doesn't think her husband is funny, either.

Over the years, Charley has had scores of jobs. He was a salesman, a janitor, a self-employed carpet cleaner. Even though he lost jobs regularly, until 4 years ago he never had a problem getting a new one. Several times in the last 3 months, Charley has mentioned suicide, always in response to a suggestion that he, like Nancy, should get on disability because of his "condition." Charley says that he would rather die first. Although he seems serious about this statement, he has no plan or means in mind.

The condition is the bipolar depression that was diagnosed 2 years ago at the time of his first and only psychotic break and consequent 4-week hospitalization. "I always got depressed," he recalls, "but that was different. That time I really went off." Remembering his grandiosity and manic behavior, he says, "I guess you do those things when you are sick." He is maintained on lithium.

A "firing" precipitated his break. He had completed an expensive cooking course and was determined to prove he could "make it" in his first cooking job. He says he hit the chef when he could no longer tolerate the man's calling him names. (His bosses have complained that Charley is too slow and talks too much.)

Since his illness, he has had fewer grand ideas—he just wants a job he can hold. When he does allow himself to dream, mostly he dreams the way he did when he was a child, quietly and by himself. He likes to daydream while he works, which affects his performance. He was fired from his last janitorial job for forgetting to lock all the doors and for not cleaning thoroughly.

Presently, Charley attends a vocational rehabilitation program, where he receives minimum wages for training in janitorial services—a job he says he already knows how to do. The program's goals are to develop the work skills and interpersonal skills needed for employment and to place him successfully in a job. Nancy is pessimistic about the outcome. She is angry because no one will tell her the results of his psychological testing. She says that if she knew for certain that Charley wasn't capable of holding a job, perhaps she wouldn't be so angry with him.

About Nancy, Charley says, "She is the best wife in the world, the same as my mother." She even worries like his mother, he says, "but I don't always like that because I don't feel like a man." The duplex they own was given to them by Nancy's Aunt Flo. Although Charley appreciates the generosity, he says, "I wanted to do that. I wanted to buy the house."

Nancy agrees that she is parental. She prefers to handle important matters herself, not trusting Charley's competence with dollars, documents, or decisions. She complains that when she sends Charley to the store for two items, he invariably comes home with one of them wrong. But most of all, she complains about not having enough money to pay the bills. "I worry and he doesn't give a damn." Charley says privately, "I worry, too, but I act like I don't because there is nothing I can do."

The couple frequently fight about Charley's compulsive lying. He tells Nancy what he believes she wants to hear, claiming he doesn't want to upset her with the truth. He says he would like to stop, but he doesn't seem able to.

Charley usually stiffens as soon as he approaches the front door of his house. "Will there be a problem? Will Nancy complain about bills? Will Michael come home from school beaten up? They will want me to solve the problems. But I can't."

Being a father has been especially difficult. Charley and his son bicker and fight like small boys. Nancy finds herself storming in, breaking them up, and scolding them both. She says that each one fights for her attention, trying to outdo the other.

Because father and son tend to relate to each other like siblings, therapists who worked with the family in the past attempted to restructure the relationship by suggesting that Charley teach Michael how to fish and play miniature golf. Charley and Michael always returned home from such outings angrily blaming each other for ruining the day. Nancy says, "The whole time they are out, I am in a knot worrying that they are going to come up the steps screaming. I am never disappointed." She wants Charley to act more like a father. Charley wants that, too. But, he says, "Sometimes you just don't think about what you're doing when you do it."

Twelve-year-old Michael is tall and gangly. When he speaks, one can hear the phlegm rattle in his chest. It seems as though his voice is echoing through the mucus. His habitually knitted brow and his glasses make Michael appear very intense. He talks about "feeling funny" and "feeling bad." He feels bad because "asthma has taken away part of my life." His theory is that God gives everyone something he or she is terrific at. He says, "I haven't found mine yet—the asthma keeps me from it. I can't be a great athlete because I can't run fast. I can't have a puppy because I would wheeze. I just want to be good at something." According to his theory, God also puts a scar on everyone. People have to overcome their scars before they can find their special thing. Michael says asthma is his scar and he is waiting to outgrow it so that he can "find himself."

In the meantime, he is unhappy and lonely. Attempts to make friends are unsuccessful. He feels that even when he tries to behave himself, it is useless because his reputation prevents the other kids from relating to him in a new way. They still tease and pick on him. If someone hits him, he neither hits back nor runs away. He just "stays."

When he is not being "silly," he is more successful in relating to adults. Always attuned to the news, he usually knows what is current in world events, politics, and business. He sympathizes with underdogs and people who are victims and talks about becoming a psychologist so that he can help them. He is fiercely patriotic and always truthful. When asked why he tells the truth when a lie would avoid trouble, he says, "I am a Boy Scout; I cannot tell a lie."

Scouting is the highlight of his life, but there is trouble there, too. Camping trips require a level of coordination, self-control, and social skills that he doesn't have. He gets reprimanded when he puts his tent up wrong or ties his neckerchief incorrectly. When this happens, he says, the other scouts laugh and he feels like a fool.

In junior high, Michael is in a learning disability class. Although learning disabilities and special classes are part of his history, the current placement was not made because of them; tests show that he has overcome or outgrown any learning disability he had. The problem that still lingers and prevents him from being "mainstreamed" is his poor social judgment. The same behaviors he calls "silly," his teachers have called "bizarre." These include touching others, making strange noises and motions, and laughing too loud or at the wrong time.

Last summer, Michael went to overnight camp. This spring, his parents received a disturbing letter from the camp. Michael was not invited back. The reason given was more than the typical foul language and mischief of 12-year-old boys. Counselors complained that at mealtimes he played with the utensils and the plates, poured things into the pitchers and the bowls, and threw food. He did not get along with the other campers and was seen as the instigator of most of the problems that occurred that summer. The staff felt that when he wanted to behave, he could, and that he willfully chose to misbehave.

Michael reports the situation differently. One moment he says that he acts "silly" because he falls under the influence of others. A moment later he suggests that he acts that way so that others will like him. Still later he says, "I don't really want to act like that. It's really kind of stupid. I don't know why I do it."

Michael is ambivalent about his sister's leaving. He agrees that it is more peaceful at home, but now his parents are fussing about him more than ever. Nancy estimates that she spends "80% of her worrying time" agonizing about what will become of Michael.

Rena, four blocks away in a basement efficiency apartment, has agonies of another sort. She is attractive, intelligent, and talented. Everyone, including Rena, always expected that she would be successful. But in the last few years, no matter how promising her beginnings, she eventually either quit or failed at everything she started.

With 31 cents in her purse and no job, she is overdrawn at the bank and can't pay her bills. She has taken loans to pay for college courses she never completed. Rena feels old and tired.

Her parents used to call it laziness when she refused to go to school and stayed in bed until midafternoon. They thought she was lazy when she dropped out of high school, got a GED, and enrolled in pre-med—only to drop out of that. They believed that if they allowed her to remain at home, she would "vegetate" and do nothing at all.

Nancy pressures Rena to "go to therapy" because she has come to believe that there must be something more seriously wrong with Rena than "laziness." Rena has agreed to go for therapy, partly because one usually does what Nancy wants. "Mother," she explains, "has a way of making you feel so bad and guilty, you finally either do what she wants or are mad because she makes you feel so bad." Rena has also agreed to go because she is lonely and confused. Unfortunately, there is a waiting list for outpatient services at the community mental health clinic—and Rena's name is at the bottom of that list.

Nevertheless, it seems that the therapeutic process has already begun. Rena writes her thoughts in her journal every day and spends hours wondering about why she is the way she is. She is happy to be interviewed because she says she needs to talk about "this stuff."

She remembers when she didn't want to talk about "this stuff" or even think about it. At 16, when the adoption agency—at her request—sent some information about her birth mother, she forced herself to not think about it. Now she intends to find out about herself, even if it means thinking about painful things.

Like Michael, Rena has some theories. The first one is that she is so accustomed to living with problems and crises that she must create them when they do not exist. "Just look at my life. It is the only way I know how to live. When things are going well, I can't stand it."

As proof, she describes her brief college experience. Her attendance was excellent; the work was easy for her. Then she met a boy. Not long after that, she dropped out—blaming it on him. She claims she merely needed an excuse to "mess up," and he was a convenient one.

She calls her second theory "the adoption." Even if her adoption explanation is a "cop out," she feels that it gives her a starting point from which to consider her life. She notes that she has patterned her life in much the same way that her birth mother did. Her birth mother didn't get along with her own parents and was a high school dropout. Like Rena, she picked boyfriends who seemed worse off than herself.

Rejection is another thing Rena thinks about. "I push people so much with my demands that they eventually drop me like a hot potato. Then I can say, 'See what they did to me. They left me out in the cold.'" Sometimes generous to a fault, but more often selfish and demanding, she offers her relationship with her adoptive parents as proof of how she forces her own abandonment.

The most recent project Rena has started is the search for her birth mother. "I want to know her—see what she looks like, talk to her. I would like to sing for my mother." Rena wonders about her birth mother's approval. "She didn't like me before. Will she like me now?"

An attorney is helping Rena through the morass of conflicting state and agency policies that keeps her from finding her birth mother. Meanwhile, she attends meetings of adoptees, birth mothers, and adoptive mothers, at which members share information and discuss feelings. Rena is usually found in the hallway asking questions of birth mothers. She asks, "Do you ever think of your kid? How could you do it? Didn't you care?"

FAMILY HISTORY

Nancy

Cute and precocious, Nancy was the cherished only child, only grandchild, and only niece of doting adults. She remembers those early years, the years before age 11, as golden. Although her mother, an exceptionally beautiful and somewhat self-centered woman, was often away socializing with a large circle of friends, there were always Aunt Flo and Gram to shower her with attention, affection, and gifts.

Little Nan was seldom childish, so the adults took her with them to the theater, the ballet, and fancy restaurants. Her manners were beyond reproach. To the delight of the grown-ups, she always cleaned her plate. She remembers, "They thought it was so cute because I ate everything and, at that age, never got fat."

Her earliest memory is of when she was 5. "I remember going to a store and getting a fried egg sandwich. I had to go a different way because I wasn't allowed to cross streets. Nobody was with me. A dog chased me home and tried to take my sandwich. I remember the smell of the sandwich and the dog chasing me. I was worried more about the dog biting my sandwich than biting me! That must have been the first clue to what food was going to be in my life."

Another memory is from the same period: "My father was a waiter. It was a big deal waiting for him to come home at night. He would bring food from the restaurant and we would all be together to eat it."

Her father was a shadowy figure. Between his job and his gambling, he was rarely home. Still, she felt closer to him than to her mother. One night, when she was 11, her parents told her that her father was leaving. It was difficult to understand—her parents never argued. Years later, she learned that the leaving was precipitated by gambling debts to "the mob." Her mother was either unable or unwilling to go.

Although Aunt Flo and Gram still bought her beautiful clothes and knit her angora sweaters, the golden years were over. Mother had to work now, so she was away more than ever—which seemed "just fine" with Mother. Nancy is convinced that her mother never wanted her, a fact that her mother denies. They moved several times in the next few years; Nancy remembers each place in great detail.

The first two summers after the marriage broke up, Nancy's father drove a thousand miles to get her and take her back with him for a visit. Her most vivid memory is from the second visit, when she was 12. She wanted to buy something at the pool, so she went to the hotel room to ask her father for money. "My father was lying in bed undressed and his 'wife-to-be' was ironing, with nothing on from the waist up. That is when I realized he was sleeping with her. Before then, I didn't know anything about that."

After that summer, her father stopped coming for her and stopped calling. He remarried and had more children, but Nancy did not find that out until later. She remembers wondering why he didn't love her. She confided only to Aunt Flo's dog. The poodle would lie by her side as she alternately wept and fantasized about her father's return. Finally, when Nancy was 14, a relative had a chance meeting with her father and reported his whereabouts. She called him immediately.

Nancy feels that if she had not initiated that contact, she would never have heard from him again. Today, when he visits Nancy (about once a year), he talks about his three wonderful children—especially his eldest daughter, Sandy. Nancy cringes every time. Her father has four children—she is the eldest. She is bitter and resentful.

When Nancy was 15, her family moved into the duplex she still lives in. Gram lived downstairs with Grandfather, and Mother and Nancy lived in the upstairs apartment. The arrangement worked well. Nancy continued to spend a good deal of time with her beloved Gram. She made friends in the new school and began to date.

By high school, Nancy was overweight. Mother, however, was still "movie star" beautiful. Nancy says, "Boys would come over to see me, but they soon liked my mother better." She felt like an ugly duckling next to her seductive mother clad in tight sweaters.

After high school, Nancy went to nursing school on a full academic scholarship. For the first time, she lived away from home. "All I wanted," she recalls, "was to take care of people." She learned how to do that in the exciting atmosphere of the hospital, where she developed lifelong friendships with other nurses and doctors. Some of those doctors are involved now with Michael's treatment.

She calls the nursing years "the best years." "I felt so good about myself, totally in control. I was a damn good nurse. I was capable of handling anything that happened."

The only nursing she has done since injuring her back was part-time "under the table" work in a nursing home. During that 18-month period, she retained none of her old confidence. She feared that at any moment a situation would arise that she could not handle. But, as usual, when emergencies did occur, she handled them quite well. Back pain and the threat of losing her disability payments because she was working "illegally" forced her to quit.

Following every flare-up of her injury, Nancy repeats the same pattern. Once the pain subsides, she feels a welling of desire to return to school for an advanced degree in nursing and to ultimately return to her profession. She calls nursing schools and fills out applications; twice she made appointments with admissions counselors.

Eventually, a pall of gloom comes over her because she again realizes the full extent of her physical limitations. The flare-ups are unpredictable and keep her off her feet for months. Even between acute phases, she is unable to sit for more than short periods without pain. The possibility of completing a graduate degree—much less maintaining a career—appear remote. When Nancy again realizes this, she relinquishes her dream and returns to earth and to the family's problems.

Charley

Charley's childhood lacked the comforts of Nancy's. He had few possessions and his clothes were never "right." He felt loved by his mother, but he was hardly the center of anyone's attention. His father, a one-time amateur boxer, was a "tough little guy." He dealt with Charley the same way he dealt with problems on the street—with his fists.

Charley's mother and father fought constantly. Although Father never hit his wife, Mother was known to have taken more than a few swings at Father. Charley remembers one night when he was 5 years old. His father came home drunk, having gambled away his money. "Mom knocked him out cold." The scariest scene from his childhood was the night that his father got out his gun to "kill" his boss, whom he accused of cheating him. Charley doesn't remember the outcome—he only remembers the gray, shiny gun.

By contrast, most memories of his mother are pleasant ones. "One day when I was about 6, I was watching Mother scrub the floor. There was an awful smell of ammonia. She stopped working, turned on the radio, and put her feet up. She said her feet were hurting. I rubbed her feet."

Another memory from the same period was from the first grade. "Whenever my friend and I would see each other, we would fall on the floor and wrestle. I remember my first-grade teacher, Miss Brown. She used to stick her long nails in our backs when she grabbed us. We had this cloak room; there were little hooks on the walls. This one time, my friend and I were wrestling in the cloak room. Miss Brown grabbed us both and hung us up on those little hooks."

When Charley was 6, his sister Pat was born. Two years later his sister Louise was born. Charley says he was a lousy brother to his cute kid sisters, always hitting them. He recalls a stunt he pulled on Pat, when he was 17 and she was 11. She was with a group of friends, and he was with a group of boys. Unexpectedly, they met on the subway. Always playing the clown, Charley took his shoes and socks off, saying that they were on backward. His companions roared; Pat was red-faced.

Like Michael, Charley was teased daily by the other kids. He got beaten up regularly, until he managed to trade a prized toy for protection from a gang of four brothers. At 18, miserable and fed up with the fighting at home and on the streets, he enlisted in the Air Force. He proudly reports that he held that job for 4 years, the longest of any job. He still talks about the Air Force shows he performed in and drops names of the famous people he met during his enlistment.

After his discharge, he went to California. Charley paints the service years and the California period with a flourish. However, when he speaks of his Hollywood adventures and the starlets he dated, the details seem vague and much less compelling than the other details of his life.

Courtship and Marriage

Nancy and Charley's first date was at a picnic in the park, arranged by mutual friends. They did not expect to be alone, but before they realized it, their friends had left for another picnic. Nancy will never forget those first few hours together. "He was so funny and handsome. He was different from anyone I had ever experienced. He told me he had been in the movies in Hollywood. He had ideas, inventions, and plans to have his own business. I believed everything he told me." Although he was only a delivery man for a florist shop, Nancy recalls, "he explained that he was learning the business to open his own shop."

Nancy promised to marry Charley, in spite of her mother's and Aunt Flo's prediction that he would never make a decent living. Nancy wanted to prove them wrong. Two years after the picnic, they were married.

Charley's mother was struck and killed by a car shortly before the wedding. His father eventually remarried; he died of a heart attack several years ago.

Their early years of marriage were relatively free from the problems that currently plague them. Although Charley went from job to job, it didn't worry them. Nancy was more than willing to support the family by working at what she loved most—nursing.

They originally had a rich social life. Over the years, however, they lost many of their friends. Nancy feels that their friends left because, as they matured, they had less and less in common with Charley, who remained a "kid."

The couple's first problem was that Nancy could not become pregnant. Because of Charley's low sperm count and Nancy's irregular ovulation, pregnancy was nearly impossible. After 4 years, doctors suggested adoption. They had been married 5 years when they adopted 6-week-old Rena. Six years later, Michael was conceived.

Rena

Gram called her the "the angel from heaven." Once again there was an only child, an only grandchild, and now an only great-grandchild as well. It was easy for the adults to dote on her—she was an exceptionally pleasant baby. At 5 months, Rena was standing. At 11 months, she could name the artist of each painting and print on Gram's walls.

Rena's early memories all include family members. She recalls playing a game with her father when she was just a toddler. She would sit on a special chair while he would go away and come back again. She recalls beckoning him to reappear. She also recalls a family vacation when she collected "teeny tiny" shells of different colors by the water's edge. When the vacation was over, she put them in a jar and took them home with her. She can still hear her mother screaming from the bathroom where Rena kept her "shells" in a jar of water, "Charley, Charley, these shells are moving!" Her father flushed what turned out to be snails down the toilet. Rena says she was very upset for a very long time.

Charley and Nancy knew that she was bright, but at first they did not realize the extent of her giftedness. At age 5, she bypassed the regular kindergarten program and entered a "mentally gifted" first grade. At a very young age, Rena began to "belt" out songs like a nightclub performer. Her parents remember other parents' asking her for her autograph after an elementary school pageant. Everyone was impressed by her talent and was certain that she would have a future in show business.

She also displayed an unusual artistic talent, wrote poetry and short stories, and had an extraordinary mechanical ability. The latter annoyed Charley, because she was able to "fix anything" and he was not.

Birthdays, a happy time for most children, were unhappy for Rena. She moped about, looking sad and distracted. Eventually, she revealed that she always thought about her birth mother on that day and wondered if her mother thought about her, too.

In grade school, there was some foreshadowing of her "not finishing anything." Then, however, when she dropped activities before completion, she always replaced them with others that were more challenging. Now she drops them in failure and despair.

The calm of her grade school years gave way to a turbulent preadolescence and adolescence. Rena says of herself at 12, "I was a different person. I was good in school and never got into trouble. All the elders loved me. I was very intelligent and could talk to anyone about anything. But, like Michael, the kids didn't like me." She spent most of her time downstairs with Gram and Great-Grandfather or with Aunt Flo.

Things were not going too well at home, either. Nancy had undergone one back operation and was facing a second. After that second operation, it was clear that she would never be able to stand the rigors of nursing again. Charley had to be the breadwinner. Michael was sick very often at that point, but the most difficult problem of all was Gram's death.

Rena's relationship with her great-grandmother had been unusually close. She spent more time in Gram's apartment than in her own family's. When Rena got yelled at, Gram would scream upstairs, "Don't touch that angel from heaven!" Several times, Gram slipped child abuse literature under the door. Rena said Gram was the only one in the whole world who ever loved her.

Shortly after Gram's funeral, Rena—who had been sharing a room with Michael—moved downstairs with her great-grandfather. It seemed a logical and convenient solution to the lack of space and privacy for a developing young girl. A year later, Great-Grandfather died, and Rena stayed downstairs alone, sleeping in Gram's bed. Her parents now regret the arrangement. They point to the deterioration in her behavior that followed.

At first, things went exceedingly well. Rena, on a whim, auditioned for a role on a proposed TV series and was one of the six finalists chosen in a national search. All the finalists were invited to New York for a screen test with a major television network. Charley was beside himself with aspirations to manage Rena and make her a star. The entire family was given the "star treatment." Unfortunately, Rena was told that she was "too cute" for the part.

Shortly after that experience, Rena won the leading role in the school play. As Dorothy in *The Wizard of Oz*, she sang and danced and won the admiration of the entire school.

When the excitement of those two events passed and life returned to normal, Rena began to cut school. Then the fighting began in earnest. She refused to go to school or to keep the downstairs apartment clean. Charley and Nancy threatened, pleaded, punished, and hit. Twice Rena ran away. When she returned, she always promised to do better.

When she was 15, she got a part in a local dinner theater. Charley and Nancy allowed her to do the weekend performances if she attended school. When she was caught cutting again, her parents had her withdrawn from the company. They feel that she has never forgiven them for that.

Eventually, Rena quit school. Now a few years older, she speaks of her shame and once more verbalizes her resolve to "do better."

Michael

Michael has been hospitalized 14 times and has spent hundreds of hours in hospital emergency rooms for asthmatic status, a type of asthma that gets out of control. (People with asthmatic status are often near death as doctors struggle to bring it under control.) When Michael has an asthma attack, Nancy works closely by phone with the pediatrician monitoring his condition; she injects him with adrenaline and helps him to breathe with a nebulizer. Michael's earliest memory is of not being able to breathe, crying, "Gimme air, gimme air." He says, "Once, an ugly lady came in and gave me a shot instead. I wanted to hit her and tell her I didn't need the shot. I am perfectly fine."

Nancy claims that Michael was born unlucky. When he was only 8 days old, he hemorrhaged from a circumcision wound. Asthma first appeared when he was 6 months old, and he was sickly and prone to high fevers throughout infancy. Nancy worried that he might not grow up at all. Now she worries about what his life will be like. Despite frequent illnesses, he was a happy baby. He walked, talked, and reached all the developmental milestones on schedule.

His worrisome health continued through the toddler stage. At 2½, he had his first grand mal seizure and has been on seizure medication ever since. Doctors hold the medication responsible for at least a portion of his behavior problems, specifically the hyperactivity, but no one is quite certain just how much of his problem can be attributed to adverse side effects.

His behavior was first identified as problematic in kindergarten. After 2 months of first grade, he was transferred from the regular classroom to a learning disabled classroom. Teachers said he could not follow instructions and seemed "lost" and confused. The report from the school psychologist stated that he had fine and gross motor coordination problems.

At 12, Michael feels that he is different from the rest of the kids. However, he refuses to accept his very real physical limitations—despite constant failure and rejection, he continues to try out for the track and softball teams. On the other hand, he acknowledges his difference and alienation and says, "Sometimes I feel that I should be in another country or in another time zone. I wish I could start my life over again." He likes the idea of having his story in a book because people "pity the underdog."

Part II

Paradigms of Clinical Social Work:

Emphasis on Diversity

2

Diversity Perspectives for Social Work Practice

Joseph Anderson, PhD
Robin Wiggins-Carter, DPA

INTRODUCTION

Culture, race, ethnicity, and diversity are intertwined and sequential concepts that have appeared in the social work and counseling literature regarding culture and clinical practice. Over the last decade the concept of diversity has included multicultural dimensions, in addition to concerns related to such particular client groups as (a) American ethnicities, with special emphasis on ethnics of color; (b) lesbian, gay, bisexual, and transgender (LGBT) clients; (c) persons with disabilities; (d) age groups; and (e) gender groups or clients with gender-related concerns. In short, diversity refers to ethnic heritage, cultural background, group affiliation, identity, and status. In this context, *identity* refers to sexual and other non-ethnic identities, and *status* refers to any biosocial or socioeconomic status, including the state of disability and social-class status.

Competence to practice with and on behalf of diversity is part of our social work professional standards (CSWE, 2002; NASW, 1996). It is also required by the reality of increasing diverse cultures in the United States and the global community. In ethnocultural diversity alone, the United States is predicted to include a majority of ethnics of color by 2050. Currently, of a population of 281,421,906 (U.S. Bureau of the Census, 2001, 2002), there are 69.1% who identify as White (not of Hispanic or Latino origin), 12.5% Latino or Hispanic origin,

12.3% as African American, 3.6% as Asian American, 0.9% as Native American and Alaska Native, and 0.1% Native Hawaiian and other Pacific Islanders.

Immigrant populations have also greatly increased our ethnocultural diversity. The last decade reflects more immigrant diversity in terms of both numbers and the variety of regions of the world from which people have emigrated. Given the increasing diversity of ethnic groups as well as differences in gender, religion, identity, status, and affiliation groups, our focus on diversity in clinical practice requires inclusive and multidimensional paradigms.

Competence in working with and on behalf of diverse populations requires more than just the adaptation of existing frameworks for practice. Clinical social workers must be prepared to expand their theory base and learn new models of practice. The paradigms presented in this chapter provide a theoretical background for understanding and identifying obstacles and strengths in the assessment of diverse populations. In addition, they recognize that diversity is not a static entity, that one's cultural identity may not be clearly defined in terms of race, gender, sexual orientation, or any one variable. It is more likely the intersection and overlapping of multiple variables that form the overall identity of individuals, thus making the use of paradigms that do not assume or impose identity from the outside important in honoring diversity.

Social workers may unwittingly use clinical practice models that are familiar and comfortable to them, without first examining the underlying assumptions and impact these models may have on treatment for the family or the individual. Not only do many of the existing theoretical models not address cultural differences, they also assume a mainstream stance. The use of deficit models that focus on individual and family pathology will always represent people of color, women, gays and lesbians, older people, and those with disabilities as having substantial and continuous difficulties. Members of these groups may be viewed as victims, needing the attention and expertise of social workers and other helping professionals.

DIVERSITY PARADIGMS

Diversity affects clinical social work practice in numerous ways. This chapter discusses three major dimensions of diversity in practice: (a) ethnocultural diversity, (b) oppression, and (c) vulnerability. It also summarizes the paradigms that have evolved within the profession to provide principles and concepts for competence in diversity practice. Perspectives and paradigms for understanding and working effectively with diversity have evolved primarily from attention to these three dimensions in practice or to particular combinations of these, as, for example, in practice with and on behalf of ethnic people of color (Anderson & Carter, 2003). Figure 2.1 depicts the paradigms emanating from these three separate and overlapping perspectives. Within the circles and their overlaps are the specific paradigms discussed in this chapter.

Central Paradigms

At the core of Figure 2.1 and central to all three perspectives are the *strengths perspective* and the *empowerment approach*. All of the discrete paradigms emphasize the strengths in and of diversity, and advocate empowerment as a central aim and process for practice. Currently, the strengths perspective encompasses a "collation of principles, ideas, and techniques" that enables "resources and resourcefulness of clients" (Saleebey, 1997, p. 15). The strengths perspective in clinical practice involves a paradigm that assumes and promotes competence in clients (Maluccio, 1981), emphasizes individual and family resilience (Fraser, 1997), and focuses on solutions rather than on problems (de-Shazer, 1985). These more humanistic models appear most consonant with social work's fundamental values regarding human worth and social justice. "Focusing and building on client strengths is an imperative of the several values that govern our work and the operation of a democratic and pluralistic society, including distributive justice, equality, respect for dignity of the individual, and the search for maximum autonomy and maximum community" (Saleebey, 1997, p. 169). Our Social Work Code of Ethics requires that we "understand culture and its function in human society, recognizing the strengths that exist in all cultures "(NASW, 1996, p. 9). The strengths paradigm provides principles and concepts that facilitate the inherent capacity of human beings for maximizing both their autonomy and their interdependence, as well as the

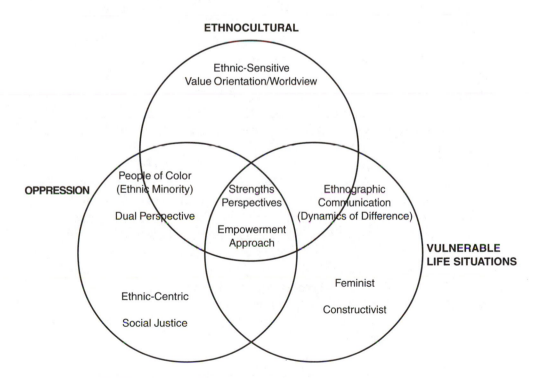

FIGURE 2.1. Social Work Diversity Perspectives and Paradigms

resourcefulness of diverse cultures for fostering survival and growth among their members.

Clinical social work with members of social and cultural groups that have survived a history of oppression in the United States taps these resources. These strengths generally evolve from three sources: (a) personal transformation qualities as a result of overcoming self-depreciating forces (Chestang, 1982); (b) family and community structures that develop self-esteem and provide a network of psychosocial and economic resources (Wright & Anderson, 1998); and (c) survival determination and skills (Hopps, Pinderhughes, & Shankar, 1995). Such strengths counter the devaluing forces of marginalization, discrimination, and oppression. Effective practice with members of such marginalized groups in oppressive conditions requires (a) the critical consciousness of the oppressor, which is rooted deep within us all (Freire, 1970); (b) the affirmation of strengths; and (c) the employment of empowerment approaches.

The empowerment approach informs the means and the ends of social work practice with marginalized diverse populations. It is "a process of increasing personal interpersonal or political power . . . [to] take action to improve . . . life situations" (Gutierrez, 1990, p. 149) and involves "the creation of structural conditions under which people can choose to 'give to' their community as well as 'take from' their community" (Breton, 1994, p. 29). This practice requires facilitation of

- Positive perceptions of personal worth, resources, and skills;
- Recognition that many of one's views do matter and are indeed valid and legitimate to voice;
- Connections with others for potential mutual aid;
- Critical analysis of the relationship between the personal and the political; and
- Strategies for social action on behalf of self and others.

Clinical practice from a strengths-based, empowerment-oriented perspective identifies and develops possibilities, resiliencies, and resources in clients and their situations. The practice models are client-centered, solution-focused, and narrative-based. An example of such practice with Nancy Shore, in the case presented in this book, would begin with listening to her story and paying attention to what it might reveal about her interests, talents, and competencies. Through purposeful conversation and questions, the practitioner encourages elaboration on stories of competence, of cultural and personal resources, and of future hopes and dreams. The client's stories of failures and inadequacies are examined, as well for, their roots, not in the client's life, but in the socially constructed discourse generated and controlled by the dominant culture.

Nancy's story's major theme is one of helplessness and powerlessness regarding her weight, her anxiety attacks, her health, her marriage, her parenting, and her career. She paints a picture of an overwhelming world from which she tends to be progressively withdrawing. From an empowerment perspective this story, in part, reflects the dominant discourse of a sexist and ageist culture and its potential effects on a woman at midlife. Nancy's strengths- and resilience-centered self-narratives become "subjugated" to the socially dominant vulnerability narratives. Thus, she sees herself primarily as over the hill, unattractive, and moving toward the purposelessness of the empty nest. In this light, it is understandable that Nancy's response would be insecurity, weakness, and vulnerability. An alternative midlife narrative would emphasize freedom, competence, the power of knowledge and lifelong learning, and feelings of being in the prime of life.

Helping Nancy to see how she has internalized parts of this cultural discourse in her self-image begins with emphasizing alternative narratives of strengths and resiliencies. This requires asking her more about her successful nursing career, her ability to take control in family crises, her courage to manage the severe recurring pain from her back injury, and her ability to parent Rena and Michael (and Charley!). This conversation would include seeking more elaboration and details about these successes: for example, "Tell me more about how you got through the day when your pain was so severe." It also includes asking exception questions: for example, "When things were going well in your life, what was different?" With the construction of positive self-narratives, the stories of helplessness and inadequacy can be deconstructed through critical questioning: for example, "Whose voice tells you that you are unattractive?" Questions such as this one are designed to identify the culturally constructed negative self-valuations.

The next step in strengths-based, empowerment-oriented practice is to encourage clients to consider solutions, possibilities, or positive visions for change. These come from such questions as, "What do you want out of life? What people or personal qualities are helping you move in this direction? What fantasies and dreams have given you special hope and guidance? How might you achieve some of your goals or recover some of these special abilities and times you have had in the past?"

Nancy Shore, in her initial narrative, did have a dream to complete a graduate nursing program. Her physical limitations, however, restricted this dream from becoming a feasible goal. But what part of this dream might possibly still be realized? What help might she receive from her resources in the health-care system, her physician friends, and others, to explore how she might develop a way to enter a new career in the health-care area that she can do within her physical limitations (for example, an online health educator)?

In empowerment practice, solutions include consideration of connections with others for participation in community activities, such as mutual aid groups. Perhaps she would be willing to participate in a support group of women experiencing midlife challenges. Or maybe she would prefer a group of people who are coping with chronic pain. These kinds of connections can involve increased critical analysis of the way in which political realities, such as sexism and ageism, may affect her sense of personal worth and power and ultimately may increase opportunities for social action designed to change potentially oppressive structures.

ETHNOCULTURAL PARADIGMS

The common defining element of the ethnocultural perspective is the relationship of ethnicity to culture. Ethnicity refers to the self-conscious collectivities of people who, on the basis of a common heritage or subculture, maintain a distinct identity among themselves and in relation to other groups in a diverse, multicultural society. This discernment of difference affects their sense of personal identity, loyalty, and belonging and their socialization into particular value orientations and normative dispostions for behavior. Two of the paradigms especially developed in social work are the *ethnic-sensitive* and *value orientation* frameworks.

Clinical social work within the ethnic-sensitive paradigm uses the concepts of ethclass and ethnic reality (Devore & Schlesinger, 1999). Ethclass concerns the intersection of ethnicity and social class. This suggests that differences in behavior, attitudes, and life chances of those within a particular social class result from ethnicity, and differences within the ethnic group result from social class status. This "ethclass" position generates identifiable dispositions and behaviors, or a particular ethnic reality. This reality includes deeply ingrained feelings, beliefs, and actions in such areas as child rearing, gender roles, and spirituality. Clinical assessment and intervention strategies require an understanding of these ethnocultural values and norms.

The values orientation paradigm can also sensitize us to certain significant ethnocultural differences (Anderson, 1997; DuBray & Sanders, 2003). Value orientations are distinguished from concrete values by their levels of generality: "A value orientation is a generalized and organized conception, influencing behavior of time, or nature of [a person's] place in it or [a person's] relation to [other people], and the desirable and undesirable aspects of people–environment and inter-human transactions" (C. Kluckhohn, 1961, p. 14). These value orientations together constitute a cultural worldview. In this paradigm several propositions determine the worldview (F. R. Kluckhohn, 1954):

1. There are a limited number of common human problems for which all people in all places must find solutions. These are
   a. Time (the temporal focus of human life);
   b. Activity (the preferred pattern of action in interpersonal relations);
   c. Human Relations (the preferred way of relating in groups);
   d. Person(s)–Nature Relationship (the way people relate to the natural or supernatural environments); and
   e. Basic Nature of Human Beings (the attitudes held about the innate good or evil in human nature and behavior).
2. Although there is variability in the solutions to these problems, this diversity is neither limitless nor random but occurs within a range of three possible solutions, or general value orientations, for each of the problems:
   a. Time (past, present, future);
   b. Activity (doing, being, becoming);
   c. Human Relations (autonomy, interdependence, hierarchy);

    d. Person–Nature (harmony, mastery, subjugation); and

    e. Basic Nature of Human Beings (neutral or mixed, good, evil).

3. All possible solutions are present in varying degrees in the total structure of every culture, and every culture will be characterized not only by a dominant profile of first-order choices but also by substitute second- and third-order choices. Differences among cultures are based on the pattern of preferences for each of these solutions in a dominant-substitute profile of values.

Table 2.1 summarizes general value orientation profiles for a select group of people with diverse ethnicity in the United States. More refined concepts evolve from a constellation of these profiles, with such variables as socioeconomic class, generation, religion, and geographic location. Also, although these profiles generally sensitize to differences, it is important to note that there are a variety of discrete group profiles subsumed under the general classifications. For instance, one finds differences between those who identify as West Indian Blacks and African American Blacks; among Japanese, Korean, Chinese, and Pacific Asian Americans; among Puerto Rican and Mexican American Hispanics; and among diverse Caucasian ethnic people.

ETHNOCULTURAL/OPPRESSION PARADIGMS

In the model presented in this chapter, there are two paradigms that overlap the ethnocultural and oppression perspectives (see Figure 2.1). These are the *people-of-color* and the *dual perspective* models. Although these frameworks share the ethnocultural perspective's sensitivity to worldview differences, they also account for how these worldviews are influenced by historical oppression, especially for minorities of color in the United States. Oppression here refers to "an institutionalized unequal power relationship-prejudice plus power" (Wambach & Van Soest, 1997, p. 243).

Doman Lum (1986, 2003) is the chief developer of the people-of-color paradigm. The framework is a conceptual effort to unify similarities among Native, African, Latino, and Asian Americans, yet to acknowledge the differences among and between these four ethnically diverse groups. From this view, practitioners draw on the positive strengths of diverse cultural beliefs and practices and are concerned about discrimination experiences that require clinical approaches sensitive to ethnic and cultural environments. Common themes require seeing individuals in collective association, especially family and community, and recognizing color, language, and behavioral characteristics, as well as racism, prejudice, and discrimination, which distinguish unique ethnic groups in a multiracial society.

The dual perspective paradigm (Chestang, 1980; Norton, 1978) similarly focuses on the ethnic minority experience and its resources and stressors for people of color. Members of these groups most often live in two worlds simultaneously, with dual experience and dual cultures as a consequence of such social conditions as institutionalized racism. Members of these groups consistently

TABLE 2.1

Comparison of Selected Ethnic Value Orientation Profiles

	Dominant Caucasian American Middle Class	African Americans	Hispanic Americans	Asian Americans	Native Americans
Time	Future>Present>Past	Present>Past>Future	Past>Present>Future	Past>Future>Present	Present>Past>Future
Activity	Doing>Becoming>Being	Being>Doing>Becoming	Being>Becoming>Doing	Doing>Becoming>Being	Being>Becoming>Doing
Human Relations	Autonomy>Interdependency>Hierarchy	Interdependency>Hierarchy>Autonomy	Interdependency>Hierarchy>Autonomy	Hierarchy>Interdependency>Autonomy	Interdependency>Hierarchy>Autonomy
Person–Nature Relationship	Mastery>Subjugation>Harmony	Harmony>Subjugation>Mastery	Harmony>Subjugation>Mastery	Harmony>Subjugation>Mastery	Harmony>Subjugation>Mastery
Basic Nature of Human Beings	Neutral>Evil>Good	Good>Evil>Mixed	Good>Evil>Mixed	Mixed>Good>Evil	Good>Mixed>Evil

Note. For a different reflection of some of these groups, see Ho (1987); for a classification of selected Caucasian ethnic groups, see Spiegel (1982).
Source: Sources here are primarily McGoldrick, Pearce, and Giordano (1982); Sue and Sue (1990); Dana (1993); and DuBray and Sanders (2003).

confront blocks that are systematically and structurally designed to restrict opportunities for goal achievement in the larger social system. Such oppressed groups may develop adaptive norms and coping strategies within their cultural world that can be at odds with society's dominant concepts of "normal," as can be found, for example in the expressive, in-your-face behavior of African Americans when engaging in conflict with Caucasians (Kochman, 1981). According to Norton (1978),

> the dual perspective is the conscious and systematic process of perceiving, understanding, and comparing simultaneously the values, attitudes and behavior of the larger social system with those of the client's immediate family and community system. It is the conscious awareness of the cognitive and attitudinal levels of the similarities and differences in the two systems. (p. 3)

Writing on the duality of the "Black experience" and the dual perspective, Chestang (1976) identified the larger, more dominant system as the "sustaining system" and the more immediate family and community environment as the "nurturing system." The nurturing system of family, friends, and the supportive institutions of the immediate community socialize people of color and diverse ethnicities to values, norms, and traditions that foster self-worth and self-actualization. The sustaining system provides resources to meet instrumental and pragmatic needs for physical survival and increases in the quality of life, such as goods and services, political power, shelter, employment and other economic resources, education, and health. This wider society is peopled by the powerful and the influential. For people of color and diverse ethnicity, these people of power most often (although not always) differ from those in one's nurturing environment in skin color, in speech patterns, in habits, in attitudes toward diverse populations, and perhaps even in language. Depending upon their experience and perception of living in these two worlds and the gaps and fences between them, people of color develop particular coping attitudes and behaviors as part of their strengths. To understand these attitudes requires a dual perspective, taking the role of the one who lives in these two spheres, as described by Chestang (1980):

> Moving back and forth between them through an invisible shield which bounds between them, so that their separation is clearly understood by those who must travel between them, although it is vaguely perceived, if at all, by those whose lives are lived primarily in one sphere. (p. 3)

OPPRESSION PERSPECTIVE

More centrally addressing oppression are practice in the *ethnic-centered* paradigm as in the Afrocentric framework, and in the *social justice* paradigm (Prigoff, 2003; Swenson, 1998; Wakefield, 1988). The ethnic-centered framework shifts the center from which to view ethnic people of color toward their intra- and innergroup relations and away from the marginalized position from which dominant cultural world views and dominant social work perspectives have historically constructed those groups.

The social justice paradigm uses Rawls's (1971) concepts of distributive justice to include equality in basic liberties and equity of opportunities and social resources. Equity implies equal distribution of resources, except to benefit those who are worse off. Clinical theories in this framework need to affirm and develop strengths, expand critical consciousness regarding social positions and power relationships (Freire, 1973), and involve the practitioner's awareness of oppression, privilege, and domination.

VULNERABLE LIFE SITUATIONS PARADIGMS

Overlapping the ethnocultural perspectives are two paradigms within the vulnerable life situations perspective. The *ethnographic* paradigm (Bein, 2003; Green, 1999) and the *communication* or "dynamics of difference" paradigm (Barranti, 2003) include ethnocultural diversity but are also applicable to multiple dimensions of difference. They focus on how the strengths and the sufferings affect the vulnerable life situations of more marginalized clients and how their experience of and response to dynamics of difference affect the helping and the service context. In short, these paradigms help practitioners discover how those who use services define themselves in their diversity and how they can identify the differences that have affected their past and current life situations. They shift focus from the "culture in the group" to the "culture in the person" (Anderson, 1997).

The ethnographic paradigm initiates in a stance of "not knowing" regarding the meaning of the client's diversity. The practitioner assumes the role of learner, with the client in the role of the authority. The ethnographic interview, as a central tool in the ethnographic approach, is a process of discovery, in which the interviewer proposes to ask focusing questions to learn the meaning of the other's culture from the client's point of view. For instance, in small group practice the practitioner may ask, "Tell us something about your culture and how you think it may influence your participation in this group." Or "Could you pretend for a moment that you're with members of your own ethnic group? Try to explain to them what this group is all about. What would you say?" (Anderson, 1997, p. 65).

Similarly, in the communication framework (Barranti, 2003; Green, 1999; Leigh, 1998) clients are considered guides into their world. The emphasis is on the awareness of, and the skill for, facilitating the process of communication, in order to cross cultural "borderlands" and lead to understanding of the differences that affect clients. Particular skills for this facilitation include (a) separating description, interpretation, and evaluation; (b) using feedback; (c) dialogic listing; and (d) metacommunicating (Gudykunst, 1991). First, the skill of consciously separating description, interpretation, and evaluation requires that practitioners label and focus on what is seen, heard, and felt. Second, as many as possible interpretations of the meaning and the intent of this experience are considered. Third, current understanding of psychological, cultural, and sociological concepts is used to make an "educated guess" in evaluation of the meaning. Using feedback involves sharing these observations and evaluations with clients to check on the nature of understanding. *Dialogic listening* is using feedback to discover whether mutual understanding is or is not occurring. *Metacommunicating* clarifyies the practitioner's messages by sharing the intent and the expectations regarding one's communication.

The paradigms that specifically address vulnerable clients (those with socially constructed devalued roles and statuses) are the *feminist* and the *constructivist* frameworks. These two paradigms focus on the needs and the issues of such "populations at risk" as people of color, women, and gay and lesbian persons (CSWE, 2002).

Within social work, the feminist paradigm (Bricker-Jenkins & Lockett, 1995; Taylor & Kennedy, 2003) envisions self-actualization as a collective endeavor and views the purpose of practice to support pro-diversity individual and collective self-actualization. This practice concerns human behavior in the social environment from perspectives of strengths, health, diversity, interdependence, and constructivism. Feminist practice relates the personal to the political through consciousness raising and facilitates processes that demonstrate egalitarian, synergetic, and nonviolent relationships. The therapeutic relationship strives to empower individual and collective capacities for healing, health, and personal and political transformation.

The constructivist paradigm (Burris & Guadalupe, 2003) emanates from the philosophical perspective of constructivism. Basic tenets of both the philosophy and the practice paradigm hold that meanings are (a) multiple and diverse, rather than singular and universal; (b) changing rather than unchanging; (c) responsive to context rather than remaining stable regardless of context; (d) interactive rather than unaffected by interaction; and (e) open to diverse interpretations. Practitioners using the constructivist lens explore the roles of language, interpretation, and meanings and their effects on people's lives as reflected in individual narrative. With the underlying assumption that reality is socially constructed, language and meaning are used for deconstructing and reconstructing dominant-defined realities of oppression and marginalization, especially in how individual private troubles and collective public issues are defined and solutions are sought.

CLINICAL SOCIAL WORK COMPETENCE
AND DIVERSITY PARADIGMS

Clinical social workers, in the context of their practice and their central values and ethics, must develop competencies for working with and on behalf of diverse populations. This competence includes consciousness of, commitment to, and confidence in understanding and serving diverse ethnocultural, oppressed, and vulnerable (or at-risk) individuals, families, and groups.

This chapter suggests the following 10 skills as central to such competence:

1. The knowledge of one's own and one's client's specific values, beliefs, and cultural practices (paradigms: ethnic-sensitive, value orientation, people of color);
2. The ability to respect and appreciate the values, the beliefs, and the practices of culturally different clients and to perceive such individuals through their cultural lenses, instead of one's own (paradigms: strengths, dual perspective, ethnic-centric, constructivist);
3. The ability to be comfortable with differences in others and thus not trapped in anxiety or defensive behaviors (paradigms: communication [dynamics of difference]);
4. The ability to control and change false beliefs, assumptions, and stereotypes (paradigms: ethnic-sensitive, dual perspective);
5. The ability to consider multiple dimensions of diversity and to recognize that one's own way of thinking and behaving is not the only way (paradigm: ethnic-sensitive, value orientation, constructivist);
6. The ability to sort through general knowledge about diverse groups to see the specific ways in which this knowledge does or does not apply to a given client situation (ethnic-sensitive, value orientation, people of color);
7. A critical consciousness to understand the causes' consequences and dynamics of all forms of oppression (paradigms: ethnic-centric, social justice, feminist);
8. The ability to let others teach us about the differences that make a difference for them (paradigms: ethnographic, communication, constructivist);
9. The ability to facilitate personal, interpersonal, and political empowerment (paradigms: empowerment, social justice, feminist); and
10. The use of self to envision and enable social and economic justice for the mutual benefit of the individual, society, and the global community (paradigms: social justice, feminist, constructivist).

As noted by Appleby (2001), many of the existing theoretical frameworks used in social work are steeped in the traditional American cultural principles of Eurocentricity, patriarchy, and capitalism. The Eurocentric worldview assumes that European-rooted values and traditions are inherently superior to all others. The patriarchy principle has led to the development of male-focused and male-developed models of human behavior that reinforce male dominance and male superiority. The capitalism principle encourages personal responsibility and individualism as precursors to success. At the very least, those who do not fit into the mainstream may be marginalized. At worst, they are pathologized and labeled deviants or outsiders. Practitioners need to be prepared to examine these assumptions and not tailor intervention strategies solely on the problem being presented. Practitioners must resist using "one size fits all" approaches and be prepared to individualize their interventions.

A number of scholars have examined cross-cultural relationships in clinical practice. Todisco and Salomone (1991), for example, have identified the following common assumptions practitioners make in cross-cultural encounters that lead to poor outcomes: "(a) all people share a common measure of what constitutes "normal" behavior, (b) there is a dependence on linear "cause and effect" thinking, (c) people of all cultures understand the intended meanings of abstract words frequently used in Western culture, and (d) counselors are already aware of their own assumptions" (p. 4). Clinical social workers must be aware of the tendency to pathologize normative behaviors that are unfamiliar to the practitioner.

SUMMARY

The paradigms presented in this chapter represent approaches that honor the knowledge, the strengths, and the abilities of diverse groups, often reframing the difficulties they present in terms of their attempts to negotiate in an oppressive society. They recognize the need to view diversity not on the basis of the difficulties that exist for certain groups or individuals, but to consider how diverse groups and individuals have historically been faced with particular challenges and have managed to successfully meet them. The challenge for clinical social work is to expand the theory base to include paradigms that will improve effective work with diverse persons and environments.

REFERENCES

Anderson, J. (1997). *Social work with groups*. New York, Longman.

Anderson, J., & Carter, R. W. (2003). *Diversity perspectives for social work practice*. Boston: Allyn & Bacon.

Appleby, G. (2001). Dynamics of oppression and discrimination. In G. Appleby, E. Colon, & J. Hamilton (Eds.), *Diversity, oppression and social functioning: Person-in-environment assessment and intervention*. Boston: Allyn & Bacon.

Barranti, C. C. R. (2003). Communication framework. In J. Anderson & R. W. Carter (Eds.), *Diversity perspectives for social work practice* (pp. 146–168). Boston: Allyn & Bacon.

Bein, A. (2003). The ethnographic perspective: A new look. In J. Anderson & R. W. Carter (Eds.), *Diversity perspectives for social work practice* (pp. 133–145). Boston: Allyn & Bacon.

Breton, M. (1994). On the meaning of empowerment and empowerment-oriented social work practice. *Social Work With Groups, 17,* 23–37.

Bricker-Jenkins, M., & Lockett, P. W. (1995). Women: Direct practice. In R. L. Edwards (Ed.), *Encyclopedia of social work* (19th ed., pp. 2529–2539). Washington, DC: NASW Press.

Burris, J., & Guadalupe, K. L. (2003). Constructivism and the constructivist framework. In J. Anderson & R. W. Carter (Eds.), *Diversity perspectives in social work practice* (pp. 199–226). Boston: Allyn & Bacon.

Chestang, L. W. (1976). Environment influences on social functioning: The Black Experience. In P. Cafferty & L. W. Chestang (Eds.), T*he diverse society: Implications for social policy* (pp. 21–42). Washington, DC: NASW Press.

Chestang, L. W. (1980). Competencies and knowledge in clinical social work: A dual perspective. In P. A. Ewalt (Ed.), *Toward a definition of clinical social work* (pp. 12–27). Washington, DC: NASW Press.

Chestang, L. W. (1982). *Character development in a hostile society*. Occasional paper. Chicago: University of Chicago Press.

Council on Social Work Education. (2002). *CSWE Educational policy and accreditation standards.* Washington, DC: Author.

Dana, R. H. (1993). *Multicultural assessment perspectives for professional psychology.* Boston: Allyn & Bacon.

deShazer, S. (1985). *Keys to solutions in brief therapy.* New York: Norton

Devore, W., & Schlesinger, E. G. (1999). *Ethnic-sensitive social work practice* (5th ed.). Boston: Allyn & Bacon.

DuBray, W. M. & Sanders A. (2003). Value orientation/world view framework. In J. Anderson & R. W. Carter (Eds.), *Diversity perspectives for social work practice* (pp. 47–58). Boston: Allyn & Bacon.

Fraser, M. W. (Ed.). (1997). *Risk and resilience in childhood: An ecological perspective.* Washington, DC: NASW Press.

Freire, P. (1970). *Pedagogy of the oppressed.* New York: Seabury Press.

Green, J. (1999). *Cultural awareness in the human services: A multi-ethnic approach* (3rd ed.). Boston: Allyn & Bacon.

Gudykunst, W. B. (1991). *Bridging differences: Effective intergroup communications.* Thousand Oaks, CA: Sage.

Gutierrez, L. M. (1990). Working with women of color: An empowerment perspective. *Social Work, 25*(2), 149–154.

Ho, M. K. (1987). *Family therapy with ethnic minorities.* Newbury Park, CA: Sage.

Hopps, J. G., Pinderhughes, E., & Shankar, R. (1995). *The power to care: Clinical practice effectiveness with overwhelmed clients.* New York: Free Press.

Kluckhohn, C. (1961). Value orientation. In F. R. Kluckhohn & F. L. Strodtback (Eds.), *Variations in value orientations* (pp. 4–28). Homewood, IL: Dorsey.

Kluckhohn, F. R. (1954). Dominant and variant value orientations. In C. Kluckhohn & H. A. Murray (Eds.), *Personality in nature, society, and culture* (pp. 72–91). New York: Knopf.

Kochman, T. (1981). *Black and white: Styles in conflict.* Chicago: University of Chicago Press.

Leigh, J. W. (1998). *Communication for cultural competence.* Boston: Allyn & Bacon.

Lum, D. (1986). *Social work practice and people of color: A process-stage approach.* Monterey, CA: Brooks/Cole.

Lum, D. (2003). People of color (ethnic minority) framework. In J. Anderson & R. W. Carter (Eds.), *Diversity perspectives for social work practice* (pp. 61–76). Boston: Allyn & Bacon.

Maluccio, A. N. (1981). *Promoting competence in clients: A new/old approach to social work practice.* New York: Free Press.

McGoldrick, M., Pearce, J. K., & Giordano, J. (Eds.). (1982). *Ethnicity and family therapy.* New York: Guilford Press.

National Association of Social Workers. (1996). *Code of ethics.* Washington: DC: NASW Press.

Norton, D. (Ed.). (1978). *The dual perspective: Inclusion of ethnic minority content in the social work curriculum.* New York: Council on Social Work Education.

Prigoff, A. W. (2003). Social justice framework. In J. Anderson & R. W. Carter (Eds.), *Diversity perspectives for social work practice* (pp. 113–120). Boston: Allyn & Bacon.

Rawls, J. (1971). *A theory of justice.* Cambridge, MA: Harvard University Press.

Saleebey, D. (Ed.). (1997). *The strengths perspective in social work practice* (2nd ed.). New York: Longman.

Spiegel, J. (1982). An ecological model of ethnic families. In M. McGoldrick, J. K. Pearce, & J. Giordano (Eds.), *Ethnicity and family therapy* (pp. 37–49). New York: Guilford Press.

Sue, D. W. & Sue, D. (1990). *Counseling the culturally different: Theory and practice* (2nd ed.). New York: Wiley.

Swenson, C. R. (1998). Clinical social work's contribution to a social justice perspective. *Social Work, 43*, 539–550.

Taylor, S., & Kennedy, R. (2003). Feminist framework. In J. Anderson & R. W. Carter (Eds.), *Diversity perspective for social work practice* (pp. 171–198). Boston: Allyn & Bacon.

Todisco, M., & Salomone, P. R. (1991). Facilitating effective cross-cultural relationships: The White counselor and the Black client. *Journal of Multicultural Counseling and Development, 19*(4), 146–158.

U.S. Bureau of the Census. (2001). *The Hispanic population in the United States*. Washington, DC: Author.

U.S. Bureau of the Census. (2002). *U.S. Census Bureau quickfacts*. Washington, DC: Author.

Wakefield, J. C. (1998). Psychotherapy, distributive justice, and social work. *Social Services Review, 62,* 187–210, 353–382.

Wambach, K. G., & Van Soest, D. (1997). Oppression. In R. L. Edwards (Ed.), *Encyclopedia of social work* (19th ed., suppl., pp. 243–252). Washington, DC: NASW.

Wright, O. L., & Anderson, J. D. (1998). Clinical social work and urban African American families. *Families in Society, 79,* 197–206.

3

Jungian Thinking and Practice

Emphasis on an Adolescent's Search for Her Guatemalan Cultural Roots

Marga Speicher, PhD

INTRODUCTION

*I*n a letter to a 14-year-old boy who considered becoming a psychoanalyst, Anna Freud speaks eloquently of the knowledge and the attitude needed to infuse the would-be psychotherapist:

> If you want to be a real psychoanalyst you have to have a *great love of the truth* [italics added], scientific truth as well as personal truth, and you have to place this appreciation of truth higher than any discomfort at meeting unpleasant facts, whether they belong to the world outside or to your own person. . . . Further, I think that a psychoanalyst should have . . . interests . . . beyond the limits of the medical field . . . [otherwise] his outlook on his patient will remain too narrow. . . . *You ought to be a great reader and become acquainted with the literature of many countries and cultures* [italics added]. In the great literary figures you will find people who know at least as much of human nature as the psychiatrists and psychologists try to do. (Kohut, 1978a, p. 474)

Search for understanding, personally and scientifically, and a knowledge base that is broad and deep: The confluence of these two streams forms the basis for solid clinical engagement and effective psychodynamic[1] practice.

Education for social workers has consistently placed emphasis on self-awareness: The practitioner needs to know what he or she brings to an encounter with a client, in terms of personal assumptions, values, and convictions; theories about life, psychological development, and functioning; pathology and therapy; and, especially, personal life experiences. Within the psychoanalytic tradition, personal analysis for the would-be analyst is a requirement. One needs to have an experience of engaging in a process of self-exploration and come to know one's vulnerabilities, woundedness, and shortcomings, as well as one's strengths. Such a process lays the foundation for a lifelong stance of introspection and self-inquiry through which the psychotherapist seeks to maintain understanding of personal psychodynamics and to separate them from the client's.[2]

Experienced clinicians stress that one needs to know as much as possible from the root fields of psychotherapy (sciences, psychology, sociology, arts and humanities, religious traditions; see Ehrenwald, 1976; Ellenberger, 1970) and from within the field of psychotherapy proper (diverse theories, diverse practice skills). When with the client, however, one needs to forget all in order to listen fully and respond from one's center. Such a stance is an ideal to which we aspire and involves a never-ending process of study and integration. What one has studied must be metabolized within oneself to become one's own.

Furthermore, the clinician needs to develop a differentiating stance toward knowledge and practice. As a reader of theoretical and clinical articles, a thoughtful clinician will reflect and explore his or her personal responses: What do these thoughts evoke in me? Where have I experienced such a phenomenon in my life? How can I integrate this thinking into my thinking? If a theoretical perspective feels foreign, the thoughtful reader will explore further. What feels foreign often contains different ideas that can expand one's worldview. The important issue is that there be reflection that leads to a considerate, differentiated, and differentiating position.

I deliberately use the term *thinking* in the title of this chapter to stress *process,* rather than product; *thinking,* rather than thought; and *theorizing,* rather than theory. Theories about human nature forever evolve. Human life is highly complex. No single theory can capture even the essential features. Theories, at their best, become guidelines in the process of seeking genuine understanding.

The theories we hold inevitably affect what we observe and how we think about observations. They can sharpen our focus when they direct our thinking but can also limit clinical inquiry when we look only through the lens of one theory, disregarding what does not fall within its sphere. Our view on the client, then, may miss salient features and become quite narrow. Jean Sanville speaks of theories as languages that we use because they are the best we have at a given time. She recommends that "our focus should not be so much on *what* theories we hold, but on *how* we hold them, whether as convictions or as provisional conveniences" (Speicher, Phillips, Sanville, & Adams, 1997, p. 23).

THE CONCEPT OF THE PERSON AND THE HUMAN EXPERIENCE

"Person" refers to a living human being with recognizable physical traits and psychological, intellectual, emotional, and spiritual qualities. These attributes may be active or dormant, more or less developed. However, in their total configuration they make the person unique; people express themselves through their qualities to the extent to which these have been developed.

Innate qualities develop as a result of a lifetime in interaction with the environment. Current thinking regards nurture as the key that can unlock innate potential, can leave it locked up but untouched, or can do outright damage to it. Just as a human being develops in the interplay of nature and nurture, a theorist's views also arise out of the mix of innate capacities with familial and cultural factors that shape his or her life.[3]

Jung was steeped in the Romantics' intellectual and emotional heritage, which valued emotional expression and experiences of nature, the soul, and the unconscious. Rejecting his father's Calvinist theology, Jung found refuge in a strong, personal connection to the natural world and to the writings of many traditions. These sources coalesced his optimistic worldview, in which he saw the potential in the human experience, yet recognized the hardships of the human struggle. Most of all, he was struck by the fecundity of the human spirit, as it appeared in the symbolism of the arts and the mythologies. Observing how human life had been lived out over the millennia, he understood the individual human being against the backdrop of what is typically human in actuality and in potential. Jung came to think of this backdrop as a dynamic field from which vital energy flows into each human life. He called this field the collective unconscious or the archetypal world.

THE CONCEPT OF THE ARCHETYPE, ARCHETYPAL IMAGES, AND ARCHETYPAL DYNAMICS

In the concept of the archetype,[4] Jung developed psychological views about the interaction between innate patterns and the outer world: Archetype is a dynamic pattern in the unconscious that becomes activated through life experiences. The dynamic of the archetype ranges across a continuum from biological through psychological to spiritual dimensions of existence, from constructive to destructive capacities. The archetype, the dynamic pattern in the unconscious, is unknowable; it becomes known in archetypal experiences and images, each such experience or image presenting a partial aspect of the archetype. Such partial and personal experience then creates a *complex* for the person. *Complex* is a constellation of psychic energy: An archetypal core is surrounded by personal dynamics.

For instance, consider the archetype of mother. It has biological, psychological, and spiritual aspects; it can be lived constructively or destructively. One's capacity for mothering develops over a lifetime in interaction of the innate potential with encounters of mothering people, as well as people in need of mothering. Any given experience of "mother" is a partial experience of the archetypal dynamic and contributes to the creation of the "mother complex" in a person. Archetypal dynamics are activated primarily in contacts with people but also in interaction with thoughts and images (e.g., in reading, observing, and seeing images of mothers and mothering). All mothering persons and depictions of mother in word, art, music, dream, and fantasy carry aspects of "mother" throughout a lifetime. For optimal development, the parents are adequate, good-enough carriers of archetypal dynamics for the young child, thus laying a foundation for the secure, solid development of the personality.

Each of us can think of personal experiences of "mother." Who was the primary mother in my life? What other people contributed to the experience of having a mother and being mothered? Were these experiences, on the whole, good enough? What was missing? What was the effect of that which was missing at various times in my life? What have I gained from experiences with images of mother and mothering in books, films, religious texts? How do people who need mothering (my children, children in general, others who long for that connection) affect me? What do they evoke? What about mothering is difficult for me? What is easy? When we explore these questions for ourselves, we come to an understanding of archetypal experiences and images related to the archetype of mother and related to the nature of the mother complex in our life. When we explore these questions with other people, we can see how these archetypal dynamics are expressed differently for each person. Such dynamics occur in every life; they take different form in different families and in different cultures.

Throughout life, a person will encounter archetypal dynamics (student, teacher, mentor, critic, judge, lover, spouse, partner, opposite, foreign, idealized, despised, hero, wise one, etc.) as these are carried by others through whom archetypal energies enter one's personal life. In psychotherapy, the therapist is a carrier, an embodiment of archetypal dynamics for his or her clients. The therapist may embody what has been missing (the absent or inadequate parent), what was overly present (the domineering or overprotective parent), what is feared (someone who has expectations, someone who judges), or what is wanted (a mentor, a helper, someone who has appreciation). The list of such archetypal functions is endless. The view of therapists as carriers of archetypal energies and functions imposes a grave responsibility on them for awareness of what they are carrying for their clients. Such awareness is essential to counteract the tendencies toward enactment or toward collusion to maintain the status quo.

Archetypal dynamics always carry constructive and destructive energies: Psychological growth involves separating from destructive energies while connecting to constructive ones. Human development progresses over a lifetime through the interplay of personal and archetypal aspects, through interaction of innate capacities with the environment, through conflict and connection between conscious and unconscious dynamics.

HISTORICAL PERSPECTIVE

Jungian thinking[5] reaches back to the work of the psychoanalytic pioneers at the beginning of the 20th century. C. G. Jung (1875–1961), a psychiatrist at a major psychiatric clinic in Zurich, Switzerland, focused his interests on under-standing the symbolic dimensions of patients' hallucinatory and delusional expressions, seeing these as communications of significance and meaning. By 1906, he became acquainted with Freud's work and entered into a period of collaborative, collegial friendship with Freud and the growing circle of psycho-analysts. Their association ended in 1913 as result of personal difficulties and professional disagreements on the nature and the contents of the unconscious.[6]

After 1913, Jung further developed his thinking on the nature of uncon-scious dynamics and the interaction with consciousness. He considered hu-man understanding of the phenomena of living to have been expressed in the arts, the mythologies, and religious traditions, as well as in pre-scientific and scientific study. He pursued cross-cultural exploration of the expressions of human psychological life through study of diverse mythologies, religious tradi-tions of East and West, tribal cultures, and medieval alchemy. These studies deepened his thinking on psychological development, pathology, and ap-proaches to healing, leading him to see typical patterns in human life, which are expressed uniquely in a given life, in a particular time and locale. Jung called these universally human patterns "archetypes."

Jung left a large body of work in essay form, collected in 20 volumes of *Collected Works* and volumes of letters (Adler & Jaffe, 1973–1975; McGuire, 1974; Meier, 2001). He never systematized the understanding of the psychic life he elaborated. Colleagues, students, scholars and clinicians of later genera-tions provide systematic accounts.[7]

Jungian views remained outside the mainstream of psychoanalytic prac-tice, frequently referred to as the work of "dissident" thinking, along with the work of Alfred Adler. Nonetheless, Jungian thinking developed to inform cli-nicians across the globe who practice psychoanalysis, psychodynamic psycho-therapy, counseling, and psycho-educational endeavors. The Jungian approach found resonance in the humanities and the arts communities (Ulanov, 1992) where symbolic thinking and its focus on access to the unconscious is valued.

Jung's (1921/1971) thinking on "Psychological Types" has entered main-stream psychology. It provides the basis for the *Myers Briggs Type Indicator*, a test widely used in career counseling, in organizations' efforts to build coop-erative work relationships, and in premarital counseling. The test aims to iden-tify a person's predisposition and preferred ways of approaching the world (e.g., through sensing, intuiting, thinking, feeling) and the primary direction in which the individual's energy flows (extravert: outward, toward the outer object; introvert: inward, toward the inner object). Understanding that differ-ent people have different predilections, one hopes, will lead to appreciation of differences (vs. judgment as "bad"), to utilizing one's strengths and developing one's weaknesses, and to working cooperatively in utilizing strengths.

Within Jungian practice, clinicians and theorists are working in several areas of theoretical knowledge and clinical application that include explora-tion of (a) the connection between personal life experiences and typically hu-man patterns; (b) clinical work with images out of dreams, fantasies, and daily life (exploration of images as providing access to unconscious dynamics and as combining affective and cognitive components); (c) the integration of concepts out of ego psychology, object relations, self psychology, and inter-subjective perspectives. For example, how do diverse theorists conceptualize a clinical phenomenon? What is similar and what is different in the concept of the ego as used in drive theory, object relations theory, and Jungian theory? For further study, see Samuels (1985); regarding perspectives on early life trauma, see Kalsched (1996). It is said that Jungian clinicians are more familiar with perspectives out of the general psychodynamic domain than clinicians from other theoretical perspectives are familiar with Jungian thinking.

The psychoanalytic historian Paul Roazen considers the splitting in the psychoanalytic field into "loyal followers" and "dissenters" to have been a most misfortunate occurrence in the early years of the 20th century (Roazen, 1984; Speicher, 1990). The intellectual feuds absorbed much psychological and intellectual energy that might have gone toward mutually enriching dialogue. The British Jungian analyst Andrew Samuels sees Jung as a "surprisingly modern thinker and psychotherapist who anticipated . . . many of the ways in which psychoanalytic and other psychological thinking has developed" (Samuels, 1985, p. 9). The list of ideas that had entered mainstream psychoanalytic thinking is long and includes (a) the clinical use of countertransference; (b) psychological development extending over the life span; (c) the transformative nature of the therapeutic process for the therapist, as well as for the patient; and (d) the therapist's personality as having central importance in depth psychology and psychotherapy (Samuels, 1985, pp. 10–11).

KEY THEORETICAL CONSTRUCTS

Jungian thinking is best understood as considering *fields of psychological processes.*[8] In writing about psychic energy, Jung used metaphors from physics. In early texts, the metaphors are from physics of the early part of the 20th century, as if psychic energy followed the laws of hydraulics. Later in life, through his friendship with the physicist Wolfgang Pauli, Jung came to see strong connections between field theory in physics and his views of archetypal energy fields (Meier, 2001; Zabriskie, 2001). A field theory approach to psychodynamics seems relevant to understanding the process nature of human psychological life.

Archetype, archetypal image, archetypal experiences, and the activation of archetypal dynamics in an individual life are fundamental components of Jungian thinking and were discussed earlier (see page 37).

Jung speaks of the *ego* as the center of consciousness, a field of conscious processes that organizes life, that orients the person to his or her inner world and the outer world, and that gives conscious direction to activities.

Beyond consciousness lies the field of the *personal unconscious,* containing all energies out of personal life experiences that are incompatible with one's orientation, everything that has been set aside, repressed, split off, considered objectionable, and rejected. The personal unconscious includes (a) what is too painful for consciousness to bear or to engage with (trauma and its residue; intrapsychic and interpersonal conflicts and their consequences); (b) what has been labeled "bad" by family, culture, society, or religious tradition; and (c) everything that is unacceptable to the ego.

The *collective unconscious* lies beyond the personal unconscious and consists of the reservoir of all typically human capacities and potential, of all archetypal energies. Every human capacity has a connection to the typically human dimension of life. (See the relation of personal experience to archetype in the example related to the mother archetype on pp. 37.)

Shadow is the term commonly used to refer to all psychological aspects that are outside of consciousness and in the unconscious, personal or collective. For example, a person reared in a very serious family, in which play was considered frivolous, will not have developed a capacity to play. This capacity will be unconscious, in shadow. For another, anger, grief, sexuality, or ambition may be repressed and in shadow. The pain of conflict or trauma is typically in shadow. What is in shadow drains a person of energy that might otherwise be available for activation and for expression of one's desires and goal-directed living. It is the work of psychological development to bring dynamics that are in shadow (in the unconscious) into the light of consciousness. Of course, there will always be aspects of psychological life that are unconscious, in shadow. The objective is to know shadow (what is unconscious) and to develop the capacity to have an ego standpoint in relation to it, neither to deny nor to enact nor to fall into shadow.

Jung's view of the unconscious is holistic: The unconscious fields are composed of energy systems containing positive and negative energies; they range across the spectrum of biological, intellectual, emotional, and spiritual capacities; they carry the repressed, rejected, split-off aspects and dynamics; they carry all potential. It is the task of consciousness, of the ego, (a) to differentiate and discriminate among these dynamic fields; (b) to integrate the energies of some fields (e.g., to resolve conflict; to work though the residue of trauma; to find ways to meet one's physical, emotional, social, intellectual, and spiritual needs); and (c) to separate from the energies of other fields (e.g., to know that hate, destructiveness, and greed are human and reside in all of us, though we do not enact them at will or impulse but develop qualities to counterbalance them).

Jung views *projection* as a major dynamic through which humans experience themselves and their environment. It is an unconscious, automatic process through which one's own unconscious psychological dynamics are perceived as being in other people. This process occurs in normal human functioning and in defensive patterns. For example, one's own unconscious anger can be projected into the other, who is then perceived as angry; people who are disconnected from their capacity for protection can project protective capacities into those from whom they expect protection. As the projecting person then comes to experience the reality of the other person (e.g., as not angry or as having no or little capacity to give protection), there is a rupture between expectation and reality. That rupture contains the potential for psychological growth: The person can come to see and own his or her feelings (anger or the need for protection) and relate to the other as that other is.

Projections that are healthy and normal at one point in life, such as the small child's projection onto the parent of capacity to give protection, are un-healthy and detrimental if encountered in an adult who projects such capacity onto a spouse or an employer. Reasonably normal development leads through gradual and repeated rupture and withdrawal of projections to perspectives in which there is increasing differentiation of reality and projection, of conscious and unconscious dimensions of psychological life. It is the psychological task of a lifetime to become continually aware of projections onto others, to pull back and to own one's own emotions, reactions, and personality traits.[9] Explo-ration of one's projections can lead to psychological growth. (Kohut speaks of the gradual process of de-idealizing the parent. Cognitive psychology speaks of the importance of unsettling cognitive structures, which can then be re-structured. Jung speaks of withdrawal of projections.)

Jung uses the term *psyche*[10] to refer to the entirety of psychological pro-cesses: conscious, personal unconscious, and collective unconscious (arche-typal fields). Jung speaks of the *Self* as the larger psychic field that lies beyond consciousness, beyond the ego, and forms the backdrop to an individual life.[11] The Jungian use of Self is totally different from the use of self in everyday language (sense of self, self-respect, etc.).

Psyche speaks in *images and metaphors* that appear in dreams and fanta-sies, in symptoms, in chance remarks, and at odd moments. Images carry cog-nitive and emotional, conscious and unconscious components. Fruitful work with images calls for focus on genuine exploration of the image with the client. Such work can bring unconscious aspects to awareness, lead to understanding of internal dynamics, and open doors to new directions. Ellen Siegelman's (1990) writing on metaphor and image in psychotherapy makes a major contribution to raising clinicians' awareness about the subtleties involved in clinical work with images.[12]

The following is an example in which work with an image involved dy-namics of current trauma and opened new directions. A woman, E. (about a year after her husband's death; psychotherapeutic work so far had centered around grief and mourning), has the image of sitting alone on a plain where a fire had burned down her house and had devastated the landscape. All is black-ened and barren. "This is what life feels like: burned down, nothing there; I am all alone." We explore together, again, the loss, desolation, and grief. Referring back to the image, I ask, "If this happened in actual life, what would you do?"—"Probably nothing, just sit there."—I then add, "Even if you did nothing at all, after some time, tiny shoots of green would emerge from the roots and from seeds that sprout."—"How do you know that?" E. asks—"Because that is how life works: There is devastation after the fire and there is new growth that will emerge in the next growing season, after some time."—E.: "That is how the physical world works. Does that apply to the spirit, too?"—"Yes, we are of the same world, nature and spirit."—E.: "I can live with that." Further exploration of the image over time led to an opening of new perspectives that, again, were further explored, alongside the ongoing grief process.

To have *psychological health*, the ego has to recognize the existence of un-conscious phenomena (the shadow), has to seek to know them and take them into account. One needs to know one's own frustration, anger, pain, trauma, desires, interests, loves, and passions. One needs to find a way to relate and give expression to them, yet also separate oneself from extreme reactions (e.g., rage). Connections to unconscious dynamics can serve to activate potential resources (qualities that were repressed or never engaged, such as initiative, nurturing, perseverance, creativity, desire, passion, etc.). In psychological health, the fields of consciousness (the ego) and of the entirety of the unconscious (personal and collective) are in dialogue and interaction; they complement each other and, together, form the basis of human development over the life span.

Psychological illness is seen as stemming from imbalanced or disturbed relations between consciousness and the unconscious. Such imbalances can be the result of trauma, of deficits in nurture, and of limited opportunity to experience and develop psychological capacities. It is the clinician's task to work with the client in the areas of those psychological processes where development has deficits or has been disturbed. For example: (a) In the case of insufficient development of ego capacities, therapeutic work supports ego development and strengthening. (b) When one is disconnected from unconscious energies, therapeutic work explores what was repressed or split off and attempts to restore those energies to consciousness. (c) If there is an excessive influx of unconscious energies (as in psychotic states, where the ego is overrun by what is typically unconscious), the therapeutic approach calls for reinstating the essential boundaries between the ego and the unconscious through psychotherapeutic treatment and psychopharmacology that restores proper cellular biochemistry.

Jungian clinicians draw on the work of many psychodynamic clinicians and thinkers (see Young-Eisendrath's [1988] review of psychodynamic thinking) when engaging in the psychotherapeutic process. They may follow the insights of Kohut (1978b, 1984), of Winnicott (1965, 1971), of various thinkers in object relations theory and in ego psychology (Goldstein, 1998), of Mitchell (1993), of Mitchell and Black (1995), or of Sanville (1991). Many Jungian clinicians follow a phenomenological approach and explore with much subtlety the phenomena of the client's experiences, images, and affects, thereby letting the data that emerge lead the way to the next level of exploration. Jungian therapists incorporate the use of nonverbal and expressive modalities[13] into the therapeutic process, in order to facilitate access to unconscious dynamics.

Jung was the first among the depth psychologists to consider *psychological development* to extend over the life span (Jung, 1931/1969, ## 749–795). His thinking on life-long development is further elaborated in the psychological process of *individuation* that involves (a) differentiation out of identity with family or culture; (b) development of a personal core, knowing oneself, having one's own standpoint; (c) development of one's personality in the best possible way; (d) knowing what is typically human and being connected to it; (e) creating a sense of meaning for one's life and developing a spiritual orientation (which is not identical with religious affiliation); and (f) living responsibly in the human community.

The question of *meaning* has a central position in Jung's work. He considered the creation of meaning for one's life to be a fundamentally human need.[14] He saw each person's answer to the question of meaning to be subjective, created out of a person's reflection and consciousness, and becoming his or her personal myth, the carrier of personal values. Considerable psychological suffering can come from the absence of a sense of meaning. The human struggle is for creation of meaning, as well as for the capacity to tolerate that which is meaningless.

ASSESSMENT

Assessment involves a directed process of understanding a person, with attention to several areas of living: the presenting problem; the history of that problem; medical, social, and psychological problems encountered; the personal history, with attention to basic needs (biological, psychological, social, spiritual; how they are met or unmet); relationships (family, school, employment, community); the structure and dynamics of intrapsychic functioning, including major defenses and areas of developmental gaps; the ability to work and derive economic support and satisfaction; one's perspective on life and living; and what gives meaning to one's life. Treatment approaches follow from such assessment and are modified as additional dynamics and problems become evident. *Assessment is always in evolution and does not yield a fixed view.* Treatment approaches, equally, are always in evolution, constituting a process that is modified in interaction with changes in assessment, psychodynamics, and outer world events.[15]

Because of space limitations, I will look at only one family member, Rena. She has not been the focus of either assessment or treatment; she has not spoken much for herself. I will highlight a few points based on the family description we have. I will deliberately use descriptive, non-technical language in an attempt to stay close to Rena's experiences,[16] and, likewise, I will phrase my theoretical speculations in everyday language. My aim is to point to how a clinician might think, rather than what theoretical term he or she may give to a phenomenon. I will add theoretical concepts to facilitate the process of conceptualizing.

Looking at Rena

Rena, age 18, is talented and bright but unable to complete what she starts. She was adopted as an infant and was adored by Gram, whom she considered to be the only one who ever really loved her. We hear nothing directly about her early life interactions with her mother, Nancy. Because Rena spent most of her time with Gram and Aunt Flo, we are left to assume that Nancy was not very involved with Rena. During Rena's early years, Nancy was fully and happily engaged in her career as a nurse.

Birthdays were sad days for Rena, though no one understood her sadness.

She now tells us that they reminded her of the birth mother, whom she missed. What were the conversations about the adoption like in the family? Was Rena missing her birth mother and missing Nancy's involvement with her? What were the years of Rena's life like before Michael's birth and before Nancy's injury? Did Rena lose the mother who was competent as a nurse and satisfied in her career at the same time she lost her place as an only child? Who was able to help her process her reactions? Did she feel left again, this time by Nancy? Did she then grow up with a sad, depressed, frustrated mother who was overwhelmed, emotionally withdrawn because of her pain and frustration? Gram's love and attention gave Rena emotional support, but, it seems, Gram was predominantly the adoring grandmother (a proper function for a grandmother) and did not provide the guidance and the structuring (functions of a parent) that any young girl needs.

As a mother, Nancy functioned well in physical caretaking but was not able to guide and direct her daughter. Never having been guided, Nancy could not guide. Not having been a playful child, she could not facilitate her daughter's playfulness, excitement, and exploration. What were her expectations of Rena? Did she expect the bright Rena to be another miniature adult, as she had been? Was she able to help Rena with goal direction and the completion of difficult tasks? Possibly, she expected Rena to just get it right, as she had done.

Rena is multi-talented and interested in musical theater. When she auditioned for a national TV series, Charley had great plans for her. To what extent was Charley taking over Rena's talents, living emotionally off Rena? If Rena had to live out Charley's dreams, she likely felt that she was losing them to him. To what extent was Nancy frightened by seeing Rena's interest in the theater, fearing a repeat of Charley's non-accomplishment? Was there anyone who could help her be a child, to enjoy performing, to work at practicing and developing structure, to be who she is? Was everyone expecting achievement from Rena? Those expectations, likely, became burdens for Rena. Did Rena, then, throw off those burdens by undermining opportunities, by not following through?

Rena moved to her great-grandfather's apartment at age 12 and lived there alone after his death. Her parents date the further deterioration of her behavior to that time. Was this move an escape from struggles in her parents' household, an attempt to return to a period of life that was conflict-free (adored by Gram as a young child), or a way to deal with Gram's death by moving into her apartment? How does she now think about this move and its meaning for her?

What are Rena's present interests, desires, and wishes? What gives her joy and pleasure? What makes her curious? Rena is now interested in psychotherapy for herself; she feels lonely and confused, and wants to talk. She is interested in finding her birth mother. At meetings of adoptees and birth mothers, she focuses on the birth mothers with the question: "Do you think of your child?" What needs are behind those questions? Since placing her name on the waiting list for psychotherapy, Rena has become more reflective; she began journal-writing. She has some theories about the roots of her problems; she is interested in understanding.

Thinking About Rena

Rena lost her birth mother shortly after birth, when she was adopted and placed in a physically and emotionally nurturing environment provided by an extended family: The archetype of mother in her caring aspects was encountered. But the archetypal energies of a mother who fully sees, guides, and directs a child were not activated. "Fully seeing" a child involves (a) seeing strengths and talents, taking delight in them, and engaging with their development; and (b) seeing weaknesses and limits, and providing direction to strengthen abilities in the weak areas.

For Rena, there is much in shadow, that is, in the unconscious: The trauma of her losses and their residue; the capacity to see herself for who she is, with strengths and limitations (vs. someone adored, for whom life does not work out); and the ability to deal with frustration and setbacks, to persist and pursue a goal. These dynamics (experiences, deficits, capacities) need to be encountered, engaged, related to, and developed so that their energies can be available for creative living in Rena's world. What has happened to her interests and talents? Have they been internally rejected, repressed, or split off after her inability to follow through undermined satisfaction in these pursuits? We do not know the degree and the direction of her desires, interest, and life energy (physical and emotional drives). Have they been rejected and repressed (are they mostly in shadow)?

In terms of intrapsychic structures, Rena lacks ego development. Ego encompasses the energies that consciousness needs to lead a life with direction, the ability to handle difficulties, perseverance, and many other qualities. Rena lacks ego capacities that are up to the tasks of encountering life as a young adult. Her lack of ego development has been apparent since latency and became increasingly troublesome during adolescence. The residue of trauma and losses, the consequences of excessive attention (Gram's doting on her), and the lack of assistance in developing perseverance may have been contributing factors.

Based on the family report (a more complete assessment needs to be developed in personal contacts), Rena does not show serious psychopathology; she seems more "lost" and directionless, in need of consolidation and development. Her search for her birth mother can be seen as an expression, (a) literally, of the need to know facts about her physical origins; and (b) metaphorically, as the search for what is missing in her life. Her question to birth mothers, "Are you thinking of your child?" can be heard symbolically as "I need someone to think about me, about who I am and what I need and am missing." Psychotherapy, it is hoped, will engage her in a process of "thinking about me," about who she is, what she is missing, what she needs, and how she can build her life.

Rena has strengths: She is bright and talented; she has a good-enough relational foundation of early nurturing; and she wants to understand herself and interrupt the cycle of behaviors through which she undermines herself. She has begun to be reflective, writing in her journal. Psychotherapy can build on and utilize those strengths.

THE THERAPEUTIC PROCESS

In anticipating therapeutic work with Rena, I can only outline an approach. The process will unfold and be modified as experiences are explored and new understanding is gained. And, within the limited space available here, I cannot address the subtleties of the process, the details of how to explore and work through. I encourage student readers with an interest in psychotherapy to read widely, to engage in conversation with experienced therapists in order to extend their repertoire of ways of exploring and working through dynamic issues and, most of all, to seek individual supervision so that they can learn the subtleties of working therapeutically.

What Will Help Rena?

The development of a good therapeutic relationship will be crucial. The therapist needs to be finely attuned to hear, see, and value those parts of Rena that others have not attended to and provide a space where Rena can express and process her frustrations, pain, and troubles. Rena wants someone "to think about me." She needs to experience that the therapist thinks about her and, more important, engages in thinking with her so that she can come to think more deeply about herself. Winnicott refers to this process as providing a holding and facilitating environment. Jung speaks of the necessity of providing a container in which the therapeutic process takes place: to move development forward, to repair the residue of earlier injuries. Within this container (facilitating environment), the therapist needs to embody basic, archetypal processes: seeing, containing, facilitating, letting Rena see Rena, aiding in exploration, and dealing with inner and outer obstacles. The therapist will carry the archetypal energies of the mother-parent-teacher-mentor who guides toward development the capacities that are dormant within the child or person needing assistance.

Projections will fall on to the therapist: projections of what is wanted and needed (the ideal mother or parent Rena never had), of what is feared (the unavailable mother or parent; the nagging, critical mother; the father who uses Rena's dreams for his own satisfaction), and of regression to the early, simple life with adoring Gram. Therapeutic progress will be dependent on sensitive work in such a heavily laden transferential field. The therapist needs to hold these projections (transferences) without stepping into them (i.e., enacting countertransference reactions), while steadily continuing to work with Rena to develop her capacities. Such work involves embodying for Rena diverse aspects of the archetypal fields of mother, parent, guiding adult: giving praise, acknowledging flaws, seeing hurt, exploring roots, looking at the obvious, pointing to the hidden background, seeing sparks of vitality, supporting development, having realistic expectations, and not imposing values, goals, or ideas. Most of all, the therapist needs to be steadily present: listening; exploring and thinking with Rena; showing patience and firmness; providing structure, containment, and freedom to Rena to be herself.[17]

Therapeutic discussions will revolve, initially, around Rena telling her story

and speaking about her current dilemmas. Her reflections can provide starting points for explorations of her life experiences. The losses she has suffered
will be talked about in many ways, repeatedly, over time. What residue have
they left? Exploration of her thoughts and emotions about the adoption and
her current search for her birth mother will be central issues. At some point,
her therapist will be able to engage her in reflecting on the metaphoric nature
of her question, "Are you thinking about your child?" but only after she has
been able to express and work through the complex reactions related to the
literal level of the question. Metaphoric exploration comes after, and in addition to, literal exploration, whether the metaphor is contained in a question, a
statement, a phrase, a bodily action, or a symptom.

Much time will be devoted to current problems and, alongside this, to
what interests Rena at present and what has interested her in the past. What is
her connection to her talents, to the creativity shown in her early life? What are
her current interests, desires? The creative talents (singing, acting, story writing,
poetry, mechanical abilities) that flourished for a while in early life may become stepping stones toward reconnecting her to hidden aspects of herself.
Or, they may turn out to have been interests of childhood that do not play an
active part in adult life. It is important that the therapist truly explore without
getting involved in countertransferential interests (a) of excessive excitement
and pushing of the talents (as her father may have done) or (b) in belittling
them because they are impractical (as Nancy may have done, out of fear of a
repeat of Charley's failure). Rena may have already internally fallen into one of
those two stances. In any event, exploring what her interests truly are will be a
slow and difficult process.[18]

It will be most important to come to understand what lies behind her
pattern of not finishing projects. How does she deal with difficulties in projects?
Did her talents and the praise she received lead her to expect that everything
should come easily, quickly? Does she lose interest when something becomes
hard, quickly assuming she cannot do it? Is losing interest a protection against
failure, against finding out she is not as good as everyone thinks, against disappointing others? Understanding what is being expressed by the phenomenon of losing interest will, at best, be slow and gradual; working with the
understanding will be equally gradual.

Pop psychology offers pat answers, and being bright, Rena can easily repeat them; what may look like understanding can be a cover-up, a defense
against genuine exploration. I imagine Rena to be a person who can easily and
superficially talk about psychological understanding. A therapist has to be respectful in dealing with those defenses: hear them, use them as starting points
for further work, never impose the therapist's own view, but, rather, help Rena
develop her own understanding.

Summary

Therapeutic work with Rena will involve the building of a solid therapeutic
relationship within which the work of psychological growth can take place:
heal the aftermath of trauma and losses, deal with the deficits in her life, fill in

developmental gaps, direct her energies to hidden or rejected qualities that contain undeveloped potential, find energies to follow through in difficulties, discover what is meaningful in her life, and connect to and give expression to what is meaningful for her. These are aspects of the process of individuation, of becoming and being the person one can be.

The therapist will be (a) looking for strengths, however hidden they may be, and for what interferes with development of those strengths; (b) working with needs and difficulties as expressed in the present, interwoven with looking back to earlier manifestations of such difficulties and of the ways in which they were dealt with in the past; (c) attending to feelings, reactions, and potentials that emerge from the unconscious; (d) maintaining awareness of how Rena interacts with friends and family; (e) helping Rena find support in the community, taking seriously that because "it takes a village to raise a child," it takes a community to support its struggling members. Such patient therapeutic work may lead Rena to create a satisfying life for herself.

APPLICATION TO DIVERSITY

Jungian clinicians practice across the globe with persons of diverse national, ethnic, and cultural backgrounds; lifestyles; and chronic illnesses and disabilities. The timeless dynamics of the archetypal dimension in human existence find expression in myriad forms, different in each culture and era. To understand how archetypal dynamics manifest in a given environment, the clinician must become familiar with the history, the traditions, and the value systems of clients and their communities. For instance, to get some understanding of an ethnic group's cultural context, I recommend listening to the people's songs and music; reading respected and beloved novels, poems, and proverbs; listening to people describe their traditions; becoming familiar with values, prohibitions, and obligations of the culture; learning some of the history; and looking at some of the myths that inform the tradition. To understand the experiences of immigrants, refugees, and other minorities, I similarly recommend reading a memoir or a fictionalized account written by a person out of the respective group (e.g., Hoffman [1989], about immigration from Poland; Cisneros [1984, 2002], about growing up Hispanic in Chicago; Santos [1999], about the mestizo experience; Ahmed [1999], about emigration from Egypt; and McBride [1996], about the biracial experience).

The Jungian clinicians will work with issues of diversity (of culture, ethnicity, socioeconomic standing, gender, lifestyle, chronic illness, or disability) fundamentally in the same manner that they work with all other issues: by *seeking understanding*. Such understanding requires that clinicians (a) have or seek knowledge about the specific issue (e.g., culture, illness, or disability) and then seek to understand each client individually through careful exploration; (b) be aware of their own thinking, perspectives, values, assumptions so as to guard against imposing their views; and (c) be committed to working with the client toward having the client gain understanding and perspectives that are connected to the core of the client's personality.

Ethnic Concerns Enter the Shore Family

The case description of the Shore family tells us nothing of its members' ethnic background; we can infer that ethnicity, whatever it may be, is not an overt issue for them. What might the impact be if ethnic concerns became an issue? Let us consider that the Shore family is Caucasian, that their traditions are "American" without much of an ethnic flavor. They live within a lower-middle-class neighborhood with conservative values and have some fears of newcomers, of immigrants that have begun to move into their neighborhood. There is not much social interaction between old-timers and newcomers.

When Rena moved out of her parents' house, she found a small apartment nearby. Struggling to earn enough money to pay her rent, she comes home regularly to have a meal, to use the washing machine, to maintain connection, yet make it clear that she lives by herself. There are fewer tensions at home; her visits are short enough to avoid troublesome entanglements.

Rena's search for her birth mother yielded results: She found a name and an address, made a connection. The birth mother, like the Shores, was Caucasian American without much ethnic connection. Rena felt assured that the birth mother had been thinking about her but an ongoing relationship did not develop. Rena learned a few facts about her birth father: The birth mother had a brief relationship with him, lost contact before becoming aware of her pregnancy, and does not know his identity or whereabouts. He was a young, handsome music student from Guatemala; he had musical talent and played in a band, in which he was the lead vocalist. He had been an interesting companion for the brief encounter with the birth mother. Rena took much interest in the bits of her birth father's life, in his country and ethnic heritage. She became interested in things Guatemalan, in Hispanic music; she attributed her musical talents to the father's genes. She began to seek out Hispanic clubs, especially the ones frequented by Central American immigrants who recently moved into the city.

Rena's interests in the world of her birth father further strained relations with the parents, who had already become anxious about Rena's search for her birth mother, and who now were quite disturbed by her interests in Hispanic culture, music, and traditions. They tried to remain supportive but became increasingly edgy as Rena looked for Guatemalan music and crafts, which she also brought to their home as small gifts. They came to feel that she was"rubbing it in" that she was of a different ethnicity. Hurt feelings led to irritability and anger; fighting arose easily over minor issues.

Thinking About Rena's Connection to the Birth Father's World

Rena's reactions have multiple components:

1. She now has a connection to an ethnic heritage that was not a live reality in her adoptive family. Such a connection meets the human need for

multigenerational history and connectedness, a link in the connections to the human family. Ethnic connection can be one part in having access to archetypal energies. The therapist will explore with Rena what meaning this connection has for her, how she will relate to the newly emerging possibilities and integrate them into her life.

2. The relation to the birth father brought reconnection to her creative musical abilities. Rena feels emotionally connected to what she sees as the birth father's gifts (her talents). It may be possible to channel that emotional energy into developing her abilities and sustaining her interests during difficulties (contrary to her former pattern of losing interest). Or, negatively, Rena may simply idealize the father's abilities without moving into developing her own. Again, careful exploration and engagement with what she discovers will lead her forward (e.g., if she re-energizes her musical interests, she will also need to develop the discipline needed for practice and study).

3. The focus on the birth father can serve to surface unresolved issues in outer life (with her adoptive parents) and in inner life (search for what is missing for her psychically). After having had conflicts with her parents for years, after having been hurt, frustrated, and angered by them, the discovery of her birth parents gives her the opportunity to direct her energies toward creating a fantasy parent in the talented Guatemalan birth father. (She maintains only limited contact with the birth mother, who is within reach and hence more likely to also disappoint, hurt, and anger her.) It is easy to focus on him, about whom she knows very little, and to create a parent whom she can idealize, a parent with whom she can connect in her imagination, who will give her an ethnic tradition, who will not rupture her fantasies because he is not within reach as a person. He can become the object of projection of wants and desires and can serve as a fantasy escape from dealing with what is missing for her, intrapsychically and interpersonally. It will be essential to deal with the unresolved personal issues (no. 3), to separate them from the genuinely ethnic (no. 1) and personal talent (no. 2) issues.

Such working through of conflicts (no. 3) needs to occur so that Rena can engage with the genuine ethnic and talent issues. It could include looking at questions like these: Whom has Rena idealized in the past? Does she have a tendency to find diverse figures to idealize for a while? The idealization will need to be received and explored, without active support and without active attempts to bring reality back into the picture. Life events (outer or inner) will occur and provide the relativizing experiences that will puncture the inflated image of the birth father. In Jungian terms, we are seeing here a projection of psychic needs, a projection that needs to be received, understood, punctured, and dissolved.

Furthermore, Rena's clashes with Nancy and Charley, triggered by her focus on her father's heritage in the present, need to be explored in terms of current problems and in terms of the residue of old problems. How much does Rena's focus on her birth father carry an expression of anger at Nancy and Charley?[19] Is the focus on the birth father also in the service of separating from

Nancy and Charley? Rena's attempts to separate from the family have been quite conflicted. Can these current conflicts also serve as a genuine separation so that she, as a separate person, can come to relate better to family and friends?

The working with the residue of old problems (no. 3) does not diminish the genuine significance of connecting to ethnic heritage (no. 1) and inherited potential (no. 2). Rena's emerging connection to the birth father's ethnic and cultural roots may develop into enduring connections, if Rena has the good fortune[20] of encountering people (teachers, coworkers, friends) who provide space in which her interests can develop. Dismissal as "it's another one of your phases" will deprive her of the opportunity to discover what her needs for rootedness are. Can she grow roots in the ethnic world of her birth father, a world uniquely hers and new and exciting, as well as in the world of her adoptive family, with all its members' limitations? Rena needs the opportunity to explore as far as she wants to without expectation and without hindrances.

Furthermore, Rena's interest in the ethnic world of the birth father can be seen as a metaphor and a symbol for connection to her internal biological and psychological roots, and can serve as one stepping stone in the process of solidifying her psychological core. Rena seems to have become energized by the search for connection to the world of the birth father. Can that vitalization awaken energy in other areas of her life? Or, will she become caught in conflicts (divided loyalties to the world of the birth father and of the adoptive family), be belittled or dismissed, be rejected as "having bad ideas" and "getting away from work"; if so, development cannot happen. Energy often awakens energy; it is hoped than this will be true for Rena.

Concluding the Perspective on Ethnic Concerns

Ethnic heritage is a part of one's lineage, one's multigenerational history, which contains conflicts, dilemmas, value systems, generational wisdom, and generational folly. Ethnic heritage can separate a person from the community at large or it can connect a person to a network of relationships. It can also be one link in the line that connects an individual to the human world at large. Known or unknown, these dynamics have an effect. A thoughtful clinician will explore them with a view toward an understanding and an enrichment of the individual life.

LIMITATIONS OF THE MODEL

Strengths and limitations are always closely related, the proverbial two sides of the same coin. Jungian thinking is strong in its holistic view of life, focus on psychological development as a lifelong process, and concern with the individual. It holds a humanist perspective and shares a connection to related fields concerned with human understanding (arts, humanities, and religious and spiritual traditions). It does not offer a very detailed account of human development (Jungians integrate views from psychodynamic thinking in general). It does not focus on approaches directly aimed at symptom relief, although such relief is part of the practice patterns of Jungian clinicians; instead, it focuses on development of the client's personality. Such an approach takes a more long-term perspective; its positive effects become visible over time. Consequently, the Jungian approach has been considered to be applicable primarily for ongoing development of functioning persons. Such an assessment is based on partial understanding, where focus on a way of working (gradual development of the personality) obscures the essential feature: a holistic view of human life. Holistic thinking can form a solid backdrop to problem-focused work. The clinician's depth psychological perspective can infuse short-term work with the spirit of recognition and appreciation of the complexity and fullness of human life when a small segment of that life is selected as a focus for clinical work.

For the clinician, Jungian thinking does not offer a detailed description or a prescription of therapeutic techniques or skills. Instead, it holds that a clinician has grave responsibility for personal development and for intensive study across a range of fields in the arts and the humanities, over and above the clinician's studies in psychology and psychodynamic and psychoanalytic theories. A more integrated personality will be better able to respond therapeutically, drawing from a wide range of knowledge and clinical skills within the psychodynamic field. On the negative side, Jungian thinking about the exploration of archetypal images and dynamics has led less experienced clinicians to fall, at times, into a didactic stance, as if teaching about archetypal dynamics would result in the activation of such dynamics.[21]

Knowledge of many ways of thinking is important; no single theory can address all facets of human life. Clinicians will serve their clients most effectively when they have a solid, humanistic worldview; when they have access to an extensive reservoir of dynamic understanding and practice; and when they can reach into that reservoir for what is useful to thier clients.

RESEARCH

Jungian clinical work falls within the domain of psychoanalytic and psychodynamic practice, about which considerable research has been done regarding therapeutic effectiveness. Hugh Rosen (1988) offers an extensive review of such research. He reports substantive findings that show effectiveness to be similar across different approaches when a positive therapeutic relationship is present that has warmth, empathic understanding, respect, and attentive interest in the patient. With that relationship as a base, therapists draw on techniques from many sources related to the problem at hand. The salient issue is not relationship *or* techniques, but relationship *and* techniques. Rosen speaks of experienced and seasoned clinicians as "virtuosos at drawing upon a variety of techniques from multiple sources . . . [while being] anchored in a unified theory and philosophy" (p. 406). Rosen concludes that the coalescence of anchoring in a unified framework and access to a wide range of techniques leads to effective clinical practice. My reading of the research literature, coupled with my clinical experience, leads me to strongly agree with Rosen. Jungian clinicians, at their best, are anchored in Jungian thinking and draw on ways of psychodynamic practice that have been established to be effective.

Beyond therapeutic gains in personality development and healing of psychological injuries and wounds, the Jungian approach offers an opportunity to deeply experience our human dynamics, to struggle with what gives meaning to our existence, to develop a personal stance toward life that will evolve throughout life. Forever a work in progress, such an endeavor is difficult to evaluate or compare: Each person knows whether his or her work in progress is personally useful and meaningful.

SUMMARY

Jungian thinking takes a holistic perspective on the person in the environment, focusing on the inner world as it unfolds in continuing interaction with the outer world. This perspective always considers conscious and unconscious fields in psychological experience; it looks at unconscious fields as consisting of rejected and repressed aspects of life, as well as of all potential. Human life has personal and archetypal (typically human) dimensions; each person is uniquely himself or herself while being connected to the heritage of humanity.

Place and time, society and culture create the environment in which the fundamentals of human nature unfold and develop into the diverse persons who share life on planet Earth. Recognition of diversities within the human commonalities and profound respect for these diversities and commonalities are essential for personal development and integrity, for cooperative living, and, of course, for ethical clinical practice.

Psychological development extends over the life span. It calls for increasing differentiation from familial and societal influences, for ongoing exploration of unconscious dynamics, for finding what gives meaning and spiritual orientation to one's life, and for connection to and responsible participation in the human community.

Thinkers, poets, artists, and healers everywhere speak of the troubles and the conflicts, the joys and the satisfactions, the love and the hate that humans have encountered over the ages. Their insights extend psychotherapists' body of knowledge so that their outlook on the patient can be wide and deep, yet focus on the needs of the present.

Development of a therapeutic stance makes substantial demands on the therapist in terms of knowledge, practice skills, and, most of all, personal integration. An ongoing attitude of self-inquiry will enable clinicians to separate their personality dynamics from those of the clients and will greatly facilitate the therapeutic engagement. To support clinicians in such work, I will simply repeat a line from Anna Freud and one from Jung. Anna Freud asks that we "have a great love of the truth, scientific truth as well as personal truth" and that we "place this appreciation of truth higher than any discomfort at meeting unpleasant facts" (Kohut, 1978a, p. 474). Jung states frankly, "Every psycho-therapist not only has his own method—he himself is that method. *Ars requirit totum hominen* [the art requires the whole person], says an old master. The great healing factor is the doctor's personality" (Jung, 1945/1966a, # 198). The clinician's personal development facilitates therapeutic process, and it gives a gift: It enriches each person's life.

NOTES

1. I use the term *psychodynamic* as referring to all approaches to psychological understanding that consider psychological processes to range across the spectrum of conscious to unconscious dimensions, including psychoanalysis, psychoanalytic psychotherapy, other psychotherapeutic approaches with a depth, psychological perspective, and psycho-educational endeavors.

   The term *depth psychology* (Jung, 1951/1976b, # 1142 [Jung's writing that appears in the *Collected Works* is referenced in this chapter by paragraph (#) number, as is customary to facilitate location of text in both hardcover and softcover editions of the *Collected Works*]; Samuels, Shorter, & Plaut, 1986, pp. 43–44) refers to all psychological approaches that consider conscious and unconscious dimensions of psychological life. Originally coined to refer to psychoanalytic theoretical perspectives that differed from Freud's theories, in current usage it is analogous to the terms *psychoanalytic field* or *psychodynamic field* and their variants.

2. It was Jung who recommended to Freud that a prospective analyst have a personal analysis (Jung, 1935/1966b, # 8; 1929/1966c, # 165). The therapist's personality structure and function are of vital importance. "Every psychotherapist not only has his own method—he himself is that method. *Ars requirit totum hominem* [the art requires the whole person], says an old master. The great healing factor in psychotherapy is the doctor's personality" (Jung, 1945/1966a, # 198). (About lifelong therapeutic process for the therapist, see Jung [1968/1976c], ## 322–323.)

3. See *Faces in a Cloud,* for Stolorow and Atwood's (1979) discussion on the interweaving of metapsychology, subjectivity, and theory construction.

4. For a detailed discussion of the development and application of the concept of archetype and archetypal dynamics, of critiques and problems, see Samuels (1985); Samuels et al. (1986); a selection of direct references from Jung is found in Sharp (1991).

5. This summary of Jungian thinking is based on numerous sources: primarily C. G. Jung, *Collected Works,* Vols. 1–20 (1953–1976); McGuire (1974); Adler & Jaffe (1973-1975); Jung & Jaffe (1961); Samuels (1985); Samuels et al. (1986); and Sharp (1991).

6. Jung disagreed with Freud's views on the primacy and exclusivity of sexual libido as internal dynamic; he considered humanity's spiritual developments as existing in their own right, over Freud's views as being a sublimation of libidinal energy. In an interview with a journalist in 1953, he stated, "I accept the facts Freud has discovered, but accept his theory only partially" (1968/1976a, # 1066).

7. For further study I recommend Brooke (1991); Hopcke (1992); Samuels (1985); Samuels et al. (1986); Siegelman (1990); Singer (1994); Stein (1998); Whitmont (1969); Young-Eisendrath & Dawson (1997); Young-Eisendrath & Hall (1991). For a direct experience of Jung's views, read Jung's reflections on his life, dictated late in life to his secretary (Jung & Jaffe, 1961), and quotations contained in Sharp (1991).

8. Early Jungian texts (along with psychoanalytic writing in general) can sound as if psychological life had defining psychic structures with specific contents.

9. Obviously, there are realities in the outer environment that need to be separated from projected qualities. In projection, the other person provides a hook onto which I then hang my picture. The critical issue lies in differentiation. What is the hook in the other? What is

the picture I hang onto it? How big a picture do I hang onto a little hook? What projections do I habitually place onto others? What are the qualities that continually evoke projections in me? Or, do I say, "I must be imagining (projecting) what I see," and I then end up denying reality?

10. *Psyche* comes from the Greek, where it refers to "soul, spirit, breath" (*Webster's New World Dictionary*, 1962, p. 1175).

11. Space limitations do not allow for elaboration. For a detailed discussion, see Samuels (1985), chapter 4; about Ego and Self, chapter 3. See also Edinger (1972), especially Parts I and II.

12. Exploration of images in literature, film, and folklore from the perspective of metaphor for psychological dynamics can vitalize psychological knowledge; metaphor and image connect affect and cognition. For illustrations, refer to audio recordings of lectures on folklore: Speicher (1996/2001, 1997/2001, 2002).

13. Drawing and sandtray work facilitate emotional expression while providing containment. Sandtray work is derived from play therapy and adapted for use with adults. See Kalff (1980); Mitchell & Friedman (1994).

14. Viktor Frankl holds the same position, and Frankl's *Logotherapy* is an existential approach to psychotherapy rooted in the search for meaning (Frankl, 1963, 1965, 1978). In recent years, the question of meaning has become more prominent in clinical thinking and writing. See Rosen (1998), for a summary of recent developments with numerous references.

15. Polly Young-Eisendrath outlines the essentials of assessment (1988, pp. 61–62) and the therapeutic process (1988, pp. 66–67) from a psychodynamic perspective, applicable across a range of theoretical perspectives.

16. Kohut stresses the importance of staying "experience-near" versus "experience-distant" (Kohut, 1984, pp. 186–187; 226, note 8). Theories and theoretical language foster the experience-distant perspective. Clinical practice has to be experience-near. For clinical work, Kohut (1984, p. 226, note 5) further speaks about using value-neutral versus value-laden language (e.g., "move away" vs. "separation"). In teaching and in supervision, I ask students, first, to describe clinical experiences in everyday language (to be experience-near) and then, and *only* then, to think conceptually and to theorize about the patient and the clinical experience.

17. Individual supervision can help beginning therapists to develop their ways of working in this manner. I suggest a careful reading of Kohut (1984, 1978b) and Winnicott (1965, 1971).

18. Working with what is unconscious, in shadow, is always cumbersome. As has been said, "The trouble with the unconscious is precisely that: it is unconscious." It is easy to say, "Explore what is unconscious (split off, repressed, rejected)," but it is very hard to do.

19. It is hoped that Nancy and Charley will also work in therapy with the issues stirred in them by Rena's reactions.

20. Good fortune and misfortune are factors that enter human experiences throughout life and play a role alongside conscious intentions, unconscious dynamics, the events of everyday life, and unusual occurrences.

21. See Plaut's discussion (1966) of the capacity to imagine as rooted in early life developmental dynamics. Development of that capacity requires sensitive attention to those early life dynamics (vs. "instruction" about images).

REFERENCES

Adler, G., & Jaffe, A. (Eds.). (1973–1975). *C. G. Jung letters* (Vols. 1–2; R. F. C. Hull, Trans.). Princeton, NJ: Princeton University Press.

Ahmed, L. (1999). *A border passage: From Cairo to America—a woman's journey*. New York: Penguin Putnam.

Brooke, R. (1991). *Jung and phenomenology*. London and New York: Routledge.

Cisneros, S. (1984). *The house on Mango Street*. New York: Vintage Books.

Cisneros, S. (2002). *Caramelo*. New York: Knopf.

Edinger, E. F. (1972). *Ego and archetype*. New York: Putnam.

Ehrenwald, J. (1976). *The history of psychotherapy*. New York: Aronson.

Ellenberger, H. F. (1970). *The discovery of the unconscious*. New York: Basic Books.

Frankl, V. E. (1963). *Man's search for meaning: An introduction to logotherapy*. New York: Washington Square Press.

Frankl, V. E. (1965). *The doctor and the soul*. New York: Knopf.

Frankl, V. E. (1978). *The unheard cry for meaning: Psychotherapy and humanism*. New York: Simon and Schuster.

Goldstein, E. G. (1998). Ego psychology and object relations theory. In R. Dorfman (Ed.), *Paradigms of clinical social work* (pp. 19–43). New York: Brunner/Mazel.

Hoffman, E. (1989). *Lost in translation: A life in a new language*. New York: Penguin Books.

Hopcke, R. H. (1992). *A guided tour of the collected works of C. G. Jung*. Boston: Shambhala.

Jung, C. G. (1953–1976). *The collected works of C. G. Jung* (Vols. 1–20; H. Read, M. Fordham, G. Adler, & W. McGuire, Eds.; R. F. C. Hull, Trans.). Princeton, NJ: Princeton University Press.

Jung, C. G. (1966a). Medicine and psychotherapy. In H. Read, M. Fordham, G. Adler, & W. McGuire (Eds.) (R. F. C. Hull, Trans.), *Collected works: Vol. 16* (## 192–211). Princeton, NJ: Princeton University Press. (Original work published in 1945.)

Jung, C. G. (1966b). Principles of practical psychotherapy. In H. Read, M. Fordham, G. Adler, & W. McGuire (Eds.) (R. F. C. Hull, Trans.), *Collected works: Vol. 16* (## 1–27). Princeton, NJ: Princeton University Press. (Original work published in 1935.)

Jung, C. G. (1966c). Problems of modern psychotherapy. In H. Read, M. Fordham, G. Adler, & W. McGuire (Eds.) (R. F. C. Hull, Trans.), *Collected works: Vol. 16* (## 114–174). Princeton, NJ: Princeton University Press. (Original work published in 1929.)

Jung, C. G. (1969). The stages of life. In Read, H., Fordham, M., Adler, G., & McGuire, W. (Eds.) (R. F. C. Hull, Trans.) *Collected works: Vol. 8* (## 749-795). Princeton, NJ: Princeton University Press. (Original work published in 1931.)

Jung, C. G. (1971). Psychological types (Vol. 6). Princeton, NJ: Princeton University Press. (Original work published in 1921.)

Jung, C. G. (1976a). Answers to questions on Freud. In H. Read, M. Fordham, G. Adler, & W. McGuire (Eds.) (R. F. C. Hull, Trans.), *Collected works: Vol. 18* (## 1065–1076). Princeton, NJ: Princeton University Press. (Original work published in 1968.)

Jung, C. G. (1976b). Depth psychology. In H. Read, M. Fordham, G. Adler, & W. McGuire (Eds.) (R. F. C. Hull, Trans.), *Collected works: Vol. 18* (## 1142–1162). Princeton, NJ: Princeton University Press. (Original work published in 1951.)

Jung, C. G. (1976c). The Tavistock lectures. In H. Read, M. Fordham, G. Adler, & W. McGuire (Eds.) (R. F. C. Hull, Trans.), *Collected works: Vol. 18* (## 1–415). Princeton, NJ: Princeton University Press. (Original work circulated in 1936; published in 1968.)

Jung, C. G., & Jaffe, A. (1961). *Memories, dreams, reflections* (R. Winston & C. Winston, Trans.). New York: Random House.

Kalff, D. M. (1980). *Sandplay: A psychotherapeutic approach to the psyche*. Santa Monica, CA: Sigo Press.

Kalsched, D. (1996). The inner world of trauma: Archetypal defenses of the personal spirit. New York and London: Routledge.

Kohut, H. (1978a). The evaluation of applicants for psychoanalytic training. In P. H. Ornstein (Ed.), *The search for the self* (Vol. 1, pp. 461–475). New York: International Universities Press.

Kohut, H. (1978b). *The search for the self* (Vols. 1–2); (P. H. Ornstein, Ed.). New York: International Universities Press.

Kohut, H. (1984). *How does analysis cure?* (A. Goldberg & P. E. Stepansky, Ed.). Chicago: University of Chicago Press.

McBride, J. (1996). *The color of water: A Black man's tribute to his white mother*. New York: Riverhead Books.

McGuire, W. (Ed.). (1974). *The Freud/Jung letters* (R. Mannheim & R. F. C. Hull, Trans.). Princeton, NJ: Princeton University Press.

Meier, C. A. (Ed.). (2001). *Atom and archetype: The Pauli/Jung letters, 1932–1958*. Princeton, NJ: Princeton University Press.

Mitchell, R. R., & Friedman, H. S. (1994). *Sandplay: Past, present & future*. London: Routledge.

Mitchell, S. A. (1993). *Hope and dread in psychoanalysis*. New York: Basic Books.

Mitchell, S. A., & Black, M. J. (1995). *Freud and beyond: A history of modern psychoanalytic thought*. New York: Basic Books.

Plaut, A. (1966). Reflections about not being able to imagine. *Journal of Analytical Psychology, 11*(2), 113–133.

Roazen, P. (1984). *Freud and his followers*. New York: New York University Press.

Rosen, H. (1988). Evolving a personal philosophy of practice: Towards eclecticism. In R. Dorfman (Ed.), *Paradigms of clinical social work* (pp. 388–412). New York: Brunner/Mazel.

Rosen, H. (1998). Meaning-making as a metaframework for clinical practice. In R. Dorfman (Ed.), *Paradigms of clinical social work* (pp. 257–288). New York: Brunner/Mazel.

Samuels, A. (1985). *Jung and the post-Jungians*. London: Routledge & Kegan Paul.

Samuels, A., Shorter, B., & Plaut, F. (1986). *A critical dictionary of Jungian analysis*. London: Routledge & Kegan Paul.

Santos, J. P. (1999). *Places left unfinished at the time of creation*. New York: Penguin Putnam.

Sanville, J. (1991). *The playground of psychoanalytic psychotherapy*. Hillsdale, NJ: Analytic Press.

Sharp, D. (1991). *Jung lexicon: A primer of terms and concepts*. Toronto: Inner City Books.

Siegelman, E. Y. (1990). *Metaphor and meaning in psychotherapy*. New York: Guilford Press.

Singer, J. (1994). *Boundaries of the soul: The practice of Jung's psychology* (Rev. ed.) New York: Doubleday.

Speicher, M. (1990). Jung, Freud, Ferenczi, and Sullivan: Their relationships and ideas (Review of the conference "Jung, Freud, Ferenczi, and Sullivan: Their Relationships and Ideas," held in New York, January 27, 1990, at the C. G. Jung Foundation of New York.) *Quadrant: The Journal of Contemporary Jungian Thought, 23*(2), 87–92.

Speicher, M. (Speaker). (1996/2001). *Through the lens of folklore: Reclaiming life*. CD recording, privately released. (Available from Lion Enterprises, 6815 Washita Way, San Antonio, TX 78256.)

Speicher, M. (Speaker). (1997/2001). *Cinderella: A story for the inner ear*. CD recording, privately released. (Available from Lion Enterprises, 6815 Washita Way, San Antonio, TX 78256.)

Speicher, M. (Speaker). (2002). *Ancient wisdom: Shaharazad the healer*. CD recording, privately released. (Available from Lion Enterprises, 6815 Washita Way, San Antonio, TX 78256.)

Speicher, M., Phillips, D. G., Sanville, J. B., & Adams, M. V. (1997). Theory, metatheory, metaphor. *Clinical Social Work Journal, 25*(1), 7–39.

Stein, M. (1998). *Jung's map of the soul*. Chicago: Open Court.

Stolorow, R. D., & Atwood, G. E. (1979). *Faces in a cloud: Subjectivity in personality theory*. New York: Aronson.

Ulanov, B. (1992). *Jung and the outside world*. Wilmette, IL: Chiron.

Webster's New World Dictionary of the American Language. (1962). Cleveland and New York: World Publishing.

Whitmont, E. C. (1969). *The symbolic quest*. New York: Putnam.

Winnicott, D. W. (1965). *Maturational process and the facilitating environment*. New York: International Universities Press.

Winnicott, D. W. (1971). *Playing and reality*. New York: Penguin.

Young-Eisendrath, P. (1988). Mental structures and personal relations. In R. Dorfman (Ed.), *Paradigms of clinical social work* (pp. 43–73). New York: Brunner/Mazel.

Young-Eisendrath, P., & Dawson, T. (Eds.). (1997). *The Cambridge companion to Jung*. Cambridge and New York: Cambridge University Press.

Young-Eisendrath, P., & Hall, J. A. (1991). *Jung's self psychology: A constructivist perspective*. New York: Guilford Press.

Zabriskie, B. (2001). Jung and Pauli: A meeting of rare minds. In C. A. Meier (Ed.), *Atom and archetype: The Pauli/Jung letters, 1932–1958* (pp. xxvii–xlix). Princeton, NJ: Princeton University Press.

4

Cognitive-Behavioral Therapy With Children and Families

Emphasis on a Russian Immigrant Family's Entry Into a New Society

Tammie Ronen, PhD[1]

INTRODUCTION

Cognitive-behavioral therapy (CBT), which in the last decade has developed into cognitive-behavioral constructivist therapy, constitutes not merely a treatment mode but rather a holistic way of life. It is also a way of thinking and of perceiving human functioning and needs as well as a way of operating within the environment in order to use the most effective means for accomplishing one's aims. CBT can be applied to families, couples, adults, children, individuals, groups, and communities, with an emphasis on the unique nature and needs of each setting (Alford & Beck, 1997; Cigno & Bourn, 1998; Graham, 1998).

CBT can be conceived as a dynamic model. It is dynamic in the way it relates to human beings, in the way it applies therapy, and in the way its therapists integrate environmental changes into the treatment. First, CBT conceives human beings as living, incessantly changing organisms (Cull & Bondi, 2001). Therapists should therefore always keep in mind the changes people are undergoing and how people may change in the future. Therapy and therapists also continually change by adapting intervention techniques and methods to the unique nature of the client. Moreover, the CBT approach undergoes constant change, both in its theoretical explanations and in clinical applications of theory.

The underlying theoretical rationale of CBT upholds that human beings' affects and behaviors are largely determined by the way in which human beings structure the world (Beck, 1963, 1976; Beck, Emery, & Greenberg, 1985). Researchers consider cognitions to be important links in the chain of events leading to normal functioning as well as to disordered behavior and psychological dysfunction (Powell & Oei, 1991). Humans start to develop their personal cognitions at birth. These personal interpretations create the human being's personal repertoire of cognitions and reflect individuals' personal schemata toward themselves and the world around them. Schemata are the meaning-making structures of cognition, which evolve to facilitate the person's adaptation to the environment (Alford & Beck, 1997). The schema concept helps organize and explain the operation of the various psychological systems, and it appears to suggest a commonality in the etiological function of these systems. Personal repertoire and schemata reflect human beings' basic belief systems and manifest themselves in individuals' automatic self-talk. Therapy addresses people's self-talk and belief systems, aiming to create changes in the basic personal repertoire and schemata.

Michael, the 12-year-old child of the Shore family, offers an illustration of these CBT concepts. From early childhood, Michael perceived himself as a sick child who could not do things that other children did. His illness and constant failure to make friends affected his personal repertoire and schemata. Based on Michael's self-talk, he tends to interpret events and people as being against him (friends do not like him, he cannot be like others), reflecting his personal schemata that people are passive and helpless and that God decides what they are good at. Michael's problems do not result directly from his medical condition or learning difficulties but, rather, from the way he chooses to interpret his life experiences and from the distorted thoughts he has developed.

THE CONCEPT OF THE PERSON AND THE HUMAN EXPERIENCE

Cognitive-behavioral and constructivist models view individuals as actively involved in constructing their own reality (Beck, 1963; Beck, Rush, Shaw, & Emery, 1979; Mahoney, 1991; Ronen, 2002). This emphasis on active dynamic involvement reflects two concepts basic to the CBT approach. First, human beings are capable of acting as their own change agents once they have acquired the appropriate skills and resources. Second, CBT emphasizes the person as a capable human being, rather than focusing on pathological response or diagnosis (Rosenbaum & Ronen, 1998).

According to the CBT approach, human beings are architects with responsibility for creating their own lives and experiences (Kelly, 1955). Problems do not constitute objective events themselves (e.g., death, depression, sickness); rather, problems can arise in how one subjectively interprets such events and how this interpretation gives rise to particular emotions and behaviors (Beck,

1976). For example, Michael's behavior would be conceptualized as an outcome of how he interprets his medical condition, his social situation, and his cognitive capabilities to learn in school.

The addition of constructivist components highlights the concept of wholeness, activity, and meaning-making process. Wholeness relates to the integration between body and mind; person and environment; and thoughts, behaviors, and emotions. Activity highlights the view of human beings as active agents, who individually and collectively construct the meaning of their experiential world (Neimeyer, 1993). The constructivist perspective offers "the idea that humans actively construct their personal realities and create their own representational models of the world" (Meichenbaum, 1993, p. 203).

The Concept of the Child and the Child's Experience

CBT with children, adolescents, and families necessitates the adaptation of basic cognitive-behavioral principles to children's developmental needs and abilities (Herbert, 2002; Ronen, 1998a, 1998b). The child is seen as someone who can be an active partner in decision making, concerning the aims of therapy, the establishment of criteria for target behaviors, and the kinds of techniques to be used (Ronen, 1998a, 1998b). The child is not a passive receptor of treatment. He or she can learn about the techniques needed for behavior change, understand their rationale, and take responsibility for their practice and application. Children are conceived of as scientists who study their own behavior, learn to identify its components, test their belief systems, and seek out effective techniques to achieve change (Kanfer, 1977). Children can be partners for learning, as long as the material is explained to them in simple, concrete words they can understand (Ronen, 1997).

Our theoretical understanding and the basic research available on development indicate that specific processes and opportunities may emerge at different ages and stages of development and differentially for boys and girls. These occur in domains such as cognitive comprehension, exposure to new experiences, establishing relationships, and perceiving and expressing emotions (Davies, 1999; Herbert, 2002; Kazdin, 1994; Ronen, 1997). Research on cognitive development, the influence of peers, and transition periods (e.g., transferring schools) suggests that children need different sorts of intervention to achieve change (Kazdin, 1993). At the youngest ages, children are more affected by their immediate environment—namely, their parents. As children grow, external events become more and more influential, reflecting children's interest in their surroundings. The child and the child's experience should therefore be conceptualized by the therapist in terms of the impact of specific experiences on the specific child of a specific gender who has a specific problem at a specific developmental stage.

Because the view of the child cannot be differentiated from that of the family, parents should be involved either in family therapy sessions with the child or joining and being an integral part of the child's therapy.

HISTORICAL PERSPECTIVE

The CBT approach essentially represents the combination of two different methods. Traditional behavior theory derived from the basic principles of learning methods. Later, cognitive theories called for the consideration of crucial cognitive and emotional components of behavior. In the main, the two methods have joined forces to formulate CBT.

In the late 1920s, behavior therapy emerged as a scientific theoretical foundation for human disorder. It began as a response to the medical model that was popular in psychology. Contrary to the medical model, behavior therapy posited (a) the view that behavior is an outcome of learning; (b) the view of persons as capable, strong, and able to change themselves; (c) that there are similar rules and explanations for the development of functional adjustment and of disorders; (d) empirically based evidence for change processes; and (e) the view of skills as crucial for behavior change. The basics of behavior therapy included three learning modes based on laboratory study and learning theories: classical, operant, and social learning.

Watson's (1970) experimental studies in his Russian laboratory and Pavlov's (1927) study of canine digestion exemplify classical conditioning that depicts the connection between stimulus (food) and response (salivating). Classical learning principles explain human habits, behaviors, and disorders. These principles comprise the source of current relaxation training and desensitization

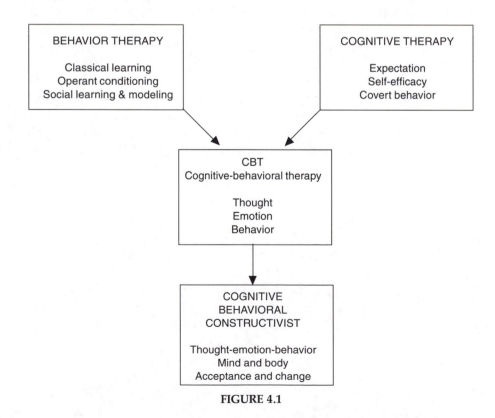

FIGURE 4.1

techniques (Wolpe, 1982). Classical conditioning offers the following explanation for Michael's behavior: He is conditioned to feel anxious, helpless, depressed, and distressed among peers. The many past occasions when children laughed at Michael conditioned him to avoid social activity. Michael's expectations of peer ridicule and rejection conditioned him to act strangely in the camp and other situations, thus creating his loneliness. In a treatment based on classical conditioning, Michael would learn relaxation as a fear-reduction technique. He would then practice desensitization to decrease his oversensitivity to and fear of athletic and social activities.

The second learning mode, operant conditioning, attributes a specific role to the environment and focuses on the person's ability to modify a behavior by changing its consequence. The basic assumption is that behavior eliciting positive outcomes will continue, whereas behavior eliciting negative outcomes will be eliminated, decreased, or made extinct. Operant conditioning pinpoints the need for environmental change, emphasizing techniques such as positive and negative reinforcement (Skinner, 1938), extinction and punishment (Hughes, 1993), and more complex programs, such as contingency contracts, token economies, and exposure techniques.

According to the operant conditioning mode, the peer response to Michael (laughter, teasing) serves as a punishment that decreases his desire to become more involved with other children, increases his sense of loneliness, and also increases his fear of relationships. Michael's behavior can be changed if we recondition him to a new pattern of behavior. One possibility for changing the outcome of his behavior targets the teacher and Michael's parents as change agents, teaching them the needed skills to gradually reinforce Michael's positive behavior. Michael is likely to repeat those positive behaviors that elicit positive reinforcement. Simultaneously, the significant adults in his life can be taught to remove attention from his undesirable negative and bizarre behavior. This would serve as a punishment, making these behaviors extinct.

The third learning mode, social learning and modeling, demonstrates that learning can occur as a result of observation and in the absence of reinforcement, either to the model or to the learner (Bandura, 1977, 1997). Bandura's social learning theory in general and his notion of vicarious (observational) learning in particular provide the basis for conceptualizing the person–environment relationship as a reciprocal process. This mode therefore perceives people as active participants in their own learning. According to the social learning mode, society clearly plays a crucial role in eliciting and generalizing Michael's distress. Michael feels better among adults than among children. Social learning treatments can help him observe other children's behavior, differentiate their behavior from his own, imitate the behavior that is usually reinforced by others, and use other children as models to acquire new skills.

The transition from the traditional behavioral learning paradigms depicted previously to those upholding cognitive learning began with the emerging interest in cognition, memory, perception, and motivation. Regarding motivation, Bandura (1977) identified the role of expectancies and self-efficacy as an important part of behavior. He viewed these concepts as central for the process of self-regulation. Research began to focus directly on the alteration of covert behavior and the role of cognitive processes in the etiology and maintenance of disorders in different populations. Ellis (1973) developed the idea of irrational thinking as the main source of human disorders. At the same time, Beck et al. (1979) started developing his cognitive model for depression. Cognitive theories evolved based on the belief that cognitive mediational processes are involved in human learning (i.e., changing automatic negative thoughts or self-talk to mediated positive ones). Clinical implications of cognitive theory include identification of thoughts, awareness of emotions elicited following those thoughts, the link between thoughts and emotions, and the view of behavior as the outcome of a process combining thoughts and emotions (Ronen, 2002). Behavior theory transformed into cognitive-behavioral theory, with a multidimensional focus on changing overt, as well as covert, behavior, such as imagery, thoughts, and emotions.

The cognitive learning rooted in Michael's behavior includes his schemata toward the world and himself. His automatic thoughts reflect his self-talk which reveals defeatist self-attitudes ("I am not good enough," "I am not like the others") and feelings of helplessness ("I cannot cope," "I still cannot find what I am good at"). Michael must learn to identify the way in which his negative thoughts elicit anxious, depressed, and lonely emotions that lead him to avoidance behavior (evading sports and social situations) and increase his negative responses to others.

Most recently, CBT has shifted again, this time toward constructivist theory. This offshoot of cognitive theory accentuates human beings' own subjective reconstructions of their objective life events and how they attribute meaning to their personal experiences (Mahoney, 1993, 1999; Nagae & Nedate, 2001). They learn to seek out their own strengths, resources, and support systems and to perceive themselves as strong and capable. Constructivism emphasizes the lack of separation between mind (brain) and body, which are linked in a natural circular system. The experience of consciousness results from biological cyclic processes (Cull & Bondi, 2001; Mahoney, 1999). Most of the components I discuss in this chapter combine the cognitive, behavioral, and constructivist orientations.

Constructivist elements in treatment, for example, would involve helping Michael to accept himself, become aware of how he conceptualizes his own life, and restructure his subjective view of life events by finding more flexible, creative, and positive meanings. For example, in reconstructing the meaning of asthma, instead of seeing asthma as a scar that damages his life, Michael can look at the scar as a symbol of heroic courage in facing adversity. He might compare himself with a fictional character, such as Harry Potter (Rowling, 1997), whose scar masked a secret past and eventually gained him notoriety and popularity. He can replace the word *scar* in his personal lexicon with *mark* or *sign*, signaling a creative challenge to discover what he might accomplish in spite of the asthma.

KEY THEORETICAL CONSTRUCTS

Behavior theory encompasses diverse key concepts, specific to the different learning modes. Stimuli, response, and conditioning depict classical conditioning, whereas operant conditioning utilizes concepts such as behavior, outcomes, extinction, and reinforcement. Social learning employs constructs such as modeling, environment, and observation. Altogether, these constructs point to the importance of the environment in conditioning one's behavior and the links between stimuli and response; behavior and outcomes; and expectancies, behavior, and environment.

In the cognitive theory of psychopathology and psychotherapy, cognition is the key to psychological disorders. The theory emphasizes several components. First, human learning involves cognitive mediational processes; therefore, thoughts, feelings, and behaviors are causally interrelated. Thought is responsible for information processing relating to the world and to oneself, and that information influences emotions, behaviors, and physiology in reliable, predictable ways. Also, this theory highlights activities such as expectations, self-statements, and attributions, which are seen as important in understanding and predicting psychopathology and psychotherapeutic change.

An important theoretical concept is the idea that human problems derive from persons' irrational, dysfunctional, and inadequate ways of thinking (Beck et al., 1979). Addressing these irrational thoughts is a key component of CBT intervention.

CBT also attributes problems to deficiencies, such as a lack of skills that impedes clients from behaving as they should. Hence, skills acquisition is conceived of as both a major, crucial component in human functioning and an important therapeutic technique.

Change encompasses another key CBT construct. CBT seeks out change, views change as an important element of therapy, and expects therapists to act as change agents. Change processes in therapy derive from attempts to convert irrational, automatic, or maladaptive emergent core schemata into more rational, mediated, or adaptive beliefs and thought processes (Ronen, 2003). During treatment, the therapist regulates and models changes step by step; maintenance processes aim to preserve the functional continuity and the sense of oneness inherent in selfhood structures (Guidano, 1995).

Rosenbaum and Ronen (1998) summarized the seven basic key features of CBT:

1. *Meaning-making processes.* These processes help clients develop a new and more suitable way of understanding and accepting their behavior.

2. *Systematic and goal-directed processes.* The therapist plans and executes treatment and designs the therapeutic hour (Beck, 1976), with an emphasis on the need to define problems, goals, expectations, means to achieve these goals, assessment, and evaluation of the process.

3. *Practicing and experiencing.* CBT constitutes not a talking therapy but

rather a doing therapy that encompasses practicing and experiencing as central components. Interventions vary and can be verbal or nonverbal, using experiential methods such as role assignments, imagery training, metaphors, writing methods, and so on (Mahoney, 1991; Ronen & Rosenbaum, 1998).

4. *Collaborative effort*. Therapist and client must enter into an alliance and collaborate on joint work, in order to achieve the goals of therapy.

5. *Client-focused intervention*. CBT should aim at treating the person, rather than treating the problem. This view focuses on the person as a whole and concentrates on the client's feelings, thoughts, and way of living, not only on the client's problem.

6. *Facilitating change processes*. This component emphasizes the important role of the therapist in pursuing effective strategies and techniques to help the client change (Rosenbaum & Ronen, 1998).

7. *Empowerment and resourcefulness*. All of the previous features actually aim to empower clients by training them in self-control skills for self-help and independent functioning.

Opening oneself up to experiences, exploring, and experimenting constitute crucial components in CBT and are achieved from within via the attentional focus. Through the process of developing sensitivity to one's own body, sensations, and emotions, therapists train clients to increase their awareness and identify internal cues related to a specific problem (Bandura, 1977; Mahoney, 1991; Ronen & Rosenbaum, 2001). Relaxation, imagery training, concentration, and self-monitoring techniques help clients open themselves up to experiences and become more aware of themselves, their emotions and sensations, and their behaviors and thoughts, as well as become more attuned to the world. These components play a crucial role both in overcoming and in accepting problems (Mahoney, 1999).

ASSESSMENT

CBT is not a collection of magic tricks that the therapist pulls out to resolve human disorders and maladaptive behaviors. Instead, CBT consists of a careful, continuous assessment process that attempts to analyze the client's needs, the therapist's knowledge about the specific problem, and the client's skills and abilities, in order to determine the treatment of choice (which will pinpoint different personal characteristics, environmental resources, and behavioral considerations).

The initial assessment draws from the role of contemporaneous determinants of behavior, rather than from early life events or the client's past (Hughes, 1993). The clinician carefully identifies objectives, target behaviors, and appropriate methods of measurement; determines the variables controlling both environment and organism; and discerns the individual thinking style and emotions controlling behavior.

Adapting Assessment Procedures to Children

Assessment of children and adolescents must be strongly anchored in developmental considerations, including the children's age, gender, and affective and cognitive characteristics (Ronen, 1998b, 2001). In the case of Michael Shore, the CBT therapist would highlight the developmental components that may influence an adolescent boy's way of thinking and behaving. Regarding cognitive considerations, for example, Piaget (1926) suggested that the age of 12 is characterized by the abstract or formal operational stage. Michael is developing an adult-like way of thinking, which clearly manifests itself in his manner of talking about himself and to adults. This preadolescent cognitive ability enables him to deal with abstract and holistic concepts. For Michael, verbal therapy would be an interesting challenge, whereas nonverbal therapy may even be insulting because he wishes to be treated like an adult.

Developmental social tasks should color the assessment and the therapeutic planning for children (Ronen, 2003). In the case of Michael, an assessment of developmental social tasks at early adolescence points to the need to help him develop social skills and self-control. Because of his medical problems and history of learning difficulties, Michael exhibits greater dependence on the family, less involvement with other children, and lower independence in his functioning than is appropriate for his age. Michael suffers from skill deficits that prevent him from developing peer relationships. His ways of thinking and behaving help him relate to adults but are not appreciated by his peers. CBT would focus on imparting Michael with skills for initiating social peer relationships, generating areas of common interest, and observing himself in comparison to others regarding appearance, conduct, and verbal communication. He would learn how to start a conversation, maintain eye contact, be assertive, and express emotion appropriately (Bornstein, Bellack, & Hersen, 1977; Gambrill, 1995).

Assessment During the Treatment Process

Assessment and evaluation encompass an integral part of the CBT intervention. Viewing therapy as a scientific process implies that clients need to constantly observe and assess their own behavior and make decisions following such observation. Assessment during therapy directs itself toward several main goals: setting targets for the next session, making changes in therapy, and learning about its efficacy.

Therapists design each session in collaboration with the client. Together, they evaluate how the client has improved and whether or not the client's expectations and goals were achieved. Thus, clients become more aware of change and can devise more appropriate expectations and goals for future change.

Assessment Tools

Means for assessment at any phase can vary. Clients' self-reports, self-monitoring, and self-ratings offer central tools in the CBT process. Therapists guide clients to carefully observe their own behaviors, emotions, and thoughts; assess and evaluate data on which to base decisions about making change; and establish targets, expectations, and goals for change. Self-assessment highlights the empirical scientific basis of CBT, as well as its reliance on self-help.

Another assessment method involves the use of structured questionnaires. To make initial decisions about the design and the goals of therapy, and to ascertain the baseline intensity, the severity, and the developmental characteristics of their difficulties, clients may complete different questionnaires at the outset to assess their behavior, thoughts, and emotions. These same questionnaires are often repeated at termination to evaluate treatment outcomes and facilitate follow-up and maintenance. These questionnaires and other self-recording methods can also be used periodically within the course of treatment to determine progress, growth, or the appropriateness of the given treatment.

Environmental reports and the therapist's observations of the client offer additional assessment methods. These may be especially valuable in dealing with children, who may not be a reliable source for self-assessment, particularly regarding acting-out or externalizing behavior problems, such as hyperactivity or aggression (Ronen, 1997, 2003). In Michael's case, acquiring peers' and teachers' objective observations of his social deficits would be one way to obtain an environmental perspective about his problems. The therapist may choose to observe a child's behavior in a natural setting such as school, either in class or on the playground among peers. Regarding internal components, such as Michael's loneliness, only the child can be a reliable resource for assessing his or her own state. Therefore, emotional components should be assessed by directly interviewing or questioning children.

Structured questionnaires, environmental reports, and self-reports may all constitute important change instruments in the process of Michael's intervention. First, to assess baseline information for making decisions about Michael's problems, the CBT approach would ascertain the environment's evaluation of Michael's behavior. For example, the therapist may ask the boy's parents to report on how often Michael left home to participate in social activities, received telephone calls, or made helpless verbal statements. The teacher would be asked to assess Michael's involvement in social activities in school. More important, the therapist would teach Michael to assess his own behaviors, thoughts, and emotions in order to promote self-control, based on self-observation and self-evaluation. Michael would observe his own and his peers' social behavior over the week between sessions (the extent to which children laughed at him and teased him; the subjects he talked about, compared to the subjects that other children talked about). By observing and reporting how children react to him, Michael can learn the extent to which children are actually rejecting him, versus how much he expects to be rejected. By assessing his own responses to peers, Michael may gain insight into the effectiveness of his behavior and can thus learn better social skills. By reporting and assessing his helpless thoughts and depressed emotions, Michael can learn about the ineffectiveness of these cognitions and affects, thereby increasing motivation to change his thinking.

THE THERAPEUTIC PROCESS

CBT is not a method that is administered to the client; rather, it is a method that is designed in collaboration with the client. No one technique or means is essential for achieving change, but the therapist must design an appropriate intervention that suits each individual client, based on his or her unique nature, hobbies, particular problem, strengths and resources, and motivation for change (Ronen, 1997; Rosenbaum & Ronen, 1998). The therapist's creative, flexible outlook will enable an openness to questions concerning the treatment of choice (Ronen, 2003). Therapists exist in a constant state of decision making, always asking themselves what the best intervention is with this specific client, with that specific problem, or in this specific situation (Paul, 1967; Ronen, 2001).

Treatment is planned, structured, and goal-directed, yet no rigid rules predetermine the length of therapy, the frequency of sessions, or the treatment location. Treatment may begin with more frequent sessions, which lessen in frequency as the client progresses. Phone calls provide between-session contact with the client. For example, asking Michael to call the therapist on each day that he was able to talk with children without them laughing at him may increase Michael's confidence, motivation, and awareness about his ability to carry on a conversation. Therapy generally transpires in the clinic but may make use of outdoor walks or natural settings for exposure exercises, or may shift to a basketball court to promote a child's motivation or to practice new skills in a concrete context (Ronen, 2003).

Because therapy is a planned, individually designed process, clinical researchers have given much attention to the construction of the intervention process. Gambrill's 12 steps are the most familiar procedure, providing guidelines for conducting the process of intervention (see Figure 4.2; Gambrill, Thomas, & Carter, 1971). These structured phases enable therapists to check and recheck the intervention process, identify their current stage, and clarify what is missing.

1. *Inventory of problem areas: Collect information about the whole spectrum of presented problems.* Collaboratively compiling the list of Michael's problems would help, first, to pinpoint all the needed problem areas to be treated (e.g., medical problems, learning difficulties, social loneliness, feelings of helplessness and hopelessness, negative thoughts about himself and his capabilities). Second, by dividing the problems into areas of difficulty, Michael can

STAGE	SUBJECT	CONTENT
1	**Inventory of problem areas**	*Collect information about the whole spectrum of presented problems.*
2	**Problem selection and contract**	*Raise clients' motivation by collaborating with them and achieving their agreement on problem areas selected for change.*
3	**Commitment to cooperate**	*Obtain the client's agreement with the process in order to facilitate compliance and motivation.*
4	**Specification of target behaviors**	*Define and analyze each behavior to decide what maintains and reinforces the problem.*
5	**Baseline assessment of target behavior**	*Collect data about the frequency and duration of the problem, to provide a concrete foundation on which to evaluate change.*
6	**Identification of problem controlling conditions**	*Identify the conditions preceding and following the problem's occurrence.*
7	**Assessment of environmental resources**	*Uncover possible resources in the client's environment.*
8	**Specification of behavioral objectives**	*Specify the behavioral objectives of the modification plan, and elicit the client's terminal behavioral repertoire.*
9	**Formulation of a modification plan**	*Select an appropriate technique for applying the most efficient program for change.*
10	**Implementation of a modification plan**	*Modify behavior and focus effort on change.*
11	**Monitoring outcomes**	*Collect information concerning the effectiveness of intervention.*
12	**Maintenance of change**	*Work to achieve maintenance and stabilization, and to help prevent relapse.*

FIGURE 4.2. Gambrill's 12 Stages of Intervention.

learn to become more aware of the kinds of problems he evidences. Third, he can become active in the decision making concerning that division into problem areas.

2. *Problem selection and contract: Raise clients' motivation by collaborating with them and obtaining their agreement on problem areas selected for change.* Michael and the therapist, together, should decide which problem to tackle first. This necessitates rating the problems from *least difficult* to *most difficult to change* and thinking about how treatment should start. Michael should be encouraged to start with a simple problem that might offer relatively immediate success, which would motivate and challenge him to work toward other, more difficult tasks for change.

3. *Commitment to cooperate. Obtain the client's agreement with the process, in order to facilitate compliance and motivation.* Involving Michael as an active partner for treatment should help him change and cope with his sense of helplessness.

4. *Specification of target behaviors: Define and analyze each behavior to decide what maintains and reinforces the problem.* At this stage, Michael would be

involved in the self-monitoring, the self-observation, and the self-rating of his own behaviors. This stage teaches him to "break down" his big problems into small, concrete behaviors that can be observed and rated. This stage helps mobilize Michael to cooperate by fostering his feelings of being active and involved, as a scientist who studies his own life.

5. ***Baseline assessment of target behavior:*** *Collect data about the frequency and the duration of the problem, to provide a concrete foundation on which to evaluate change.* Assessing each behavior will help Michael accept a more rational view of his conduct and surrounding events. For example, if Michael records each instance of peers laughing at him (when it happened, what happened beforehand, how long they laughed, what they said, and his response), this information will help him consider better ways to behave and learn about the change he has achieved. By establishing baseline reports of his medical symptoms, he will be able to compare his baseline condition to his condition at termination and later be able to differentiate actual increases in symptoms from his own expectations of symptom increase.

6. ***Identification of the problem controlling conditions:*** *Identify the conditions preceding and following the problem's occurrence.* Observing ongoing events will help Michael understand the conditions controlling his behaviors. He can learn to link his friends' laughter to his actions in certain situations. He then might notice that his strange behavior at camp resulted in children's hasty withdrawal from him.

7. ***Assessment of environmental resources:*** *Uncover possible resources in the client's environment.* Although Michael comes from a multiproblem family, his parents care for him and, with supervision and training, can participate in his change process by helping him cope better.

8. ***Specification of behavioral objectives:*** *Specify the behavioral objectives of the modification plan, and elicit the client's terminal behavioral repertoire.* Together, Michael and the therapist should make decisions concerning the targets of his behaviors, in order to facilitate beginning to work toward achieving those goals. Such targets may include becoming more involved in a sports activity that he is capable of performing, taking part in social activities, trying to make friends, feeling better about himself, having more positive thoughts about his strengths and resources, behaving better in different settings, and so on.

9. ***Formulation of a modification plan:*** *Select an appropriate technique for applying the most efficient program for change.* Various techniques can be selected with Michael. Cognitive techniques would work toward changing his automatic thoughts and would reconstruct a positive way of thinking using self-talk, self-recording, and self-evaluation. Experiential techniques would work toward increasing his awareness to internal cues and his ability to identify his emotions. Relaxation, imagery, and exposure techniques would help him overcome his fears; social skills techniques would be used to improve his ability to interact with friends; and self-control techniques would help him become more independent.

10. ***Implementation of modification plan:*** *Modify behavior and focus effort on change.* Therapy should start by selecting one goal, clarifying the appropriate technique, and beginning to implement it.

    11. *Monitoring outcomes: Collect information concerning the effectiveness of intervention.* Throughout the entire process of therapy, Michael should be encouraged to monitor his behavior. Monitoring will help in collecting data and making decisions on how to proceed; it also will help challenge Michael to put forth more effort for change, as he becomes more aware of the progress he has already made.

    12. *Maintenance of change: Work to achieve maintenance and stabilization, and to help prevent relapses.* It is not enough to look at changes. Therapy should continue until maintenance is achieved and the new behavior becomes an integral part of Michael's life.

    After making a list of Michael's problematic areas, Michael and the therapist will need to decide on the first goals of therapy. If Michael and his therapist decide to start working toward changing the outcomes of his medical problem, the first goal should be to teach him to differentiate the feelings of stress and anxiety relating to his asthma from the thought of impending catastrophe. Second, he must learn to cope with the anxiety and to decrease it. Third, the family must resist maintaining his avoidance behavior by ceasing to reinforce it. Fourth, he must be taught how to deal with his social situation and to develop social skills (Ronen, 2003).

    CBT advocates the selection of intervention strategies with a high probability of success; sequential steps that match available skill levels; clear, relevant means of monitoring progress; practice opportunities; and maintenance and follow-up periods (Gambrill, 1995). Homework assignments constitute an integral part of most CBT interventions, due to the strong need to exercise and apply knowledge from the intervention setting to the natural environment (Ronen, 2003). The therapeutic setting is linked not to time sequences (once weekly) but rather to role accomplishment. Therapy is terminated not when the problem decreases but only when clients prove their ability to maintain their achievements and generalize them to other settings and problem areas.

    CBT therapists regularly use a large variety of techniques. Mahoney (1991) viewed the appropriate use of techniques as a ritualized method of human relatedness and communication or as a stylized language for expressing and exploring the ongoing narratives of life processes. CBT consists not only of a talking process but also of an experiential and practical course (Mahoney, 1999; Ronen, 1997; Rosenbaum & Ronen, 1998). Creative indirect techniques assist therapists in overcoming difficulties in the treatment process, help clients surmount obstacles in therapy, and apply more effective treatments to the clients' specific life purposes. Techniques can also be adapted to various client settings (e.g., family, group, individual).

    Michael could enjoy a combination of treatment methods. Behavioral social skills would improve his ability to interact with others, and cognitive-behavioral methods would decrease his anxiety and fear related to coping with friends, sports, and his medical condition. Cognitive techniques would change his misconceptions about his helplessness and his passive way of waiting for things to happen. Constructivist methods would help him accept himself the way he is and become more aware of his needs.

With Michael, mutual selection of the least problematic area for the first stage of intervention should be the modus operandi. His choices might include becoming involved in gradual physical exercise, finding a pet he could raise, learning social skills, working toward changing his automatic thoughts, learning to take active steps toward identifying his special talent(s), or working toward changing his self-concept.

Without collaboration or creating a good alliance and agreement for change, it will be difficult for Michael to trust the therapist and start the journey toward investing efforts toward change. Agreeing to collaborate should lead Michael to select a small step that he can gradually work toward achieving. His achievement of that first step will facilitate his motivation to invest effort toward more difficult, major changes.

APPLICATION TO DIVERSITY

Let us assume that the Shore family is a Russian family that has recently immigrated to the United States. An immigrant's entry into a new society is a gradual process characterized by fear, stress, anxiety, and crisis (Shuval, 1982). Immigration involves a mutual process of adaptation, socialization, and accommodation, to which immigrants respond diversely. These changes occur at physical, psychological, social, and cultural levels. Immigrants require coping mechanisms to adapt and adjust to the new society. However, the coping mechanisms that served the family members in their country of origin often do not help them in their new country. New coping strategies must also be developed, in order for the family to adapt to the new society (Shuval, 1982).

The Shore family evidences multiproblem maladjustment, even without new immigrant status. If we add the characteristic of recent immigration to their case, the Shores are exposed to new familial, as well as individual, stresses, in addition to their pre-existing problems.

For the parents, who immigrated to improve their family life opportunities, adjustment to a new society was a difficult process. As older adults without knowledge of the English language, and as members of a single family alone in its new place, Nancy and Charley are in crisis. They are luckier than most; they earn an income from renting out the apartment downstairs and have no mortgage because their house was a gift. However, they are unemployed and therefore have few opportunities to meet people. At their age, they find it difficult to become accustomed to a new lifestyle; the big city confuses them with its variety of options, large stores, modern television, and modern, democratic way of life in general. They also fear what will happen to their children in this new world. They feel disconnected, isolated, and weak. Formerly authoritative figures in Russia, suddenly Nancy and Charley find themselves dependent on Rena and Michael. The children must talk for them, go to the bank with them to translate, and deal with shopping, schools, and other issues that used to be their jurisdiction. These changes naturally disrupt the homeostasis at home—specifically, the roles and the relationships within the family. The collision with modern democratic culture confuses the whole family, causing feelings of uncertainty about family members' behavior and even shame about their past.

Rena and Michael sense the family's dependence on them and, feeling more independent and mature, tend to ignore their parents' wishes and demands, making their own decisions without consulting the parents. Nancy and Charley feel as if they have lost control over the children.

Michael, who was about to overcome his learning difficulties in Russia, faces difficulties in acquiring the language. The gap in the learning material between Russia and the United States causes him to feel helpless, and he regresses to a previous stage of learning difficulties. He refuses to study, complaining that he is unable to keep up and refusing to share his difficulties with his parents "because they do not understand anything." He starts to skip school and develop disobedience disorders, both at school and at home. Having always suffered from social rejection, Michael tries to ingratiate himself with others by disallowing all symbols of Russian culture and customs that were important to his parents. He feels even more different from others than he did in the past. He is ashamed of his parents and does not want them to attend parent–teacher meetings or class events, leading to more family crises and arguments. In addition, Michael's anxiety, stress, and fear have exacerbated his asthmatic symptoms. His medical condition has worsened, thus increasing his avoidance behavior.

Treating Michael now should involve four main settings: family therapy, school consultation, and group and individual treatments. There is an urgent need to work with the family as a whole to strengthen the members' cohesion and support of each other, facilitating their return to coping as one unit. Through role-play, the family members need to practice traditional family roles and communication, where the parents regain their control and the children accept that authority. Functioning like a family, with structured roles and a clear differentiation between parents and children, is necessary both for the parents and for the children. A crucial step toward adjustment involves family support, which will not occur until Michael and Rena learn to obey and respect their parents for who they are, no matter where they came from and how poorly they speak the local language.

The second intervention setting will be the therapist's intervention with the school. Peer support is an important adjustment-promoting factor for Michael. One means to achieve this consists of helping Michael meet other immigrants in his school who can share their feelings about this process and toward whom he can develop a sense of belonging. Another means would be to work with Michael's class and help the children accept him as a member, fostering his attempts to become acquainted with his new classmates. Michael's obedience problems, as well as the new version of his learning difficulties, seem to result from stress and fear related to immigration. Therefore, these problems may recover spontaneously once Michael feels better and more adjusted to his new home.

Michael's social problems, however, did not begin when he came to the United States. These chronic behaviors and social skill deficits imply that, even if other children do stop laughing at him, he does not possess the skills to socialize with them. He therefore needs social skills training, which can best be attained in a group setting that will enable him to practice and apply the skills in vivo.

As mentioned before, CBT is a dynamic therapy that focuses on the personal meaning making of the client. Consequently, CBT with a new immigrant does not basically differ from other modes of CBT, because the first step of treatment would be to very carefully learn what Michael's problems mean to him. The therapist must ascertain how Michael conceives himself as a new immigrant and what changes the immigration rendered in his life, his behavior, his thoughts, and his feelings. In what way does Michael make it easy for himself by placing blame on the immigration and thus releasing himself from responsibility? Inasmuch as CBT conceptualizes individuals as active and reactive in their environment, it is very important initially to obtain details on how Michael used to live and cope in Russia, the changes immigration caused to his life, the cultural differences he perceives and what they mean to Michael and his family, and Michael's goals concerning his new country.

Only after understanding how Michael conceives and conceptualizes his life in the United States can decisions be made about how to begin therapy. Treatment should combine goals relating to long-standing problems that are unrelated to immigration, problems that increased because of immigration, and problems with an onset after moving, which resulted from immigration.

Individual therapy should also target Michael's misconceptions about his ability to cope, adjust, and live a normal life in the United States. Michael must learn to differentiate between the problems he has to learn to live with (some breathing difficulties and some learning difficulties) and the way he copes with these in order to avoid their increase and generalization. He needs to learn self-control skills to improve his independent behavior with friends, with himself, and with his family.

Usually, with 12-year-old adolescents, therapy should focus on verbal treatment. However, as a new immigrant with language difficulties, Michael may benefit more from an integration of creative techniques with verbal therapy. He would be a good candidate for using metaphors and imagery training, where he could visualize himself with friends, happy, enjoying life, and coping in the future. Such methods may enable him to consider other possibilities that are open to him in the future and might help him focus on experiencing his emotions, rather than on just talking about them. Relaxation and fear-reduction techniques could also contribute to Michael's functioning.

The added issue of immigration necessitates different priorities and decision-making processes. The first goal should focus on the new crisis resulting from the immigration. Timely intervention will help prevent the crisis from becoming chronic. The immigration-related problems show good potential for change because they are new, and the family, in its history back in Russia, has shown an ability to cope. Change can be incurred by treating and strengthening the family members, helping them obtain social support, and changing their misconceptions about their inability to adjust.

The second priority consists of those pre-existing problems that impede adjustment to the new country and whose reduction may facilitate adjustment and adaptation. These problems consist of Michael's loneliness, which necessitates the acquisition of social skills, and Michael's school avoidance, due to his feeling that learning difficulties prevent him from progressing.

Third, Michael's basic problems warrant treatment: his attribution of all his difficulties to his asthmatic disorder, his lack of self-control skills, and his sense of helplessness and hopelessness.

In sum, CBT with Michael, the new immigrant, basically does not differ from CBT with a Michael whose family has lived in the United States for generations. There is no need to modify the treatment; rather, this approach's focus on personal meaning making will allow for the necessary adaptations. The therapist will, in the course of conducting CBT according to the guidelines outlined in this chapter, learn in detail about Russia, the way people think and behave differently there, and, most of all, what the differences between Russia and the United States mean for Michael.

LIMITATIONS OF THE MODEL

The CBT model has demonstrated effective change processes, yet it also has some deficiencies concerning its suitability to a large range of clients. CBT necessitates a high level of motivation, cooperation, and involvement. Treatment combines exercises, training, and demonstrations within sessions and homework assignments in the natural environment. It is therefore impossible to achieve change with a client who does not wish to change. Hence, CBT best suits compliant individuals. Unmotivated clients can be treated if therapy includes a preliminary stage of working toward increasing motivation. Often, people cooperate once they believe in their ability to achieve change. In the case of unmotivated clients, rather than working toward the first goal of therapy, treatment should first be directed to increase self-efficacy and motivation.

The two most common criticisms of the model concern its reliance on high-order cognitive skills and its aspiration for change, even when some human disorders cannot be modified. With respect to the first criticism, reliance on high-order cognitive skills, professionals view CBT as a verbal therapy and therefore question its applicability to clients from a low socioeconomic background or to young children. I reject this criticism. The cognitive-behavioral therapist must learn to creatively and flexibly adapt the treatment to the client's needs, whatever these may be. Therapists must initially become expert in the unique characteristics of specific developmental stages, cognitive stages, socioeconomic strata, and diverse cultures. Consequently, therapists can flexibly adapt and adjust cognitive and behavioral techniques into nonverbal, creative modes such as imagery, play, music, and so on (Ronen, 2003).

The second criticism concerns an aspiration for change even when some human disorders cannot be modified. Indeed, CBT focuses mainly on change processes, constantly seeking to study what has changed and to what extent. This continuous search for change may create the undesirable belief that clients should always aim to change as quickly and as extensively as possible. This attitude places stress on both the client and the therapist. However, with the recent addition of constructivist therapy to this therapeutic genre, the stated criticism can be countered by summoning the distinction between acceptance and change as therapeutic goals. Constructivism emphasizes living with, accepting, and opening oneself up to experiences. This new approach allows for a focus on disorders that cannot be easily resolved but rather necessitate that the client learn how to live with them. Therapists today need to augment CBT by attempting to apply therapeutic work directed toward accepting and opening oneself up to experiences.

With the development of constructivism and of creative modes for change, CBT can now relate to emotional disorders through relaxation, imagery, attentional focus exercises, and other nonverbal methods aiming to help clients explore, experiment, and open up, rather than merely change themselves. Much work remains regarding the application of CBT for special populations and various disorders; I believe this will be a major focus of this model in the next few years.

RESEARCH

As a scientific model, CBT necessitates assessment, evaluation, outcome studies, and research as an integral part of the intervention process. Applied research comprises the main empirical trend in CBT. Single case designs predominate among CBT research on children, trying to identify unique intervention modes to suit different ages and problems, such as in the areas of traumatic experiences (Brandell, 1992; Ronen, 1996a), selective mutism (Carlson, Kratochwill, & Johnson, 1999; Ronen, 2003), or fear reduction (Kanfer, Karoly, & Newman, 1975; Ronen, 1996b).

Most of CBT research examines the efficacy of CBT applications to clients. Many such studies have demonstrated effective outcomes for cognitive therapy in treating depressive disorders (Beck, 1963, 1976; Beck et al., 1979), anxiety disorders (Beck et al., 1985; Marks, 1969, 1978, 1987), and aggressive disorders (Kazdin, 1994).

Research on CBT has also investigated intervention packages, in an attempt to evaluate the efficacy of the model for change (Bornstein et al., 1977; Gambrill, 1995; Ronen, 1997, 2003).

Research encompasses an integral part of CBT. In its early stages, CBT research focused mainly on proving its efficacy (Beck, 1963, 1976; Beck et al.,

1979), whereas now, empirical efforts have shifted to the study of more theoretical basic components, such as the role of emotion, the role of therapeutic relationships, and the underlying mechanisms enabling change (Kanfer & Schefft, 1988; Mahoney, 1999; Rosenbaum, 1999; Safran & Segal, 1990; Swell, 1995).

SUMMARY

This chapter presents the main components of CBT, particularly how they deal with children and how they may be applied with the Shore family. CBT constitutes an educational therapeutic intervention that is characterized by a nonstop process of making decisions about the optimal treatment for the specific client, with the specific problem, at the specific stage of development, in the specific environmental context. The advantages of CBT lie in its ability to relate to all areas of human functioning: human thoughts, emotions, and behaviors. It enables adaptation and adjustment of the treatment to the individual client, couple, family, or group.

The difficulties in applying CBT lie in the fact that the treatment necessitates the client's active participation. It is very difficult to treat someone who is not interested in learning or changing. Such clients necessitate significantly more effort to develop and maintain motivation. Kanfer and Schefft (1988) state that everyone is motivated, and that it is our responsibility as therapists to find out toward what they are motivated and to develop and work toward increasing that motivation.

Another advantage of the model lies in its aim to empower clients and develop self-control and self-help. CBT looks for and increases clients' support systems, strengths, and resources to help them help themselves. This client-empowerment perspective involves adapting treatment to the changing needs of society and culture, while adjusting the treatment to diverse clients. Indeed, CBT's combination of behavioral, cognitive, and constructivist therapies implies a flexible, dynamic model for change that encompasses diversity as an integral part of treatment. Each client is considered to be unique and different, with treatment focusing on a client's personal meaning making. Therapists should always ask themselves: In what way does my client's personal, historical, physical, psychological, gender, socio-environmental, familial, cultural, and social characteristics change my considerations in assessment and intervention?

Adapting treatment to the clients' unique backgrounds and mobilizing clients' forces in relating to their own diversity components (e.g., disability, race, sexual orientation, age, culture) enable therapists to use clients' positive forces and capabilities and empower them for the process of change.

NOTE

1. The author would like to express her appreciation to Dee B. Ankonina for her editorial contribution.

REFERENCES

Alford, B. A., & Beck, A. T. (1997). *The integrative power of cognitive therapy.* New York: Guilford Press.

Bandura, A. (1977). *Social learning theory.* Englewood Cliffs, NJ: Prentice Hall.

Bandura, A. (1997). *Self-efficacy: The exercise of control.* New York: Freeman.

Beck, A. T. (1963). Thinking and depression. *Archives of General Psychiatry, 9,* 324–333.

Beck, A. T. (1976). *Cognitive therapy and the emotional disorders.* New York: Meridian.

Beck, A. T., Emery, G., & Greenberg, R. L. (1985). *Anxiety disorders and phobias.* New York: Basic Books.

Beck, A. T., Rush, A. J., Shaw, B. F., & Emery, G. (1979). *Cognitive therapy of depression.* New York: Guilford Press.

Bornstein, M., Bellack, A. S., & Hersen, M. (1977). Social skills training for unassertive children: A multiple-baseline analysis. *Journal of Applied Behavior Analysis, 10,* 183–195.

Brandell, J. R. (1992). Psychotherapy of a traumatized 10-year-old boy: Theoretical issues and clinical considerations. *Smith College Studies in Social Work, 62,* 123–138.

Carlson, J. S., Kratochwill, T. R., & Johnson, H. F. (1999). Sertraline treatment of 5 children diagnosed with selective mutism: A single-case research trial. *Journal of Child and Adolescent Psychopharmacology, 9,* 293–306.

Cigno, K., & Bourn, D. (Eds.). (1998). *Cognitive-behavioural social work in practice.* Aldershot, England: Ashgate/Arena.

Cull, J., & Bondi, M. (2001). Biology/psychology of consciousness: A circular perspective. *Constructivism, 6,* 23–29.

Davies, D. (1999). *Child development: A practitioner's guide.* New York: Guilford Press.

Ellis, A. (1973). *Humanistic psychotherapy: The rational-emotive approach.* New York: McGraw-Hill.

Gambrill, E. (1995). Helping shy, socially anxious, and lonely adults: A skill based contextual approach. In W. O'Donohue & L. Krasner (Eds.), *Handbook of psychological skill training: Clinical techniques and application* (pp. 247–286). Boston: Allyn & Bacon.

Gambrill, E., Thomas, E. J., & Carter, R. D. (1971). Procedure for sociobehavioral practice in open settings. *Social Work, 16,* 51–62.

Graham, P. (1998). (Ed.). *Cognitive behaviour therapy for children and families.* Cambridge, England: University Press.

Guidano, V. F. (1995). A constructivist outline of human knowing processes. In M. J. Mahoney (Ed.), *Cognitive and constructive psychotherapies: Theory, research, and practice* (pp. 89–102). New York: Springer.

Herbert, H. (2002). The human life cycle: Adolescence. In M. Davies (Ed.), *The Blackwell companion to social work* (pp. 355–364). Oxford, England: Blackwell.

Hughes, J. (1993). Behavior therapy. In T. R. Kratochwill & R. J. Morris (Eds.), *Handbook of psychotherapy with children and adolescents* (pp. 181–220). Boston: Allyn & Bacon.

Kanfer, F. H. (1977). The many faces of self-control, or behavior modification changes its focus. In R. B. Stuart (Ed.), *Behavioral self-management* (pp. 1–48). New York: Brunner/Mazel.

Kanfer, F. H., Karoly, P., & Newman, P. (1975). Reduction of children's fear of dark by competence-related and situational threat-related verbal cues. *Journal of Consulting and Clinical Psychology, 43,* 251–258.

Kanfer, F. H., & Schefft, B. K. (1988). *Guiding the process of therapeutic change.* Champaign, IL: Research Press.

Kazdin, A. E. (1993). Psychotherapy for children and adolescents: Current progress and future directions. *American Psychologist, 48,* 644–656.

Kazdin, A. E. (1994). Psychotherapy for children and adolescents. In A. E. Bergin & S. L. Garfield (Eds.), *Handbook of psychotherapy and behavior change* (4th ed., pp. 543–594). New York: Wiley.

Kelly, G. A. (1955). *The psychology of personal constructs.* New York: Norton.

Mahoney, M. J. (1991). *Human change processes: The scientific foundations of psychotherapy*. New York: Basic Books.

Mahoney, M. J. (1993). Introduction to special section: Theoretical developments in the cognitive psychotherapies. *Journal of Consulting and Clinical Psychology, 61,* 187–193.

Mahoney, M. J. (1999). *Constructive psychotherapy: Exploring principles and practical exercises.* New York: Guilford Press.

Marks, I. (1969). *Fears and phobias.* New York: Academic Press.

Marks, I. (1978). *Living with fear.* New York: McGraw-Hill.

Marks, I. (1987). *Fears, phobias and rituals.* New York: Oxford University Press.

Meichenbaum, D. H. (1993). Changing conceptions of cognitive behavior modification: Retrospect and prospect. *Journal of Consulting and Clinical Psychology, 61,* 202–204.

Nagae, N., & Nedate, K. (2001). Comparison of constructive cognitive and rational cognitive psychotherapies for students with social anxiety. *Constructivism, 6,* 41–49.

Neimeyer, R. A. (1993). An appraisal of constructivist psychotherapies. *Journal of Consulting and Clinical Psychology, 61,* 221–234.

Paul, G. L. (1967). Outcome research in psychotherapy. *Journal of Consulting Psychology, 31,* 109–118.

Pavlov, I. P. (1927). *Conditioning reflexes* (G. A. Anrep, Trans.). New York: Liveright.

Piaget, J. (1926). *The language and thought of the child.* London: Routledge & Kegan Paul.

Powell, M. B., & Oei, T. P. S. (1991). Cognitive processes underlying the behavior change in cognitive behavior therapy with childhood disorders: A review of experimental evidence. *Behavioural Psychotherapy, 19,* 247–265.

Ronen, T. (1996a). Constructivist therapy with traumatized children. *Journal of Constructivist Psychology, 9,* 139–156.

Ronen, T. (1996b). Self-control exposure therapy for treating children's anxieties. *Child and Family Behavior Therapy, 18,* 1–17.

Ronen, T. (1997). *Cognitive developmental therapy with children.* Chicester, England: Wiley.

Ronen, T. (1998a). Direct clinical work with children. In K. Cigno & D. Bourn (Eds.), *Cognitive-behavioural social work in practice* (pp. 39–59). Aldershot, England: Ashgate/Arena.

Ronen, T. (1998b). Linking developmental and emotional elements into child and family cognitive-behavioural therapy. In P. Graham (Ed.), *Cognitive-behaviour therapy for children and families* (pp. 1–17). Cambridge, England: Cambridge Press.

Ronen, T. (2001). Collaboration on critical questions in child psychotherapy: A model linking referral, assessment, intervention, and evaluation. *Journal of Social Work Education, 37,* 91–110.

Ronen, T. (2002). Cognitive-behavioural therapy. In M. Davies (Ed.), *The Blackwell companion to social work* (2nd ed., pp. 165–174). Oxford, England: Blackwell.

Ronen, T. (2003). *Cognitive constructivist psychotherapy with children and adolescents.* New York: Kluwer/Plenum.

Ronen, T., & Rosenbaum, M. (1998). Beyond verbal instruction in cognitive behavioral supervision. *Cognitive & Behavioral Practice, 5,* 3–19.

Ronen, T., & Rosenbaum, M. (2001). Helping children to help themselves: A case study of enuresis and nail biting. *Research on Social Work Practice, 11,* 338–356.

Rosenbaum, M. (1999). The self-regulation of experience: Openness and construction. In D. Dewe, T. Cox, & A. M. Leiter (Eds.), *Coping, health and organizations* (pp. 51–67). London: Taylor & Francis.

Rosenbaum, M., & Ronen, T. (1998). Clinical supervision from the standpoint of cognitive-behavioral therapy. *Psychotherapy, 35,* 220–229.

Rowling, J. K. (1997). *Harry Potter.* London: Warner Brothers.

Safran, J. D., & Segal, Z. V. (1990). *Interpersonal process in cognitive therapy.* New York: Basic Books.

Shuval, J. T. (1982). Migration and stress. In L. Goldberger & S. Breznitz (Eds.), *Handbook of stress: Theoretical and clinical aspects* (pp. 677–691). New York: Free Press.

Skinner, B. F. (1938). *The behavior of organisms.* New York: Appleton-Century-Crofts.

Swell, K. W. (1995). Personal and construct therapy and the relation between cognition and affect. In M. J. Mahoney (Ed.), *Cognitive and constructive psychotherapies: Theory, research, and practice* (pp. 121–138). New York: Springer.

Watson, J. B. (1970). *Behaviorism.* New York: Norton.

Wolpe, J. (1982). *The practice of behavior therapy* (3rd ed.). New York: Pergamon Press.

5

Behavioral Child Therapy

Emphasis on an African American Family Living in a High-Risk Community

Joseph A. Himle, PhD
Daniel J. Fischer, MSW
Jordana R. Muroff, MSW

INTRODUCTION

The focus of this chapter will be to describe methods of behavioral assessment and specific behavioral interventions to address these problem areas. The main interventions discussed in this chapter are parent behavior management and social skills training, including how these interventions may be modified to fit an African American family. Research in support of these interventions and limitations of the model are also presented.

THE CONCEPT OF THE PERSON AND THE HUMAN EXPERIENCE

The central concepts behind behavior therapy are that a person's behavior is shaped by the contingencies present in his or her environment, and that new behavior can be acquired through altering these contingencies, as well as through observational learning and modeled behavior. Behavior therapy is based on the empirically supported notion that an individual's behavioral response is influenced by social consequences that have followed that person's behavior during prior, similar circumstances. In short, people learn to respond to their environment as a result of previous experience. Behavior, both appropriate and inappropriate, followed by reinforcement, is likely to be repeated, whereas behavior that elicits negative consequences is likely to decrease in frequency. Over time, these positive and negative social consequences shape the ways individuals interact with their world.

Individuals who experience harsher environmental circumstances, such as poverty, abuse and neglect, a negative peer group, and parents with ineffective disciplinary styles, are likely to develop more personal and social problems. Behavior therapy attempts to modify the relationship between behavior and environmental responses, in an effort to attain more socially valid outcomes. By reducing or eliminating the inadvertent reinforcement of inappropriate behavior, and rewarding more appropriate behavioral responses, the therapist is able to assist clients in making observable changes in the way they interact with their social environments.

Of key importance, however, is the therapist's ability to distinguish between changeable and nonchangeable environmental circumstances. The therapist must be able to determine whether key contingencies maintaining behavior can be modified. For example, in the case of the Shore family, Michael's peers may persistently provide reinforcing social attention to Michael when he makes inappropriate noises in class, despite the teacher's efforts to reduce the environmental incentive to continue speaking out of turn. This would make it important for the social worker to arrange other environmental incentives to increase Michael's pro-social behavior in class. In short, interventions should target environmental factors that can be effectively altered to produce desired change and outcome.

HISTORICAL PERSPECTIVE

The historical foundations of contemporary child behavior therapy began in the 1950s and 1960s with many classic works by Skinner (1953, 1969) and others (Eysenck, 1960; Lazarus, 1958; Wolpe, 1958). Skinner's notion of radical behaviorism, with its central theory that behavior is maintained by the contingencies in the social environment, shaped many of the early applications of child behavior therapy. A good number of these applications of child behavior therapy focused on mentally retarded and other severely impaired youths (Doubros, 1966; Doubros & Daniels, 1966). Interventions were typically delivered in institutional or classroom environments, in which it was thought to be essential to rigorously apply reinforcement and other strategies to modify problematic behavior. In the mid to late 1960s, early work using these interventions for youths without severe impairment or cognitive deficits began to appear in the literature (Patterson, 1968). During this period, the field of applied behavior analysis began to establish itself as an important movement in addressing behavior problems in youths (Baer, Wolf, & Risley, 1968). Patterson, Reid, Jones, and Conger's (1975) work with antisocial youths was instrumental in moving the focus of behavioral therapy from the child to the family context and extending interventions to the home environment. Substantial growth in the application of behavior therapy for youths took place throughout the 1970s, in which several studies demonstrated the effectiveness of behavioral interventions for a growing number of problems, including autism (Lovaas, Koegel, Simmons, & Long, 1973), classroom behavior management (O'Leary, Becker, Evans, & Saudargas, 1969), and family treatments (Patterson et al., 1975). The 1980s brought the development of a behavioral-systems perspective that Mash (1989) described as viewing child behavior problems as a function of interrelated response systems within the family. The behavioral-systems perspective considers the entire family situation when assessing the impact of a change in any single variable and posits that behavioral interventions are likely to lead to multiple outcomes (e.g., readjustments of relationships). Many of the interventions discussed in this chapter address child problems from a behavioral-systems perspective. More recent advances in child behavior therapy have focused on making interventions more prescriptive to problem type, manualizing these approaches, and increasing the developmental sensitivity of child behavioral treatments (Holmbeck, Colder, Shapera, Westhoven, Kenealy, & Updegrove, 2000; Ollendick & King, 2000).

KEY THEORETICAL CONSTRUCTS

The primary theoretical foundation of child behavioral practice rests on the notion that the social environment determines an individual's behavior. A central construct in child behavior therapy is that it is empirical in nature. This evidenced-based approach drives the selection of assessment and intervention strategies. Functional behavioral assessment is used to develop individualized treatment strategies aimed at producing desired behavior change. Continued assessment and data collection throughout the intervention phase help the therapist and the client monitor progress and make appropriate modifications to further enhance treatment outcomes.

Child behavior therapy is based on the principle of ABC, wherein *antecedent* events elicit a *behavioral* response that is maintained or eliminated by resulting *consequences.* Therefore, effective child behavior therapy (parent behavior management, social skills training) influences behavior change either by addressing the events that occur before a given behavior or by modifying the consequences that follow the behavior.

In the case of parent behavior management, modification of antecedents focuses on helping parents anticipate a child's misbehavior. By anticipating problematic behavior, parents are able to adjust the antecedents of misbehavior (e.g., assigning a chore with ample time to complete it before a favored television show comes on, rather than just prior to it) to facilitate a desired behavioral outcome (e.g., completing the chore). Typical intervention strategies designed to address behavioral antecedents include scheduling, instructions, modeling, and verbal and physical prompts.

In the case of social skills training, the child or adolescent learns to identify events that elicit anger and peer conflict, yet develop strategies for altering or avoiding the anger-producing situations. However, it may not always be possible to alter antecedents to problematic behavior. Therefore, a second focus of behavioral intervention is to change the consequences that result from a given behavior, in order to influence the likelihood of that behavior happening again. Attending to the connection between consequences and behavior is referred to as *contingency management.* Further discussion of the key theoretical constructs of child behavior therapy is included in the "Assessment" and "Therapeutic Process" sections of this chapter.

ASSESSMENT

The three elements of behavioral assessment (antecedent, behavior, and consequences) can be seen in the Shore family. For example, an antecedent to conflict between Charley and Michael may be when Charley corrects his son's casting technique on a fishing trip. This may serve as a trigger for a disrespectful comment (behavior) from Michael toward his father, which in turn may elicit a countering negative comment from Charley that cycles into a conflict that ends the trip (consequence). Michael has likely learned to respond to unpleasant requests from his parents by making disrespectful comments or by refusing to comply altogether. This pattern of behavior probably persists because it often succeeds in allowing Michael to escape or avoid unpleasant tasks. Conversely, Charley's yelling and critical statements likely persist because they usually result in people eventually giving in to his demands.

In the case of the spiraling argument between Michael and Charley, Michael's argumentativeness may help him to avoid or delay compliance with his father's instructions, whereas Charley's yelling may eventually succeed in Michael's yielding to his request. However, it is likely that if both parties fail to reach their desired behavioral outcome, the argument will become noxious for both, thus ending the fishing trip and allowing Charley and Michael to escape the unpleasantness of the conflict. Understanding the antecedents, the behaviors, and the consequences of Charley and Michael's problematic interactions is one example of many areas of Shore family functioning that require a thorough behavioral analysis.

The first step in completing a behavioral analysis is to select and operationally define specific target behaviors for change. A behavior therapist should always first consider addressing behaviors that are dangerous to the child or to others. In Michael's case, his social behavior, which leaves him picked on and physically assaulted by his peers, would be a good choice for an early focus of a behavioral analysis and intervention plan. A second consideration for choosing target behaviors involves selecting those most relevant to the child and to the parents. Conflicts between Michael and his father are clearly identified by all parties as a source of significant concern. A third factor of interest in prioritizing targets for analysis and change is the degree of interference caused by the behavior in school, family, and community functioning. Michael has experienced significant functional impairment from his impulsive behavior and his inappropriate social conduct in a variety of settings, making these behaviors important targets for early assessment and change. A final issue of importance in selecting behavioral targets relates to the likelihood that a behavioral intervention would yield a satisfactory result. Clearly, clinical impressions suggest that families are at risk for dropping out of treatment if initial attempts at change fail. Failure to persist when meeting resistance may be especially important for the Shore family, given Charley's difficulty in persisting when times are tough.

Once a target behavior is selected, the process of operationalizing the selected problem begins. Labels for problematic behaviors, such as disrespectfulness, having a bad attitude, or mischievousness, are redefined as observable, measurable, and specific. The ultimate goal of this process is to subject the behavior to an intervention plan aimed at producing positive social change.

For example, Charley may describe Michael as a "social misfit" when speaking of his son's problem of being bullied at school. The term *social misfit* does not reveal clear targets for change, whereas interrupting peers during lunch conversation, making annoying sounds in class, and pushing classmates in the hallway are examples of operationalized problem behaviors that are ready for intervention.

Once specific behaviors are selected, the next step in behavioral assessment is data collection. Baseline measurements of the frequency, the duration, and the intensity or severity of the problem behavior are completed. Baseline measurements are often obtained through naturalistic observations by the therapist and through parent, teacher, and child data collection. These baseline assessments are used to establish the nature of the intervention and also to set the stage for behavioral change goals. Data collection extends throughout the intervention and maintenance portions of treatment, allowing the therapist to make appropriate modifications to the initial intervention plan.

Discussion thus far has focused on the child's behavior. Behavioral assessment should also include attention to the bi-directional nature of parent–child conflicts, with the goal of identifying change targets for both the parents and the child. Using the Shore family as an example, imagine that Charley and Michael are watching a program on television. Charley gets up to go to the kitchen and on the way notices Michael's messy room. Charley returns and says to Michael, "When are you ever going to get around to cleaning your room?" Michael ignores Charley. Charley responds by saying that he is going to ground Michael for 2 weeks if the boy doesn't get started right away. Michael states, "I don't care." Charley counters by screaming at Michael, "You are useless . . . you never do anything I ask you to do!" Hearing the commotion, Nancy comes into the room, calls them both "children," and tells them that she will take care of cleaning the room. It is too much work for Michael to do by himself anyway.

This multi-directional interaction pattern illustrates the need for assessment that extends beyond focus on the child to include target behaviors for change in the parents. For example, Charley's method of giving commands to Michael may be a target for change. Also, Nancy's involvement at the end of the interchange clearly undermines Charley's authority and allows Michael, once again, to avoid complying with his father. The ultimate outcome of this multi-directional assessment would likely be that each member of the family would have a list of behaviors to increase or decrease when faced with family conflict.

THE THERAPEUTIC PROCESS

Michael's central behavior problem in the home is parent–child conflict. Although there is no clear behavioral description of the conflicts between Michael and Charley, one can assume that deficits in communication, problem solving, and child compliance with rules and expectations are present. It is apparent that Nancy, Charley, and Michael have struggled in developing consistent lines of family authority. The therapeutic process with the Shore family would begin with a functional analysis of the factors that contribute to and maintain the family disturbance. This analysis includes several factors, the characteristics of the child and the parents, overall family circumstances, and specific behavioral factors. Michael has several characteristics that may contribute to his misbehavior, including his severe chronic illness, learning disabilities, hyperactivity, social-skills deficits, and impulsivity. Nancy and Charley each have significant characteristics that make effective parenting challenging. Nancy struggles with depression, anxiety, chronic pain, and obesity. Charley has been diagnosed with bipolar disorder, has difficulty with goal-directed behavior, and is socially immature.

Behavior Management of Parent–Child Conflict

It is apparent that Charley has little authority in the home and that parent and adolescent conflicts have been a persistent pattern, starting with Rena and continuing now with Michael. In addressing parent–child conflicts, the behavioral clinician must determine the primary source of conflict, which is often related to issues of independence, school performance, and compliance with home-based rules.

Effective behavior management involves keeping the connection between behavior and consequences clear. Three central components are involved in establishing this connection. First, parents must learn to be specific regarding rules and behavioral expectations for their children. Second, parents must learn to respond immediately to child behavior, in order to establish strong connections between behavior and consequences. Consistency of parental follow-through and delivery of consequences, both positive and negative, is the final step

A central problem in the case of the Shore family is the lack of a unified parental coalition between Nancy and Charley. In order to establish specific expectations for Michael, the behavioral therapist must first encourage Nancy and Charley to reach agreement on household rules. One specific strategy aimed at reaching this agreement is to ask each parent to develop a list of relevant behavioral expectations for the son. When completed, these two lists would be compared, and the expectations common to both lists would form the core household rules. Once rules and developmentally appropriate expectations have been established, the next step would be to work with the parents to develop consistent, predictable consequences for rule adherence and violations. Parents often over-rely on punitive measures in dealing with their child's problematic behavior, resorting to severe punishments to "send a message" to the child, in an effort to completely eliminate the likelihood of the misbehavior's reoccurring. Severe punishments are usually ineffective and inconsistently delivered. Parents who favor punitive approaches often resist the idea of providing positive incentives for desired behavior, viewing positive incentives as bribery or, at minimum, unnecessary. An unbalanced approach favoring negative over positive consequences often leads to an angry, frustrated, demoralized child who ultimately is less likely to comply with parental expectations.

Once a basic set of household rules is established, a collaborative family meeting is held, which focuses on refining these expectations and clarifying a specific behavioral contingency management program. Many youngsters expect unencumbered access to multiple activities, privileges, and material goods. Parents often feel obligated to provide these things to their children, regardless of their children's behavior. If the youth misbehaves, parents may take away these privileges in a punitive effort to address misbehavior. Behavioral contingency management pairs desired and preferred privileges with the appropriate behavior. The advantage of this approach is that privileges, which are under parental control, are available to the child based upon his or her compliance with appropriate expectations and rules. Thus, this system of management not only helps to re-establish parental authority but also aids in teaching self-responsibility to the child. A behavioral contingency management program could be established with the Shore family using several strategies, including token economy, behavioral contracting, response cost, and the use of grounding.

Token Economy

There are three steps to developing a token economy program. In step one, the parents and the child identify specific expectations and rules for the child's behavior. In step two, the parents and the child develop a list of preferred privileges or rewards that are under the parent's control. This list should have both tangible and social rewards and may include many of the things the child has taken for granted. It is important for the therapist to help parents anticipate their child's resistance to the token economy system. In step three, the family must determine what type of token will be used, how many tokens are earned for each identified behavior, and the cost of each privilege or reward.

In the case of the Shore family, the parents may identify several behavioral responsibilities for Michael. These may include completion of specific chores, talking respectfully to adults, complying with his asthma treatments, getting himself dressed on time for school in the morning, and going to bed at an established time without argument. The difficulty of the task and the likelihood of compliance would determine the number of tokens he earns for complying with each of these expectations. The more difficult the task, the more tokens he earns. The privilege list for Michael, which should incorporate both daily and weekly rewards, could include the following items: television; staying up ½ hour later at night; choice of a special snack; being driven to school; miniature golf; a subscription to a current events magazine or newspaper; fishing trips; and items specific to his involvement with the Boy Scouts. The cost of each privilege is determined by the relative cost to Nancy and Charley and the value of each privilege to Michael. Michael would earn tokens whenever he does something on the responsibility list. If possible, tokens should be delivered immediately upon completion of the task. If Michael wanted something from the privilege list, he would have to pay with his earned tokens. Michael would not be able to do anything on the privilege list until he earned enough tokens. The list of responsibilities and rewards could be modified as needed to keep the program novel and the rewards salient.

Behavioral Contracting

A behavioral contract is a written agreement between the parents and the child, which specifies a task or a responsibility to be completed by the child and a privilege earned upon task completion. In using a behavioral contract with the Shore family, the therapist would again need to develop a list of specific responsibilities and privileges for Michael. Once these lists have been established, the first behavioral contract would be implemented by selecting a low-difficulty task and a privilege of moderate value. For example, the parents would inform Michael that access to the evening newspaper is contingent upon whether he clears the dinner table immediately after dinner. This requirement would then be written on the behavioral contract signed by Nancy, Charley, and Michael, indicating that he has been informed of the arrangement. Both Michael and his parents would be given a copy of the contract, which would remain in effect for 1 to 2 weeks.

Response Cost

In most successful behavioral contingency management programs, rewards and privileges are not sufficient in managing child misbehavior and establishing parental authority. In addition to rewards, punishments may also be required to maintain appropriate child behavior. Response cost is an approach that, when combined with either a token economy system or behavioral contracting, can be an effective parental strategy for child misbehavior. Response cost involves the loss of tokens or privileges for specific acts of noncompliance or for other violations of family rules. Combining response cost with a token economy program should be implemented after at least 1 to 2 weeks of successful use of the token economy program.

For example, Nancy and Charley might choose "do not swear at my parents" as the behavioral target. Once the problem behavior is identified, the parents should select a privilege that is meaningful to the child and that can be easily withheld should the child engage in the identified problem behavior. The behavioral contract would be written to include this if/then arrangement, be reviewed with the child, and be signed by all.

Grounding and Work Details

Grounding is the withholding of all preferred activities and privileges in response to problematic child behavior. There are several common mistakes that parents may make when using grounding. First, when some parents say their child is grounded, this refers to the child's being restricted to the home. Although this may limit access to some preferred activities, the child is still able to play video games, watch television, and use the computer, which often diminishes the effectiveness of the grounding consequence. A second common error in the use of grounding occurs when parents ground their child but are unable to monitor him or her, which means that the child is often able to violate the grounding restrictions without penalty when the parents are away. A third problem for most parents is that they have trouble following through with extended groundings. A child grounded for 1 week may stay grounded for only a few days, as parents fail to enforce the grounding once they are no longer angry with the child. Another problem is that some parents use grounding only when they are extremely angry with their children and, as a result, are unreasonably harsh in establishing the duration of the punishment. Therefore, children see the parents as unreasonable and overreactive, thus focusing on the parents' behavior rather than on their own. Finally, parents often add time to a 1-week grounding because of some other infraction, so 1 week becomes 2, and 2 weeks become 3, until it feels like the child is grounded for life. These common mistakes limit the effectiveness of this consequence and further decrease parental authority.

Combining grounding with an assigned work detail can produce these desired effects. This strategy requires that the child perform an assigned work detail in order to gain back access to privileges. The length of the grounding is determined by the difficulty of the work detail (which is matched to the severity of the misbehavior) and the child's timeliness in completing the task.

In the case of the Shore family, the following strategy could be put in place: Nancy and Charley inform Michael that swearing is against the rules of the house. If Michael uses swear words in an argument, he will be given an assigned work detail. Nancy and Charley will inform Michael that once the work detail is assigned, he is grounded from all privileges and is under "house arrest" until the work detail is completed to his parents' satisfaction. In combining grounding with work details, Charley and Nancy should be instructed to focus on withholding privileges rather than feeling compelled to make Michael do the assigned task in a timely manner. How quickly the task is completed and, ultimately, the duration of the grounding are under Michael's control. Thus, instead of simply withholding privileges, Nancy and Charley are able to shift the responsibility for the punitive consequence back to Michael and therefore avoid the struggle for control.

Communication Skills Training

Until this point in the behavior therapy with the Shore family, the emphasis in treatment has focused on parent-driven interventions. Once a plan of action has been implemented in order to re-establish a parental coalition and parental authority, the behavior therapist should focus attention on improving communication and developing family problem-solving skills. In making this shift, the therapist must attend to the fact that treatment to this point has been applied *to* Michael, not *with* Michael. Therefore, the next phase of treatment would focus on building rapport with Michael. This is crucial, as success in the next phases of the intervention program require his willingness to collaborate with the therapist and his parents in an effort to reduce parent–child conflict.

Once rapport with the child has been established, communication skills training and family-based problem solving are introduced. Communication skills training focuses on replacing obstructive styles of parent–child communication with more facilitative alternatives. In family-based problem solving, the behavior therapist teaches parents and youths to clarify negotiable and non-negotiable rules. Once negotiable rules have been identified, the therapist assists the family in developing a strategy designed to arrive at mutually agreeable expectations. Examples of non-negotiable rules may include no physical aggression, no swearing, and no substance use. Negotiable rules might include curfew times, household chores, and activities with friends.

Communication skills training with the Shore family would involve three specific steps. In step one, the behavior therapist presents a list of examples of common communication errors to the family. This list should include interactions observed during earlier sessions, as well as suspected errors. For example, in the Shore family, sarcasm, blaming statements, denial of responsibility, name calling, and dredging up the past are among the communication problems that are likely present. The second step is to have the family and the therapist brainstorm alternative facilitative communication strategies. The therapist should keep the list of negative patterns in view during the session. The family discusses each negative pattern and, guided by the therapist, uses the positive communication methods identified during the brainstorming session to address each problematic interaction pattern. Roles may be reversed to facilitate generalization and greater understanding of the perspective of others. The facilitative patterns are then posted for use during future clinic sessions and in the family home.

Step three involves maintaining the focus on communication throughout future sessions. At all subsequent sessions, the communications list should be posted and quickly reviewed at the beginning of the visit. The therapist should closely monitor family communication and point out any communication errors observed, with the family practicing positive alternatives on the spot. In this way, all opportunities for improving family communication are utilized.

Family-Based Problem Solving

Family-based problem solving involves a five-step process. First, families are taught to define the problem to be addressed. This step can be somewhat challenging, because families often state problems in global, nonspecific terms (e.g., "Our problem is that he is irresponsible and never does anything we ask him to") instead of as behaviorally specific single-problem statements (e.g., "Even with reminders, he will not clean his room"). Next, family members brainstorm possible solutions to the problem. It is important that families avoid evaluating solutions as these are introduced, in order to facilitate the development of a full list of possible solutions. Third, families are instructed how to evaluate the benefits and the drawbacks of each possible solution and to select the best mutually agreeable option. In step four, families develop a plan for implementing and providing rewards or consequences for follow-through with the agreed-upon solution. Finally, in step five, families are encouraged to evaluate the outcome of the chosen solution and to select an alternative, if necessary.

Social Skills Training

One of the most challenging difficulties the Shore family is experiencing concerns Michael's social isolation and inappropriate social behavior in school, at camp, and with his Boy Scout troop. Clinical attention may be needed in order to help Michael develop friendships and increase his pro-social behavior. Michael has developed a reputation as a troublemaker and is often the recipient of social ridicule and peer violence. These problems are leading to considerable functional impairment, as evidenced by Michael's loneliness and the fact that he is still assigned to a classroom for learning disabled children, even though his learning difficulties have long been resolved. It appears that the most pressing priority for Michael is to improve his peer relationships, given that he often comes home beaten up and spends most of his time alone.

Behavioral techniques for improving peer relationships usually begin with several strategies for establishing a few close friendships (Frankel, Cantwell, & Myatt, 1996). As informal neighborhood play has been progressively overshadowed by parent-led organized activities, such as scouting and sports teams, new methods have developed to provide the opportunity for children to spend extended informal time together (Ladd, 1992). These informal meetings, or "play dates," are crucial to the development of friendships (Ladd, 1992). Research suggests that structured activities such as scouting or sports teams do not go far toward helping a socially rejected child make friendships (Ladd & Price, 1987), with the exception of providing an opportunity to make arrangements for later play at a peer's home (Parke & Bhavnagri, 1989). However, these "play date" arrangements are of little value if the rejected child exhibits negative social behavior during the meetings. These arranged meetings also require parents to exhibit certain pro-social behaviors: interacting with other parents to arrange transportation and building relationships so that parents feel comfortable leaving their children under each others' care. In addition, parents must have skills in supervising the play date at some distance, remaining able to redirect negative interactions, while providing a comfortable environment with suitable activities. It is likely that Nancy and Charley fall short of accomplishing these objectives.

Socially rejected children often have substantial difficulties managing several aspects of peer relations during unstructured play opportunities. They are often bossy, inflexible, and argumentative; fail to follow the game rules; and rarely consider other children's wishes when choosing activities. The first task of a behavioral therapist in working to help children establish appropriate friendships is to complete an assessment of the child's social strengths and weaknesses. This task is often accomplished by observing the child in session, through parent and teacher reports, and by observing the child's social interaction in his or her natural environment (e.g., school, playground, home). Socially rejected children may be observed interfering with other children's activities, awkwardly attempting to join activities at inappropriate times, and engaging in disruptive behavior that draws negative attention. Michael has been observed making strange noises, talking too loudly, using foul language, throwing food, and instigating conflicts with his peers. These behaviors likely persist because they result in Michael receiving attention, and some notoriety, albeit for negative behavior. Positive social attention in the form of praise from parents, teachers, and peers, likely eludes Michael.

The social skill assessment would also focus on Michael's social strengths. These strengths could include honesty in relating to others, compassion for peers who are struggling (e.g., "underdogs"), and a fund of knowledge about current events. The goal of the behavior therapist would be to intervene to increase the frequency of already established pro-social skills, establish new pro-social skills, and decrease undesirable social behavior. Typically, the therapist would utilize in-office role-play to rehearse one new desirable social behavior at a time. Focus on too many deficits would likely demoralize the child and the parents, leading them to believe that the situation is hopeless. The therapist and the child could rehearse essential skills needed during play dates, including negotiating mutually enjoyable activities, managing conflict, learning appropriate hosting behaviors (e.g., offering snacks, having suitable options for play available), and selecting appropriate topics for conversation.

Managing conflict is another social skill that needs attention in Michael's case. Problems with negotiating conflict are apparent in Michael's activities with Charley. Outings for fishing or miniature golf can reliably be expected to end in an unresolved argument. It is likely that Charley has not modeled appropriate compromise and conflict-resolution strategies for his son. Essential skills in managing conflict in a social activity include seeking compromise, backing away from one's position to maintain a comfortable atmosphere, and choosing activities that would be unlikely to prompt a dispute. Backing down or redirecting conflict during a play date is especially important for the host. Effective parents can also help children in conflict find a solution or move on to another activity. Clinical impressions suggest that many socially rejected children hold too closely to their position in a dispute or, conversely, give in so readily that peers see them as pushovers. Clearly, there are situations wherein a socially rejected child should stand his ground, but a minor dispute about a judgment call in a backyard basketball game may not be the time to do so. One effective strategy for resolving conflict during a play date is to help the socially rejected child brainstorm potential solutions to the conflict, evaluate them with his peer guest, and select the most desirable solution from both perspectives. It is likely that Michael has little experience with backing down from a dispute or in generating an array of potential solutions for a social impasse.

Also of relevance for Michael is to develop new skills for social entry. Michael likely has difficulty timing his attempts to join in potentially enjoyable activities (e.g., conversations, games, sporting events). Clearly, for a boy like Michael, joining in activities that are already underway may be a valuable skill because he is not likely to be included when activities are initially arranged. Role-plays of various scenarios, based on joining opportunities from Michael's life, would be a valuable opportunity for social rehearsal in the office. Once rehearsed in the office, assignments would be given to attempt to join activities, with a homework recording form provided for Michael to record his experiences. Subsequent sessions would include review of successful and unsuccessful attempts to join in.

Inviting skills are also important for children attempting to establish friendships. Many socially rejected children do not make clear invitations, due, in part, to lack of social skills and also because unclear invitations may serve to buffer the negative effects of a clear rejection. Once again, behavioral rehearsal of appropriate invitations for play dates can be done in the therapist's office. Collaboration with parents regarding their responsibilities in facilitating social encounters for their child is essential. Many parents feel anxious or awkward about discussing the logistics of a play date for their child, and successful strategies for this situation can be rehearsed in the office.

Another important component of most social skills programs relates to conversational deficits. One key conversational skill is the ability to ask open-ended, other-centered questions. Socially rejected children are often self-centered in their conversational style (e.g., "I really like astronomy"), as opposed to other-centered (e.g., "What do you like to do?"; Barkley, 2000). Asking questions that are open-ended usually requires a child to listen well to the response and to respond with a follow-up question to get more information (e.g., "What do you like about that video game?"). This process of asking about the interests and the activities of a conversational partner usually results in discovering topics of mutual interest that can be explored further. In addition to asking questions, it is also crucial for children to offer information about their own interests but to do so while attempting to avoid bragging and dominating the conversation. In addition to asking questions, providing verbal reinforcement to a conversational partner in the form of occasional compliments or praise is another valuable method to enhance social success. Finally, appropriate eye contact and body positioning can also be rehearsed. Michael may need help with several of these conversational skill areas, although his success in conversing with adults suggests that he may have some of these skills in his repertoire. Michael may need special help with how to participate in social interactions that involve larger groups of children, given his problems with acting out in class and on scouting trips. Michael's disruptive classroom behavior is especially critical to attend to, because it is undoubtedly annoying to his peers and is largely responsible for his reputation as a troublemaker. More socially appropriate ways to contribute to the classroom discussion (e.g. raising his hand, offering comments about the material, offering help to others) can be modeled, rehearsed, and assigned as homework.

Finally, any social skills program for Michael should include attention to managing bullying and teasing. Michael gets beaten up regularly by his classmates. When this happens, he often stands there and takes the beating, without attempting to fight back or run away. These physical altercations likely begin with teasing from other children. A central skill in responding to teasing is to take the reinforcement out of the situation so that the child inflicting the teasing finds it less attractive. One method involves agreeing (at least partially) with the teasing. For example, if a peer teased Michael by saying, "You are a loser, you have no friends" he may respond by saying, "Yeah, you're right, I could have more." Another method is to make fun of the tease. For instance, Michael might say, "I've heard that one a million times, that is old as the hills!" (Coie & Dodge, 1988). Above all, the most important strategy is to not show how much the tease hurts (Perry, Williard, & Perry, 1990). Michael likely reinforces the teasing by trying to tease back and failing or by displaying how much the teasing bothers him. Establishing a group of friendly peers at school, such that bullies may be less likely to single him out for teasing, could also be helpful. These strategies may succeed in reducing the number of physical altercations that Michael is involved in. However, there will likely be a need to utilize other strategies. One obvious strategy is for Michael to avoid the children who bully and to seek help from a responsible adult when appropriate. Regularly reporting these altercations to his parents and a school administrator would likely help reduce them.

APPLICATION TO DIVERSITY

This section will consider diversity issues and how such influences are applicable to the concepts and the theoretical constructs presented here—specifically, social-skills training and parent behavior-management training. This section will also consider how the therapeutic models under discussion would be applied differently if the Shore family were African American.

The Shore family's sociodemographic characteristics of being White and lower middle class may influence the therapeutic process. For example, social class may influence clinician and client expectations of the therapeutic process. The literature suggests that clients of lower socioeconomic status have the expectations that therapists will be active and will provide advice, which are not typical of those shared by clients of middle-class backgrounds (Garvin & Seabury, 1997). In addition, some mental health clinicians may also have low expectations of clients of lower socioeconomic status, assuming that they are not open to psychotherapy, which may then prove to be true through self-fulfilling prophecy (Garvin & Seabury, 1997).

To better understand the role of race and class in the application of behavior therapy, it is important to explore the development of such behavioral treatments. Behavior therapy, developed and practiced by predominantly White scientist–practitioners (Neal-Barnett & Smith, 1996), is mainly based on research with middle- to upper-class European Americans (Forehand & Kotchick, 1996). Despite the acknowledgment that culture is an important consideration in the delivery of behavior treatment, this issue has essentially been ignored in behavior therapy research, especially as it relates to the influence of cultural values on parenting (Forehand & Kotchick, 1996). In addition, most parent-rated behavioral assessment instruments were developed almost exclusively with middle- to upper-class European American families (Forehand & Kotchick, 1996). Given that the values and needs of middle-class European American families may differ from those of people with diverse racial or ethnic backgrounds and socioeconomic status, the universal application of child behavioral-management programs and instruments may not be appropriate. For instance, the "competencies" and behaviors that poor urban parents value may be distinct from those valued by middle- to upper-class parents (Ogbu, 1985; from Forehand & Kotchick, 1996, p. 193). Therefore, clinicians need to place added emphasis on the collaborative aspect of assessment and intervention development, rather than focusing specifically on prescriptive procedures.

Cultural differences in competencies and social skills may be an important consideration in social-skills training. For example, among social groups characterized by economic instability and financial strain, compliance may be emphasized, whereas social groups with greater financial prosperity and stability may stress independence and assertiveness (Forehand & Kotchick, 1996; Harkness & Super, 1995). Thus, life circumstances and socioeconomic status may influence which social skills are most needed. Assessment must be individualized to include those competencies, behaviors, and social skills valued by specific families for specific situations. It is important when working in these situations that clinicians not only understand their own values but take care not to impose these upon their clients.

If the Shore family were an African American family living in a crime-ridden neighborhood, what treatment considerations would be critical to the therapeutic process? As discussed in the "Assessment" section, behavioral analysis is an important aspect of an effective behavioral intervention. It is important that culture and environmental factors be considered in this process. The initial step in behavioral analysis is the identification and operationalization of those specific maladaptive and adaptive behaviors that will be targeted for change. As noted, behavior therapists must consider behaviors that put the child at risk. It may be even more critical for a behavior therapist working with an African American child living in a crime-ridden neighborhood to consider environmental characteristics and to target behaviors that further increase the child's risk of harm. For example, social behavior that leads to teasing and physical assault may be particularly problematic when living in such an environment, where the tendency toward violence is already inflated. Michael's peers and members of his community may be more likely to own, carry, or use weapons, given an orientation toward survival and living under constant threat. Being perceived as having poor judgment or lacking social acumen may lead to social isolation due to concerns around safety and survival. Persons may be less likely to immediately trust. Therefore, reliance on family networks, close friends, and church affiliations for social support with proven loyalty may be the norm. In an effort to enhance the therapeutic relationship in such circumstances, it is crucial that the clinician acknowledge these multiple systems and attempt to utilize them in intervention development.

Such cultural and environmental factors need to be incorporated into the development of behavior-management plans and response costs. Although we advocate that parents adopt a positive approach to managing children's behavior, culturally specific parenting styles need be acknowledged and understood. African American parents often believe that parental authority is a deterrent to child misconduct (McGoldrick & Giordano, 1996). Physical punishment and emotional withdrawal are more commonly seen as acceptable forms of discipline among the African American community (Forehand & Kotchick, 1996; McGoldrick & Giordano, 1996). In addition, African American parents more closely monitor their children's whereabouts, have greater influence over peer selection, and are usually more authoritarian than their White counterparts (Gillmore, Catalano, Morrison, Wells, Iritani, & Hawkins, 1990; Giordano, Cernkovich, & Demaris, 1993; Peterson, Hawkins, Abbott, Catalano, 1994; Wallace & Muroff, 2002). African American parents living in a crime-ridden environment may have stronger concerns associated with altering this style. Because the tendency is to have a more authoritative style, the idea of moving toward a reward-and-privileges orientation may prompt concerns that being less authoritative might reduce protection and increase vulnerability to harm. It is important for behavior therapists to acknowledge these concerns. Joining and collaboration between the behavior therapist and the family are critical.

However, despite the increased cultural acceptance of physical punishment, clinicians should not feel compelled to design behavioral interventions with greater reliance on corporal discipline. Conversely, a clinician who summarily dismisses all physical punishment as unethical and inappropriate will find it difficult to maintain ongoing therapeutic relationships with families whose cultural background supports this approach. However, cultural support for corporal punishment does not relieve clinicians of their professional responsibility to assess and report physical abuse.

The implementation of behavior plans may also be influenced by culturally specific social network characteristics. African Americans have historically relied on family, friends, religion, and their community for social support. There is a relatively high percentage of single-parent, female-headed households in the African American community. Other family members (i.e., grandparents) may live in the same household as well. It is critical that behavioral contracts clearly indicate which adult figures are established as parental authority figures. It is important that a unified coalition be established between the parental authority figure(s) and other adult figures who reside in the home. Other adult figures must agree not to alter contracts without the established authority figures' agreement.

An added dimension to behavioral treatment with African American families living in crime-ridden environments includes the complex balance between living in mainstream culture and maintaining a cultural identity. There may be significant distinctions between the social skills necessary for success on the street, in the home, at school, and when interacting with the majority culture. Such social skills may contradict each other, and using a set of social skills from one domain in another setting may lead to rejection, ostracism, or even physical violence. Behavior therapists need to be cognizant of social expectations that are characteristic of various domains. This issue again highlights the importance of a collaborative therapeutic style, whereby the client and his or her support network join with the clinician in determining the necessary social skills needed for success in various settings.

Finally, in working with African American families, it may be helpful for behavior therapists to include African American motivational speakers and to utilize videotape, audiotape, or print media featuring African American models of successful parenting and use of social skills (Neal-Barnett & Smith, 1996).

LIMITATIONS OF THE MODEL

Although parent behavior-management training and social-skills training have been shown to be effective interventions, several limitations of these treatments exist. First, outcomes are often incomplete, especially in relation to the impact of these interventions on everyday functioning (e.g., academic performance, peer relations, social competence). Second, there is a paucity of research focusing on adolescents, using parent behavior-management and social-skills interventions; that which is available indicates that adolescents do not respond as well compared to younger children (Dishion & Patterson, 1992). Third, there are a limited number of appropriately trained clinicians available to deliver these treatments, and opportunities to receive such training are scarce (Kazdin, 1997). Finally, as noted in the previous section, the application of these interventions across a range of subjects from varied ethnic and socioeconomic groups is limited. Clearly, research focusing on delivering these interventions to more diverse groups is needed.

RESEARCH

Child behavior management has received extensive evaluation in numerous randomized clinical trials, particularly for youths with conduct problems (Kazdin, 1997; Mabe, Turner, & Josephson, 2001). These studies include children of various age ranges and degrees of severity of oppositional behavior (Kazdin, 1997; Mabe et al., 2001). Research has typically compared behavior management training to no treatment, wait-list control conditions, or to other viable treatment options, such as individual or family therapy (Kazdin, 1997; Mabe, et al., 2001). Overall, research supports the efficacy of behavior management treatment in improving child behavior problems and reducing family conflicts (Barkley, Edwards, Laneri, Fletcher, & Metevia, 2001; Kazdin, 1997; Mabe, et al., 2001; Marcus, et al., 2001; Patterson, Dishion, & Chamberlain, 1993; Serketich & Dumas, 1996). Serketich and Dumas (1996) conducted a meta-analysis of 26 controlled studies of parent behavior-management training with antisocial youths and found substantial support for this intervention, producing large treatment effects for both the child and the parents. This meta-analysis also found that several studies demonstrated that treatment gains were maintained over follow-up periods of 2 months to 1 year (Serketich & Dumas, 1996). Long, Forehand, Wierson, and Morgan (1994) conducted a follow-up study of behaviorally disordered children whose parents had participated in a behavior-management training program and reported that treatment gains had been maintained 10 to 14 years after treatment was completed. Overall, research indicates that behavior-management training is an effective, durable intervention for child behavior disorders, which produces lasting benefits for both the child and his or her parents. The program described in this chapter to help the Shore family reduce parent–child conflicts was modeled after an 18-step parent management-training program developed by Barkely, Edwards, and Robin (1999).

Several studies of behavioral social skills training for youths with socialization problems have reported improvement on measures of social adjustment (Berner, Fee, & Turner, 2001; Flanagan, Povall, Dellino, & Byrne, 1998). The social skills program described in this chapter was largely modeled after the intervention designed by Frankel, Cantwell, and Mayatt (1995), which reported superior outcomes compared to a wait-list control for a 12-week group social-skills training program targeting socially rejected youths. This program has also been found to be effective for youths with attention deficit hyperactivity disorder and oppositional defiant disorder (Frankel, Myatt, Cantwell, & Feinberg, 1996). A recent meta-analysis by Magee, Kavale, Mathur, Rutherford, and Forness (1999), including 35 studies of youths with emotional or behavioral disorders, given interventions that included a social-skills training component, found a relatively modest effect size overall. Larger effect sizes were found for approaches that focused on teaching and measuring specific skills, as opposed to more global interventions. Outcomes were further enhanced when skills-training programs were integrated across several settings, including the home, the school, and the playground. This meta-analysis confirmed the common clinical belief that social skill programs are not particularly effective in improving social outcomes for youths if they are limited to small group sessions in the clinic.

SUMMARY

The Shore family presents two significant opportunities for child behavioral interventions, parent management training and social-skills training. Although no therapeutic model is perfect, child behavioral interventions would likely be helpful to the Shore family. However, it is important to note that this chapter addressed only a few of the many behavioral treatment approaches that may have been relevant to each member of the Shore family. Clearly, well-tested behavioral interventions exist for many problems relevant to the Shore family, including those designed to address anxiety disorders, depression, bipolar disorder, anger management, marital conflict, and weight management. It is likely that behavioral clinicians would include many of these interventions in an overall treatment plan for the Shore family. Intervening to address Nancy's and Charley's individual mental health concerns would likely enhance the outcomes obtained with interventions designed for Michael's problems. The child behavioral interventions discussed in this chapter offer practical, time-limited, empirically tested, and durable approaches to Michael's social and behavioral difficulties. It is again important to note that behavior therapy is mainly based on research with middle- to upper-class European Americans. However, it is clear that culture is an important consideration in the delivery of this treatment. Further research is needed to understand how best to tailor behavioral treatment for families from diverse cultural and socioeconomic backgrounds.

REFERENCES

Baer, D. M., Wolf, M. M., & Risley, T. R. (1968). Some current dimensions of applied behavior analysis. *Journal of Applied Behavior Analysis, 1,* 91–97.

Barkley, R. A. (2000). Taking charge of ADHD: The complete, authoritative guide for parents (Rev. ed.). New York: Guilford Press.

Barkley, R. A., Edwards, G., Laneri, M., Fletcher, K., & Metevia, L. (2001). The efficacy of problem-solving communication training alone, behavior management training alone, and their combination for parent-adolescent conflict in teenagers with ADHD and ODD. *Journal of Consulting and Clinical Psychology, 69,* 926–941.

Barkley, R. A., Edwards, G. H., & Robin, A. L. (1999). *Defiant teens: A clinician's manual for assessment and family intervention.* New York: Guilford Press.

Berner, M., Fee, V. E., & Turner, A. D. (2001). A multi-component social training program for pre-adolescent girls with few friends. *Child and Family Behavior Therapy, 23,* 1–18.

Coie, J. D., & Dodge, K. A. (1988). Multiple sources of data on social behavior and social status. *Child Development, 59,* 815–829.

Dishion, T. J., & Patterson, G. R. (1992). Age effects in parent training outcomes. *Behavior Therapy, 23,* 719–729.

Doubros, S. G. (1966). Behavior therapy with high level, institutionalized, retarded adolescents. *Exceptional Children, 33,* 229–233.

Doubros, S. G., & Daniels, G. J. (1966). An experimental approach to the reduction of overactive behavior. *Behaviour Research and Therapy, 4,* 251–258.

Eysenck, H. J. (Ed.). (1960). *Behavior therapy and the neuroses.* New York: Pergamon Press.

Flanagan, R., Povall, L., Dellino, M., & Byrne, L. (1998). A comparison of problem solving with and without rational emotive behavior therapy to improve children's social skills. *Journal of Rational-Emotive & Cognitive Behavior Therapy, 16,* 125–134.

Forehand, R., & Kotchick, B. A. (1996). Cultural diversity: A wake-up call for parent training. *Behavior Therapy, 27,* 187–206.

Frankel, F., Cantwell, D. P.,& Myatt, R. (1996). Helping ostracized children: Social skills training and parent support for socially rejected children. In E. D. Hibbs, & P.S . Jensen (Eds.), *Psychosocial treatments for child and adolescent disorders: Empirically based strategies for clinical practice* (pp. 595–617). Washington, DC: American Psychological Association.

Frankel, F., Myatt, R., Cantwell, D. P., & Fineberg, D. T. (1996). Parent-assisted transfer of children's social skills training: Effects on children with and without attention-deficit hyperactivity disorder. *Journal of the American Academy of Child and Adolescent Psychiatry, 36,* 1056–1064.

Garvin, C. D., & Seabury, B. A. (1997). *Interpersonal practice in social work: Promoting competence and social justice* (2nd ed.). Boston: Allyn & Bacon.

Gillmore, M., Catalano, R., Morrison, D., Wells, E., Iritani, B., & Hawkins, J. (1990). Racial differences in acceptability and availability of drugs and early initiation of substance use. *American Journal of Drug & Alcohol Abuse, 16,* 185–206.

Giordano, P. C., Cernkovich, S. A., & Demaris, A. (1993). The family and peer relations of Black adolescents. *Journal of Marriage and the Family, 55,* 277–287.

Harkness, S., & Super, C. M. (1995). Culture and parenting. In M. H. Bornstein (Ed.), *Handbook of parenting: Biology and ecology of parenting* (Vol. 2, pp. 211–234). Mahwah, NJ: Erlbaum.

Holmbeck, G. N., Colder, C., Shapera, W., Westhoven, V., Kenealy, L., & Updegrove, A. (2000). Working with adolescents: Guides from developmental psychology. In P. C. Kendall (Ed.), *Child & adolescent therapy: Cognitive-behavioral procedures* (pp. 334–385). New York: Guilford Press.

Kazdin, A. E. (1997). Parent management training: Evidence, outcomes, and issues. *Journal of the American Academy of Child and Adolescent Psychiatry, 36,* 1349–1356.

Ladd, G. W. (1992). Themes and theories: Perspectives on processes in family–peer relationships. In R. D. Parke & G. W. Ladd (Eds.), *Family–peer relationships: Modes of linkages* (pp. 3–34). Hillsdale, NJ: Erlbaum.

Ladd, G. W., & Price, J. M. (1987). Predicting children's social and school adjustment following the transition from preschool to kindergarten. *Child Development, 58,* 1168–1189.

Lazarus, A.A. (1958). New methods in psychotherapy: A case study. *South African Medical Journal, 32,* 660-664.

Long, P., Forehand, R., Wierson, M., & Morgan, A. (1994). Does parent training with young noncompliant children have long-term effects? *Behaviour Research and Therapy, 32,* 101–107.

Lovas, O. I., Koegel, R., Simmons, J. Q., & Long, J. S. (1973). Some generalization and follow-up measures on autistic children in behavior therapy. *Journal of Applied Behavior Analysis, 6,* 131–166.

Mabe, P. A., Turner, M. K., & Josephson, A. M. (2001). Parent management training. *Child and Adolescent Psychiatric Clinics of North America, 10,* 451–464.

Magee, M. M., Kavale, K. A., Mathur, S. R., Rutherford, R. B., & Forness, S. R. (1999). A meta-analysis of social skill interventions for students with emotional or behavioral disorders. *Journal of Emotional and Behavioral Disorders, 7,* 54–64.

Marcus, B. A., Swanson, V., & Vollmer, T. R. (2001). Effects of parent training and child behavior using procedures base on functional analyses. *Behavioral Interventions, 16,* 87–104.

Mash, E. J. (1989). Treatment of child and family disturbance: A behavioral-systems perspective. In E. J. Mash & R. A. Barkley (Eds.), *Treatment of childhood disorders* (pp. 3–36). New York: Guilford Press.

McGoldrick, M., & Giordano, J. K. (1996). *Ethnicity and family therapy.* New York: Guilford Press.

Neal-Barnett, A., & Smith, J. M. (1996). African American children and behavior therapy: Considering the Afrocentric approach. *Cognitive and Behavioral Practice, 3,* 351–369.

Ogbu, J. U. (1985). A cultural ecology of competence among inner-city blacks. In M. B. Spencer, G. K. Brookins, & W. R. Allen (Eds.), *Beginnings: The social and affective development of Black children* (pp.45–66). Hillsdale, NJ: Erlbaum.

O'Leary, K. D., Becker, W. C., Evans, M. B., & Saudargas, R. A. (1969). A token reinforcement program in a public school: A replication and systematic analysis. *Journal of Applied Behavior Analysis, 2,* 3–13.

Ollendick, T. H., & King, N. J. (2000). Empirically supported treatments for children and adolescents. In P. C. Kendall (Ed.), *Child & adolescent therapy: Cognitive-behavioral procedures* (pp. 386–425). New York: Guilford Press.

Parke, R. D., & Bhavnagri, N. P. (1989). Parents as managers of children's peer friendships. In D. Belle (Ed.), *Children's social networks and social supports* (pp. 241–259). New York: Wiley.

Patterson, G. R. (1968). *Living with children.* Champaign, IL: Research Press.

Patterson, G. R., Dishion, T. J., & Chamberlain, P. (1993). Outcomes and methodological issues relating to treatment of antisocial children. In T. R.Giles (Ed.), *Handbook of effective psychotherapy* (pp. 43–87). New York: Plenum Press.

Patterson, G. R., Reid, J. B., Jones, R. R., & Conger, R. E. (1975). *A social learning approach to family intervention: Families with aggressive children* (Vol. 1). Eugene, OR: Castalia.

Perry, D. G., Williard, J. C., & Perry, L. C. (1990). Peer perceptions of the consequences that victimized children provide aggressors. *Child Development, 61,* 1310–1325.

Peterson, P., Hawkins, J., Abbot, R., & Catalano, R. (1994). Disentangling the effects of parental drinking, family management, and parental alcohol norms on current drinking by African American and European American adolescents. *Journal of Research on Adolescents, 4,* 203–227.

Serketich, W. J., & Dumas, J. E. (1996). The effectiveness of behavioral parent training to modify antisocial behavior in children: A meta-analysis. *Behavior Therapy, 27,* 171–186.

Skinner, B. F. (1953). *Science and human behavior.* New York: Macmillan.

Skinner, B. F. (1969). *Contingencies of reinforcement.* New York: Appleton-Century-Crofts.

Wallace, J. M., & Muroff, J. R. (2002). Preventing substance abuse among African American children and youth: Race differences in risk factor exposure and vulnerability. *Journal of Primary Prevention, 22,* 235–261.

Wolpe, J. (1958). *Psychotherapy by reciprocal inhibition.* Stanford, CA: Stanford University Press.

6

Play Therapy
Across the Life Span

Emphasis on a Second-Generation,
Middle-Class Japanese American Family

Daniel S. Sweeney, PhD

INTRODUCTION

Not all issues can be expressed in psychotherapy through words. To assume that a family, whether collectively or individually, can verbally articulate intrapsychic and relational issues may well be shortsighted. In general, the assumption that therapy should be limited to verbal and cognitive processing is somewhat insular. When children are involved in the process, this viewpoint is developmentally inappropriate. Persons of all ages can benefit from expressive and projective interventions, such as play therapy.

There are numerous theoretical approaches in the use of play therapy with children; my own approach is primarily a child-centered play therapy one. Although its title stems from its foundation in person-centered theory, the approach fundamentally points to a simple child *focus*. The child-centered play therapist does not focus on problems, symptoms, diagnosis, or prescriptive techniques.

Play Therapy

Play therapy is based upon the fundamental truth that children do not communicate in the same way that adults do. Adult communication requires both verbal abilities and abstract thinking skills. Children do not communicate this way; they communicate though play. The basis for doing play therapy is fundamentally to honor children by entering their world of communication, rather than forcing children to enter the adult world of verbalization. Landreth (2002) asserts that children "playing out" their experiences and feelings is the most natural dynamic and self-healing process in which children can be involved. Given the opportunity, adolescents and adults can benefit from the same process of expression, apart from compelled verbalization.

Landreth (2002) defines play therapy as a

> dynamic interpersonal relationship between a child (or person of any age) and a therapist trained in play therapy procedures who provides selected play materials and facilitates the development of a safe relationship for the child (or person of any age) to fully express and explore self (feelings, thoughts, experiences, and behaviors) through play, the child's natural medium of communication, for optimal growth and development. (p.16)

Sweeney (1997) expands upon the crucial elements contained within this definition. Play therapy involves a dynamic interpersonal *relationship*. Relationship is the basis for therapeutic healing; it should be without question that therapeutic relationships be dynamic and interpersonal. The play therapist should be *trained in play therapy procedures.* Play therapy is not simply providing play media while using talk therapy. Attending a brief workshop or reading a book about play therapy does not make a play therapist. Training is essential. *Selected play materials* should be provided—not a random collection of toys. In play therapy, the play is the child's language and the toys are the child's words. The *development of a safe relationship* is facilitated by the play therapist. This does not involve following the agenda of the therapist. Referred children already feel disempowered and out of control. The child needs to be given the opportunity to *fully express and explore self*. Finally, play therapy allows the children to use their *natural medium of communication, play*.

Filial Therapy

Family play therapies essentially attempt to creatively engage the entire family in the therapy progress. Filial therapy is one such form, an empirically supported parent training program. Developed by Bernard Guerney and his colleagues in the early 1960s, filial therapy is an innovative approach to the treatment of disturbed children, in which parents conduct play sessions at home, thus becoming the agents of therapeutic change (Guerney, 1964). The underlying rationale for filial therapy is based on the hypothesis that if parents can be taught to assume a role similar to a therapist, they can conceivably be more effective than a professional, because the parent naturally has more emotional significance in the life of the child. In addition, the anxiety symptoms learned by the child in the presence or under the influence of parental attitudes can be more effectively unlearned or extinguished under facilitative parent–child conditions (Guerney, Guerney, & Andronico, 1966).

Sweeney and Skurja (2001) provide an additional rationale for the use of filial therapy:

> Families who seek professional therapeutic input are often motivated not only by the challenges of disruptive child behavior, but also by the increasing stress in the parenting process. Children may be presented as "out of control" and the parents sense their own loss of control as well. Both parent and child are in need of an intervention that will establish or re-establish balance to the chaotic system. Many parent training programs available focus on behavior management or control. Behavioral interventions for children who act out can be useful. However, if a child's behavior is primarily a reflection of emotional turmoil and unmet needs, behavior controls will not have a lasting impact. It becomes necessary to provide a therapeutic experience that touches the child at emotional and relational levels while empowering the parents to be the change agent for the child, themselves, and their relationship.
>
> In the parent training process, Sweeney (1997) asserted that "rules without relationship equals rebellion" (p. 166). Parents can employ the most researched, effective, and developmentally appropriate rules of parenting and behavior management; but if the parent–child relationship is poor, the result will involve minimal compliance and potential rebellion. It is relationship that creates the environment for emotional expression and problem solving. Filial therapy provides this opportunity. (p. 176)

The filial therapist must be a mental health professional who has been trained in play therapy, group therapy, and filial therapy. It is beyond the scope of this chapter to discuss the filial process in detail. Interested readers are referred to Landreth's (2002) book, *Play Therapy: The Art of the Relationship*. Readers interested in exploring other forms of family play therapy are referred to *Play in Family Therapy* (Gil, 1994). (See also www.a4pt.org, the Association for Play Therapy, for additional resources.)

Rationale for Using Play Therapy

The dynamics of play therapy and filial therapy are similar in many ways and therefore have similar benefits and rationale. The following qualities of play therapy–based interventions have been adapted from Sweeney (1999):

Play therapy interventions give expression to nonverbalized emotional issues. Both children and adults often express their emotional turmoil through acting-out behaviors, usually because they do not have a safe place to express these emotions elsewhere. Because play is the language of childhood and provides a nonverbal means of communicating, therapeutic play experiences provide a safe medium for expression.

Play therapy interventions have a unique sensory and kinesthetic quality. Play, by its very nature, is sensory and kinesthetic. Clients who have encountered trauma need such therapeutic interventions, because trauma itself is sensory in nature.

Play therapy interventions create a therapeutic distance for children. It is often easier for emotionally wounded clients to "speak" through the metaphor of the play than it is to verbalize their pain. The therapeutic distance that play therapy interventions provide creates a safe place for abreaction to occur. The play therapy setting allows repressed issues to be relived. The negative emotions attached to these repressed issues can then be experienced as a means to achieve resolution and mastery.

Play therapy interventions teach and provide opportunities for boundaries and limits. Boundaries and limits define relationships, providing the necessary rules for engagement and connection with others. Limits are needed to provide a safe world for clients in which to grow. A specific limit-setting model is used in play therapy and filial therapy. An example of this limit-setting is on page 116 in the case study material.

Play therapy interventions provide a unique setting for the emergence of therapeutic metaphors. Unexpressed emotional needs can find facilitated expression through the metaphorical and fantasy quality of the play experience.

Play therapy interventions may be effective in overcoming a client's resistance. Clients who may be resistant to participating in psychotherapy may be more open to a "therapeutic" experience that does not compel verbalization and disclosure. The therapeutic play experience, because of its non-threatening and engaging qualities, can captivate the reticent client and allow self-expression through an alternative medium of communication.

Play therapy interventions provide a needed and effective communication medium for the client with poor verbal skills. Clients with the additional burden of developmental language delays or deficits, social or relational difficulties, and substantial physiological challenges can find expression in play where verbal therapies may fail.

Conversely, play therapy interventions can cut through verbalization used as a defense. For the verbally sophisticated client who uses the adult skills of intellectualization and rationalization as defenses, the therapeutic play experience may cut through these defenses.

Play therapy interventions create a place for the client to experience control. The client who is in crisis or has experienced trauma often feels the loss of control. Therapeutic play experiences provide an opportunity for the client to be empowered. This results from the client being allowed to take control in the client-led play therapy experience, while being affirmed and understood by a therapist who promotes the client's role of director and choreographer in the play experience.

The challenge of transference may be effectively addressed through play therapy interventions. The presence of an expressive medium creates an alternative object of transference, making it possible for the transference to occur between the client and the play media, rather than between client and therapist. Transference issues then can be safely addressed, in which play media may become objects of transference or the means through which transference issues are safely addressed.

Finally, deeper intrapsychic issues may be accessed more thoroughly and more rapidly through play therapy intervention. Gaining access to underlying issues and unconscious conflicts is a challenge for any counselor. Although certainly not a comprehensive list, the qualities of using play therapy generate an atmosphere where deep and complex intrapsychic issues can be safely approached.

THE CONCEPT OF THE PERSON AND THE HUMAN EXPERIENCE

The theoretical constructs of child-centered play therapy are unrelated to the child's age, physical and psychological development, or presenting problem. Instead, they are related to the inner dynamics of the child's process of relating to and discovering the self that the child is capable of becoming (Landreth & Sweeney, 1997). Development is viewed, in the child-centered approach, as a flowing, dynamic journey, a maturing process of *becoming*.

The client-centered approach views all persons as having a formative tendency; given an appropriate environment, personal and relational capacity can develop. Children and families can grow and heal when a growth-producing climate is provided, free from agenda and constriction. This is the basis for child-centered play therapy. The fundamental constructs of personality, as described by Rogers (1951), are (a) the person, (b) the phenomenal field, and (c) the self.

The *person* is all that a child is, consisting of self-perceptions that include thoughts, feelings, and behaviors, as well as physiological considerations. Children interact with and respond to their personal and continually changing world of experience. The *phenomenal field* is composed of everything that is experienced by the child. These experiences include everything happening within a person at a given time (conscious or unconscious, internal as well as external), including perceptions, thoughts, feelings, and behaviors. The *self* is the differentiated aspect of the phenomenal field that develops from the child's interactions with others.

Play and filial therapy experiences become phenomenal fields through which children and families can discover self and others in relation to self. Not only are the family members' emotional and behavioral expressions consistent with their concept of self, but the play therapy experience facilitates positive change in self-concept. This can dramatically affect family relationships.

HISTORICAL PERSPECTIVE

The history of play therapy begins with Sigmund Freud's (1909) classic case of "Little Hans" and Freud's attempt to apply psychoanalytic therapy to children. Hug-Hellmuth (1921) focused on play as being foundational in child therapy, providing her child clients with play media. Melanie Klein (1955) saw play as a technique that could be equated with the free association used with adults, and Anna Freud (1946) viewed play as a means for establishing a therapeutic alliance.

Levy (1938) developed release play therapy, which took a structured play therapy approach in working with children experiencing specific anxiety-provoking circumstances. Structured play therapy (Hambidge, 1955) expanded upon this approach. Taft (1933) and Allen (1934) developed relationship play therapy, which focused on the curative value of the emotional relationship between the therapist and the child, using play.

A student of Carl Rogers, Virginia Axline (1947), developed non-directive play therapy (also called child-centered play therapy), based on the principles of client-centered therapy. Landreth (2002) is the current leader in this approach and has developed the Center for Play Therapy at the University of North Texas, the largest play therapy training center in the world (www.center forplaytherapy.com).

Filial therapy was introduced in the 1960s as an innovative adaptation of child-centered play therapy, which involved training parents to be therapeutic agents with their children, using child-centered play therapy skills (Guerney, 1964). Landreth (2002) adapted a 10-week model of filial therapy (discussed on page 119–120).

Numerous theoretical and technical approaches to play therapy have been developed over the last 2 decades, including Jungian, Gestalt, Adlerian, and many other adaptations. See O'Connor and Braverman (1997), for a theoretical and technical description of each of these approaches.

KEY THEORETICAL CONSTRUCTS

The success or failure of any therapeutic intervention rests upon the development and the maintenance of the therapeutic relationship. Moustakas (1959) believed that "through the process of self-expression and exploration within a significant relationship, through realization of the value within, the child comes to be a positive, self-determining, and self-actualizing individual" (p. 5).

In the child-centered approach to play therapy, the child is the focus, rather than the presenting problem. Therapists who concentrate upon diagnosis and evaluation risk losing sight of the members of the family. Such could be the case with the Shore family, where symptoms and circumstances are both colorful and complex. The therapeutic relationship, therefore, should be intentionally focused upon a present and living experience. Landreth (2002) further illustrates this point, perferring the

person of the child	rather than	problem
present	rather than	past
feelings	rather than	thoughts or acts
understanding	rather than	explaining
accepting	rather than	correcting
child's direction	rather than	therapist's instruction
child's wisdom	rather than	therapist's knowledge (p. 86)

The focus of the play therapist is on the inner person of the child, on what the child is capable of becoming, as opposed to the child's way of being in the past. For example, the individual members of the Shore family are the focus, not the "problem" for which they have been referred. Essentially, knowledge about the "problem" is considered unnecessary in establishing a therapeutic relationship with the Shores and could well be a substantial distraction.

"Maladjustment" is viewed within the context of the developing relationship and results from a state of incongruence between the self-concept of family members and their experiences. Goal setting in the child-centered play therapy approach must take into consideration this perspective on maladjustment. Just as labels are generally eschewed in the person-centered process, the term *goal* is somewhat inconsistent with child-centered philosophy. Goals are evaluative and imply specific externally established achievements required of the client. Family members should be related to as persons to be understood, as opposed to persons with goals to be achieved. The child-centered philosophy renders the establishment of treatment goals contradictory.

There are, however, broad therapeutic objectives that are consistent with child-centered theory. Landreth (2002) suggests the following:

> The general objectives of child-centered play therapy are consistent with the child's inner self-directed striving toward self-actualization. An overriding premise is to provide the child with a positive growth experience in the presence of an understanding supportive adult so the child will be able to discover internal strengths. . . . To that end, the objectives of child-centered play therapy are to help the child: (1) Develop a more positive self-concept; (2) Assume greater self-responsibility; (3) Become more self-directing; (4) Become more self-accepting; (5) Become more self-reliant;

(6) Engage in self-determined decision making; (7) Experience a feeling of control; (8) Become sensitive to the process of coping; (9) Develop an internal source of evaluation; and (10) Become more trusting of himself. (pp. 87–88)

Within the framework of these general objectives, all family members in play therapy interventions are free to work on specific self-identified problems. The identification of such problems, however, is not a result of the therapist's direction, suggestion, or implication.

Like individual play therapy, filial therapy is structured to reject a specific problem-solving focus and to enhance relationship (in this case, it is the parent–child relationship). Landreth (2002) outlines the objectives of filial therapy:

> To strengthen and enhance the parent–child relationship by helping parents (a) understand and accept their children; (b) develop sensitivity to their children's feelings; (c) learn how to encourage their children's self-direction, self-responsibility, and self-reliance; (d) gain insight into themselves in relation to their children; (e) change their perception of their children; and (f) learn child-centered play therapy principles and skills. (p. 371)

ASSESSMENT

Each member of the Shore family knows and struggles with loneliness routinely. In their own ways, Nancy, Charley, Rena, and Michael have continued to struggle for autonomy and identity in this world but have been cruelly oppressed by circumstances and poor choices—and have thus felt unfairly isolated. In his discussion of loneliness, Moustakas (1974) poignantly states, "It is the terror of loneliness, not loneliness itself but loneliness anxiety, the fear of being left alone, of being left out, that represents a dominant crisis in the struggle to become a person" (p. 16). It is into this lonely place where so many clients reside that therapists must be willing to enter and be instruments of healing.

Conceptualizing the Shore family's case from a child-centered play therapy approach takes a very different perspective from the case history offered in "The Case." This section begins with the statement "The problems of the Shore family are common ones." This very statement assumes a therapeutic position that is problem-centered. Moustakas (1959) correctly notes that most therapeutic relationships with children involve problem-centered interactions. Child-centered play therapy, however, as its title asserts, focuses on the child. As such, the development of a relationship with the Shore family that is "Shore-focused," rather than problem- or diagnosis-focused, is central.

Assessment and diagnosis do not play a significant role in the child-centered approach to play therapy. Person-centered therapy views diagnosis and evaluation as distracting and potentially detrimental to the client (Rogers, 1951). The psychometric and background information that may be available on the Shore family, though interesting, is not considered foundational in the conceptualization and treatment planning of their case. The assessment of the

Shore family, therefore, involves attempting to understand them in the here and now, as well as how they perceive themselves. This will enable the Shores to view themselves and their situation differently.

The Shore family members' self-concepts and perceptions of each other are more important than is formal assessment. As the Shores resolve the incongruence between these perceptions and their experience (resulting in "maladjustment," as previously noted), they are able to "own" their own feelings and behaviors and feel in greater control, more empowered, and more congruent.

Assessment, however, is not entirely eschewed in the child-centered approach. Insurance companies or referral sources may require assessment to determine diagnosis. In addition, pre- and post-testing for process and outcome studies are current priorities in the play therapy field.

THE THERAPEUTIC PROCESS

Discussion of the therapeutic process should begin with the role of the child-centered play therapist. The therapist's role can be summarized in Axline's (1947) eight basic principles, as revised and extended by Landreth (2002). The therapist

1. Is genuinely interested in the child and develops a warm, caring relationship.
2. Experiences unqualified acceptance of the child and does not wish the child were different in some way.
3. Creates a feeling of safety and permissiveness in the relationship, so the child feels free to explore and express himself or herself completely.
4. Is always sensitive to the child's feelings and gently reflects those feelings in such a manner that the child develops self-understanding.
5. Believes deeply in the child's capacity to act responsibly, unwaveringly respects the child's ability to solve personal problems, and allows the child to do so.
6. Trusts the child's inner direction, allows the child to lead in all areas of the relationship, and resists any urge to direct the child's play or conversation.
7. Appreciates the gradual nature of the therapeutic process and does not attempt to hurry the process.
8. Establishes only those therapeutic limits necessary to anchor the session to reality and which help the child accept responsibility. (pp. 84–85)

The relationship that emerges as the therapist communicates this type of acceptance and understanding is powerful. When the play therapist responds sensitively to the inner emotional part of the child by accepting and reflecting feelings, whether verbally or non-verbally expressed, the child can begin to recognize his own inner resources.

The following is a brief summary of the therapist's responsibilities during a therapeutic play experience:

- *Set the stage*—This primarily involves preparing the play setting. This expresses the importance of the process to the clients (and the importance of the child) and creates an environment in which the process can occur.
- *Let the client lead*—Clients need to have the control to take the lead. This is empowering and creates the opportunity for them to manage, within the play, what has often been unmanageable in their lives.
- *Be verbally active*—Being verbally active allows clients to know that the therapist is dedicated to building the therapeutic child relationship.
- *Reflect the client's feelings*—Through reflection of feelings, the therapist acknowledges and affirms the client's emotions. This creates a safe and caring atmosphere for the client to play out internalized and externalized behaviors tied to emotional turmoil.
- *Be facilitative*—The role of director and choreographer of the therapeutic process should belong to the client. Therapist responses and actions should facilitate rather than prescribe.
- *Set limits*—Clients of all ages are frequently desperate for an environment marked by consistent boundaries. Therapists (and parents) need to learn limit-setting skills. Limit setting is facilitative, as clients do not feel safe or accepted in a completely permissive environment. (See Landreth's [2002] ACT limit-setting model.)
- *Offer encouragement, not praise*—Praise leads people (to do what they otherwise might not do because they want to please) and reinforces an external locus of evaluation. Children, frequently accustomed to negative external evaluations, need to learn an internal locus of evaluation based upon encouragement, which involves acknowledging the child's power and effort.
- *Join in the play, as a follower*—Although play sessions are "child- and family-centered," therapists should be encouraged to actively join their clients in the play, at the request and the lead of the clients.
- *Avoid questions*—Questions tend to take the focus off the play behavior and thus take children out of the lead. Questions also result in a shift from emotions, play, and fantasy to the cognitive process of thinking.
- *Avoid teaching*—Although there is a place for psychoeducational work, the therapeutic play should not involve this dynamic. It places the therapist in the expert role and takes the lead away from clients.
- *Avoid evaluation*—Evaluative statements deprive the child of inner motivation. Clients do not learn self-direction, self-evaluation, and responsibility when the therapist evaluates or provides solutions.
- *Return responsibility*—Clients must discover and develop their own inner resources. If therapists make the decisions, clients miss the opportunity of expressing their own creativity and learning responsibility.
- *Match the client's affect*—Therapeutic responses (both verbal and non-verbal)

should be congruent with the client's expression of emotion. This should include intensity and frequency of emotional expression.
• *Use short responses*—Because lengthy responses disrupt the therapeutic flow and the client's focus, therapeutic response should be succinct. If responses are too long, clients may focus on the therapist instead of on their own emotional expression.

The course of treatment with the Shore family will fall within the parameters of the philosophies noted previously. Individual play therapy is recommended for Michael; he is said to be "unhappy and lonely," feels "funny" and "bad," and has poor social judgment. Play therapy is an effective intervention with which to treat such poor self-concept.

The brief case example in Table 6.1 illustrates the play therapy process. The child's and the therapist's activities and responses are not meant to reflect a typical play therapy session but offer clarification to the points made previously.

A related intervention for use with the Shores is filial therapy. Filial therapy focuses on relationship, a dynamic sadly lacking in the Shore family. Although this therapy has traditionally been used with children who are 12 years old and younger, the skills apply to all parent–child relationships. Considering the apparent developmental level of Michael and the attachment losses of Rena, filial therapy can be considered an appropriate intervention. Once the parent–child relationships are developed and strengthened (a focus of filial therapy), discipline and limit setting, so clearly needed in this family, can truly be effective.

In the case of the Shores, the primary focus of filial therapy would be the father–son relationship between Charley and Michael. Previous therapists have reportedly worked on "restructuring" this relationship. It is suggested that the issues go deeper than a superficial restructuring, and that filial therapy can address the issue. The benefits for both child and parent (noted in the "Research" section on page 20) should prove powerful for both Michael and Charley.

APPLICATION TO DIVERSITY

A play therapy approach to treatment is inherently helpful when working cross-culturally. Although the play media differs, children in every culture play. Glover (1999) suggests that

> play therapy is ideal for working with children who may have a different cultural background than the therapist. . . . When the therapist does not have a specific structure in mind, the children are allowed to explore the issues which are most significant to them. (p. 279)

In this section, the Shores are conceptualized as a second-generation, middle-class Japanese American family, living in an urban area. Both parents have college degrees.

TABLE 6.1
An Example of the Play Therapy Process

Therapist: Michael—you can see that there are a bunch of toys in here, and you can play with any of them in a lot of the ways you'd like to.	The child-centered play therapy approach is permission-giving. The therapist respects the child's ability to make decisions and take the process where it needs to go.
Michael: (Looks around at the various materials in the room but does not move toward anything)	Michael may be expected to be somewhat cautious. His life situation is out of control and it is unusual for an adult to give him control.
Therapist: Looks like you're wondering what to do. In here, you can decide.	Reflecting the child's actions and affect are key in play therapy. The therapist's response is already promoting Michael's self-responsibility. The words *in here* punctuate that this is a place where the child is in control.
Michael: (Looking over at the easel) Can I paint?	By seeking permission, Michael is looking for approval, something he likely lacks in the Shore family context. As he makes his own decisions, Michael will not only feel empowered, but also develop an internal source of approval and locus of control.
Therapist: Sounds like you've got something in mind. In here, you can decide.	In some ways, Michael is really not asking a question. He is saying that he wants to paint. By not answering his question, the therapist continues to allow Michael to have the lead.
Michael: (Angry that the paint is dripping) Damn it—I messed up!	Any emotion should be acceptable for expression. This may be a reflection of Michael's basic self-perception.
Therapist: You're really mad that didn't turn out the way you wanted.	Acknowledging the feeling conveys understanding and acceptance. By the therapist not focusing on Michael's messing up but rather on the fact that Michael is upset at the product, the focus is kept on his feelings and not on the action.
Michael: (Still angry, dips the paintbrush in the paint and throws the paint at the therapist)	
Therapist: Michael, you're really upset, but the paint is not for throwing, the paint is for the paper. You can throw the ball (pointing at ball).	This is an example of the therapeutic limit-setting model used in play therapy. The ACT model, developed by Landreth (2002), is a highly effective tool in the playroom. It includes (1) A—Acknowledging the child's feelings (it is important to begin limit setting by continuing reflection and acceptance); (2) C—Communicating the limit (in a neutral and non-punitive manner); and (3) T—Targeting an acceptable alternative (which recognizes that the child still has a need to express self and can do so within acceptable boundaries). Limits that are set objectively, with acceptance, without disapproval are most often received and complied with.
Michael: (Picking up a family of toy bears and speaking in almost a whisper) I wonder what I can do with these.	

TABLE 6.1
Continued

Therapist: (Also in a whisper) Looks like you have something in mind.	The therapist's response is short and matches the affective level of the child. It continues to follow the lead of the child. Also, it may be tempting to interpret Michael's play with an animal family as relating to his real family. This may be the case, as he can project behaviors and emotions onto the toys. The setting provides this freedom, but the therapist who enters into an interpretive mode will compromise the communication of empathy and the child's direction of the process.
Michael: (Buries toy bears in the sandbox)	
Therapist: You're covering those up—can't even see them.	Simple tracking of the child's behaviors should continue throughout the process, which shows interest and investment. Note that the therapist has not actually identified the toys (this should occur only after the child does), and is waiting for the child to give further detail or ascribe meaning and motivation.
Michael: Why are you talking so weird?	The child should see the therapist as interacting differently.
Therapist: I sound kind of different to you.	Rather than responding to Michael's adjective, the therapist responds to the underlying message. It is different!

The therapist working with this family would be well advised to consider Ho's (1992) assertation that in therapy with

> children whose cultures do not endorse open expression of feelings, especially to a non-kin member, play sometimes can be a child's only form of communication. Playing in therapy permits children to verbalize conscious material and associated feelings safely and to act out unconscious conflicts and fantasies. (p. 127)

Ho further suggests that those strongly allied to the "Asian work ethic" may view play as a frivolous activity, noting that "Asian parents may not consider play as productive to solving their children's problems, which they think often center around too much play and not enough serious work" (p. 128).

If this is the case with the Japanese American version of the Shore family, its members may need to be therapeutically educated. Huang and Ying (as cited in Gibbs & Huang, 1998) found that it is important to educate parents as to the efficacy of play, especially when working with parents who stress academic excellence. Because education is valued in Japanese culture and both Shore parents have college degrees, the educational component of filial therapy can be highlighted. A primary educational goal of filial therapy includes the teaching of parenting skills to be used within the family, as opposed to establishing a dependent counseling relationship.

Pederson (1997) proposes that the Western approach to counseling essentially focuses on helping persons feel more pleasure and less pain, more success and less failure. He suggests that this one-directional approach does not consider the two-directional balance that is sought in Asian cultures. Defining and restoring balance are central to effective counseling in non-Western families. This is a key element to play therapy, which allows the client to lead in the process and thus gain self-mastery and balance.

Because many non-Western cultures emphasize the family over the individual, family interventions may be particularly effective and appropriate within such collectivistic groups (Aponte, Rivers, & Wohl, 1995). However, many therapists are at a loss for how to incorporate children and adolescents into the therapy process without compelling them to verbally engage or relegating them to the corner with a few toys and some crayons. Hu and Chen (1999) note that for Asians, "the family unit has been the strongest social unit to provide guidance, support, and help to individuals" (p. 31). Therapy interventions such as filial therapy keep the focus within the family, promoting both child and parent autonomy through a process of interdependence and mutual activity.

Seeking the help of a therapist may be somewhat taboo, or at least may be resisted, in family-focused cultures. The idea of being open and intimate with a stranger about family difficulties can risk bringing shame upon both the family group and the larger collective (Ponterotto, Casas, Suzuki, & Alexander, 1995). Considerable shame is already evident in the Shore family in its members' reaction to (a) Nancy's extreme concern about her appearance and the loss of esteem associated with the loss of her career; (b) Charley's bipolar diagnosis and the loss of his dreams; (c) Rena's promising beginning and subsequent letdown; and (d) Michael's feeling of being so different from other children. Play therapy that is person-focused, along with filial therapy and its strengths-based focus on relationship enhancement, can possibly mitigate shameful family challenges.

Japanese Americans in general have a strong ethnic identity (Ibrahim, Ohnishi, & Sandhu, 1997). Self-respect, dignity, self-control, and humility are important qualities. Glover (1999) notes that respect is given to elders, and that independence and self-directedness may be viewed as aggressiveness and stubbornness. Applying this to the Shore family, Rena's push for independence would take on considerable added meaning. Because Asian American parents may expect their children to repress strong emotions in obedience to parental authority and family honor (Sandhu, 1997), a therapeutic intervention that does not force verbal betrayal may be particularly helpful.

In work with the Japanese American population, Nagata (as cited in Gibbs & Huang, 1998) reported that play therapy was an effective and important form of therapy. The use of play therapy allows themes to emerge that are unlikely to be expressed in traditional family therapy or with the use of behavioral treatments. For this reason, Nagata stresses the importance of clearly delineating the goals of the therapy to the parents.

For example, filial therapy would train the Shores in the use of play therapy skills as a means to establish and strengthen the parent–child relationship.

They must be convinced that play therapy is a legitimate intervention, and that these skills can be taught and used by them. Charley and Nancy may report that they already play with Michael and therefore question the validity of training that revolves around play. It would be imperative to educate them about the meaning of children's play, the value and the efficacy of play therapy, and to stress the difference between "regular" parent–child play and the special play times that are a part of the filial therapy training process.

The Shores would be instructed to interact with Michael in much the same way as in the case example given previously. A small collection of toys, representative of the same basic categories found in the playroom, is stored and used only for this special play time with Michael. These can be adapted to include materials that the Shores see fitting their Japanese American culture as well. The recommended filial therapy format is in a group setting. The Shores surely feel alone in their challenges, and the dynamic of a shared group experience is invaluable.

The filial therapist must be trained and experienced as both a play therapist and a group therapist. The 10-week filial therapy model developed by Landreth (2002) is the recommended format. With ancillary stressors, it would be difficult for the Shores to commit to a longer format. The 10 weeks should be considered a minimum because of the substantial amount of material covered. The duration is also crucial so that they can be supervised adequately in their skill development and so that proper support can be given as they deal with emotionally charged parenting and family issues.

LIMITATIONS OF THE MODEL

A play therapy approach is considered to be uniquely suited to a wide variety of therapeutic situations. Families from different socioeconomic strata and ethnic backgrounds can benefit from play therapy interventions, because these issues would not alter the play therapist's beliefs, philosophy, theory, or approach to children and families. Landreth and Sweeney (1997) state,

> empathy, acceptance, understanding, and genuineness on the part of the therapist are provided to children [families] equally, irrespective of their color, condition, circumstance, concern, or complaint. The child [family] is free to communicate through play in a manner that is comfortable and typical for the child [family], including cultural adaptations of play and expression. (p. 25) [italicized words added]

A key limitation in the play therapy approach can emerge out of an insular approach to treatment planning that may occur when the therapist does not consider additional and adjunct therapeutic interventions. Recognizing the family's developmental level and systemic circumstances, additional interventions may include family therapy, behavior management, pharmacotherapy, cognitive-behavioral therapy, group therapy, art therapy, and any of the other approaches discussed in this book. Obviously, the child and family therapist utilizing any of these interventions must receive adequate training and supervised experience.

Addressing Michael's various needs provides a good example of the necessity to coordinate the interventions. He takes anti-seizure medication, which may be partially responsible for his behavior problems. Anti-seizure medications are frequently used for psychiatric purposes, so it is likely that adjusting or adding to Michael's medication regimen may be necessary. The need for a psychopharmacological intervention is clear. There is no medication, however, that impacts self-esteem. This must be addressed psychotherapeutically; play therapy intervention may be particularly valuable. The benefit of medication or play therapy alone does not equal the benefit of the two combined.

RESEARCH

Play and filial therapy have been demonstrated to be effective treatments for children and families. Ray, Bratton, Rhine, and Jones (2001) conducted a meta-analysis of play and filial therapy studies, which demonstrated that treatment groups performed better than non-treatment groups. These results were stronger than in a previous child psychotherapy meta-analytic study by Weisz, Weiss, Han, Granger, and Morton (1995).

Child-centered play therapy specifically has been shown to be an effective intervention, and contrary to the myth that it is a long and meandering process, the research literature supports its efficacy in short-term usage (Axline, 1948; Bills, 1950; Crow, 1989; Johnson, McLeod, & Fall, 1997; Oualline, 1975). Kot, Landreth, and Giordano (1998) demonstrated positive results using an intensive model of short-term, child-centered play therapy with child witnesses of domestic violence. Other intensive work using child-centered play therapy includes that by Tyndall-Lind, Landreth, and Giordano (2001) and Jones (2000).

Consistent, significantly positive results have also been found in research with Landreth's (2002) 10-session filial therapy model. This model has been demonstrated to improve children's self-concepts, reduce children's behavioral problems, improve children's emotional adjustment, and increase children's desirable play behavior. In addition, the 10-session model has been demonstrated to significantly decrease parental stress, increase parental empathy and acceptance, and improve the family environment.

Using a pre- and post-test control group design, the Landreth filial therapy model has been studied and has been demonstrated to be effective with a wide variety of child and parent populations, including single parents (Bratton & Landreth, 1995), incarcerated mothers (Harris & Landreth, 1997) and fathers (Landreth & Lobaugh, 1998), non-offending parents of children who were sexually abused (Costas & Landreth, 1999), children with learning disabilities (Kale & Landreth, 1999), chronically ill children (Tew, Landreth, Joiner & Solt, 2002), child witnesses of domestic violence (Smith, 2000), Chinese parents (Chau & Landreth, 1997; Yuen, 1997), Korean parents (Jang, 2000), and Native American parents (Glover & Landreth, 2000). Several studies yielding significant results have also been done with non-parent paraprofessionals, including undergraduate student trainees (Brown, 2000) and high school students conducting play sessions with at-risk preschool and kindergarten students (Jones, 2001; Rhine, 2000).

SUMMARY

All persons experience a need to feel understood and accepted. The issue of loneliness, which seems so prevalent in each member of the Shore family, involves this need to be understood and accepted. In the context of play therapy interventions, clients experience a consistent and accepting response from the therapist, regardless of their presenting problem. In addition, clients are allowed "dialogue" about these issues in a natural and non-threatening medium of communication. The variety of play therapy interventions allows clients to process issues on both an intrapersonal and an interpersonal level.

Play and filial therapy interventions honor diversity in the therapeutic context. Because play is a universal and cross-cultural language (toys and games may differ, but all children in all cultures engage in play), diversity is respected. Because filial therapy takes this cross-cultural language and teaches it to parents in a way that empowers them to be the positive instigators of change (reducing the therapist's role of expert), diversity is respected. Because play and filial therapy promote independence, yet value interdependence within families, diversity is respected.

Play therapy further gives voice to the millions of children in need of being heard. It honors children and families. It benefits therapists as well, as a gifted and skilled child therapist will almost always make a gifted and skilled adult therapist. For the sake of children, families, and the profession—it is time to join in the play.

REFERENCES

Allen, F. (1934). Therapeutic work with children. *American Journal of Orthopsychiatry, 4,* 193–202.

Aponte, J. F., Rivers, R. Y., & Wohl, J. (1995). *Psychological interventions and cultural diversity.* Boston: Allyn & Bacon.

Axline, V. (1947). *Play therapy.* New York: Harper & Row.

Axline, V. (1948). Some observations on play therapy. *Journal of Consulting Psychology, 11,* 61–69.

Bills, R. (1950). Nondirective play therapy with retarded readers. *Journal of Consulting Psychology, 14,* 140–149.

Bratton, S., & Landreth, G. (1995). Filial therapy with single parents: Effects on parental acceptance, empathy, and stress. *International Journal of Play Therapy, 4*(1), 61–80.

Brown, C. (2000). *Filial therapy with undergraduate teacher trainees: Child–teacher relationship training.* Unpublished doctoral dissertation, University of North Texas, Denton.

Chau, I., & Landreth, G. (1997). Filial therapy with Chinese parents: Effects on parental empathic interactions, parental acceptance of child, and parental stress. *International Journal of Play Therapy, 6*(2), 75–92.

Costas, M., & Landreth, G. (1999). Filial therapy with non-offending parents of children who have been sexually abused. *International Journal of Play Therapy, 8*(1), 43–66.

Crow, J. (1989). Play therapy with low achievers in reading. *Dissertation Abstracts International, 50*(9A), 2789.

Freud, A. (1946). *The psychoanalytic treatment of children.* London: Imago.

Freud, S. (1909). *The case of "Little Hans" and the "Rat Man."* London: Hogarth Press.

Gibbs, J. T., & Huang, L. N. (1998). *Children of color: Psychological interventions with culturally diverse youth.* San Francisco: Jossey-Bass.

Gil, E. (1994). *Play in family therapy.* New York: Guilford Press.

Glover, G. (1999). Multicultural considerations in group play therapy. In D. Sweeney & L. Homeyer (Eds.), *Handbook of group play therapy* (pp. 278–295). San Francisco: Jossey-Bass.

Glover, G., & Landreth, G. (2000). Filial therapy with Native Americans on the Flathead Reservation. *International Journal of Play Therapy, 9*(2), 57–80.

Guerney, B. (1964). Filial therapy: Description and rationale. *Journal of Consulting Psychology, 28*(4), 303–310.

Guerney, B., Guerney, L., & Andronico, M. (1966). Filial therapy. *Yale Scientific Magazine, 40,* 6–14.

Hambidge, G. (1955). Structured play therapy. *American Journal of Orthopsychiatry, 25,* 601–617.

Harris, Z., & Landreth, G. (1997). Filial therapy with incarcerated mothers: A five week model. *International Journal of Play Therapy, 6*(2), 53–73.

Ho, M. K. (1992). *Minority children and adolescents in therapy.* Newbury Park, CA: Sage.

Hu, X., & Chen, G. (1999). Understanding cultural values in counseling Asian families. In K. Ng (Ed.), *Counseling Asian families from a systems perspective.* Alexandria, VA: American Counseling Association.

Hug-Hellmuth, H. (1921). On the technique of child analysis. *International Journal of Psychoanalysis, 2,* 287.

Ibrahim, F., Ohnishi, H., & Sandhu, D. S. (1997). Asian American identity development: A culture specific model for South Asian Americans. *Journal of Multicultural Counseling and Development, 25,* 34–50.

Jang, M. (2000). Effectiveness of filial therapy for Korean parents. *International Journal of Play Therapy, 9*(2), 39–56.

Johnson, L., McLeod, E., & Fall, M. (1997). Play therapy with labeled children in the schools. *Professional School Counseling, 1*(1), 31–34.

Jones, E. (2000). The efficacy of intensive individual play therapy for children diagnosed with insulin-dependent diabetes mellitus. *Dissertation Abstracts International, 61*(10A), 3907.

Jones, L. (2001). Effectiveness of filial therapy training on high school students' empathic behavior with young children. *Dissertation Abstracts International, 63*(2A), 508.

Kale, A., & Landreth, G. (1999). Filial therapy with parents of children experiencing learning difficulties. *International Journal of Play Therapy, 8*(2), 35–56.

Klein, M. (1955). The psychoanalytic play technique. *American Journal of Orthopsychiatry, 25,* 223–237.

Kot, S., Landreth, G., & Giordano, M. (1998). Intensive child-centered play therapy with child witnesses of domestic violence. *International Journal of Play Therapy, 7*(2), 17–36.

Landreth, G. (2002). *Play therapy: The art of the relationship* (2nd ed.). Philadelphia: Brunner-Routledge.

Landreth, G., & Lobaugh, A. (1998). Filial therapy with incarcerated fathers: Effects on parental acceptance of child, parental stress, and child adjustment. *Journal of Counseling & Development, 76*(2), 157–165.

Landreth, G., & Sweeney, D. (1997). Child-centered play therapy. In K. O'Connor & L. Braverman (Eds.), *Play therapy: Theory and practice.* New York: Wiley.

Levy, D. (1938). Release therapy in young children. *Psychiatry, 1,* 387–389.

Moustakas, C. (1959). *Psychotherapy with children: The living relationship.* New York: McGraw-Hill.

Moustakas, C. (1974). *Portraits of loneliness and love.* New York: Prentice-Hall.

O'Connor, K., & Braverman, L. (Eds.). (1997). *Play therapy theory and technique: A comparative analysis.* New York: Wiley.

Oualline, V. (1975). Behavioral outcomes of short-term nondirective play therapy with pre-school deaf children. *Dissertation Abstracts International, 36*(12A), 7870.

Pedersen, P. (1997). *Culture-centered counseling interventions: Striving for accuracy.* Thousand Oaks, CA: Sage.

Ponterotto, J. G., Casas, J. M., Suzuki, L. A., & Alexander, C. M. (Eds.). (1995). *Handbook of multicultural counseling.* London: Sage.

Ray, D., Bratton, S., Rhine, T., & Jones, L. (2001). The effectiveness of play therapy: Responding to the critics. *International Journal of Play Therapy, 10*(1), 85–108.

Rhine, T. (2000). The effects of a play therapy intervention conducted by trained high school students on the behavior of maladjusted young children: Implications for school counselors. *Dissertation Abstracts International, 62*(10A), 3304.

Rogers, C. (1951). *Client-centered therapy.* Boston: Houghton Mifflin.

Sandhu, D. S. (1997). Psychocultural profiles of Asian and Pacific Islander Americans: Implications for counseling and psychotherapy. *Journal of Multicultural Counseling and Development, 25,* 7–21.

Smith, N. (2000). A comparative analysis of intensive filial therapy with intensive individual play therapy and intensive sibling group play therapy with child witnesses of domestic violence. *Dissertation Abstracts International, 62*(7-A), 2353.

Sweeney, D. (1997). *Counseling children through the world of play.* Eugene, OR: Wipf & Stock.

Sweeney, D. (1999). Foreword. In L. Carey, *Sandplay with children and families.* Northvale, NJ: Aronson.

Sweeney, D., & Skurja, K. (2001). Filial therapy as a cross-cultural family intervention. *Asian Journal of Counseling, 8*(2), 175–208.

Taft, J. (1933). *The dynamics of therapy in a controlled relationship.* New York: Macmillan.

Tew, K., Landreth, G., Joiner, K., & Solt, M. (2002). Filial therapy with chronically ill children. *International Journal of Play Therapy, 11*(1), 79–100.

Tyndall-Lind, A., Landreth, G., & Giordano, M. (2001). Intensive group play therapy with child witnesses of domestic violence. *International Journal of Play Therapy, 10*(1), 53–83.

Weisz, J., Weiss, B., Han, S., Granger, D., & Morton, T. (1995). Effects of psychotherapy with children and adolescents revisited: A meta-analysis of treatment outcome studies. *Psychological Bulletin, 117,* 450–468.

Yuen, T. (1997). Filial therapy with immigrant Chinese parents in Canada. *Dissertation Abstracts International, 58*(3-A), 0756.

7

Crisis Intervention and Diversity

Emphasis on a Mexican Immigrant Family's Acculturation Conflicts

Elaine P. Congress, DSW

INTRODUCTION

A crisis intervention model is most effective in working with families such as the Shores. Crisis events can include life-cycle transitions, such as entering adolescence, or sudden, unexpected crises ("bolts from the blue," Pittman, 1987), such as sudden disability or unemployment. At this point the Shore family is experiencing multiple life transition crisis events, as Michael approaches adolescence and Rena moves toward becoming independent of her parents. The Shore family has also experienced traumatic crisis events: Nancy's recurring back injury, Charley's unemployment, and Michael's persistent asthma attacks. Their marriage began with a crisis; Charley's mother was killed by a car shortly before the Shores' marriage.

This chapter will focus first on crisis intervention theory and how this model can be particularly effective in working with individuals and families. Skills and techniques especially important for clinicians using a crisis intervention model will be addressed. Families, as well as individuals, can experience crises; their responses to crisis events will be discussed in the context of the Shore family. The Roberts (2000) seven-stage model for crisis intervention work will be applied to the Shore family. In the "Application to Diversity" section, I take a culturally diverse perspective, applying the crisis intervention model to the Sanchez family (a.k.a. the Shores).

The use of a crisis intervention model is particularly helpful to social workers who daily work with clients and their families who have experienced traumatic events. Violence in all forms (family, community, and national) is on the increase. Social workers frequently see families affected by unemployment, child abuse, HIV/AIDS, suicide attempts, sexual assault, and substance abuse. Recent years have witnessed escalating costs of mental health treatment. Short-term models, such as task-centered therapy (Reid & Fortune, 2002), solution-oriented treatment (DeJong & Berg, 2002), and crisis intervention treatment (Roberts, 2000), are viewed by many as less costly and also more effective.

THE CONCEPT OF THE PERSON AND THE HUMAN EXPERIENCE

The crisis intervention model is an optimistic one. The individual in this paradigm is viewed as possessing the capacity for change and growth. Crisis and the reactions to crisis are seen as short-lived. The expectation is that, after a short course of treatment, the individual will be stronger and better able to cope with future crises. Underlying this belief is the assumption that individuals have the capacity within themselves to develop plans for coping with crisis events and to recover completely from traumatic experiences.

An important concept is the "perception of and response to the crisis event" (Parad, 1965, p. 171). Each person has a unique reaction to a crisis event. What one person may view as a major crisis, another may not see as a crisis at all. For example, losing one's job may be particularly traumatic for a young married man with several young children whose wife is unemployed, whereas another young man with no family responsibilities may view unemployment as providing an opportunity to pursue activities that he did not have time for previously.

HISTORICAL CONTEXT

Even though he did not coin the term, Lindemann (1944) is often credited with being the father of crisis intervention. In his work with survivors of the 1943 Coconut Grove fire, Lindemann was especially interested in the survivors' acute grief reactions, which he noted were natural and expected reactions to a loss. He found that the severity and the length of the bereavement process were dependent on the survivor completing a series of phases that Lindemann (1944) called "grief work." Caplan (1964) first used the term *crisis intervention* and noted that a hazardous event upsets the usual homeostasis of individuals and that their usual defenses do not work. Their reactions, fortunately, are time limited and, with treatment, individuals can be restored to their previous level of functioning.

Rappaport (1962) was the first to note that a crisis can be perceived as a loss, a threat, or a challenge. Those who experience crisis as a loss usually demonstrate depressive symptoms, whereas those who experience crisis as a threat demonstrate anxiety symptoms, and those who experience crisis as a challenge often perceive it as providing a new opportunity. Parad (1965) pointed out that the client must perceive the event as stressful in order for it to be a crisis. Golan (1978) noted that a client is most amenable to help immediately following a crisis event.

In the 1960s crisis intervention was the treatment choice at a burgeoning number of suicide-prevention programs. Following the 1963 Community Mental Health Centers Act, mental health programs (in which 24-hour crisis intervention and emergency services were components) were created throughout the country. Crisis intervention services have also been used in rape counseling centers (Congress, 1992). Natural and human-caused disasters have increased the use of crisis intervention services.

The Roberts (1990, 2000) seven-step crisis intervention model that will be used to describe work with the Shore family builds upon the models developed by Caplan (1964), Golan (1978), and Parad (1965). All of these models address immediate problems and focus on resolving problems with a limited number of contacts. Most recently, the solution-based approach has been applied to crisis intervention work (Greene, Lee, Trask, & Rheinscheld, 2000). This approach builds upon the strengths perspective and supports the belief that individuals, even after a major crisis, can find solutions to help themselves recover from the crisis and return to their previous or improved levels of functioning.

KEY THEORETICAL CONSTRUCTS

Crisis intervention treatment is usually short term, with sessions held over a 6- to 12-week period. This intervention stems from a "functional" model that focuses on structure and time limits, about which the client is informed in the beginning of treatment. Differing from many traditional psychotherapeutic models, crisis intervention involves specific action steps. Roberts (2000) has emphasized a rapid establishment of the relationship between client and worker. From the very beginning, the social worker must establish and maintain a clear and specific focus, based on the precipitating crisis event. Throughout the course of treatment the client is encouraged to seek auxiliary forms of help, outside the context of the professional relationship. Assessment and treatment are inextricably connected and treatment begins in the first session. Crisis workers must be flexible and eclectic in their approach. The "50-minute hour" does not exist; some sessions may be longer, others shorter, depending upon the sequence of activities covered.

ASSESSMENT

Applying crisis intervention treatment to families is not a new concept; Parad (1965) writes about therapists entering into the life situations of families to help them mobilize resources to cope with crisis events. Crisis events are usually personal, in that one family member is primarily affected (e.g., loss of a job, a diagnosis of AIDS, or a severe automobile accident). Yet if one family member experiences a crisis, all family members are affected by the event. This is true for sudden crisis events, as well as life-cycle transition crises. Individuals pass through different life-cycle events (Erickson, 1963), as do families (Carter & McGoldrick, 1999). Difficult transitions may produce family crises. Similar to the disequilibrium that an individual experiences when encountering a crisis, a family crisis threatens its own usual equilibrium. As a result, coping mechanisms fail for families and the individuals that comprise them.

Carter and McGoldrick (1999) identified six stages of the family life cycle, the transition between which often produces crisis.

Stage 1 Between Families: The Unattached Adult
Stage 2 The Joining of the Couple Through Marriage: The Newly Married Couple
Stage 3 The Family With Young Children
Stage 4 The Family With Adolescents
Stage 5 Launching Children and Moving On
Stage 6 The Family in Later Life

Social changes, including the rise in the number of unmarried parents, divorces, and remarriages, necessitate modification of these stages. It should be noted that these stages may be different for poor or culturally diverse families. Some of these differences will be addressed later.

Family Life Cycle Crises

Each of the Carter and McGoldrick (1999) stages will be considered in the context of the Shore family. During Stage 1, the key developmental task for the Unattached Adult focuses on separating from the family of origin (dependent upon one's culture), developing intimate peer relationships, and establishing work roles. Charley, for example, was separated from his family by joining the Air Force and seems to have achieved some success there, though the time immediately after he went to California and tried to establish a movie career seems less certain. Nancy was able to pursue an education in nursing and sought a career away from home until she was injured. There were many challenges when the Shores first became engaged. Nancy's relatives predicted that the marriage would not work, doubting that Charley could support a family. Charley's mother was struck and fatally hit by a car before the wedding.

The first years of marriage are reported to be relatively problem-free for the Shores in Stage 2, the Joining of the Couple. Charley did not work steadily but was supported by Nancy's work as a nurse. The first problem that emerged was Nancy's failure to become pregnant; Charley's low sperm count and Nancy's irregular ovulation may have been a source of great stress, contributing to marital disappointment and conflict.

Stress continued as the Shores entered Stage 3, the Family With Young Children. Growing from two to three members, the long-awaited adoption of Rena constituted a life-cycle transition crisis event in the family. Often when a couple becomes parents, grandparents become more involved, sometimes producing conflict within families. Even when it was discovered that Rena had such special talents, additional stress was placed on the family members as they sought appropriate resources for their exceptional child. Michael's arrival as an unplanned child with significant health problems further exacerbated the stress for the family during this stage.

Arguably the most significant family crisis, however, occurred around the transition to adolescence in Stage 4, the Family With Adolescents. Adolescence is frequently characterized by emotional turmoil as the child strives to become more independent, while continuing to need the structure and guidance of adults. Often, adolescents seem to prefer any other parents but their own; Rena may have had some fantasies about what her birth mother would have been like. The decision to live downstairs with her grandparents indicates some estrangement from Nancy and Charley. Other family crisis events occurred at the same time: Nancy's back injury worsened, she became disabled, and Charley had to become the breadwinner. The family's stress during this stage was compounded by Michael's adolescence, which was plagued by asthma, behavioral problems, and learning disabilities.

The case study of the Shores ends as Rena seeks to become more independent, moving the family toward Stage 5, Launching Children and Moving On. She began this transition in early adolescence when she moved downstairs to live with her grandparents. Her decision to live alone in the apartment even after they died produced continued conflict with her parents, reflecting the ambivalence of all parties about her becoming more independent. Rena probably felt rejected when Charley and Nancy demanded that she move out on her 18th birthday. Despite her feelings, Rena's ability to live independently of her parents is a testament to her strength.

Bolts-From-the-Blue Crisis Events

In addition to life-cycle transition crises, the Shore family has experienced several "bolts from the blue" (Congress, 1996; Pittman, 1987) crisis events. Most notable among them are Nancy's back injury and subsequent disability, Charley's chronic unemployment, Michael's life-threatening asthma, and Rena's aggressive behavior. When crisis events happen to individuals, all family members are affected.

The Shore family has proven its resiliency by surviving many crises. Its members could have benefited from crisis intervention treatment at several points in their family life cycle. Rena's attempt to physically harm Nancy, followed by Charley's retaliation and beating of Rena, is an example of an appropriate opportunity to utilize crisis intervention treatment. The following application has been conceptualized as if a social worker had been enlisted to intervene directly after this event.

THE THERAPEUTIC PROCESS

Roberts (2000) proposes a seven-step crisis intervention model that is particularly helpful for working with families that are experiencing multiple crises.

Step 1—Conduct a Crisis Assessment (With Special Attention to Lethality)

Direct questions about the history of homicidal or suicidal behavior are necessary to assess a threat to the client or others. Assessment includes questions about motivation, access to a means of doing harm to the self or to others, and family history of violence. In the Shore case, the social worker learned that the family violence had already been reported to Child and Family Services by a neighbor; an investigation into the case is already underway. Both Charley and Rena were able to contract with the worker that they will not physically attack another family member again.

In addition to violence to others, the social worker should assess for suicidal risk among the family members. Statements of hopelessness ("I wonder if I can go on") demand follow-up with more direct questioning. None of the Shore family members speak specifically about depression or suicide, yet the social worker must evaluate each member. As an adolescent, Michael may be most at risk because there is some indication that he is feeling increasingly withdrawn because of his health problems and school difficulties. Rena's "laziness" and staying in bed until midafternoon may be indications that she, too, is struggling with a mood disorder.

Step 2—Make Psychological Contact and Establish a Relationship

A critical step in the beginning of all therapeutic relationships involves establishing rapport and building trust (Biestek, 1957). This is especially important in crisis work because the course of treatment is so short. Establishing trust, however, may be difficult with individuals (and even more so with families) in crisis. Individuals and families may express feelings of anger, anxiety, fear, or depression that can detrimentally affect communication. Although it has been noted that people in crisis are often less defensive (Parad & Parad, 1999), the emotional overlay of their communications may make establishing contact difficult. Active, empathetic listening helps establish rapport. It is necessary to explore what has happened with a minimum of direct probing, questioning, or confrontation, because these activities often negatively impact developing rapport.

A challenge for the social worker using a crisis intervention model with a family is that each member may express the crisis differently. In order to establish rapport with each member and with the whole family, the worker may see part of the family or one member separately. Often in crisis intervention work, a particular member is scapegoated. This may be true with the Shores; Rena is currently seen as causing all the problems.

Step 3—Identify the Dimensions of the Problem

At this stage the social worker asks direct questions and observes family interaction in order to gain greater understanding of the nature of the problem. Clarifying the problem is essential when a family is faced with developmental life-cycle crises. This is apparent with the Shore family, which may view Rena as the major problem without understanding that each member has a role in the family conflict. After establishing a relationship, the social worker treating the Shore family could ask each member to describe his or her understanding of the family problem. For example, each member would tell the story of Rena's attack on Nancy and Charley's subsequent retaliation. The worker might be surprised to hear that each member has a very different version.

Nancy feels bewildered by the event, believing that Rena's attack was unprovoked. Her disappointment and sadness are palpable, and she longs to return to the past when the family was closer. She is angry with Charley for hitting and bruising Rena, and embarrassed by the subsequent investigation by Child and Family Services.

Charley, on the other hand, feels justified in his actions. Rena has been increasingly difficult to manage; lunging at Nancy was the "last straw." He believes that Nancy is overprotective of Rena; if Nancy had been stricter with their daughter, this event would never have happened. Charley believes Rena should shape up or get out. He secretly believes that she would be more respectful had she been their biological daughter.

Rena believes that her parents do not really want her because she is adopted—this is the reason they were so anxious to have her move downstairs with her grandparents. Why else would they be so eager for her to continue to live apart from the family, demanding, now, that she leave the home when she turns 18? Rena attacked Nancy out of frustration; she could no longer tolerate her mother's nagging. Charley had no to right to strike her. Rena fears her father and is convinced that he never loved her.

Michael is weary of the arguments between his parents and Rena. He does what he can to stay "on the sidelines." He believes that if they would not be on her "case" all the time, there would be no more fights. He sometimes feels invisible and believes that his parents do not understand him. They want him to be a super boy-man because he is their only biological child. He feels depressed about the future, not knowing what he will do when he grows up. He has learned that the best way to deal with his parents is to avoid them. Sometimes he wishes he could just disappear.

It is apparent that each member of the family has a very different perspective on the nature of the family's problems. Not surprisingly, each member also seems to be struggling with his or her own issues.

Step 4—Encourage the Exploration of Feelings and Emotions

During this stage, the social worker should seek individual family members' emotional reactions to the crisis event. The social worker needs to be accepting of different family members demonstrating diverse emotional reactions, including depression, angry outbursts, fearfulness, anxiety, somatic complaints, or paranoia. Providing an opportunity to ventilate feelings can be very therapeutic for individuals and families.

Nancy is profoundly hurt and sad that her daughter attempted to strike her. Nancy always felt especially close to Rena. Her daughter's recent quest for independence is especially upsetting to her mother. Nancy simply does not understand why her only daughter, her special child, has turned against her.

Whereas Nancy is hurt and sad, Charley expresses anger. How dare his daughter attempt to strike her mother, especially after everything they have done for her! He was secretly glad when Rena began to live downstairs with her grandparents; Rena's absence in the household made for less conflict. Seeing Rena as such an ungrateful child, he has difficulty remembering happier days.

Rena expresses anger that her parents are trying to interfere with her life; she wants to be as far way from them as possible. She would be content to remain downstairs in her grandmother's apartment forever. Her parents, however, have told her that she must leave the apartment when she turns 18. Rena feels betrayed and left out. She is already fearful about how she will support herself when she has to move out. She believes that her birth mother would have been nicer.

Michael expresses feelings of resentment toward his older sister. He feels that she is the preferred child because of her musical and intellectual abilities. Sometimes he feels that life is hopeless, and he wants to lie down and die. Prior to crisis intervention treatment, Nancy and Charley did not realize the extent of Michael's depression. Aware that suicide risk among adolescents is a major concern, the social work clinician was able to elicit depressed feelings from Michael that may require immediate intervention.

Step 5—Explore and Assess Past Coping Attempts

In this phase, the social worker assesses the individual and family strengths that have helped them resolve conflicts in the past and will provide support in the future. For example, the social worker can ask the family members about previous events, how they felt, and what actions they took to cope with the crisis. Asking a client to report his or her past successes tends to reinforce past coping skills, provides hope to deal with the current crisis, and paves the way for future successes. When working with a crisis that involves an entire family, previous coping strategies have to be explored at both the individual and the family levels.

The Shore family is accustomed to arguments between Nancy and Rena. Rena has run away from home twice. But the incident in question was the first time physical violence occurred; Rena lunged at Nancy, Charley pulled Rena away and beat her. The social worker asked the Shores how they had been able to keep their arguments from getting physical in the past. She learns that in the past, Nancy would retreat to her room when Rena started arguing. This action, though initially infuriating to Rena, broke the physical tension between the two of them. Rena typically would leave the house and take a walk around the block, cursing to herself about her fate. Michael would generally be found in his room during these altercations, his music playing loudly. Charley found refuge in front of the television, waiting for things to return to normal. Two or 3 days later, the tension would subside and things would feel relatively "normal" again. The social worker would then validate the family's success in keeping their arguments non-violent and underscore the strategy of maintaining physical distance as a means to de-escalate arguments.

The social worker would then spend time learning about each individual family member's strengths and personal repertoire of coping strategies. Discussion about successes in coping with past crises should always be linked with the present. The social worker learns that Charley was raised in an atmosphere of family violence. Yet unlike his father, until the incident in question, Charley never dealt with family conflict through violence. The social worker can explore with Charley how he felt during his difficult childhood and what outlets he had for expressing his anger, apart from violent measures. Nancy was educated as a nurse, which provided continued job opportunities. She was able to cope with her back disability, which had incapacitated her for weeks and months at a time. Rena's intelligence and talent have provided her with many opportunities. She possesses the strength to live independent of her family in the downstairs apartment. Michael has been able to survive repeated asthma attacks; there is hope that as he grows older, proper medication might diminish or eliminate them. He relates well to adults and demonstrates a facility on computers that may provide job opportunities in the future.

As a family unit, the Shores have considerable strength. They have stayed together through many hard times, including unemployment, fertility problems, health problems, and life-cycle transition crisis. They have worked hard as parents: coping successfully with having a child who has chronic, life-threatening asthma and finding special opportunities for Rena after discovering that she was a gifted child.

Step 6—Generate and Explore Alternatives and Specific Solutions

The social worker should ask the family members about possible ways to re-solve the crisis situation, including a thorough discussion of each possibility. If the family is "stuck," even after gentle probing, the social worker can suggest different alternative solutions. For example, Nancy believes that Rena should move back upstairs because she is not mature enough to live by herself. Rena is adamantly opposed to this solution because she feels that she wants to live as far away as possible from her mother. Charley, who usually tries to avoid what he calls "mother–daughter spats," takes a definite stand. He fears that if Rena moves back upstairs, Nancy and Rena will "kill each other." Michael does not care where Rena lives; he just wants her to stay out of his room.

Step 7—Develop an Action Plan

The seventh and final step involves developing an action plan. An individual or a family crisis often perpetuates an overflow of emotions that impairs cogni-tive decision making. By helping a family consider alternatives, the social worker aids in the restoration of cognitive functioning. Generating alternatives involves three steps. First, the family must have a realistic understanding about what happened and what led up to the crisis. Second, all family members must un-derstand what the crisis means to them and how it challenges their own expec-tations. Finally, unfounded beliefs need to be clarified; in addition, homework assignments can be given to lead to new experiences (Roberts, 2000). Each family member must participate in this process, as well as in generating alter-natives to resolve the crisis.

As individuals and as a family, the Shores need to understand what led up to the conflict between Rena and Nancy, and Charley's subsequent retaliation. Both parents need greater understanding of adolescent developmental issues that may be especially complicated with adoptive families. Both parents, but especially Nancy, must accept that Rena will never be the perfect latency-age child she once was. As an adolescent adopted child, Rena feels unwanted. Her feelings of loss were aggravated by the loss of her grandmother. Rena needs a greater appreciation of Nancy and Charley's efforts to succeed as parents.

As treatment nears the final stages, the Shores agree that it is best for Rena to continue living downstairs. They will decide about her moving to her own apartment when she turns 18 at a later date. Rena has decided to accept a part-time job in the neighborhood, giving her more independence and per-haps lightening the financial strain on the family. Charley is mandated to at-tend anger-management classes as a result of the beating incident. Rena and Nancy agree to "walk away" and "get some space" when arguments begin, to ensure that their disagreement does not need to be expressed physically. The social worker makes a socioeconomic intervention and refers the family for food stamps to ease the family's financial strain.

A major concern that has surfaced during crisis intervention treatment is Michael's depression. The social worker was insistent that Michael should have an immediate psychiatric evaluation. As a result of this evaluation, Michael was referred for ongoing counseling.

The final stage of crisis intervention treatment also involves plans for follow-up. Treatment lasted only 10 weeks, but the Shore family was told that its members could return for further treatment, if needed.

APPLICATION TO DIVERSITY

The United States is becoming increasingly diverse. It is estimated that by the mid-2000s the majority of Americans will be from countries other than Western Europe. Even now, one zip code in Queens, New York, reports residents from over 125 countries (*National Geographic,* 1998). Working with families from diverse backgrounds presents an ongoing challenge for social workers. The following guidelines have been helpful to social workers who work with culturally diverse families (Devore & Schlesinger, 1996). Social workers should

1. Examine and understand their own cultural background. Before beginning to work with clients and families from other backgrounds, social workers must examine the way in which their own cultural beliefs affect their attitudes toward families whose values may differ markedly from their own.
2. Invite clients to talk about their own cultural backgrounds. With the multiplicity of cultural backgrounds of their clients, social workers may despair that they will ever be able to understand the different cultures. Social workers cannot know about every culture. In fact, social workers who think that they know a great deal about different cultures are at risk of making generalizations and stereotyping different clients. Asking clients to share their cultural beliefs serves to engage clients and demonstrates understanding and respect.
3. Focus on strengths, rather than on deficits, in working with culturally diverse families (Saleeby, 1997). Many families have strengths that have often helped them cope with multiple crises. Crisis intervention workers need to focus on what families are doing right and what they have accomplished (Kaplan & Munoz, 1997). Social workers who respect and support clients' strengths are often the most successful with culturally diverse families.
4. Avoid generalizations. Each individual family is unique. (The *culturagram*, a family assessment tool developed to help social workers individualize culturally diverse families, is discussed later.)

The crisis intervention model is particularly effective in working with culturally diverse families. Immigrant families, especially, have likely endured many crises, among them dislocation and relocation to a new community. The crisis intervention model produces positive results with a minimum expenditure of time and money, a consideration that may be particularly important to an immigrant family with limited resources.

Culturagram

In order to provide culturally competent services, social workers must avoid making generalizations about specific cultural groups, which can deny the uniqueness of each family and lead to prejudicial stereotyping. For example, an undocumented Mexican family that arrived in the United States last week is sure to be quite different from a Puerto Rican family that has been in the United States for 20 years. The culturagram (see Figure 7.1), a family assessment tool, was developed to help clinicians individualize and understand culturally diverse families (Congress, 1994, 1997, 2002). Neither the ecomap (Hartman & Laird, 1983) nor the genogram (McGoldrick & Gerson, 1985), two widely used family assessment tools, focus solely on culture. The culturagram is particularly helpful in working with culturally diverse families that have experienced crisis. The following cultural aspects are addressed in the culturagram.

Reasons for relocation. There is often a sense of loss and a longing for familiar homes, families, friends, and communities left behind, as well as anxiety about adjusting to the new country. The crisis of relocation may be more acute if the relocation was forced because of economic, political, or religious oppression in the country of origin and the client cannot return.

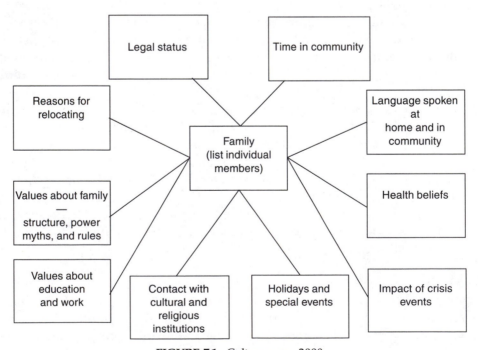

FIGURE 7.1. Culturagram—2000

Legal status. Fear of discovery and deportation may produce another crisis event, especially if the client and the family are undocumented.

Length of time in the community. Anxiety about deportation for non-citizens has increased since September 11, 2001. The length of time one has been in the country may be significant; often a family member may become more acculturated the longer he or she lives in the United States. Often one member may have lived in the United States longer than another, leading to family conflict in terms of acculturation.

Language spoken at home and in the community. In many cases one language is spoken at home and another language in the community. Sometimes a crisis occurs when members have a different facility and interest in speaking their native language or English.

Health beliefs. Illness and the need for treatment may be particularly stressful for culturally diverse families, in which health beliefs and practices differ from traditional Western medicine.

Impact of crisis events. In general, families may experience a crisis in many different ways. Certain crises may be more stressful for some families than for others, depending on their cultural background as well as specific family beliefs. For example, the rape of a teenage girl is certainly a crisis event for any family. Yet a Puerto Rican family with whom I worked found this event particularly stressful, because it meant that the girl was no longer a virgin and would never find someone to marry. In addition, the death of a grandparent may be particularly traumatic for culturally diverse families, in which the older person is venerated and depended upon for major decisions. The impact of each individual crisis event on culturally diverse families requires exploration.

Holidays and special events. Holidays and special events may provide support for the culturally diverse family. Yet, at times, these events may produce more stress and crisis because of sadness stemming from missing relatives or differing customs.

Contact with cultural and religious institutions. The social worker needs to explore cultural and religious supports that the client has used in the past and can continue to use, as well as additional sources of support.

Values about education and work. Beliefs about work and education may create stress and produce crisis for the culturally diverse family. First, skills learned in the country of origin may not be easily transferred to a highly urbanized, technological society like the United States. Resulting unemployment may produce a financial crisis for the family. Also, women may be able to find jobs easier than men. Men may be unemployed or employed in positions for which they are overqualified. These factors place additional stress on men who have traditionally been "breadwinners" and their families. Culturally diverse families often put much hope in the educational system, although school structure, special education programs, and educational policies may be particularly threatening for the immigrant family. For example, immigrant families often want siblings to stay together, whereas schools in the United States stress separating and individualizing each student, including twins (Congress & Lynn, 1994).

Values about family structure, power, myths, and rules. Conflict between family values found in the country of origin and those common to the United States may cause conflict. Many immigrant families come from hierarchical backgrounds in which male members hold absolute authority. A challenging crisis for many immigrant families often occurs around the life-cycle transition of adolescence. Immigrant parents, for example, may expect teenage girls to help with housework and child care, whereas adolescent girls may chose to spend leisure time with their peers. Such a crisis can cause culturally diverse families to present for crisis intervention treatment.

Application to the Shore Family

In this section I will apply the Roberts (2000) crisis intervention model to the Shore family (which will become a Mexican immigrant family named Sanchez for this illustration). The Sanchez family came to the United States from Mexico 5 years ago. For the sum of $2,000, a "coyote" (a person who is paid money to help an immigrant cross the border) had helped them enter the United States over the Rio Grande border. The families eventually made their way to New York City, where relatives had told them opportunities abound. Even though Carmen (Nancy) had received special training as a nurse in Mexico City, her pay there was so inadequate that she could not support her family. In the United States she is unlicensed, as well as undocumented, and therefore unable to secure work as a nurse. Juan (Charley) has loved acting since he was a young child. He dreams of being in telenovellas and being a star.

At first, Juan and Carmen were unable to have children. This was particularly embarrassing for Juan because having a large family is culturally accepted. However, there was a solution. A young unmarried girl in their neighborhood had a child, Rosa (Rena). The Sanchezes took her in. Surprisingly, Rosa turned out to be a gifted child, even though her mother had been considered slow and her father was unknown. Miguel (Michael) has had severe asthma since infancy. His grandmother tried to treat his asthma with various herbs, but nothing seemed to help. Their small, overcrowded, roach-infested apartment in Queens has not helped his asthma condition. Juan and Carmen came to the United States to better their situation, but their financial and health problems led to discouragement. Because of their undocumented status, they have difficulty securing even menial employment and are ineligible for social service or health-care services.

The Sanchez family managed to cope with all these stresses until Rosa reached adolescence. She was especially close to her grandmother, who would frequently tell Rosa stories about her birth mother (the daughter of her grandmother's friend). Rosa believes that the Sanchez family does not understand her. The family conflict and crisis began shortly after her grandmother died. After a recent argument, Rosa lunged at Carmen; Juan tore his daughter away and struck her several times in the face, bruising her badly. The argument was a familiar one: Rosa wanted to drop out of school, take a full-time job, live on her own, and perhaps someday return to Mexico to find her birth mother. Like many immigrants, Mr. and Mrs. Sanchez believe that the family is paramount and that Rosa should devote her time and energy to the family, rather than to her own personal pursuits. In addition, they believe that any income Rosa earns from a job should be used to help the family, especially because both parents are unemployed.

Like other immigrant families, the Sanchez family believes that education is the key to success in the new country. The parents were very upset when their birth son, Miguel, demonstrated learning problems, but were most respectful of the school's decision to put him into special education. Often, teachers and other school personnel are seen as experts whom parents would never question about placement decisions for their child. When working with culturally diverse families around school issues, a social worker can help make the family members aware of their rights to question and advocate for what they see as the most appropriate placement for their child (Congress, 1990).

Use of the Crisis Intervention Model With the Sanchez Family

The first step in applying the Roberts (2000) crisis intervention model involves conducting a crisis assessment, especially in terms of lethality. After learning of the violent incident between Juan and Rosa, the social worker called Child and Family Services to report Juan's physical abuse. An investigation of the incident is underway. The social worker must also rule out the possibility of suicidal intent. There is some evidence that Hispanic adolescent girls are at greater risk for suicide (Zayas, Kaplan, Turner, Romano, & Gonzalez-Ramos, 2000). It is important to assess for depression and inquire about previous suicide attempts, as this may increase the risk that Rosa will choose this alternative as a way of coping with feelings of loss over the death of her grandmother and ongoing conflict with her parents. In conducting a suicide and homicide assessment during crisis intervention work, the social worker should assess all family members, not only the one considered the identified patient. Sometimes the quieter child or the family member who is not the identified patient may have a serious mental health problem that is overlooked. By directly questioning Miguel at the beginning of family crisis intervention treatment, the social worker learned that Miguel is depressed and consequently referred him for a psychiatric evaluation.

The second step involves making psychological contact and establishing the relationship. Families that are undocumented may be particularly fearful that information they share with the worker will then be given to INS and will lead to their deportation. The social worker must work very hard to try to establish a relationship with the family and individual members. *Personalismo* (a personal relationship) has been seen as particularly useful in establishing a relationship with Hispanic clients (Congress, 1990). A poor Mexican family may view a middle-class Anglo social worker as very different from its members; language barriers can further impede the development of a relationship.

Carmen may be the most easy to engage because of her previous experience in the health field. Juan may be very distrustful that a female social worker will attempt to tell him what to do. Rosa may believe that the social worker will ally with her parents. The Sanchez parents may believe that the social worker will support Rosa because they perceive that the social worker favors an Anglo value of independence over their value of family.

The third step involves identifying the dimensions of the problem. Each member has a different view as to the cause of the problem. Both the Sanchez parents feel deeply disrespected; Rosa is too influenced by her U.S. peers and should put her family first. They worry that she has turned away from their family and their church. Rosa feels that her parents are old-fashioned, that they think they are still in Mexico and are not accepting of U.S. ways. Juan firmly believes that it is the right of the father to discipline his children in whatever way he sees fit. He is also deeply upset that he is not able to support his family. Carmen feels that her role as a wife and a mother is to hold the family together. She feels very threatened that Rosa should want to leave the household; Carmen feels that this reflects on her worth as a mother. Miguel is caught in the middle. He believes that his parents don't understand how difficult it is to straddle two cultures, as he and Rosa must. He also agrees that Rosa should have more respect for her parents.

The fourth step involves encouraging the exploration of feelings and emotions. When the social worker first saw the Sanchez family, there was a great deal of outpouring of emotional expression. Mrs. Sanchez cried and screamed; during the first session she had an *attaque* (Congress, 1990). Attaques are behavioral states characterized by extreme hyperkinetic, convulsive movements. This conversion disorder occurs in Hispanic women and usually represents a reaction to stress (Roberts, 1990). Mr. Sanchez expressed anger that Rosa was breaking up the family by not helping her mother with household chores. He will not tolerate his daughter's disrespect. Miguel seemed aloof and had little to say about his feelings. Rosa was initially silent and distrustful, fearing that the social worker would identify with her parents. As the therapy progressed, she was able to identify feelings of rejection and a sense that she does not belong in this family.

The fifth step involves exploring and accessing past coping attempts. Like many immigrant families, the Sanchez family demonstrates many strengths. Despite great adversities, Carmen had pursued a nursing education in Mexico. The family was able to survive the stresses of immigration and also negotiate

Rosa's entry into a gifted class. Despite extreme poverty, unemployment, and health problems, the family has been able to stay together. The social worker helped the Sanchez family identify the ways in which its members had been able to cope with various stresses in the past.

The sixth step includes generating and exploring alternatives and specific solutions. The social worker had each family member generate an alternative plan. Rosa wants to quit school, get a job, and move out with a friend. Carmen and Juan want her to stay in the household. No one feels understood. There is much concern about Miguel's school progress, and it is noted that he is very depressed. The parents received information about the risks of adolescent suicide, and Miguel was referred for a psychiatric evaluation. At first, they were reluctant to have Miguel evaluated, fearing that he would be considered *loco*, perhaps eventually leading him to be removed from the household. The social worker, however, was able to reassure the family that a psychiatric evaluation would be helpful.

A major ongoing concern for the family is economic. Both Juan and Carmen have difficulties finding work because of their undocumented status. Furthermore, Carmen's chronic back pain prevents her from finding work as a child-care worker. Socioeconomic interventions are often very important in crisis work with poor, culturally diverse families. The social worker made a referral to a social service agency that specializes in providing assistance to undocumented families. The services include a food bank and pro bono legal assistance (to help with their immigration status).

The seventh and final step involves developing an action plan. A compromise is finally reached. Rosa is to remain at home with the family. She will stay in school, take a part-time job at a nearby market, and be able to keep and save the money she earns. She agrees to talk with the family's priest and help Carmen with the household duties on weekends. She will show her father and mother respect; in turn, she asks for understanding from her parents. Juan and Carmen will also talk with the priest to get support for their concerns. Carmen agrees to talk with other mothers in her neighborhood who are struggling with "letting go" of their adolescent children. Juan will continue to participate in the Child and Family Services–mandated anger-management class. Together, the family members agree to reinstitute the regular prayer time they used to take together. When arguments occur, they agree to try some of the social worker's suggestions (take a break from each other, go to opposite ends of the apartment, or take a walk and talk about it 30 minutes later). The family hopes Rosa will remain at home and enjoy more independence.

LIMITATIONS OF THE MODEL

The crisis intervention model pre-supposes the ability to communicate verbally and, as a result, would not be helpful with individuals whose severe cognitive impairment affects such ability. In addition, crisis intervention treatment may not be appropriate with individuals who are psychotic and cannot engage in secondary-process verbal communication. These clients may need medication and hospitalization as an alternative to crisis intervention treatment. A final concern is the limitation in terms of suicide or homicidal risk. The first step of the model assesses lethality; an individual in need of emergency hospitalization would preclude crisis intervention treatment.

A particular caveat with culturally diverse families is that the treatment must be in the language understood by the family. Crisis intervention treatment is not indicated with families in which the social worker is not able to communicate in the family's language. The social worker must adapt the crisis intervention model to the needs of the culturally diverse individual or family.

RESEARCH

There have been several demographic studies of agencies that use the crisis intervention model. Roberts (1995) compiled a national directory of crisis hotlines, and I (Congress, 1992) have studied different types of rape counseling centers.

Many research projects have tested the effectiveness of crisis intervention treatment with different populations in diverse settings (Cocoran & Roberts, 2000). A review of recent social work literature includes the following articles that document the efficacy of crisis intervention services with people victimized by domestic violence (Cocoran, Stephenson, Perryman, & Allen, 2001; Mancoske, Standifer, & Cauley, 1994), inpatients in a psychiatric hospital (Anthony, 1992), residential treatment clients (Hartmann & Sullivan, 1996), people who have experienced trauma (Bell, 1995), and children in a psychiatric day center (Robb, 1990).

The consensus is that crisis intervention treatment is effective, especially when there has been a crisis event that impedes the client's ability to use prior ways of coping. Current treatment is especially concerned with outcomes. A multifaceted crisis assessment scale has been seen as particularly helpful in assessing the severity of the dysfunction associated with a crisis event (Roberts, 2000). However, the effectiveness of crisis intervention with culturally diverse families has been minimally studied and requires further research (Congress, 2000).

SUMMARY

Crisis intervention treatment can be very useful in working with families from diverse backgrounds. Social workers, however, must be flexible in adapting crisis intervention methods to their clients and families. Families from different cultures often handle crisis events in many different ways. Social workers need to guard against making generalizations about people from specific cultures. The culturagram can be useful in helping social workers individualize families with whom they are working.

Crisis intervention treatment is helpful in working with culturally diverse families for a variety of reasons. First, this type of treatment is short term and solution-focused: two aspects of crisis intervention treatment that often appeal to culturally diverse families. Many families may have come from backgrounds in which mental health treatment was not readily accepted or available. A method that quickly moves to a solution may be viewed as more helpful than long-term models that focus on increasing one's psychological understanding of behavior. Also, because many culturally diverse families have limited incomes and health insurance coverage, the short-term aspect of crisis intervention treatment can be especially appealing. Furthermore, crisis intervention treatment often includes socioeconomic interventions that may be of special importance for families with limited incomes. Finally, culturally diverse families, especially immigrants, often experience many crises associated with leaving a familiar community and immigrating to the United States. Here, they are often forced to accept employment with inadequate pay, and they face the lack of available public social services. These factors may increase the number of crisis events they encounter, stemming from unemployment, poor health, and poverty. Crisis intervention services can often make an important difference for culturally diverse families that are struggling to survive in a challenging environment.

REFERENCES

Anthony, D. (1992). A retrospective evaluation of factors influencing successful outcomes on an inpatient psychiatric crisis unit. *Research on Social Work Practice, 2*(1), 56–64.

Bell, J. (1995). Traumatic event debriefing: Service delivery designs and the role of social work. *Social Work, 40*(1), 36–43.

Biestek, F. (1957). *The casework relationship.* Chicago: Loyola University Press.

Caplan, G. (1964). *Principles of preventive psychiatry.* New York: Basic Books.

Carter, B., & McGoldrick, M. (1999). *The expanded family life cycle: Individual, family, and social perspectives* (3rd ed.). Boston: Allyn & Bacon.

Cocoran, J., & Roberts, A. (2000). Research on crisis intervention and recommendations for future research. In A. Roberts (Ed.), *Crisis intervention handbook: Assessment, treatment, and research* (pp. 453–486). New York: Oxford Press.

Cocoran, J., Stephenson, M., Perryman, D., & Allen, S. (2001). Perceptions and utilization of a police-social work crisis intervention approach to domestic violence. *Families in Society, 82*(4), 393–398.

Congress, E. (1990). Crisis intervention with Hispanic clients in an urban mental health clinic. In A. Roberts (Ed.), *Crisis intervention handbook: Assessment, treatment, and research* (pp. 221–236). Belmont, CA: Wadsworth.

Congress, E. (1992). Unmet needs, service delivery, and practice issues with rape victims. *The Justice Professional, 7*(1), 1–15.

Congress, E. (1994). The use of culturagrams to assess and empower culturally diverse families. *Families in Society, 75*, 531–540.

Congress, E. (1996). Family crisis—life cycle and bolts from the blue: Assessment and treatment. In A. Roberts (Ed.), *Crisis intervention and brief treatment: Theory, techniques, and applications* (pp. 142–159). Chicago: Nelson Hall.

Congress, E. (1997). Using the culturagram to assess and empower culturally diverse families. In E. Congress (Ed.), *Multicultural perspectives in working with families* (pp. 3–16). New York: Springer.

Congress, E. (2000). Crisis intervention with culturally diverse families. In A. Roberts (Ed.), *Crisis intervention handbook: Assessment, treatment, and research* (pp. 430–449). New York: Oxford Press.

Congress, E. (2002). Using the culturagram with culturally diverse families. In A. Roberts & G. Greene (Eds.), *Social workers' desk reference* (pp. 57–61). New York: Oxford Press.

Congress, E., & Lynn, M. (1994). Group work programs in public schools: Ethical dilemmas and cultural diversity. *Social Work in Education, 16*(2), 107–114.

DeJong, P., & Berg, I. (2002). *Interviewing for solutions* (2nd ed.). Pacific Grove, CA: Brooks Cole.

Devore, W., & Schlesinger, E. (1996). *Ethnic-sensitive social work practice* (4th ed.). Boston: Allyn & Bacon.

Erickson, E. (1963). *Childhood and society.* New York: Norton.

Golan, N. (1978). *Treatment in crisis situations.* New York: Free Press.

Greene, G., Lee, M., Trask, R., & Rheinshceld, J. (2000). How to work with clients' strengths in crisis intervention: A solution-focused approach. In A. Roberts (Ed.), *Crisis intervention handbook: Assessment, treatment, and research* (pp. 31–55). New York: Oxford University Press.

Hartman, A., & Laird, J. (1983). *Family oriented treatment.* New York: Free Press.

Hartmann, D., & Sullivan, P. (1996). Residential crisis services as an alternative to inpatient care. *Families in Society, 77*(8), 496–501.

Kaplan, C., & Munoz, M. (1997). Poor minority adolescents and their families. In E. Congress (Ed.), *Multicultural perspectives in working with families* (pp. 61–75). New York: Springer.

Lindemann, E. (1944). Symptomatology and management of acute grief. *American Journal of Psychiatry, 101,* 141–148.

Mancoske, R., Standifer, D., & Cauley, C. (1994). The effectiveness of brief counseling services for battered women. *Research on Social Work Practice, 4*(1), 53–63.

McGoldrick, M., & Gerson, R. (1985). *Genograms in family assessment.* New York: Norton.

National Geographic. (1998, September). All the world comes to Queens.

Parad, H. (1965). *Crisis intervention: Selected readings.* New York: Family Service Association of America.

Parad, H., & Parad, L. (1999). *Crisis intervention book 2: The practitioner source book for brief therapy.* Milwaukee, WI: Family Service Association.

Pittman, F. (1987). *Turning points: Treating families in transition and crisis.* New York: Norton.

Rappaport, L. (1962). Crisis-oriented short-term casework. *Social Service Review, 41,* 31–43.

Reid, W., & Fortune, A. (2002). Task centered treatment. In A. Roberts & G. Green (Eds.), *Social workers' desk reference* (pp. 101–112). New York: Oxford Press.

Robb, E. (1990). *Crisis intervention in a children's psychiatric day treatment program: Its beneficial characteristics.* Unpublished doctoral dissertation, Smith College.

Roberts, A. (1990). *Crisis intervention handbook.* Belmont, CA: Wadsworth.

Roberts, A. (1995). *Crisis intervention and time-limited cognitive treatment.* Thousand Oaks, CA: Sage.

Roberts, A. (2000). An overview of crisis theory and crisis intervention. In A. Roberts (Ed.), *Crisis intervention handbook: Assessment, treatment, and research* (pp. 3–30). New York: Oxford Press.

Saleeby, D. (Ed.). (1997). *The strengths perspective in social work practice.* New York: Longman.

U.S. Census Bureau. (2001). *Statistical abstract of the United States: 2001* (121st ed.). Washington, DC: Author.

Zayas, L. H., Kaplan, C., Turner, S., Romano, K., & Gonzalez-Ramos, G. (2000). Understanding suicide attempts by adolescent females. *Social Work, 45*(1), 53–63.

8

Group Work

Emphasis on the Role of Gender

Charles Garvin, PhD

INTRODUCTION

This chapter differs from many of the other chapters in this book, in that group work is not a specific theory but a context used to help individuals enhance or resolve problems in their social functioning. Social workers have employed all of the theories portrayed in this book, as well as in the other volumes in this series, to enable groups to better fulfill the purpose of helping individuals. Group workers have also drawn from social psychological theories, such as role theory and small group theory (Garvin, 1987). In addition, group workers think in systems terms and utilize concepts derived from social ecology. They do not see the group as isolated from its social environment, but rather in interaction with it. Organizational- and community-level theories are called upon to help us understand this phenomenon.

CONCEPT OF THE PERSON AND THE HUMAN EXPERIENCE

Regardless of theoretical predisposition, group workers hold similar views regarding the person and human experience. They see people as inherently social organisms who require interaction with other people to survive and develop. This idea can be noted in early childhood, when infants focus on human faces and seek to have their needs met through the ways they communicate with others, particularly parents. Group workers view the family as a group (an especially important one). Some even see later group experience as, at least in part, a recapitulation of family dynamics (Yalom, 1995).

This need to interact with others in groups is manifested throughout life. In young children, the most important group is typically the family. In some societies in which families live in close proximity, this type of peer group may be composed of cousins or other children with whom one shares a family "identity."

As the individual moves through childhood, other groups become salient, such as peer groups that assemble either informally or formally (e.g., in classrooms). In adulthood, the individual typically affiliates with many groups in such institutions as colleges, unions, places of employment, churches, and communities. Groups are often formed for specific purposes, such as social action, social support, or to pursue a mutually held interest like sports or music.

Groups are where individuals develop close and meaningful relationships with others, but they also fulfill a number of other functions for the individual, including the following:

- The individual learns about social norms through the rules of the group, the expressions of the members, and the sanctions imposed by the group for violations of norms.
- The individual acquires new behaviors through observing others in the group and through trying out new behaviors in the group.
- The individual is helped to express and identify emotions by observing others in the group express emotions and hearing them name their own emotions.
- The individual learns to express feelings of closeness to others in the group by observing others doing this in ways that are approved in the group.
- Individuals are helped to develop a self-understanding by receiving feedback from other group members.
- Individuals develop an understanding of culture and develop a broader worldview by listening to other members' contributions. Individuals learn ways of seeking changes in both the group and the external environment, individually as well as together with other group members, by observing others in the group and by discussing this issue in the group.

HISTORICAL PERSPECTIVE

Group work in social work had its beginnings in agencies that were developed to help immigrants in urban communities cope with the poor conditions they found there. Another population in need consisted of people who migrated from rural parts of the country to the city. Both groups sought economic opportunities in the rapidly industrializing cities. Examples of these agencies were the Young Men's Christian Association, organized in the United States in 1851; the Young Women's Christian Association, organized in 1866; and the Boys' Clubs of America, organized in 1906. Ethnic and religious institutions, such as the Catholic Youth Organization and the Jewish Community Centers, also established agencies. Such organizations, according to Schwartz (1971), "looked to the face-to-face group to restore opportunities for the good life taken from people by the speed and ruthlessness of post–Civil War industrialization."

Settlement houses, first created in England, quickly spread to the United States. By 1900 there were more than 400 settlements in the United States. The settlement was founded on the idea that workers could best help people suffering from urban conditions and a lack of preparation for urban life by participating in their community life. Thus, settlement workers lived in the settlement houses and worked with community residents to create a broad variety of activities to meet their needs.

Settlement workers came from a variety of professional backgrounds, including education, social work, and psychology, as well as most of the liberal arts fields. They sought theories that were compatible with their goals. Notable theories included the work of Mary P. Follett, a political scientist; John Dewey, who developed ideas referred to as progressive education; and Eduard C. Lindeman, who was interested in the role of community groups in a well-functioning democracy.

Social work schools were slow to relate to these developments. One of the first was Western Reserve University (now Case Western Reserve University), where Mildred Chadsey developed a course in group work in 1923. A number of people worked on efforts to conceptualize group work, including Clara Kaiser, Wilbur Newstetter, Margaret Williamson, and Grace Coyle. In 1935, the National Conference of Social Work agreed to institute a section on group work, and several of the papers that were delivered at that meeting set the group work agenda for the years to come. For example, Coyle spoke about the dual functions of transmitting cultural values to individuals, while helping people transform these values through democratic processes. Newstetter took on issues of defining group social work. The next year, the National Association for the Study of Group Work was formed.

After World War II, the United States moved into a more politically conservative period. Group workers followed the political trend and focused less on the social reform functions of groups and more on clarifying practice theory and the movement of practice into new settings. There was also a debate as to whether group work was an educational or a social work specialization. At the 1946 meeting of the National Conference on Social Work, Coyle's argument, that group work as a method falls within the larger scope of social work as a method, was supported (Trecker, 1955). This consensus led to the formation of the American Association of Group Workers (AAGW), a professional membership organization, with membership based on professional training.

Group work continued to be predominantly practiced in community agencies during the 1940s and 1950s, although group workers began to explore the techniques they were developing in psychiatric settings, hospitals, family agencies, correctional institutions, and schools. The use of groups in the psychiatric treatment of World War II veterans contributed to this process.

Several forces drove the evolution of group work in the 1960s and 1970s.

One was the strengthened commitment of government to solve such problems as delinquency, poverty, and mental illness. The War on Poverty and the Civil Rights Movement caused social workers to see problems in new, often more sociological perspectives. This led to the awareness that no single method could do the job. An effective approach required that individual, group, family, and community interventions be employed in some comprehensive fashion. Thus the concept of a social work generalist method arose, based on a vision of the worker dealing with systems in interaction.

As group work was more widely practiced in treatment-oriented settings, group work theorists sought to develop approaches and concepts that supported this trend. For example, in the 1950s, Vinter conceptualized the development of treatment goals for individuals to be accomplished in groups and stated that these goals should be the outcomes of individual diagnoses (Vinter, 1959). Vinter saw the group as a means for achieving treatment goals, rather than the group experience being an end in itself. He was concerned about demonstrating the effectiveness of group work practice. Vinter and others, including William Schwartz (1961), developed precise formulations as to what group work skills entailed.

These kinds of discussions led to the conclusion that group workers had begun to diverge in their approaches to their work. Papell and Rothman (1966) performed an important service when they developed a typology that captured some of the diversity that had emerged. They identified three models that they termed *social goals, remedial,* and *reciprocal.* The social goals approach views social work as a "cause." Because of its relevance to struggles for human rights, the social goals model continues to influence contemporary thinking about group work. The remedial model emerged during the movement of group work into clinical settings and focused on treatment goals for individuals. In this model, the group was viewed as a means and a context to attain such goals. The reciprocal model focused on enhancing the process whereby individuals, groups, and larger social systems engaged each other to undertake activities of mutual benefit. The workers in this method are described as *mediators.* As such, they are involved in the ways a group member seeks to use the group, the expectations the group places on the members to ensure its own survival, the pressures the group places on the agency, and the agency requirements transmitted to the group and its members.

In the ensuing years since Papell and Rothman (1966) completed this analysis, other approaches to group work have been created. These approaches have drawn upon several orientations, including cognitive-behavioral, feminist, narrative, object relations, gestalt, social cognition, and social-ecological ideas. Nevertheless, it seems plausible that the conceptual differences identified by Papell and Rothman still explain differences among workers.

A force in the development of group work in the last 25 years is the International Association for the Advancement of Social Work with Groups (AASWG). This organization was created in 1978 by group workers who were concerned about the lack of attention to strengthening the knowledge base of group work and educating practitioners for group work. This lack appeared to be a consequence of the absorption of group work into generalist curricula in schools of social work, a dearth of group work content at conferences, and the presence of few group work articles in journals. These group workers also perceived that group work practice was poor when performed by people without quality group work education.

KEY THEORETICAL CONSTRUCTS

In view of the plethora of ways of working with groups, some group work writers have identified essential elements of social work practice with groups. Among these are Middleman and Goldberg (1987), who state that this practice "must focus on helping members to become a system of mutual aid." This means that a main source of help for each member comes from other members, and the task of the social worker is to help members understand this dynamic and to strive for a group in which mutual aid is strengthened.

The second element is that the group worker should utilize group processes to help the members and the group to attain their purposes. The interactions among the members are one of the most important of these processes. The worker helps the members listen attentively to each other and communicate with one another in direct and honest ways. Communications occur through a variety of verbal and nonverbal means, including solving problems, determining norms, and expressing feelings.

The third element is the worker's efforts to move the members and the group to greater degrees of autonomy, in which each entity is likely to function effectively in the absence of the worker. Group autonomy is not always possible, because some members require a long period of support. On the other hand, some groups evolve into self-help groups that can carry on without a professional.

The fourth element is the worker's recognition that groups go through phases. Beginning phases require members to initiate relationships with one another, determine individual and group purposes, and establish group norms. Middle phases require addressing power and control issues, and determining and carrying out group tasks and activities. Ending phases involve evaluating the group experience, assessing progress in attaining goals, choosing future services that may be needed, and separating from the group.

One idea that is commonly used to explain how groups help people change is that groups can create a set of therapeutic factors (Bloch & Crouch, 1985; Yalom, 1995). Bloch and Crouch define a *therapeutic* or *curative factor* (the latter is their preferred term) as "an element of group therapy that contributes to improvement in a patient's condition and is a function of the actions of the group therapist, the other group members, and the patient himself [sic]" (p. 4).

In discussing therapeutic factors, we use Bloch and Crouch's (1985) typology. There are other typologies; however, Bloch and Crouch's attempts to be theoretically neutral. In addition, they draw upon the extensive research litera-ture to substantiate the existence of such factors and the power of factors to create change in group members.

The first factor is "instillation of hope." Hope stems not only from the therapist but from other group members as they express optimism about the outcome of the group experience. Group workers have observed that mem-bers, as a result of group discussion, are likely to correct both undue pessi-mism and unrealistic expectations.

The second factor, "universality," comes about as members begin to real-ize that their situations and problems are not unique and that others have similar concerns and feelings. Many clients with problems such as alcoholism, mental illness, and criminal behaviors are likely to feel stigmatized. A sense of universality can help reduce their feelings of alienation.

A third factor, "guidance," involves the provision of information and ad-vice to a member from the group worker and group members. Many social work groups are created to provide this input, such as groups for parents, can-cer patients, people about to be released from inpatient facilities, and potential foster parents. Members of these types of groups often have had experiences that they can share, which are often more credible to others in the group be-cause they share similar backgrounds.

The fourth factor, "altruism," describes the way a member's self-concept is enhanced because of helping other members. This factor has been described by Bloch and Crouch(1985) as follows:

> Altruism operates when the patient: offers support, reassurance, sugges-tions, or comments to help other group members; shares similar problems with the purpose of helping other members; feels a sense of being needed and helpful; can forget about himself [sic] in favor of another member; and recognizes that he [sic] wants to do something for a fellow member. (p. 192)

Altruism is unique to group work as compared to individual work, although it occurs for somewhat different reasons in family work, as part of the responsi-bility family members have for one another. It represents an important value to foster in society—namely, that we have responsibilities for each other. It also reflects the long-standing value placed upon mutual aid by social workers with groups

The fifth factor, "learning from interpersonal action," is defined as "the attempt to relate constructively and adaptively within the group, either by imi-tating some behavior or responding to other group members" (Bloch & Crouch, 1985). This specifically happens as members clarify their relationships to oth-ers in the group or try out new ways of interacting with other members.

The sixth factor is "vicarious learning." The group provides many oppor-tunities for members to observe how other members act or describe how they acted under specified circumstances. Sometimes this occurs when simulations such as role-plays are deliberately introduced to provide models. It may also occur spontaneously, as the member attends to how others in the group respond to group events.

The seventh factor, "insight," occurs when the group members learn something important about themselves. This results from the feedback members provide to one another about how they behave, view themselves, and think about what causes them to act as they do and how they think others see them. Members often accept this kind of feedback more readily from others in the group than from a professional group worker because of the similarity in their backgrounds and experiences.

The eighth factor, "acceptance," refers to the idea that the members value the group, identify with it, and see themselves as important to other members. Many members of treatment groups have felt rejected in social situations. The therapeutic group may be one of the few places where they feel fully accepted. This is different from acceptance by professionals, whom clients often see as being "paid" for their concern. The other members do not "have to" express caring, yet, as group workers will attest, it almost always emerges. One of the main tasks of the worker, nevertheless, is to foster caring and to work to remove barriers that stand in the way of its existence.

The ninth factor, "catharsis," refers to an emotional release of feelings, such as anger, affection, or sorrow. Treatment groups typically develop norms that support the expression of emotions. Members observe other members expressing themselves in this way, and members are helped by each other to feel safe and accepted, no matter what emotions are expressed. Anger often requires a more mature group. Members in a new group may think it is unacceptable to express this emotion and may also be frightened by its expression unless the group has become a safe place to deal with it.

The tenth factor, "self-disclosure," refers to a member sharing personal information with the group. In groups, a unique type of disclosure is for the members to reveal how they think and feel about the group and its members. In groups in which a sufficient degree of trust has been established and some members have initiated the self-disclosure process, a member's self-disclosure may be the first time he or she has told others about traumatic life events.

ASSESSMENT

Before clients enter a group, it is prudent for the group worker to assess their experiences, thoughts, and feelings related to groups. The following questions are posed:

- What have been the clients' previous group experiences? Specifically, in what kinds of groups have they held membership? Were these groups satisfying or dissatisfying? What roles did they play in these groups?
- What do the clients think the group work experience will be like? What are their expectations? What do they look forward to, as well as what do they fear?

- How do clients see themselves as behaving in groups? Are they assertive or passive? How do they develop relationships in groups? Do they talk a great deal or seldom?

It is impossible to state that group work should be used with people who have particular diagnoses, whereas individual work should be used with others. Groups, however, do have a special value for clients who wish to work on intimacy and relationship issues. The group provides the opportunity for members to experiment with different ways of relating to others and to obtain feedback on and support for their efforts. Thus the presence of these issues should be assessed.

Several circumstances must be assessed in referring clients to groups. One is whether the client wishes to be in a group. Some are very concerned about confidentiality issues. Others have too much anxiety about group membership. Still others may find the need to share the attention of the worker with other members as too stressful.

It is possible that the client may wish to be in a group, and the group worker also sees this as desirable, yet an appropriate group is not available. As we shall discuss later, an effective group is based on creating a group with a suitable set of members. Even if an appropriate set of potential members is available, the clients may not be available at the same time or be able to travel to the location of the group.[1]

THE THERAPEUTIC PROCESS

Groups progress through phases over time, with specific therapeutic processes pertinent to each phase. The simplest formulation is to divide the group into a pre-group phase, a formation phase, a middle phase, and an ending phase. These phases will differ depending on whether the group is short-term (e.g., six sessions) or long-term (e.g., 6 months or more) and whether the group content is highly prescribed or is determined from moment to moment on the basis of the interactions taking place. Obviously, there is quite a discrepancy between six sessions and 6 months. It is impossible in a short chapter to discuss the developmental variations in each type of group, so only the most general principles are presented.

We recommend that group experiences be offered to members of the Shore family. Nancy has many issues concerning her role in the family and might like to utilize a group of women whose members are struggling to handle the many stresses they experience in their families. I will use Nancy's likely experiences in a group to illustrate how these experiences may vary at different stages of group development. Charley also might benefit from a group of men whose members are unable to meet the standards they have set for themselves and who are exploring their views of manhood. Rena could benefit from a short-term group of adults dealing with their identities as persons who have been adopted. Rena could also benefit from a longer-term group of young adults who are confused about their goals as independent adults. Michael might be helped by membership in a peer group working on social skills.

Pre-Group Phase

One of the first activities of the group worker prior to the first meeting of the group is to determine who to invite to join the group, a process known as "group composition." At times, the group is composed of people who already constitute a group, referred to as a "natural group." Examples of such groups are people living together in an institution or adolescents in a gang. At other times, the group worker selects members for the group, referred to as a "formed group."

Some of the characteristics group workers consider in choosing members are age, social class, social skills, gender, ethnicity, and how the individual is likely to behave. Gender and ethnicity are particularly important, because the dynamics of the group are affected by gender composition and cultural expectations. This is especially true when the person is a member of an oppressed group, such as African Americans, Native Americans, Asians, or Latinos. A general principle is to not compose a group in which a person, by virtue of ethnicity or gender represents a small minority of one or two within the group. This person may experience little in common with other members and may be seen as a representative of a particular group rather than as an individual. The only female African American in a group is often asked what all women or African Americans think or feel!

Sometimes group workers will create a group in which all members are of a single ethnicity or gender. This can enhance the members' work on identity issues or provide them with a high degree of social support.

Of equal importance is the gender composition of the group. Martin and Shanahan (1983), in their discussion of this topic, make the following points:

1. Even without interpersonal interaction (e.g., verbal exchanges), females are negatively "evaluated" in all-male groups and in groups in which they are tokens.
2. The quantity and the content of verbal interaction in groups vary with the sex composition of the group and by the gender of the participant. For example, women talk less frequently and are talked to less frequently in mixed groups than in all-female groups; men in all-male groups tend to concentrate on competition and status topics, whereas females in all-female groups focus on personal, home, and family topics.
3. Females are perceived less positively than males, even when they are equally influential.
4. "Solo" or "token" females, in otherwise male groups, tend to fare poorly.

In summarizing some of the literature on this subject, we concluded the following (Garvin, 1997):

In contrast to the many stresses with which women have to cope, men experience much that is valuable in mixed groups. Men are more likely to be "personal" and less competitive and disagreeable under these circumstances than when in all-male groups. Nevertheless, group leaders find that they have to discourage men from talking too much and from becoming overly competitive with one another in mixed groups.

Finally, in all-male groups, the worker must help the men accept more intimacy and self-disclosure than they might otherwise adopt. They must similarly be helped to deal with too much competition and conflict.

Two other variables to consider in group composition are the purpose of the group and the likelihood the group will become a cohesive one. The composition must support the purpose. Examples are a group to help Native American adolescents work on their identity, in which all members were of that ethnicity; a group to help men and women develop more comfortable relationships with each other, which had an equal number of men and women; and a group to help people develop safe ways of dealing with angry feelings, in which all members sought help with this type of problem. A group is more likely to become cohesive if the members can find other members whom they see as similar in some ways to themselves.

Finally, the group worker will determine the size of the group. Most writers have recommended that treatment groups have about seven members. This number can vary, depending on the purpose of the group. Smaller groups demand and produce intimacy, and pressure is usually exerted to have everyone participate. Larger groups allow some members to have a low level of participation, although having the group divide into subgroups will sometimes offset this.

Members are more likely to benefit from the group if they are prepared for it; thus, we strongly urge group workers to have a meeting with each member individually before the group begins (Garvin, 1997). A pre-group individual meeting allows members to discuss their reactions to group placement (Northen, 1969) and to learn about the rationale and the process of the treatment (Goldstein, Heller, & Sechrest, 1966). Because many problems deal with relationship issues, the group worker should explain that the group will work on these in ways that will transfer to interactions outside the group (Yalom, 1995).

Formation Phase

During the formation phase, the group members in conjunction with the group worker clarify the purpose of the group, determine group and individual goals, decide on group norms and rules, start to form relationships, and deal with member ambivalence about the group experience. Both the members and the group worker will gather information to choose effective ways of attaining goals. In treatment groups this is seen as an assessment process. The members and the group worker are essentially engaged in a contracting process. Whether in oral or written form, the contract consists of an agreement on goals and the means of reaching them, rules to be followed, fees, time and frequency of meetings, and mutual obligations of members and the group worker. If agreement among members does not occur, this becomes an issue for the entire group to face and to seek to resolve in ways that are therapeutic for members.

During this formation phase, Nancy will have an opportunity to talk about the stresses she experiences in the family. She will be likely to learn that other women in the group have similar problems. This will help her to feel less isolated in her struggles and to experience a sense of relief that she is not unique in this respect. Others can provide her with empathy and support. She will also have the opportunity to formulate specific goals, such as identifying strategies for coping with Rena or enrolling in a weight-reduction program.

Even though goals were discussed individually during the pre-phase interview, when the members were confronted with the reality of what the other members were like, they may wish to rethink their individual purposes. Thus, a *group* discussion of goals and purposes is essential.

Norms and rules must also be discussed. Norms regarding confidentiality, honest communication, and attendance are fundamental. Other norms should relate to group purpose. If members, for example, have problems with violence, a rule might be that no one is permitted to strike or threaten others. If members have problems with substances, a rule might be that members are not to use these substances just prior to or during a meeting.

Members are likely to approach the group with ambivalence. This is because they might be anxious about whether others will accept them and whether they will find the group content upsetting. On the other hand, if they have volunteered to join the group, they may have positive feelings about the group. A discussion of these feelings can reinforce positive expectations and alleviate fears.

Some treatment groups are involuntary, in that members are forced to come by an external source. Examples of external sources are court orders, the threat of losing one's job, or fear that a spouse will terminate a marriage if the individual does not obtain treatment. Some agencies, particularly residential ones such as hospitals, prisons, and even schools, insist that individuals attend a treatment group. These types of groups are discussed extensively by Rooney (1992) and Garvin (1997). A basic principle of work with such groups is to find a common ground between agency and member purposes, so that the members become willing to participate. The members' reactions to forced attendance must be recognized, discussed, and, ultimately, respected.

From the beginning, the group worker should be conscious of developing relationships among the members and between the members and the group worker. The former is often attended to through the use of an activity (sometimes called an ice-breaker) that promotes informal interaction among the members. In a more formal treatment group, members are usually encouraged to tell something about themselves in an initial "go around" and to discover similarities among each other. The group worker should remember that the basic principles of empathy, genuineness, and warmth (Schulman, 1978) are as important in group situations as they are in one-to-one helping.

When members clarify purposes, begin to relate to one another, establish goals, and create ground rules, they are ready to focus on the methods they will utilize to reach these goals. This is a sign that the group is moving into its middle phase.

Middle Phase

During the middle phase, the group develops a number of group conditions that will help accomplish its purposes. These include members taking on leadership roles, creating group and individual tasks, and determining ways of solving group and individual problems. Norms must be established for dealing with disagreements and conflicts.

A process that occurs in many groups early in the middle stage is that, after initial agreements have been reached, the group enters a period of conflict. Garland, Jones, and Kolodny (1965) refer to this as a "power and control" phase, whereas Sarri and Galinsky (1985) call it a "revision" phase. At this time the leadership of either the group worker or the members is challenged, and goals and activities are questioned.

As groups face internal conflicts, the group worker must support the group so that cohesiveness does not seriously decline, thus jeopardizing the future of the group. Cohesiveness can be maintained by helping the group to learn constructive ways of resolving conflicts, review leadership patterns, and reformulate goals.

After "revision" phases, the group returns with new energy to its tasks. The group worker should recognize, however, that this greater sense of closeness might cause members to see only their commonalties, rather than their differences. The group worker should be sensitive to members' needs to maintain their individuality. We shall now discuss in general terms the ways that group workers help members attain their goals, help create a group that is conducive to individual goal attainment, and help the members to manage forces outside of the group. Although the group worker is responsible for being aware of the forces that affect the group and for helping the members cope with these forces, we also believe members are responsible, to the extent their abilities will allow, for what happens in the group. The concept of *empowerment* is important here, as members learn to take charge of their lives and seek change in forces that impede them from doing so (Lee, 2001).

The group worker will help members attain their goals through interacting with individual members during group sessions and through facilitating the emergence of group conditions that will be beneficial to members. We assert that the latter should be the primary vehicle for individual change; we agree with virtually all group workers that the main emphasis should be on helping the group to become a strong system of mutual aid, in which members help one another. Nevertheless, there are times when the group worker's interaction with a member is timely and when the group worker can model ways that members can help one another.

The following are some of the main ways group workers interact with members for therapeutic purposes:

- Group workers point out an irrational belief, such as that the member must be loved and respected by everyone (Ellis & Harper, 1975).
- Group workers enhance members' awareness of themselves or others through making a psychological interpretation or pointing out how a member attributes causes of events.
- Group workers reinforce desirable behaviors, such as complimenting a member for something the member has done.
- Group workers model a behavior through actually participating in a role-play or through expressing empathy and warmth when this is appropriate.
- Group workers help members deal with feelings, sometimes in tangible ways, such as helping members to relax.
- Group workers can express values that will be useful to a member. Schwartz referred to this type of expression as "lending a vision" (Schwartz, 1961).
- Group workers can make assignments to members. When the assignment will take place outside of the group, it is often referred to as "homework." Another assignment in the group is to ask the member to take part in a role-play.

The essence of group work is to help the group to be the main source of therapeutic change for its members. Group interactions can have a major impact on how members view reality. We are more likely to see things in a particular way if several other people also see it that way. This is a two-edged sword, as members can also collectively support "false" views. Thus, when there is some question as to the accuracy of the members' views, the group worker will inquire as to how other group members see the same event.

One of the main tools used by group workers in treatment groups is the "process commentary." This is introduced by the group worker or one of the members by calling attention to an interaction that has just occurred in the group.[2] This type of attention usually leads to an examination of what one member said, what the intent was, how it was perceived by another, and what the second party intended by her or his response. The ultimate question is whether these initial and subsequent responses help the members to realize their relationship goals. When this movement forward is not the case, members can experiment with other responses and subject these, in turn, to the same kind of examination. As the members learn this type of reflection in the group, they can apply it to relationships outside of the group (Garvin, 1997).

One of the most important processes used in group treatment is "problem solving." At times, the "problem" is one related to an individual member; at other times, it is a group problem, such as whether a particular rule should be adopted. In the former situation, the group should not impose a solution on a member. It is beneficial to use the well-accepted phases of problem solving: clear specification of the problem, collection of information relevant to the problem, identification of alternative solutions, evaluation of alternatives, selection of the most desirable alternative, and implementation of that solution.

Social workers have made a major contribution to the group therapy field through their recognition that therapeutic processes may be rooted in activities other than discussion.[3] Group workers have used a variety of media, such as games, crafts, music, drama, cooking, and dance, to help members understand themselves and others better, communicate their feelings, and increase their self-esteem (Middleman, 1968).

During the middle phase of the group, Nancy will be helped to examine the ways that she interacts with Rena that result in conflict. She will consider, with input from other group members, ways of responding to Rena that will lead to a reduction of conflicts. She is likely to be given the opportunity to observe other members role-playing the use of these ways and then enter into the role-play herself and obtain feedback as to how well she is using these skills and how she might improve on this. She is also likely to report to the group the information she has obtained about weight-reduction programs. The members will help her make the decision as to which program to join. After this, they will support her participation in the program and will help her address any barriers to participation she may encounter.

The members will also point out to Nancy how she interacts with them and how she behaves in the group. At times, Nancy may have interactions with other group members that replicate her way of relating to Rena. When members point this out, the effect will be very powerful, as Nancy receives immediate "here and now" feedback from people she cares about and who care for her.

Ending Phase

A variety of ending circumstances are possible in a group, such as all members terminating together or some members leaving the group while others continue. Members may also leave because they have accomplished their purposes or because they do not see the group as helping them. We cannot deal with all of these circumstances here but have discussed them more thoroughly elsewhere (Garvin, 1997). The ending phase may be accomplished in one session in a short-term group or over several sessions in a long-term group. In general, the group worker seeks to accomplish the following when the group ends for some or all of the members:[4]

- Members evaluate the group in relationship to achievement of its goals. This can be accomplished through discussion or through the use of simple questionnaires that are summarized and discussed.
- Members seek to understand and cope with their feelings about termination.
- Members seek ways of maintaining the beneficial changes resulting from the group experience.
- Members explore how to utilize the skills, the attitudes, and the knowledge

gained through the group in a broader array of circumstances than the ones discussed during the previous sessions.

• Members identify new experiences and services to draw upon and to continue the process of learning and personal growth.

When Nancy has attained her goals, she will be helped to terminate from the group, which is likely to be ongoing. The members will review the progress Nancy has made in attaining her goals. They will help her express her regrets on leaving the group because of the relationships she has made there. They also will hold a small ceremony to mark her departure.

APPLICATION TO DIVERSITY

The diversity issue that we have chosen for this chapter is gender.[5] Social workers and others engaged in therapy have understood too little about differences in the socialization and the societal treatment of men and women. The ways in which women have been oppressed in many social institutions have also not been taken into account. Although there has been progress, women still are disadvantaged in many work situations, are frequently treated in sexist ways in social situations, and are usually the ones victimized in cases of domestic violence.

Many theories of development have been created as though male development were the norm as to what is healthy for all human beings. These theories have discussed issues such as goal orientations, socialization of emotions, and the responses of people to competition and power, as if both men and women progress in the same way (DeChant, 1996).

With reference to this issue, we have stated elsewhere (Garvin & Reed, 1983), that

> a sex role perspective alone emphasizes the complementarity of male and female roles, but ignores the process of power and prestige ordering that occurs when men and women interact. There is considerable evidence that women's and men's roles are not valued equally by society, that men's contributions are more valued than women's not only monetarily, but also in terms of status and prestige, and that these status differences influence male and female behaviors in group settings. . . . People who have more status display both verbal and nonverbal behaviors that indicate more dominance and power (they talk more often, address the entire group, are less personal); those with lower status are more deferent verbally and nonverbally. Those socialized for higher status positions often resist accepting this view of themselves and its possible consequences, and may fear that role change will lead to a loss of some advantages associated with the higher status. Those with lower status are likely to have incorporated some of the consequences of this position into their self-image and worldview. Self esteem is often low, they may feel very isolated, and are more likely to blame themselves for their circumstances.

A difficulty in exploring this issue is that it is difficult to disentangle genetic effects from those of socialization. Nevertheless, there is a rapidly growing literature that creates new insights into this topic. Social workers, and certainly group workers, must study this or take the risk of doing a vast disservice to clients, especially female ones (DeChant, 1996; Reed & Garvin, 1983).

Obviously, much more can be said about the subject of gender, but the previous material should alert the reader to some of the salient issues. Let us now apply the subject of a gendered analysis to answer the question, "How would the paradigm under discussion be adapted to assist family members, especially those who are women, if the worker were appropriately sensitive to gender issues and gender oppression and if one or more of these family members received group work services?"

- Social justice and social change are major goals. This implies a critique of the status quo and a view of a socially just world for women and girls. This may initially be approached by raising the consciousness of group members about gender as a source of oppression in the family, the agency, the community, and the larger society.
- One of the value issues for the group involves an examination of feminist values, theory, and knowledge. This does not imply that a treatment group becomes a study group, but that these issues are raised whenever appropriate to the content of the group. These values emphasize women's strengths and are validated by learning from women's experiences.
- The group should engage in self-reflection and consciousness raising. This includes observance of one's gendered socialization. Another topic to which attention should be paid is examining one's sources of both privilege and disadvantage. A White woman, for example, may be confused by how her Whiteness privileges her and how her gender is a source of oppression.
- The group should pay attention to process. We have stated earlier that this is an important tool in group work. It has special meaning as the group members examine their processes because these reflect gender attitudes within the group.
- The group should recognize that the personal is political. This means that members are helped to see how their difficulties are often maintained by gender discrimination occurring in larger systems, such as the family and the workplace. Too often, women blame themselves for failings to which societal factors contribute.
- Power issues should be examined so that members, in affirming ways, can use power (see Reed & Garvin, 1996, p. 34). In practice, power is usually reframed as power *with* others, rather than power *over* others; as arising from collective processes, rather than from individual achievement. Group psychotherapy can provide an arena in which participants can practice alternative forms of power and also where they can learn to recognize and confront manifestations of power differences that are unhealthy or oppressive.

- The group should incorporate regular and continuous mechanisms for examining gendering and other culturally based assumptions and processes.
- The meaning of words and symbols should be examined when these maintain gender-based oppression. These include beliefs about the family, religious teachings, and perceptions of biological factors.
- The group should examine and strengthen relationships among women, including mother–daughter relationships.

A number of the women in the Shore family have problems that can be viewed through the lens just described. Nancy describes herself as "grossly obese." This can have a personal component in terms of her actual weight. It also reflects social stereotypes about the female figure, stereotypes that are often imposed on women by men with whom they interact. A feminist-oriented group would be especially attuned to discussing such societal issues and will help members confront such societal stereotypes when they occur.

Nancy also has the role of "trying to get everything fixed." Women in families are often pressured by society to carry a role overload of solving all the problems in the family. Assuming the responsibilities of landlord adds to this overload. Nancy is also depressed, which is often a response of women who face their oppressive circumstances by turning their emotions inward.

Rena and Nancy often see each other as adversaries. They do not see the possibilities inherent in their shared roles as women and the ways they can support one another. Rena's desire to have a positive coalition with another woman is also reflected in her search for her birth mother.

Charley assumes that he has the right to impose his will on Rena through the use of force. Charley seems to assume a stereotypical male role that demands self-sufficiency. The idea of accepting help is repellant to him. He resorts to lying, rather than admitting any inadequacies to his wife.

These are only a few of the gender-related issues and their personal and social antecedents that might be considered in a group work experience, in which gender sensitivity and feminist insights on the part of the group worker are important. We have discussed in the course of this chapter the possible ways in which a group work experience could be beneficial to members of the Shore family.

RESEARCH

The scientific findings that inform group work practice come from three sources. One is research on groups conducted by social scientists. The second is research on group work by social workers. The third is research on group therapy by investigators from allied professions.

Because group research is so voluminous, group workers often utilize one of several volumes in which authorities in the field present excellent summaries of research. These summaries are organized around such phenomena as communication processes, member interactions, interpersonal attraction, co-hesion, power, interpersonal influence, group culture, group development, and group norms (Forsyth, 1999; Hare, Blumberg, Davies, & Kent, 1995; McGrath, 1984).

Increasingly, group workers are employing well-developed research tools to examine both processes and outcomes of social work groups. Although much of the research is quantitative, an increased interest exists in employing quali-tative research but in a more rigorous fashion than these case studies were previously presented. It is likely that even the case study approach will borrow ideas from such fields as anthropology, which seek to validly capture not only a series of events but the meaning that participants attach to these events. Group workers have also been employing single-system methods to examine data collected over time from a single system such as a group (Toseland & Rivas, 2001). This can be applied to changes in individual members or to the group as a whole. Single-system methods compare baseline data to post-intervention data.

An important contribution was made by Toseland and Siporin (1986), who reported on studies comparing group to individual treatment. They reported that group treatment was found to be more effective than individual treatment in 25% of the studies reviewed, and that individual treatment was not found more effective than group treatment in any of the studies. However, group work was found to be the most efficient use of resources. This review did not identify any clear findings as to the types of problems for which group work was the most effective approach. In a subsequent report, Toseland and his col-leagues did find that group work is likely to be more effective than individual for increasing social support and less effective for intense interpersonal prob-lems (Toseland, Rossiter, Peak & Smith, 1990).

Reports on the effectiveness of group work are presented in most of the issues of the journal *Social Work With Groups*. In addition, many group work-ers publish the results of their work in the *International Journal of Group Psycho-therapy*. Group workers draw on the extensive research literature on group psychotherapy. Bednar and Kaul (1994) have periodically summarized this lit-erature and in a recent publication reiterated their assertion that group treat-ment has been shown to be effective in a broad array of circumstances. A recent publication by Beck and Lewis (2000) moved the entire field of group psycho-therapy research forward, with a large volume presenting information on re-search approaches to studying group processes, particularly in psychotherapeutic groups.

LIMITATIONS OF THE MODEL

One of the main problems in offering a group work service is the difficulty in arranging a time and a place that make it possible for the potential members of the group to attend. This is one of the reasons for creating groups that "meet" over the telephone or the computer. Another is that, although choosing members to be in a group is not an exact science, the potential compatibility of members is important. It can also add to the difficulty of forming a group if the potentially "right" array of people is not available, with reference to time and place.

Agency conditions also create difficulties. Many agencies were not designed to have a meeting room that is appropriate for a small group. In addition, the value of group work may not be appreciated, and groups may meet in places that have the distractions of people passing through, or members in residential settings may be called out for other appointments, as if the group were incidental to their treatment.

There is also the assumption in some settings that group work skills are not important and that anyone can conduct a group. This leads to groups that are not focused and whose purposes and methods are unclear to participants, who are simply asked "What do you want to talk about today?" with no parameters for the discussion to take place.

SUMMARY

This chapter stressed the idea that group work is important because humans are social beings and live much of their lives in groups. The history of group work illustrates how this understanding was used to create a large number of institutions and educational activities devoted to group work. Out of this, a number of important concepts evolved, such as mutual aid, group process, and achieving autonomy through groups. Group development became a central concept, as well as the idea that over time, groups conducted for therapeutic purposes draw upon a set of therapeutic factors that can emerge in groups.

This chapter takes the reader through the stages of group development and the nature of group worker and group tasks in each stage. Finally, the chapter illustrates the special issues that emerge when we seek to understand how gender diversity affects the nature of the group experience. The chapter concludes with a discussion of how research is used by group workers and the limitations these workers face in their practice.

NOTES

1. Increasingly, group workers are creating groups in which members communicate over the telephone or on computers. This allows people to form a group even if they cannot meet at the same place or at the same time. This topic goes beyond the scope of this chapter, but an extended discussion of it may be found in Meier (in press).
2. This is also referred to as "here and now" focus.
3. Group workers usually refer to this as "the program."
4. These steps are not necessarily in the order in which they occur.
5. We go further in our thinking than taking only gender into account. Our perspective is informed by feminist ideas that see women as oppressed by social institutions oriented to maintaining male power. Thus, a feminist perspective takes seriously the concept that "the personal is political" and that the solutions to individual problems should be understood within a social context, and therapeutic goals should include both individual and social change.

REFERENCES

Beck, A. P., & Lewis, C. M. (Eds.). (2000). *The process of group psychotherapy: Systems for analyzing change.* Washington, DC: American Psychological Association.

Bednar, R. L., & Kaul, T. (1994). Experiential group research. In A. E. Bergin & S. L. Garfield (Eds.), *Handbook of psychotherapy and behavior change* (4th ed., pp. 631–663). New York: Wiley.

Bloch, S., & Crouch, E. (1985). *Therapeutic factors in group psychotherapy.* New York: Oxford.

DeChant, B. (Ed.). (1996). *Women and group psychotherapy: Theory and practice.* New York: Guilford Press.

Ellis, A., & R. A. Harper (1975). *A new guide to rational living.* North Hollywood, CA: Wilshire Book.

Forsyth, D. (1999). *Group dynamics* (3rd ed). Belmont, CA: Wadsworth.

Garland, J. A., Jones, H. E., & Kolodny, R. (1965) A model for stages of development in social work groups. In S. Bernstein (Ed.), *Explorations in group work* (pp. 17–71). Boston: Boston University School of Social Work.

Garvin, C. D. (1987). Group theory and research. In *Encyclopedia of social work* (18th ed.,Vol. 1, pp. 682–696). New York: National Association of Social Workers.

Garvin, C. D. (1997). *Contemporary group work.* Boston: Allyn & Bacon.

Garvin, C. D., & Reed, B. G. (1983). Gender issues in social group work: An overview. In B.G. Reed and C. D. Garvin (Eds.), *Groupwork with women/Groupwork with men: An overview of gender issues in social groupwork practice* (pp. 5–18). New York: Haworth Press.

Goldstein, A., Heller, K., & Sechrest, L. (1966). *Psychotherapy and the psychology of behavior change.* New York: Wiley.

Hare, A. P., Blumberg, H. H., Davies, M. F., & Kent, M. V. (1995). *Small group research: A handbook.* Norwood, NJ: Ablex.

Konopka, G. (1949). *Therapeutic group work with children.* Minneapolis: University of Minnesota Press.

Lee, J. A. B. (2001). *The empowerment approach to social work practice: Building the beloved community* (2nd ed.). New York: Columbia University Press.

Martin, P. Y. & Shanahan, K. A. (1983). Transcending the effects of sex composition in small groups. *Social Work With Groups, VI,* 19–32.

McGrath, J. (1984). *Groups: Interaction and performance.* Englewood Cliffs, NJ: Prentice-Hall.

Meier, A. (in press). Group work with technology mediated groups. In C. D. Garvin, L. Gutierrez, & M. Galinsky (Eds.), *Handbook of social work with groups.* New York: Guilford Press.

Middleman, R. R. (1968).*The non-verbal method in working with groups.* New York: Association Press.

Middleman, R. R., & Goldberg, G. (1987). Social work practice with groups. In A. Minahan (Ed.), *Encyclopedia of social work* (8th ed., pp. 714–729). Silver Spring, MD: National Association of Social Workers.

Northen, H. (1969). *Social work with groups.* New York: Columbia University Press.

Papell, C. P., & Rothman, B. (1966). Social group work models: Possession and heritage. *Journal of Education for Social Work, 2*(2), 66–77.

Reed, B. G., & Garvin, C. D. (Eds.). (1983). *Groupwork with women/Groupwork with men: An overview of gender issues in social groupwork practice* (pp. 5–18). New York: Haworth Press.

Reed, B. G., & Garvin, C. D. (1996). Feminist thought and group psychotherapy: Feminist principles as praxis. In B. DeChant (Ed.), *Women and group psychotherapy: Theory and practice* (pp. 15–49) New York: Guilford Press.

Rooney, R. (1992). *Strategies for work with involuntary clients.* New York: Columbia University Press.

Sarri, R., & Galinsky, M. (1985). A conceptual framework for group development. In M. Sundel, P. Glasser, R. Sarri, & R. Vinter (Eds.), *Individual change through small groups* (2nd ed., pp. 70–86). New York: Free Press.

Schulman, E. D. (1978) *Intervention in human services* (2nd ed.). St. Louis, MO: Mosby.

Schwartz, W. (1971). Social group work: The interactionist approach. In *Encyclopedia of social work* (Vol. 2, pp. 1252–1263), Edwards, Ed. New York: National Association of Social Workers.

Schwartz, W. (1961). The social worker in the group. In *New perspectives on service to groups* (pp. 7–29). New York: Columbia University Press.

Toseland, R., Rossiter, C., Peak, T., & Smith, G. (1990) Comparative effectiveness of individual and group interventions to support family caregivers. *Social Work, 35*(3), 209–219.

Toseland, R., & Siporin, M. (1986). When to recommend group treatment: A review of the clinical and research literature. *International Journal of Group Psychotherapy, 36*(2), 171–201.

Toseland, R. W., & Rivas, R. F. (2001). *An introduction to group work practice* (4th ed.). Boston: Allyn & Bacon.

Trecker, H. B. (Ed.). (1955). *Group work: Foundations and frontiers*. New York: Whiteside.

Vinter, R. D. (1959). Group work: Perspectives and prospects. In *Social work with small groups* (pp. 128–149). New York: National Association of Social Workers.

Yalom, I. D. (1995). *The theory and practice of group psychotherapy* (4th ed.). New York: Basic Books.

9

Constructual Marital Therapy

Emphasis on a Chinese Immigrant Family

Marshall Jung, DSW

INTRODUCTION

Constructual marital therapy (CMT) is a complex, comprehensive, and pragmatic model of therapy designed to help couples in conflict. *Constructual* is derived from the Latin word *construct,* meaning "to build up." This paradigm, in a systematic manner, builds upon and allows for the integration of other theoretical concepts and models of practice. CMT describes the foundation upon which a successful modern relationship is built: love, trust, hope, friendship, and respect. It is defined here as "the covenant marriage" and is inclusive of all unions. I will present the principles of practice and the rationale from which those principles were derived for use in clinical interventions. Each feature of the CMT framework draws from those models of practice and theory deemed appropriate for conceptualization, diagnosis, planning, or intervention. The model allows freedom for therapists to select from their own body of knowledge and experience in theoretical concepts and principles of practice that lead couples to travel together on a clear and harmonious path (Jung, 1993).

Constructual marital therapy assumes that there must be many ways to approach couples in therapy, for each couple brings its members' personality characteristics, psychological profile, developmental history, expectancies, gender orientation, and cultural background. Practitioners face the challenge of adapting to the unique requests and characteristics of their clients, while collaborating with them in selecting suitable interventions. CMT allows for that kind of adaptation.

Like most models in the field of couple's therapy, CMT was originally designed to meet the needs of Western couples. With this in mind, the model will be applied to the Shore family. The case vignette will be used to demonstrate theoretical, philosophical, and spiritual concepts; principles of practice; and techniques underpinning the model. The model will then be applied to the Wongs, a "traditional Chinese immigrant family," highlighting the cultural issues that must be addressed and how the CMT can be easily adapted to take into consideration those factors.

THE CONCEPT OF THE PERSON AND THE HUMAN EXPERIENCE

Dignity, integrity, goodness, and the desire to give and receive love are inherent at birth. Given a supportive, understanding, and nurturing environment in which to grow, children are loving, playful, curious, and fascinated with the wonder and the beauty that surrounds them. They ask for nothing but to be loved for being themselves. If their natural gifts are recognized and affirmed, they will grow into loving, responsible, and charitable adults, filled with gratitude for their family, friendships, and opportunities.

Unfortunately, many children face several issues impeding them from developing into loving human beings. These issues include child abuse, institutional racism, poverty, mental illness, developmental and learning disabilities, and physical and medical problems. These impediments can perpetuate fear, trauma, and psychological insecurities, robbing people of their self-respect and placing them in an emotional prison. However, a silent voice within each human being calls that individual to live a life of integrity, a life that honors the authentic self, a life that lives in hope.

Human growth and development are not linear, predetermined, or static; they are evolutionary, developmental, and unpredictable. Human development is a constant process of change, a process of constructing, deconstructing, and reconstructing reality. This process is contained within and heavily influenced by our physical characteristics, personality, gender, intelligence, vulnerabilities, predispositions, and the culture in which we are raised. However, how we ultimately organize and interpret our perceptions and internalize our values, beliefs, and attitudes is unique to each individual and remains a mystery.

We must learn to acclimatize and adapt to the constant changes that take place around us, if we are to grow intellectually, emotionally, interpersonally, psychologically, and spiritually. We must also learn to integrate our life experiences if we are to find solitude, recognize and appreciate our uniqueness, and discover the reasons for our existence. This process of integration includes finding peace with the past, learning to live in the present, and remaining hopeful toward the future.

HISTORICAL PERSPECTIVE

The field of couple's therapy is rooted in three sources: (1) Sigmund Freud and his medical and scientific approach to mental illness (Freud, 1904; Freud, 1940); (2) the application of systems theory to understand families, beginning with Gregory Bateson's 1952–1962 research project on communication (Bateson, 1971); and (3) pastoral counseling.

Freud's psychoanalytic model of treatment of chronic mental illness moved the approach to working with the mentally ill out of the Dark Ages and opened the door for exploring individual dysfunction from a scientific, rather than a religious, perspective. Numerous theories evolved from his work in an effort to try to understand human growth and development. These theories and the models were later applied to couples and families; they included psychoanalytic couple and family therapy (Bader & Pearson, 1988; Jurg, 1975; Nadelson, 1978; Scharff, 1995), behavioral couple and family therapy (Fallon, 1988; Greer & Zurilla, 1975; Jacobson & Margolin, 1979; Lester, Beckham, & Baucom, 1989; Stuart, 1980), cognitive couple and family therapy (Ables, 1977; Baucom & Epstein, 1990; Ellis, Sidrel, Yeager, DiMattia, & Di Giuseppe, 1989), and gestalt couple and family therapy (Hale, 1978; Hatcher & Himelstein, 1978).

The main shift from viewing individual dysfunction from an intrapsychic phenomenon to a systemic perspective began in the 1950s and 1960s with the efforts of the Palo Alto family researchers. Major contributors of the family therapy movement include Nathan Ackerman in New York; Murray Bowen in Topeka and Washington, D.C.; Lyman Wynne and Margaret Singer at the National Institute of Mental Health in Bethesda; Carl Whitaker in Atlanta; Salvador Minuchin and E. H. Auerswald at the Wiltwyck School in New York State; Theodore Lidz and Stephen Fleck at Yale; and Gregory Bateson, Don Jackson, Jay Haley, John Weakland, Paul Watzlawick, John Bell, and Virginia Satir in Palo Alto (Hoffman, 1981). Family therapists believe that the etiology of individual dysfunction is embedded in the family system rather than in the person. Attempts at reconciling or integrating the two perspectives followed, with paradigms such as object relations (Scharff & Scharff, 1987; Slipp, 1995), contextual (Boszormenyi-Nagy & Spark, 1973; Goldenthal, 1996), and multimodal theory and practice (Lazarus, 1981).

Pastoral counseling is rooted in religion, with priests, pastors, and rabbis helping and giving advice to couples on ways to reconcile differences and live in spiritual and interpersonal harmony. These religious leaders recognized the need for more knowledge and skills to help couples, and looked to the family therapy movement for guidance and assistance. Under the leadership of the American Association of Marital and Family Therapists, graduate schools for marriage and family therapy emerged in the 1960s and 1970s. Participation in the movement immediately broadened and began to include anyone seeking a professional degree to assist children, couples, and families in distress.

Constructural marital therapy presents a conceptual framework for understanding marriage and marriage development. Within this framework, treatment begins with the premise that therapists must have numerous models of practice at their disposal when working with couples, and that depending on their clients' unique characteristics, particular issues, circumstances, and defined needs, a treatment model and a method must be based on a "goodness of fit." During the course of therapy, additional models can be integrated into the treatment process.

CMT is centered on love, trust, hope, friendship, respect, and commitment. These concepts are clearly defined in collaboration with the couple. The relationship and its development are shared and discussed. CMT provides therapists with a conceptual framework, in which the issues brought to treatment and circumstances in which they are surrounded can be addressed based on phenomena, rather than on theoretical formulations. For example, if a spouse is ambivalent about remaining in the marriage, individuation therapy using a cognitive or an affective approach may be warranted. In another example, a couple recognizes there is no love in the relationship, but the partners wish to remain together because of their children. In this case, accommodation therapy with a mediation or solution-focused approach can be suggested. In short, CMT is an eclectic, adaptive, collaborative, phenomenally based model of practice.

KEY THEORETICAL CONCEPTS

Constructual marital therapists define modern *marriage* as two individuals coming together freely, based on love, to seek an intimate union for its own sake. Such a relationship consists of the respective autonomy of the two partners and the "we psyche," or their psychological and emotional interdependence. This interdependency becomes more pronounced the longer the members of a couple remain together. It can either guide them to greater internal freedom and discoveries regarding themselves or put them into a psychological and emotional prison, in which they become lost and alienated from their essence. The main task of covenant relationships is the ability to negotiate differences, without attempting to control the other partner. There are six stages leading toward a successful and enriching relationship, defined here as a covenant marriage, through which couples pass as they resolve their differences. The phases are evolutionary but not mutually exclusive, with no particular time limit in which to pass through them. Couples can also move back and forth between stages.

The marital journey begins with the enchantment phase, in which couples "fall in love." In this phase the relationship is based primarily on feelings and romantic love. Partners believe they have found someone who knows, understands, and accepts them completely and unconditionally. There appear to be no differences but rather a sense of oneness. This phase is followed by the disenchantment stage, in which partners recognize their differences (differences that foster feelings of disappointment and create discord). The third, or negotiation, stage is the most difficult. Most couples who seek therapy have remained in this stage. In this phase, partners attempt to resolve their apparent areas of conflict and the marriage is tested. This is where the "hard work" begins, to build a mutually enhancing relationship. To successfully negotiate this phase, partners must learn to enter into discussion with maturity, understanding, and support. In the fourth, or integration, stage, there is relatively little discord, with partners being mutually loving, respectful, and encouraging. If partners don't take their relationship for granted and continue to grow in warmth and affection, they enter into the fifth, or enhancement, stage. Remaining in this phase guides the couple into the sixth, or covenant, stage, in which the partners are living the vows they exchanged and keeping the promises they made to each other to love, honor, cherish, and nurture one another on a daily basis.

The most pronounced means of demonstrating love is the making of loving sacrifices. Such sacrifices establish a relationship in which partners continually take into consideration the feelings, needs, and beliefs of the other, leading to a freeing, rather than a confining, transactional process. This process allows for the flexibility in problem solving that is required for spouses to adapt and accommodate to the main differences they bring into the relationship. Areas of difference include beliefs, habits, values, personality traits, religion, expectations for the relationship, life goals, money management, desire for and needs of children, and expectation for involvement with extended family. In every relationship, adaptation and accommodation can and will be met to some degree with a "bargaining process." In other words, couples will problem solve differences either by finding something that is mutually acceptable or by trading—that is, We will do it your way this time and my way the next time. Although necessary, this latter process is not nearly as enhancing to the relationship as solving problems by giving out of love.

By making loving sacrifices, a relationship is perpetuated that allows for true acceptance of differences, thus encouraging each partner to be whoever he or she can be in the world. In relationships where loving sacrifices do not exist, partners often believe that they accept differences (when in fact they have only accommodated, often begrudgingly). In such relationships, resentment often builds because the accommodation leads to emotional distancing. However, when the giving of a loving sacrifice is received, the partner's thoughts, feelings, and beliefs are validated. This creates feelings of warmth, kindness, and generosity in the receiver, which in turn instills the desire to want to give back, not out of guilt or obligation, but out of a feeling of love. The giving of a loving sacrifice provides tangible evidence to the receiver that he or she is loved. Such evidence makes the receiver feel special and will help each person feel safe and united.

The giving of a loving sacrifice also facilitates trust. Recognizing the tangible evidence of love, partners feel safe in being themselves. This creates an atmosphere in which partners feel they are able to share their deepest, most sensitive thoughts, feelings, and insecurities. When profound trust has been established, spouses know that what is being said can be taken at face value. Each trusts that the other is always acting in good faith and toward a goal of enhancement of the partner.

Finally, in the giving of a loving sacrifice, the giver loses something and in some instances will suffer from the loss. For example, one partner might experience tremendous sadness and loss because of a move made for the other partner's professional advancement. However, at a deeper level, the person who made the sacrifice loses nothing and is actually enhanced, because of the most wonderful feelings engendered from having sacrificed out of feelings of love.

A loving relationship must be based on affectionate, rather than "romantic," love and lived in the ordinary, rather than the extraordinary. This affection is expressed in friendship. In such a context, the expression of affection can be demonstrated in numerous ways—an expression of gratitude, a loving touch, or a thoughtful comment, to name a few.

Loving relationships must also be based on expressions of mutual respect. By treating each other in such a manner, the partners honor each other and themselves. Consequently, the relationship grows not only in love but also in dignity and integrity. The essence of each person is recognized, cherished, and affirmed. The relationship is also enriched by mutual admiration, allowing each partner to influence the other.

Finally, a marriage must be founded on hope, because one does not know what the future holds. This hope looks to the future, based on love and trust that partners will fulfill the promises made to each other. Thus hope is anchored by commitment, in the giving or pledging of the partners' word to one another.

Causes of Conflict

Couples normally seek treatment only after having tried for an extensive period of time to reconcile their conflicts. Consequently, they are often caught in a "negative spiral syndrome." The first coil of the spiral is disagreement. If this is not resolved, it can lead to anger, leading to criticism, leading to the need to control the relationship, leading to defensiveness, leading to insecurity, leading to the absence of trust, leading to the absence of friendship, leading to the absence of respect, leading to the death of love. The sequencing of these feelings and behaviors might not follow in this order and could be concurrent. Nevertheless, if this dysfunctional pattern of interacting does not reverse, the partners will be pulled further into the negative spiral into which they have been drawn.

The problems brought to treatment can generally be classified into two major categories: foundational and interpersonal. Foundational issues are ones that threaten the foundation or the very integrity of the marriage, eroding at a very deep level the couple's love, trust, friendship, respect, hope, and commitment. Interpersonal issues are ones that impede the successful reconciliation of significant unresolved issues. They tend to be developmental or situational issues.

Principles of Practice and Techniques

Constructual marital therapists have a primary set of practice principles from which to draw clinical interventions. These principles are derived from other therapeutic models, particularly structural and strategic family interventions, and from clinical experience. The following principles of practice are general guidelines for therapists working with distressed couples. Each principle of practice can be translated into numerous techniques or interventions. The list can be as long as the social worker's imagination.

1. Join with clients.
2. Build positive connections between partners.
3. Prevent one partner from dominating the session.
4. Maintain neutrality.
5. Create a positive and safe therapeutic atmosphere.
6. Identify and build on strengths.
7. Begin with the presenting problems.
8. Accept the role as expert.
9. Avoid non-negotiable issues.
10. Be cautious in using feeling statements.
11. Avoid accepting one-sided views.
12. Support but do not rescue a client experiencing distress.
13. Work on one problem at a time.
14. Schedule change-oriented interventions.
15. Translate feelings into actions.
16. Quickly involve both spouses in treatment.
17. Direct relationships toward symmetry.
18. Control the session.
19. Avoid being center stage in the session; have the clients do the work.
20. Move from content to process.

ASSESSMENT

The Shores represent a multiproblem family being challenged by issues associated with loss, abandonment, unemployment, chronic medical problems, disillusionment, inability to successfully complete developmental tasks, and poor self-esteem. Consequently, "negative entropy," or randomness based on feelings and perceptions of powerlessness and helplessness, is manifested at all levels in the Shore family: in each individual, between the parents, and within the family as a unit. Thus the family members respond to stressors at the "instrumental," rather than the secondary or primary, level of emotions, reacting to, rather than being present with their fears, insecurities, and vulnerabilities. Their situation is chronic. The Shore family has lived for years in a circular pattern that reinforces crisis and chaos.

In the marital subsystem, Charley and Nancy remain fixed in the negotiation phase of marital development, having accommodated to their inability to work collaboratively to resolve differences and the emotional distance they now experience. Nancy's comment that she "has less and less in common with Charley, who remained a kid," alludes to the possibility of her also remaining in the disillusionment stage. They are deeply entrenched in the negative spiral syndrome, reflected in part by the couple's many conflicts, deep feelings of frustration, frequent critical remarks, profound feelings of insecurity, and Nancy's need to control their relationship.

The foundation upon which the relationship rests is fragile. However, the fact that Nancy supports Charley's acting activities because it makes him happy and his statement that "she is the best wife in the world" allude to the caring feelings that still remain between the two. The depth of their care probably remains hidden beneath the daily upheavals and the fact that they have a hierarchal, rather than an egalitarian, relationship, with Nancy treating Charley as one of her children. Nancy states clearly that she doesn't trust Charley. Included in that mistrust is Charlie's inability to understand and nurture Nancy's emotional insecurities. Furthermore, given Nancy's continued criticism, it would be hard to imagine that Charley would trust Nancy with his emotional insecurities and vulnerabilities. The partners no longer relate as friends but as parent and child. Finally, with comments like, "He has remained a kid," it appears that Nancy no longer respects Charley as an adult partner, able to meet her needs as an individual, a wife, or a mother. He, on the other hand, appears to admire her competency, especially in crisis situations. Unfortunately, his feelings of failure prevent him from respecting himself.

Although the couple faces many chronic problems, and at times feels desperate and overwhelmed, the integrity of the marriage persists. This is reflected in the care the partners demonstrate toward one another and the fact that neither appears to be contemplating a divorce. Their concerns therefore remain in the interpersonal category, with the partners needing to resurrect their loving feelings and rediscover the trust, friendship, and respect that existed earlier in the relationship. Accomplishing these tasks would require establishing a collaborative, egalitarian, and supportive relationship, as well as resolving the long-standing problems and differences with the family members.

The partners' individual insecurities also contribute to the dysfunctional patterns in the marriage and family. Their insecurities are reflected in the three dimensions in which people engage the world: cognitively, emotionally, and behaviorally. Cognitively, several of Nancy fears are rooted in "expectancies." This is illustrated in her fear of having recurring flare-ups of a back injury, fear of having problems associated with the apartment they are renting, and fears concerning Rena's future. Nancy also has faulty "assumptions," including her belief that she should be able to fix her children's problems or follow all the suggestions given to her by social workers. These "core" beliefs trigger "primary" fears, to which she reacts with extreme anxiety and panic attacks. This situation is often followed by becoming behaviorally immobilized. Another negative circular pattern of behavior may begin with a problem with one of her children, which in turn triggers negative thoughts that lead to distorted perceptions, which lead to primary feelings of fear, which lead to overwhelming anxiety, which leads to her being incapacitated, which reinforces her feelings of inadequacy, which triggers more negative thoughts. The same could be said of Charley. He, for example, has negative perceptions of himself, which trigger feelings of inadequacy and helplessness that manifest in incompetent behavior, which reinforces his negative perceptions of himself.

Despite the numerous problems faced by Nancy and Charley and their seeming inability to resolve them while living in chaos, the partners possess many strengths upon which they could rely to find peace and harmony again in their marriage and family. They have demonstrated competency, love, and concern for one another and their children, as well as an ability to overcome adversity. They have also demonstrated resiliency by finding success and happiness despite their unsupportive parents and unhappy childhoods. Nancy has demonstrated professionalism, intelligence, and the capacity to establish and maintain lifelong friendships. Charley is resourceful, adaptive, and proud, as demonstrated by his desire to be self-sufficient despite his disability. Both are sensitive, well meaning, courageous, sociable, diligent, and responsible.

The early phase of their marriage was very stable, with Nancy enjoying her work, Charley being able to find and maintain jobs, and both enjoying an enriching social life. The family began to deteriorate when Nancy lost her capacity to work regularly. Unemployment prevented her from continuing to be the stabilizing force in the family and kept her from enjoying what she loved most, caring for patients. The family didn't have the resources to compensate for this tragedy. Over time, the marriage turned into a pseudo-mutual relationship, appearing to be stable, but in reality being fragile. The marriage had changed from being mutually supportive, cooperative, and egalitarian to one in which Nancy felt she had outgrown Charley and could no longer rely upon him for support. The weakness in the marriage only amplified Nancy's feelings of being overburdened and helpless. Furthermore, Michael's physical, social, and psychological problems and Rena's struggle to find her identity and her place in the world compounded matters, aggravating Nancy's feelings of incompetence and helplessness and the discord in the marriage. Finally, Charley's inability to find and sustain jobs because of his disability added further stress and strain on the family, depleting it even more of positive energy.

THE THERAPEUTIC PROCESS

In the beginning phase of therapy, emphasis is placed on joining, creating a positive atmosphere, clarifying and working on treatment goals, and developing a template upon which therapy will be based. That template includes the way in which issues will be addressed, identifying themes that will be high-lighted throughout the process, and the sequencing of issues. The emphasis in the middle phase of treatment is on working through the clients' various pre-senting problems. The ending phase of treatment is focused on anchoring the changes that have been made and formulating plans for continued growth.

In the beginning, I will remain central to the sessions, but as treatment proceeds, I will move toward the periphery. Also, I will normally remain in control of the sessions, orchestrating them in a manner that provides stability, safety, and affirmation, inviting collaboration and cooperation. Therapy is, however, a process of trial and error, with therapists offering interventions, monitoring their usefulness, and, if not effective, suggesting others.

After the Shores shared their stories and articulated what they desired from treatment, I would summarize and reflect back what they had shared, adding positive dimensions that they had not taken into consideration. I might say to Charley, for example, that I thought his frustration with his inability to help Michael was caused, in part, by the tremendous love he feels toward his son and by the helplessness he experiences at being unable to guide Michael into realizing his full potential.

To join with and create a positive atmosphere for Nancy, I might state that her fears and anxieties are warranted, knowing that a serious problem may arise again from her back injury, that tenants are often irresponsible and de-manding, and that Rena has a propensity for having personal crises. To join further, I might ask why she feels so anxious about Rena having a crisis; then, following her response, I would add that I thought it spoke to the depth of care and love she felt for Rena. After hearing their stories, I might join with the partners by congratulating them for raising such beautiful children and then proceed to share the strengths I perceive in them. I might also join with Char-ley by highlighting his integrity, giving examples of how I see it manifested. I would, for example, point out his diligence and his perseverance at efforts to fulfill his dream of being a comedian, despite the adversity he encounters, and in the fact that he continues to seek gainful employment. These interventions would send the family a metacommunication-level message that I want to cre-ate a safe environment in which they can express their vulnerabilities and in-securities and that I understand and empathize with their pain, problems, and difficulties.

In the initial session I would give special attention to the marital dyad by sharing my observations of their marital development. I would convey that I didn't know their truth, that only they did, but that I was simply sharing my observations, based on their comments and my clinical expertise. I would ex-plain my paradigm for an enriching marriage, indicating how love, trust, friend-ship, and respect had been eroded in their relationship. I might then try to build a bridge between the partners by making a comment such as, "It must be sad for both of you that your hopes and dreams for the marriage have not been fulfilled." If one or both acknowledge that I was correct, I would have them share those sad feelings. I then would let them know that sadness is a dimen-sion of love, that it is associated with care and the loss of something or someone special. These efforts would be aimed at helping the partner either resurrect or be more in touch with the loving feelings they have toward one another.

I might also attempt to build other bridges between the partners by highlighting their similarities, indicating that both are sensitive, caring, courageous, diligent, and competent. If necessary, I would give examples. To Nancy, I could say that by her own admission, she was an excellent nurse, and that when a crisis occurs, she always rises to the occasion. I would suspect she would downplay the latter, indicating that she always waits until a crisis arises before responding. I might counter with, it doesn't matter if she waits; the fact is that she responds competently. I might further amplify my observations by asking Charley to validate my perceptions. To Charley, I might refer to the time during military service when he felt competent. These cognitive restructuring interventions would be aimed at empowering the clients, providing a strength, rather than a deficit, base for their working together. If these interventions were not successful, I might use a solution-focused approach to accomplish the same results.

I would also recommend to the couple that Nancy take full responsibility for helping Rena and that Charley do the same for Michael. Nancy is therefore not to intrude on Charlie and Michael if they are having difficulties nor is she to make any suggestions as to how her husband should parent. The rationale would be that by her own admission, Nancy feels overburdened, implying that she would like to rely on Charley for help. I would also suggest that if it were necessary, I could take a few minutes during their sessions to provide Charley with a consultation. These recommendations serve the following six purposes. First, they create a normal boundary between the parents. Second, they take the negative expectancy away from Nancy, which will, it is hoped, reduce her anxiety. Third, they send a message to Charley that I think he is competent and capable of being an effective parent, thus, I hope, helping him to feel better about himself. Fourth, they elevate Charley to an egalitarian position with Nancy as a parent, providing the basis for them to collaborate and cooperate in the future. Fifth, if Charley is successful, his self-esteem might improve, providing a basis upon which Nancy might begin to reestablish respect for him. Finally, by offering Charley consultation, I block Nancy's tendency to intrude on Charley's relationship with Michael and thereby remove one of Charley's negative expectancies. I would also be modeling for Charley how to be in a collaborative relationship, something to which Nancy could readily identify because of her nursing background.

Before ending the session, I would provide the basis upon which the partners could rebuild their marriage by asking them to define love. During our discussion, I would be sure to highlight its giving aspect. I would also suggest that the overall goals of therapy should be the recapturing of their loving feelings and developing an enriching relationship.

In closing, I would suggest homework assignments and share that therapy is work in progress. I would clarify my role in the treatment process, making it clear that it was incumbent upon me to remain neutral. Finally, I would summarize the issues they wished to be addressed in therapy, but before proceeding to resolve them, I would recommend that they take a short break from the marriage. In so doing, they would refocus on themselves and on what they desire personally and for the relationship. This intervention is aimed at reducing anxiety by having them divorce themselves from any expectations of one another. I then would give the following four assignments. First, they are to write 25 attributes that they either like, admire, or love in themselves. This assignment is directed at empowerment and helping them to recognize their strengths. Second, they are to write 25 attributes they either like, admire, or love in their spouse. This recommendation is aimed at rekindling positive feelings and laying the foundation upon which to establish an affectionate relationship. Third, they are to list five things they are willing to do to contribute to the well-being of the other. This exercise is a change-oriented intervention, aimed at helping them take responsibility for their part in contributing to the unhappiness in the relationship. It is also aimed at helping to build trust. Finally, they are to list five things they desire from the relationship. This suggestion is aimed at providing a path on which the marriage can proceed. It can also be used to foster affective ties. All the exercises are aimed at helping clients reduce their level of stress while regaining feelings of control over their lives.

In the second session I would address the homework assignments, attempting to build bridges, highlight and build on strengths, reduce stress, and encourage hope. I would then proceed toward helping to resolve the partner's presenting problems, asking them to each select one they'd like to address. Working on one problem at a time helps clients feel more in control and less overwhelmed.

To assist Nancy, I might use Socratic dialogue in guiding her to positive, rather than negative, perceptions of herself, particularly emphasizing her competency and caring attitude. These two attributes would be highlighted throughout treatment in order to become part of the "core thoughts." I would, for example, ask Nancy if she was a competent nurse. I suspect she would say yes. I then would ask how she managed to address all the unexpected situations on her job. Following her response, I would ask if she applied the same body of knowledge and skills to her family crises. Again, I suspect she would say yes. I then would ask if she was proactive as a nurse and used contingency plans for possible emergencies. If she said yes, I would amplify her competency by highlighting the fact that she has the body of knowledge and skills not only to handle emergencies but also to prevent them. I then would ask what contingency plans she could make to prevent serious problems arising with her tenants. I would also ask if she could consider using Charley as a sounding board, just as she might have done with her former colleagues. The latter suggestion would be used to build a bridge between the partners and to elevate Charley's stature in the relationship. Thus I would maximize the opportunity for the intervention to succeed.

To address Nancy's anxieties associated with Rena's problems, I would use a cognitive restructuring intervention by suggesting that her anxieties are associated with her sensitivity and care for her daughter. Her anxiety therefore represents at a deep level how much she loves Rena. If she agreed, I would proceed to have her share those loving feelings with me. During the course of our conversation, I might ask Charley how he felt hearing the depth of love Nancy had for their (inclusive language) daughter. The aim of this intervention would be to redirect Nancy's sharing of sensitive feelings from me to Charley and thereby connect the two in intimacy. I would conclude this sequence by asking Nancy how she might feel sharing her loving feelings with Rena.

To assist Charley in recognizing that he was "somebody," I might use cognitive restructuring, followed by affective interventions. I might, for example, use Socratic dialogue to guide him into recognizing the depth of love he has for Michael. It would begin with the question "Do you love Michael?" followed by describing all the things he loved about his son. I then would comment that it appeared that Charlie loved his son in spite of the disrespect Michael has shown him. I would then ask if that were true. If he said yes, I would ask what that said about him. I would be sure to suggest that it meant Charley knew how to love unconditionally. If he agreed, I would ask what it felt like not being able to help Michael with his poor self-esteem. In so doing, I would be helping Charley learn how to stay with and process his feelings rather than react to them. I then would ask how he felt sharing his sensitive feelings with me. If he indicated that it was a nice experience, I would ask if he could be present to his son's struggles in the same way without trying to solve them, indicating the importance of simply listening, supporting and being available to our children's pain. I would be cognizant of the fact that at a metacommunication level, I would be sending the same message to Nancy, hoping she'd use it to engage Rena in the same manner.

I would continue with Charley by asking whether he loves Michael for what he does or for who he is. If Charley said the latter, I would suggest that maybe that same view could be applied to him and that who he is could be more important than what he does. I then would refer to the 25 attributes Nancy loved, admired, or cared about in him and the 25 things he loved, admired, or cared about in himself. I would also add to those lists the positive attributes I saw in him. Finally, I'd highlight this sequence of interventions by stating that I saw him as being a "somebody," a man filled with love, care, and integrity. I would close the session by including Nancy in the discussion on Charley's positive qualities. This intervention would be aimed at having the couple relate as two adults, rather than as parent–child, and at having Nancy engage Charley in a supportive, rather than a critical, manner.

During subsequent sessions, and as we entered the middle phase of treatment, we would continue to address their issues systematically, maintaining balance by alternating between their individual concerns. The themes of the couple being competent, sensitive, and caring would continue to be interwoven throughout therapy. I would also take every opportunity to build bridges between the partners, aiming to connect them in an egalitarian, supportive, and intimate manner. Finally, I would continue to use a variety of interventions to assist the couple, such as solution-oriented questions, Socratic dialogue, and reflective listening. Emphasis would remain on working with Nancy's and Charley's emotions. To illustrate the latter, for example, I would work with Charley on reconciling the loss of his unfilled dream of becoming a star.

I would approach the subject of Charley's unfilled dreams by highlighting their importance, indicating that dreams flow from our souls and reflect the creative, imaginative, and innocent dimensions of us. I would explain further that dreams call us to be the people we were created to be and that dreams do not necessarily have to be fulfilled to be enriching. I'd state that this is why, in part, I think he continues to daydream at work. However, I would also discuss the difference between participating in and living in our dreams, with the latter turning into fantasy—frustrating rather than enhancing us. I would ask if he would share his feelings regarding his unfilled dreams of becoming a star. The aim of this reflective listening intervention would be to guide him from his secondary into his primary level of emotions associated with this subject. I suspect he would express feelings of loss, sadness, and loneliness. If this was the case, I would ask Nancy how she felt listening to Charley share his emotions. The aim of the intervention would be to shift Charley's sharing of feelings with me to Nancy, thereby bridging them in the intimacy of sadness. If successful, I would ask Nancy to share her feelings associated with the loss of her ability to work full time as a nurse. These series of interventions would be aimed at continuing to help the partners learn to process, rather than react to, their painful emotions, providing an atmosphere in which they could be intimate while safely grieving losses and disappointments.

In the middle phase of treatment, the focus would be on working more directly with the issues that impede the couple from moving into the integration and enhancement phases of marriage. A solution-focused approach, using the lists that indicate what they want from the marriage, would be used for this purpose. Together, we would look to the future, exploring solutions for building a loving, trusting, friendly, and respectful relationship, rather than dwelling on the past and what went wrong or on the present and what keeps them trapped. Again, the themes of competency, care, and integrity, used throughout treatment, would continue to be woven into the discussions, along with the knowledge and the skills demonstrated in resolving previous issues and concerns.

The ending phase of treatment would focus on highlighting the strengths of each spouse and of the relationship, and on examining the changes they've made and how these came about. It would also focus on what they could do to continue growing personally, while building an enriching relationship between themselves and their children. These interventions would be aimed at anchoring the gains made by the couple and fostering a proactive rather than a reactive stance at problem solving and relationship building. With this in mind, the closing session would be used to summarize the treatment process.

During the session prior to the termination interview, Nancy and Charley would be asked to think about, discuss, and write down their perceptions of what occurred during therapy, highlighting changes and the reasons for them. That document would be the basis for our last meeting. Following the sharing and discussion of that information, I would offer my impressions of what happened during the course of therapy. My observations would be contained in a one-page summary report, given to them at the end of our meeting. It would be a reminder of what happened in therapy and could be used as a reference. It would also serve as a "certificate of completion" and a "document of affirmation," affirming the goodness in themselves, the marriage, and the family.

APPLICATION TO DIVERSITY

For this discussion on diversity, the White, lower-middle-class Shores will be transformed into the Wongs, a lower-middle-class Chinese immigrant family. Mr. and Mrs. Wong are a traditional Chinese couple that had an arranged marriage in Canton before immigrating to the United States and starting a family. They exhibit the same presenting problems as the Shores. However, issues associated with immigration, intergenerational cultural conflicts, and, especially, Chinese culture compound their problems. I preface this section with the acknowledgment of tremendous intragroup diversity within Chinese culture. For the purpose of discussing issues of diversity, I focus on cultural commonalities, but it is not my intent to oversimplify complex characteristics and behaviors within a given group. American society, for example, emphasizes individuation, self-esteem, and independence, whereas Chinese culture emphasizes interdependence, self-effacement, and loyalty. American society emphasizes freedom, equality, and autonomy, whereas Chinese culture emphasizes tradition, reciprocity, and connectedness. American society is heavily influenced by Judeo-Christian morality, whereas Confucian ethics and, secondarily, Taoism and Buddhism provide the basis for Chinese values. In providing marital therapy to traditional Chinese couples, practitioners must take into consideration these factors as well as the fundamental differences between the foundations upon which American and Chinese marriages are based.

The relationship between partners in American marriages tends to be egalitarian, with the foundation of the marriage resting on love, trust, friendship, and respect. Every modern marriage is unique, with couples being responsible for designing and building them. The desire for most modern couples is to seek an "intimate" union, a relationship that is safe, supportive, nurturing, enriching, joyful, and encouraging. To achieve such a relationship, they must be skilled at negotiating differences without being controlling.

Traditional Chinese marriages, on the other hand, are based on role expectations, function, and accountability to the extended family, all dictated by tradition and Confucianism. The foundation of the relationship rests on loyalty, responsibility, and respect. The marriage is highly structured and basically concerned with having and nurturing children. Marriage is the means of carrying on the family lineage, supporting older relatives, and maintaining the connection with ancestors. Furthermore, the relationship between spouses is hierarchical, with the wife being in the subservient position. In such marriages there is no "I," only "we," and the "we" is an extension of the family, the community, and the culture. Finally, the relationship is based on devoted, rather than intimate, love. If partners honor their respective roles, they have an enriching relationship.

Another major issue that must be taken into consideration when providing therapy to Chinese couples is the fact that Chinese culture is shame rather than guilt based—shame being the feeling associated with violating a family, a community, or a cultural norm. This perspective is rooted in Confucianism, which dictates how individuals should behave in their respective roles. To not honor one's role is to bring shame or "loss of face" on the individual, as well as to his or her family, extended family, and ancestors.

Finally, Chinese culture emphasizes what one does and not what one says or how one feels. Again, importance is placed on behavior or code of conduct. The Chinese do not have a history of expressing their personal feelings toward one another. If they do experience negative feelings, such as anxiety, frustration, or depression, they tend to express them psychosomatically, in the form of headaches, backaches, and other forms of physical discomfort.

Constructual marital therapy is a culturally sensitive model of practice, allowing for the integration of any conceptual framework to which clients can identify—in this case, Confucian ethics. Therefore, the eight Confucian principles—devoted love, justice, respect loyalty, honor, responsibility, altruism, and wisdom—can easily be used in the therapeutic process.

In providing therapy, practitioners must take into consideration what their clients expect from treatment. Many Chinese expect therapists to be authority figures, experts, and information providers. Practitioners must also take into consideration the method of practice to which their clients can most readily identify. For the Chinese, that might be a cognitive-behavioral approach. For these reasons in the marital therapy paradigm, marital mediation is ideally suited for Chinese couples. It is rooted in cognitive and social exchange theory and offers what Chinese expect from treatment. It is, for example, an active, brief, and practical approach that follows a logical progression. It is concrete, informative, directive, and task-centered. Therapists are authority figures, experts, educators, and role models, who emphasize the couple's strength, while providing a therapeutic environment that is warm, respectful, and supportive. Finally, the following 11 stages of the mediation are processes to which the Chinese couple can easily identify:

1. socialization,
2. collaboration,
3. problem identification,
4. role clarification,
5. defining conflict parameters,
6. establishing an agenda,
7. selecting treatment interventions,
8. examining settlement alternatives,
9. assessing options,
10. final bargaining, and
11. formalizing, implementing and monitoring a final settlement (Jung, 1999).

Therapists can weave strength-based themes, such as integrity, courage, and perseverance, throughout the therapeutic process. I could, for example, join with the Wongs by acknowledging the courage it must have taken to leave their home in China to make a new start in the United States. I could also join by indicating that I know that among Chinese, seeing a therapist can evoke feelings of shame and that it takes a great deal of courage to come and share their difficulties with a stranger. Finally, I could say they have demonstrated perseverance by coming to therapy and not giving up on the many problems they have with their children.

Although mediation therapy has a goodness of fit with Chinese couples, it does present one major cultural bias: the requirement of an egalitarian, collaborative, and cooperative relationship between partners. This concern, therefore, must be addressed in the initial session.

Conceptually, the concern can be defined as a "cultural dilemma." To reconcile such dilemmas, couples must challenge rather than react to them. Psychologically, the psyche can adhere to ambivalences for only a relatively short period of time if these are addressed directly, then must reconcile them. Spiritually, culture is something to which we identify, but it does not define us. Therefore, the reconciliation of major dilemmas speaks to our integrity, as well as to a deeper and more profound definition of ourselves and our place in the world.

A fundamental ethical principle of social work practice is the client's right of self-determination. This principle would be introduced at the beginning of treatment with the Wongs. I would explain why I was suggesting mediation as the treatment of choice, indicating that it requires partners to work collaboratively, as well as be willing to negotiate differences by bargaining (giving up something to gain something else). Part of the responsibility of therapists in the mediation process is to assist couples in finding common ground or a basis for which they would want to cooperate. With the Wongs, for example, I might suggest that they may want to cooperate to help their children learn respect and responsibility or to save further embarrassment from having to work with other professionals, such as teachers and school counselors. Or, I might say to Mr. Wong that therapy might help him save further embarrassment from his mental illness and unemployment.

Following this discussion, I would share with the partners that the mediation process may seem contrary to their beliefs and their usual manner of relating, and, therefore, they may be faced with a cultural dilemma. I then would close the discussion by asking whether or not they would be willing to be in a type of marriage that is different from what they are accustomed to—namely, an egalitarian relationship. This intervention is aimed not only at supporting the clients' right to self-determination, but also at appealing to their "pragmatism," a philosophical stance that underpins Chinese culture. If they answer in the affirmative, they would have reconciled their dilemma and accepted my invitation to work collaboratively.

Following this series of interventions, I would proceed to the remaining nine phases of the mediating process. I would begin Phase 3 by asking the

Wongs to each develop a list of behavioral changes and then prioritize these from most to least important. This would be followed by Phases 4 and 5, with the further clarification of my role and the defining of conflict parameters. I might suggest, for example, that they work only on issues directly related to the relationship with their children, excluding for the moment their relationships with friends or extended family. This suggestion would be aimed at reducing expectancies and would thereby reduce the anxiety associated with the relationship and the therapeutic process. We then would proceed with Phases 6 and 7 by establishing an agenda, followed by selecting treatment interventions. I might, for example, suggest a communication and problem-solving approach, with the aim of offering a process with which they could easily identify. Phases 8 and 9 would follow, by our examining settlement alternatives and assessing options. Mr. Wong, for example, may agree to be more helpful with the children (sending a message that he is concerned about his wife) if she would "complain less" (demonstrating to him respect). A homework assignment may be suggested to help clarify the specifics of their requests. Finally, we would conclude this series of interventions with Phases 10 and 11, final bargaining and formalizing their agreements. The latter may take the form of a written contract appealing to the couple's sense of formality, an attitude in Chinese culture that is pervasive.

LIMITATIONS OF THE MODEL

The most immediate limitations of constructural marital therapy, or any other therapy, are the skill, the training, the experience, and the judgment of the therapist. Because CMT is a multifaceted, multidimensional, and eclectic approach to working with distressed couples, practitioners can easily become overwhelmed in its complexity. This in turn may result in interventions becoming a hodgepodge of trial-and-error techniques. Unlike some models that are linear in their methodology, using templates that offer standard and clear operating procedures, CMT requires practitioners to be imaginative, creative, and adaptive. Although the model offers guiding principles of practice, the more experienced the practitioner, the more he or she will recognize the exceptions to the rules. Furthermore, the model claims the ability to integrate various methods and models of practice, but does not articulate clear guidelines for how this can be accomplished. Consequently, this knowledge can be acquired only with experience and excellent supervision. Finally, the model does not address the issue of "goodness of fit" and what therapeutic style would best lend itself to its use.

RESEARCH

In general, the effectiveness of marital therapy, like other approaches to practice, is inconclusive because of problems in research design, reliability, and validity.

The two paradigms to marital therapy that emerge from the literature as being the most promising are the behavioral and the conjugal relationship enhancement approaches (Jacobson, 1978). This is due, in part, to the fact that the presenting problems of clients are organized around clearly defined symptoms and the approach to addressing them around clearly defined templates, upon which interventions are made. Unlike these two approaches—and given that CMT is dynamic rather than linear, is assessment rather than diagnostically based, and is client rather than model centered—developing a valid and reliable research design to measure its effectiveness would be extremely challenging.

Although no formal studies have yet been undertaken on the effectiveness of CMT, clinical observation, case studies, supervision, and self-reporting by clients give evidence to its usefulness. This is not surprising in lieu of the evidence that change in clients is to a large extent predicated on the nature of the therapist–client relationship (Blundo, 2001), to which this model plays particular attention. Transparency, collaboration, empowerment, active empathy, and integrity provide the foundation upon which it is built. Nevertheless, it is hoped that scholars will take upon themselves the inclusion of CMT in their research endeavors.

SUMMARY

Constructural marital therapy is a dynamic, sophisticated, and respectful approach to working with distressed couples. It accentuates competency, taking into consideration attitude, knowledge, and skills in its conceptual framework. Emphasis is on elasticity and adaptability, with practitioners possessing a variety of methods and models of practice upon which to draw, in order to meet the unique needs of their clients. Because of the focus on client strengths and clinician adaptability, the model is well suited to work with people from diverse backgrounds. CMT recognizes, respects, and uses the knowledge and the abilities that couples bring to therapy. Thus, the model is collaborative, strength based, and eclectic, allowing for flexibility and creativity in efforts to assist those whom it was designed to serve.

REFERENCES

Ables, B. S. (1977). *Therapy for couples.* San Francisco: Jossey-Bass.

Bader, E., & Pearson, P. T. (1988). *In quest of the mythical mate: A developmental approach to diagnosis and treatment in couples therapy.* New York: Brunner/Mazel.

Bateson, G. (1971). *Steps to an ecology of mind.* New York: Ballantine Books.

Baucom, D. H., & Epstein, N. (1990). *Cognitive-behavioral marital therapy.* New York: Brunner/ Mazel.

Blundo, R. (2001). Learning strengths–based practice: Challenging our personal and professional frames. *Families in Society: The Journal of Contemporary Human Services, 82,* 296–304.

Boszormenyi-Nagy, I., & Spark, G. M. (1973). *Invisible loyalties.* New York: Harper & Row.

Ellis, A., Sichel, J. L., Yeager, R. J., DiMattia, D. J., & DiGiuseppe, R. (1989). *Rational-emotive couples therapy.* New York: Pergamon Press.

Fallon, I. R. H. (Ed.). (1988). *Handbook of behavioral family therapy.* New York: Guilford Press.

Freud, S. (1904). Psychoanalytic procedure. In J. Strachey (Series Ed.), *The standard edition of the complete psychological works of Sigmund Freud, Vol. 7*, 247–255. London: Hogarth Press, 1953.

Freud, S. (1940). An outline of psychoanalysis. In J. Strachey (Series Ed.), *The standard edition of the complete psychological works of Sigmund Freud, Vol. 23*, 139-301. London: Hogarth Press, 1964.

Goldenthal, P. (1996). *Doing contextual therapy: An integrated model for working with individuals, couples, and families.* New York: Norton.

Greer, S. E., & Zurilla, D. (1975). Behavioral approaches to marital discord and conflict. *Journal of Marriage and Family Counseling, 1*, 299–316.

Hale, B. J. (1978). Gestalt techniques in marriage counseling. *Social Casework, 59*, 428–433.

Hatcher, C., & Himelstein, P. (Eds.). (1978). *The handbook of gestalt therapy.* New York: Aronson.

Hoffman, L. (1981). *Foundations of family therapy: A concept and framework for systems change.* New York: Basic Books.

Jacobson, N. S. (1978). A review of the research on the effectiveness of marital therapy. In T. J. Paolino & B. S. McCrady (Eds.), *Marriage and marital therapy* (pp. 395–444). New York: Brunner/Mazel.

Jacobson, N. S., & Margolin G. (1979). *Marital therapy.* New York: Brunner/Mazel.

Jung, M. (1993). *Constructual marital therapy: Theory and practice.* New York: Gardner Press.

Jung, M. (1999). The application of marital mediation to Chinese American immigrants. *Family Therapy, 26*, 1–12.

Jurg, W. (1975). *Couples in collusion.* New York: Aronson.

Lester, G. W., Beckham, E., & Baucom, D. H. (1989). Implementation of behavioral marital therapy. *Journal of Marital and Family Therapy, 2*, 189-200.

Nadelson, C. C. (1978). Marital therapy from a psychoanalytic perspective. In T. J. Paolino & B. S. McCrady (Eds.), *Marriage and marital therapy* (pp. 89–164). New York: Brunner/Mazel.

Scharff, D. E., & Scharff, J. S. (1987). *Object-relations family therapy.* New Jersey: Aronson.

Scharff, J. S. (1995). Psychoanalytic marital therapy. In N. S. Jacobson & A. S. Gurman (Eds.), *Clinical handbook of couple therapy* (pp. 164–196). New York: Guilford Press.

Slipp, S. (1995). Object relations marital therapy of personality disorders. In N. S. Jacobson & A. S. Gurman (Eds.), *Clinical handbook of couple therapy* (pp. 458–470). New York: Guilford Press.

Stuart, R. B. (1980). *Helping couples change: Aa social learning approach to marital therapy.* New York: Guilford Press.

10

Integrative Family Therapy

Emphasis on a Middle-Class African American Family in Suburbia

Marlene F. Watson, PhD

INTRODUCTION

*I*ntegrative family therapy now seems to be a major trend in the field; however, it was once regarded as "selling-out"—not remaining true to the purity of the hard-won traditional models of family therapy. In the beginning, family systems therapists diligently fought not only to distinguish family therapy from individual therapy but also to differentiate themselves from one another. Thus it appears that the field of family therapy, like the adolescent in a family, needed to establish a separate identity before recognizing and acknowledging the legitimacy of an integrative family therapy approach (Nichols & Schwartz, 2001).

In my early years of training, I rigidly adhered to the strategic-structural approach, expecting it to be the solution to all therapeutic problems with all families. However, at the same time I struggled with the notion of the family system as "the problem." For example, I was keenly aware of the role of race in my own life, as well as in that of my family. In addition, I knew firsthand that African American families were negatively impacted by social practices of institutionalized racism, prejudice, and discrimination.

Consequently, I began to question approaches that did not go beyond the family to understand problems with techniques primarily aimed at symptom relief, particularly with African American families when race was an organizing principle in their lives. Moreover, I began to question approaches that did not deem it necessary to validate the impact of race on the social and psychological development of African Americans, given society's long-standing negative view of African American individuals and families.

Because helping families to gain insight into their problems was not a specific goal of the strategic-structural approach, I often felt limited when working with African American families. I specifically felt limited because of my basic belief that African American individuals and families need to reconnect with their psychological side (I contend that as a result of slavery and racism, African Americans disconnected their psychological wires in order to survive). These observations moved me to revisit my earlier roots in psychology and to reclaim insight as a virtue. Promoting clients' understanding of the sociocultural forces that help to shape their lives seemed to be a way of empowering these families to make informed decisions about their individual and family functioning.

According to Nichols and Schwartz (2001), there are three very different forms of integration: *eclecticism, selective borrowing,* and *specially designed integrative models.* Eclecticism refers to the free use of various models and techniques. In selective borrowing, one is dedicated to a particular approach but occasionally employs methods from other approaches. The specially designed integrative models usually draw on several approaches to create one integrative approach.

An important value of the integrative family therapy perspective is that it removes the "one approach fits all" blinders from therapists, allowing therapists to consider the full range of human complexity and the multiplicity of influences on human interaction. Another important value of the integrative family therapy approach is that it gives the therapist flexibility. Finally, the integrative family therapy approach encourages therapists to critically assess both theory and practice.

My particular practice of integrative family therapy relies heavily on the intersystem model that was set forth by Weeks (1989) as a theoretical frame. In addition, it encompasses the dynamics of power and privilege related to issues of race, gender, class, sexual orientation, ethnicity, culture, religion, and spirituality. The intersystem model was developed mainly for the treatment of couples and integrates elements from the three core approaches to therapy: the *individual,* the *interactional,* and the *intergenerational* (Weeks, 1989). To these three approaches I would add a fourth, which would be the *contextual.*

The integrative approach identified previously addresses the various influences on the course of family development. Essential to this approach is the idea that no individual is an island unto herself or himself. Rather, each individual and each family is a part of a larger social network. As such, each person influences and is influenced by the whole unit.

THE CONCEPT OF THE PERSON AND THE HUMAN EXPERIENCE

The concept of the person and the human experience is an integral component of the integrative family therapy model that I espouse. Individuals are seen as both actors and reactors who exist in a complex system of biopsychosociocultural influences. Individuals are also seen as resilient beings with possibilities for regeneration.

The intersystem model focuses on the couple as a system consisting of two individuals. The individual is of vital importance in the assessment and treatment of couples and families from this approach. The individual's coping and defense mechanisms, life-cycle position, ethnicity, and intrapsychic dynamics are attended to and assessed. Each individual has his or her own unique family of origin history (Weeks & Treat, 1992). Also, the individuals who compose the family unit each have their own unique history, based on their racial identity (just as immigrant family members can have different levels of acculturation, individuals can have different levels of racial identity), gender identity, sexual identity, class identity, personality style, expectations, relationships with other family members, and birth order.

To not see the Shore family members as individuals might obscure the therapist's understanding of each person's contribution to the problem, as well as each person's strengths, given that each individual has a unique history. Conversely, knowledge of each individual may seduce the therapist into taking one person's side. For example, the therapist may be tempted to side with Nancy as the victimized person because Charley has been diagnosed with bipolar depression. Rather than reinforce Nancy's views of Charley's incompetence and of her role as the person "trying to get everything fixed," the therapist could use his or her knowledge of the individual context to better understand the assignment of Nancy's and Charley's roles in the family and of their acceptance of those roles. The therapist should also use the individual context to identify and strengthen significant factors that enable individuals and, consequently, families to withstand and rebound from crisis and challenge (Walsh, 1998).

The individual and the family have resources within them for healing. Thus individuals and families are basically competent systems that need help seeing the obstacles that are interfering with their competence. If barriers to accessing their competence are removed, then individuals and families can reclaim their competence (McDaniel, Lusterman & Philpot, 2001). For instance, Nancy demonstrates remarkable strength and competence during times of crisis but is overwhelmed by the fear of something bad happening at other times, preventing her from claiming personal competence. Both Charley and Michael have dogged determination and persistence, which are major strengths; however, they tend to invest their energies into unrealistic goals (Charley's goal of becoming a star and Michael's goal of running track and playing softball), preventing them from claiming personal competence. Rena has natural gifts—intelligence and talent—but believes she is destined to "mess up" or to repeat her birth mother's mistakes, preventing her from claiming personal competence.

HISTORICAL PERSPECTIVE

In the founding era of family therapy, clearly articulated schools of thought were kept separate and distinct; most family therapists became disciples of a particular school. Each school of family therapy highlighted a particular area of family life. For example, experientialists encouraged people to feel, behaviorists encouraged people to reinforce positive actions, and Bowenians encouraged people to think for themselves. Mostly, family therapy models were competitive and ignored the insights of other approaches (Nichols & Schwartz, 2001).

During the 1980s, family therapists began experimenting with integrative models of therapy. However, the overall integration movement happened like a quiet revolution. The integration movement may have gone largely unrecognized because many seasoned family therapists gradually, and sometimes unconsciously, incorporated aspects of different theories. Not until they were asked to describe their approach did these therapists become aware that they were borrowing from other approaches (Nichols & Schwartz, 2001).

Furthermore, the integrative movement may have been both overshadowed and inspired by the feminist movement. The feminist movement gave rise to a major critique of the traditional models in the field of family therapy and sparked a cultural movement. Thus it may be that the critical lens of the feminist movement also caused family therapy purists to look more critically at the limitations of their own theories.

Some family therapists, who found their approach lacking, endeavored to create something more comprehensive. *Metaframeworks,* which brings together key ideas from the various schools and connects them with a set of overarching principles, is one example of an all-encompassing model. Another example of a model designed to increase comprehensiveness is the integrative problem-centered therapy model, which ties together several different theories in sequence and establishes a decision tree for moving among the various approaches (Nichols & Schwartz, 2001).

Family therapy has evolved from competing schools to cross-fertilization among the different models, to adding concepts and methods from the fields of psychology, sociology, social work, and biology. The ecosystemic approach reflects family therapy's shift toward deconstructing the wall and building a bridge between the individual, the family, the community and other larger systems. The ecosystemic approach is integrative or eclectic (the terms *integrative* and *eclectic* are used interchangeably in some family therapy circles today) and allows the family therapist to create a flexible and effective way of doing therapy. The ecosystemic approach uses a very broad lens to capture the environment that influences individual and family development, including the individual, the family, and larger systems, such as work systems, health-care systems, social services and legal systems, gender issues, religion, ethnicity, and culture (McDaniel, Lusterman & Philpot, 2001).

Although family therapists in the 21st century do not regard eclecticism as a patchwork of various theoretical models and concepts as did family therapists of the 1970s, the debate over eclecticism and integration is not dead. Regardless of one's epistemology about eclecticism and integrative therapy, a conceptual focus is required in the practice of eclectic therapy. Therapists must guard against the practice of unfocused eclecticism (Nichols & Schwartz, 2001).

According to Weeks (1989), most attempts to develop an integrative family therapy model in the earlier years were limited to combining schools of thought and methods. Hence, they lacked originality and, at best, were eclectic and not truly integrative. From the perspective of Weeks and Treat (2001), the new efforts toward integration in the field of couples therapy fail to achieve their goal due to the lack of a coherent theory and, therefore, continue to be eclectic, missing the mark of integration. Although eclecticism may lead to greater unity, true integration creates a whole out of parts. In order to create a coherent integrative family therapy model, at least two constructs are needed— the foundational and the integrational. The foundational construct lays the groundwork for the integration of concepts, methods, and ideas from the various schools and requires close scrutiny of the philosophical assumptions on which the theory is built. The integrational construct produces a collective lens through which to view a variety of phenomena that has been articulated in different theories (Weeks, 1989).

KEY THEORETICAL CONSTRUCTS

An underpinning of the intersystem model is the theory of interaction proposed by Strong and Claiborn, as cited by Weeks (1989). According to the theory of interaction, individuals are open systems who are social and who behave in ways that attempt to enhance their sense of control. There is both an intrapsychic and an interactional component to the model. The intrapsychic component is composed of three elements: interpretation, definition, and the ability to predict what others desire. Thus individuals interpret or give meaning to their communication with others, define their communication with others according to how they wish to be seen and how they see others in the relationship, and rely on their ability to predict what will cause a desired outcome from others, based on their interactional history (Weeks, 1989).

The interactional component has two elements: congruence and interdependence. Congruence is achieved if the feedback from others matches the individual's desired or preferred definition. When the individual's desired definition differs from that of others, the relationship becomes incongruent and the result is tension. The individual's tolerance for incongruence is a function of her or his interdependence. In fact, the individual's perceived level of interdependence is directly correlated with that individual's tolerance for incongruence. Furthermore, the individual with less power in a relationship is more likely to acquiesce in order to restore the relationship congruence (Weeks, 1989).

In the intersystem model, individual symptoms are regarded as behaviors that develop as a result of some relationship incongruence. Although all parties share in the development of individual symptoms, each tends to point the finger at the other through attributions or beliefs about the other's motives (Weeks, 1989).

Nancy seems to attribute Charley's "failures" at home and at work to male inadequacy. As a result of their interactional history, she predicts that Charley cannot be trusted with "dollars, documents, or decisions." She also predicts that she has to handle all important matters in order to achieve a positive outcome. Charley seems to attribute Nancy's anxiety to "female worry" (women not being able to handle the facts of life and worrying about things that they have no control over). Resulting from their interactional history, Charlie predicts that Nancy cannot handle hard reality, so he tells her what "she wants to hear." Both Nancy's and Charley's behaviors seem to be attempts to enhance their sense of control in the relationship. However, their behaviors function to keep them both from seeing themselves favorably in the other's eyes, resulting in relationship stress.

The contextual dimension must be central to the therapeutic process because external social and political forces affect individual and family functioning. Race, ethnicity, gender, class, sexual orientation, and religion represent salient group membership, and each of these groups, both separately and collectively, has a powerful effect on life experiences.

Culture dictates family norms and rules. Culture also confers power and privilege upon some individual family members, yet contributes to the oppression of others. It is therefore necessary to explore and understand how the family's culture, as well as the larger culture, influences both the individual's oppression and the individual's tolerance of oppression within the family. Because I am an advocate of social justice, I believe in the necessity of exposing culturally sanctioned oppression because it undermines basic human rights. Despite the fact that African American men and women have endured harsh realities of racism and oppression, maintaining Black silence about child abuse and domestic abuse within African American families is wrong. It does little to ensure racial survival and prevents the optimal development of African American individuals and families.

Power and control are key elements of culture. Cultural awareness alone does not lead to effective treatment of families. Issues of power and control—specifically, historical cultural practices of male domination and female subordination—have definite and sometimes deleterious effects on individual and family functioning. Culture is at the center of individual and family expectations; however, cultural expectations may result in obligations that lead to constraints for both the individual and the family.

Individuals make sense of their world through their beliefs. Sociocultural factors greatly influence the individual's belief system. An individual's emotional and behavioral functioning is clearly related to his or her belief system (Hines, 1998). Beliefs based on sociocultural learning can encourage individuals and families to be hopeful, or, alternatively, they can rob individuals and families of meaning and purpose. Oppressed individuals and families frequently suffer from deprivation of both "bread" and "spirit," culminating in hopelessness (Aponte, 1994).

People may find themselves in situations that prevent them from feeling or behaving differently. The options that they see available to them, given their circumstances, may appear very limited. In this way, individuals, couples, and families may become constrained because they see limited options or because they have developed belief systems that limit their options (Breunlin, Schwartz & Mac Kune-Karrer, 1992). For example, some African Americans may be constrained by the belief that Whites are smarter, based on theories of intelligence (i.e., the Bell Curve). Likewise, some Caucasians may be constrained by the belief that Blacks are naturally more athletic.

Although constraints can be present at any of the four levels (individual, interactional, intergenerational, and contextual) of a human system, constraints at the contextual level are likely to be of long standing. When constraints have existed for a long time, the problem becomes more deeply seated because the individuals involved despair of their capacity to solve it (Breunlin, Schwartz & Mac Kune-Karrer, 1992). For instance, slavery and its twin companion—racism—constrained the intimate relationship between African American women and men; and from the hot debates about the Black female–male relationship, the Black woman and the Black man seem convinced that the other will not change and, therefore, each is fearful of the other. Unfortunately, their fear of the other creates a barrier that constructs yet another constraint that affects the institution of Black marriage.

Most people do not consciously understand that social realities related to context can produce psychological constraints. Presupposing that any American who wants to achieve can achieve frequently leads to victim blaming from both the victimized persons and others.

Therapists must be able to see through the family's mask and not label the family members as resistant when they appear cautious about taking risks or feel hopeless about removing the constraints in their lives (Breunlin, Schwartz & Mac Kune-Karrer, 1992).

The contextual lens in therapy is instrumental to the therapist maintaining a strength-based stance because it helps the therapist to have a greater appreciation of the web of constraints in a family's life. The strength-based position helps the therapist to be respectful and optimistic, yet at the same time to assess the obstacles that block the individual's, the couple's, or the family's success (McDaniel, Lusterman & Philpot, 2001).

Hope is essential to life. Therefore, it is crucial to the therapeutic process. The therapist's sense of hope about the family's ability to change is very important. It has been documented that hope has a positive effect on individuals' ability to cope with stress (Walsh, 1998). Thus it stands to reason that a sense of hope will help the therapist to have a positive outlook in therapy. With a positive outlook, the therapist is in a better position to develop a collaborative relationship with the family, as opposed to creating another constraint in the life of the family. Within the context of a collaborative relationship, the therapist and the family are more likely to develop a spirit of cooperation in which they struggle together against the constraints in the family's life, instead of against each other (Breunlin, Schwartz & Mac Kune-Karrer, 1992).

ASSESSMENT

People express their hopes, dreams, pain, and suffering through individual and family stories. Thus, people need to tell their stories, and therapists need to listen. Individual and family testimony leads to revelation. In turn, revelation leads to enlightenment, a necessary step toward change.

Self-analysis or self-confrontation requires a sense of safety, trust, and control. If fear replaces self-analysis and safety, trust and control are absent, and the individual's threshold for experiencing strong emotions is severely lowered, activating defensive mechanisms that protect the individual from intense feelings. Some individuals (afraid of strong emotions or afraid of their relationships "falling apart") have difficulty voicing their thoughts and feelings. In such cases, it is incumbent upon the therapist to develop a collaborative relationship with her or his clients, enabling them to tell their stories and confront their problems.

Couple and family therapy approaches are inherently systemic and require an understanding of each person's contribution to the problem. Although this perspective is valuable and has merit, therapists are cautioned against assigning equal blame and promoting equal compromise without first assessing issues of power and privilege as they pertain to gender, race, class, and religion in the family, regardless of the family's culture.

An oppressed person may demonstrate complementary behavior, but that does not mean that the oppressed person has equal responsibility for the development of the problem. Rather than trying to prove that each person is equally responsible for the problem, it is more important to expose oppression in families and work toward creating more socially just or ethical family relationships.

At the individual level of the intersystem approach, attention is given to individual development and personality styles, individual defense mechanisms, and individual stressors. The goal of assessment at the individual level is to understand the personal dynamics, including identity and personality style, that directly affect the way an individual relates to others (Hof & Treat, 1989). For example, at the individual level, Michael's behaviors (touching others, making strange noises and motions, and laughing too loud at the wrong time) have been attributed to poor social judgment; however, it would be important to assess organic causes, particularly because some of these behaviors could be manifestations of neurological disorders.

At the interactional level, the focus is on the relationship. Based on the assumption that all individuals have three basic interpersonal needs (the need to belong, the need to have a sense of control, and the need for love; Weeks, 1989), the purpose of assessment at this phase is to understand how these needs manifest and contribute to relationship functioning. Some of the areas of exploration at the interactional level are communication skills, degree of affect, nonverbal communication, conflict-resolution skills, decision-making skills, and responsivity versus reactivity (Hof & Treat, 1989).

Without the contextual lens as an overarching frame of reference at the interactional level, the assessment may yield an incomplete picture, lead to more blaming of the victimized person, or may inadvertently help to maintain the status quo. Cultural norms and expectations help to determine patterns of communication, expressions of anger and affection, power distribution, gender roles, and implicit or explicit couple and family contracts.

At the intergenerational level the emphasis is on the extended family and the multigenerational context. The intent of assessment at this level is to understand issues such as legacies across the generations, loyalties, cut-offs, unresolved losses, and the impact these issues have on the individual and on his or her relationship functioning (Hof & Treat, 1989).

Couple and family therapists have given little attention to siblings, despite their focus on the intergenerational dimension in therapy. Siblings have a powerful effect on the individual's development of identity and personality. More specifically, siblings influence an individual's relationship to her or his children, intimate partners, friends, and coworkers (Watson, 1998). Race, class, and culture significantly influence sibling relationships, determining whether siblings are close, distant, or equal. Furthermore, culture governs the family rules and norms that affect sibling relationships (McGoldrick, Watson & Benton, 1999), thereby setting the stage for the individual's emotional system, because sibling relationships are as formative as parent–child relationships (Watson, 1998).

Again, the contextual dimension is extremely important when considering the intergenerational level because of the role culture plays in determining how individual family members behave and how their behavior reflects on the entire family. Culture also influences family myths that are passed down through the generations victimizing and contradictory intergenerational messages and dysfunctional family patterns. Individual family members may feel helpless to change these myths, messages, and patterns. A contextual framework can help the individual, the couple, and the family to separate cultural learning from a damaged self-perspective.

The purpose of assessing the contextual level is to give therapists a better understanding of those cultural factors, which provide the emotional map for individual and family functioning, enabling therapists to have a better understanding of their clients and resulting in improved treatment outcomes.

Therapists should carefully assess and challenge inequities in individual and family functioning, regardless of the presenting problem. As members of society, we are exposed to social inequities that become a part of the psyche, resulting in emotional and behavioral constraints for individuals and families.

THE THERAPEUTIC PROCESS

A comprehensive and complete understanding of the intersystem model can be found in the books *Treating Couples: The Intersystem Model of the Marriage Council of Philadelphia* (Weeks, 1989) and *Couples in Treatment: Techniques and Approaches for Effective Practice,* Second Edition (Weeks & Treat, 2001). Offered in the following sections are organizing principles in the process of my integrative family therapy practice: structure, therapist–client relationship, the collaborative contract, information gathering, hypothesizing, goal setting, and change strategies and interventions.

Structure

The integrative model proposed in this chapter involves several aspects. One of the most integral is the use of more than one theory and the employment of techniques from different approaches. A therapeutic process that is comprehensive, multidimensional, multilayered, and flexible helps the therapist to avoid conceptualizing and treating the family within narrow parameters (Weeks & Treat, 2001).

A systemic perspective is also critical to the therapeutic process. It allows the therapist to work with problems by addressing the contexts in which they occur. It provides a broader understanding of the complex nature of human behavior and keeps the therapist from seeing only one level of the human system as the cause of a problem. On the other hand, a systemic perspective may suggest that individuals are equally healthy or unhealthy (Weeks & Treat, 2001). Thus, a systemic perspective may enable therapists to overlook oppression and serious personality disorders in families. Therapists who assume a neutral stance under the guise of systemic therapy, pretending that each family member has equal power, are also acting as though relationships develop outside of any larger historical and sociopolitical context (Del Vecchio, 1998).

The four levels or systems (individual, interactional, intergenerational, and contextual) provide information about human development and conditioning and point to the constraints that limit functioning and maintain problems. An integrative family therapist must be able to simultaneously view the multisystemic context of the problem, use techniques and questions that impact on the various levels, and fluidly move among the levels and between varied change strategies.

Therapist–Client Relationship

The therapist–client relationship should acknowledge the client's strengths and seek to empower the client through knowledge and strategies that the client can then use to access her or his competence. The effort to validate the client's strengths and to empower the client begins with the first session. The social worker describes the therapeutic approach, including the importance of the therapist–client relationship. The client is also asked to share any concerns about the therapist–client relationship, in order to attempt a solution before the client decides that it is not a good match (the act of doing this may increase the client's sense of hope and may help to empower the client to attempt other solutions). At the end of the first session the client is asked, "What do you think about us being able to work together?" If the client states that he or she believes that we could work together, the beginning of a collaborative working relationship is established.

The Collaborative Contract

The collaborative contract helps to establish the family's role as a shared participant in the therapeutic process. In a collaborative process, each person respects the other's area of expertise. Each person becomes a valued member of the team, which increases each individual's commitment to finding a way out of the present difficulty.

The collaborative contract also helps to establish the therapist's role as team facilitator. The therapist is therefore entrusted to explore each individual's understanding of the problem and the interpretive meaning that each person gives to the problem. Furthermore, the therapist is expected to be impartial—to show understanding and empathy for all perspectives—yet expose oppression and identify constraints on any or all of the four levels (individual, interactional, intergenerational, and contextual) that prevent families from reaching their optimal potential. The therapist must have a positive outlook to inspire hope and help the family realize its own natural healing resources.

Gathering Information

The therapist needs to have a clear and comprehensive picture of the individual, interactional, intergenerational, and contextual factors as they relate to constraining behaviors, thoughts, and feelings. The therapist may be required to share knowledge about the systemic nature of problems and the impact that each of the four systems, individually and collectively, has on problem development and the potential for change.

Information gathered at the individual level is generally concerned with understanding the individual's intrapsychic dynamics, as well as the physical health of the person. In addition, the therapist is interested in the meaning that each individual gives to the problem and what each individual thinks about the other's perception of the problem (circular questions may be used to elicit such feedback). Individual family members' responses reveal information about each person's interpretive framework, relationship definition, and predictions of the other members' behavior (Weeks & Treat, 2001).

The interactional level of inquiry is concerned with the family's functioning. The specific focus of inquiry is on communication patterns, conflict-resolution skills, emotional contracts, interlocking cognitive distortions, and inappropriate or blocked emotions. Special consideration should be given to how family members use attributional strategies to avoid taking personal responsibility by blaming other people or external events (Weeks & Treat, 2001).

The intergenerational component is focused on family-of-origin issues that may contribute to the couple's stalemate. Because couple's therapy may be an ineffective process for resolving deeply entrenched intrapsychic issues, therapists may consider concurrent individual therapy for each partner (Hollander-Goldfein, 1989).

Extended family members, regardless of where they live, can powerfully influence an individual's relationship with others. Boyd-Franklin and Franklin (1998) caution therapists against treating African American individuals, couples, or families in isolation from the extended family because extended family members can exert incredible pressure. They argue that a careful genogram and the inclusion of key family members will help to prevent extended family members from sabotaging treatment.

The contextual level is most directly concerned with the sociopolitical and the sociocultural structures that impact the individual, the interactional, and the intergenerational dimensions of human development and family functioning. Therapists are urged to attend to the relationship between the family and societal injustices.

Hypothesizing

Hypothesizing is a shared endeavor between the therapist and the family. It involves the therapist sharing some basic ideas about the nature and the causes of the problem (Weeks & Treat, 2001) and engaging the family in a dialogue about the hypotheses (including the family's disagreement). Although the therapist elicits the family's feedback, the direction of the conversation is ultimately determined by the therapist's own assumptions. If a therapist assumes family deficiency, the family will be guided to discuss its pathology, and its strengths will remain hidden. Thus, the questions asked by the therapist influence what is learned about the family, for both the therapist and the family (Bruenlin, Schwartz & Mac Kune-Karrer, 1992).

Goal Setting

An integrative approach allows the therapist to tailor the goals of treatment to the family without being constrained by the treatment goals within a unidimensional model. However, there are three important steps to goal setting: (a) gather a clear statement of each person's view of the problem and what each person wants from the others and from therapy; (b) gain knowledge of attempted solutions so that the family's problem-solving abilities are integrated into realistic, success-promoting goals; and (c) formulate the collected data in a meaningful, organized way (Groome, 1989). The objective of goal setting is to have the family members take into account how the four systems influencing them constrain them from changing.

Change Strategies and Interventions

Change strategies and interventions may be formulated for each system of assessment. Within an integrative approach, the therapist can use any combination of strategies, techniques, and approaches. However, the therapist needs to have a clear focus with respect to all the systems. The therapist must have an awareness of where to intervene first, the family's readiness for work in different problem areas, and how to sequentially build on success (Weeks & Treat, 2001).

APPLICATIONS TO DIVERSITY

For the purposes of applying integrative family therapy, assume that the Shore family is a middle-class African American family living in a suburban neighborhood. Nancy is 43, overweight, depressed, and employed as a pediatrician in a community clinic. Charley is 51, overweight, depressed, and unemployed. He flunked out of medical school, working in various pharmaceutical sales positions until his last job 2 years ago. He was asked to leave that job because of poor performance. The children are Rena, 18, who graduated from a private high school but dropped out of Howard University after completing one semester, and Michael, 12, who was recently diagnosed with Tourette's syndrome, after being expelled from his private school for accidentally hitting (Michael said it was a mistake) his White female teacher.

Nancy is the older of two sisters, and Charley has a younger and an older brother. Nancy came from a working-class family in the South, and Charley came from a middle-class professional family in the North. Charley's father is a doctor, and his mother is a teacher. His older brother is a lawyer. His younger brother, a computer analyst, died from AIDS. Neither of Nancy's sisters went to college, and both work inside the home.

Nancy frequently argues with Charley, claiming that he does not help around the house or with the children. Nancy complains about Charley giving money to Black charities when he is not bringing in any income. Charley complains that Nancy never thinks what he does around the house is good enough. He also complains that Nancy will not join the "right" Black organizations for her status as a doctor. Charley grew up in the elite "Jack and Jill" organization for middle-class Black youths, and his parents belonged to "Black society."

Nancy and Charley disagree about parenting. Nancy believes Charley is too hard on Michael (trying to force him into sports when he prefers to play computer games) and that he is too easy on Rena (not trying to force her to go back to college). Charley believes that Nancy babies Michael, yet stays on Rena's back.

Nancy's parents divorced after their youngest child graduated from high school. Nancy's mother discovered that her husband was gay right after the birth of their youngest child but did not want to disrupt the family. Nancy's father died from AIDS several years ago. Charley's parents are still married. Nancy's mother is the only family member living in the area. Charley resents Nancy's closeness with her mother.

Nancy and Charley both believe in religion but attend different churches. Charley goes to a Methodist church and Nancy attends a nondenominational church with her mother. Charley resents Nancy taking their children to her church because he believes the membership consists of ex-addicts and homo-sexuals.

African American Family Diversity

African American families are frequently regarded and treated as a monolithic group (Watson, 2000). Class differences are especially ignored, reinforcing the commonly held belief that problematic Black families are low-income families living in a crime-infested urban neighborhood. Family therapists may acknowl-edge race as a context when assessing and treating African Americans but often fail to acknowledge class differences in general and within-family class differences in particular.

The multiproblem, middle-class African American Shore family poignantly illustrates class differences within the family. Nancy and Charley basically grew up in two different worlds. It was just assumed that Charley, a member of the Black elite, would succeed, continuing the legacy of generations of African Americans who are well-bred examples of the Black race. Because Nancy was smart, family members sacrificed to enable her success. However, Nancy's suc-cess was regarded as the entire family's success, resulting in her internaliza-tion of a "debt" owed to the family. Thus, class is an important filter for each partner's expectations of self, marriage, and family.

Race and Individual Development (Individual System)

No African American can escape racism, regardless of class, socioeconomic status, education, and income (Boyd-Franklin & Franklin, 1998). Family thera-pists should explore racial identity with African Americans and the impact of race on the psychosocial development of African Americans. Family therapists should not assume that all African Americans consciously understand the ef-fects of race on their individual development and, consequently, on their inter-actions with others (Watson, 2000).

Rena was challenged with the authenticity of her Blackness at a histori-cally Black college. Charley encouraged Rena to go to a Black school, but once there, Rena felt as if she did not belong. Not knowing how to deal with such intense racial feelings and not trusting her parents to understand, Rena simply refused to return after completing her first semester.

Although race was largely at the heart of the elite Black community of Charley's upbringing, race was rendered invisible by the emphasis placed on high achievement. Charley first began to feel Black when he entered medical school. In medical school he experienced frequent racist assaults that he internalized as his own inadequacy. He then became depressed and eventually flunked out of medical school, disappointing both his family of origin and his new wife.

Race was always present in Nancy's working-class family in the South. She was accustomed to accepting racism and moving on. Although Nancy experienced racism in medical school, she felt she had to "keep on keeping on." She had difficulty talking about race and discouraged Charley from doing so.

African American girls are seen as faring better than African American boys in a racist society. African American boys are disproportionately placed in special education classes and are labeled more often as aggressive or hyperactive (Boyd-Franklin & Franklin, 1998). Michael's behavioral problems may have been viewed as social maladjustment, without any exploration of a physical cause. Hence, it is crucial for the therapist to explore the racial experiences of African American women, men, girls, and boys, both within and outside the family.

The emphasis on the individual system allows the therapist to explore racial identity. Such exploration assists the integrative family therapist in better understanding the racial identity of each member of the family, helping to avoid assuming that racial identity is the same for each family member. By exploring racial identity, the therapist facilitates the family's discussion of race and the way in which it affects family members' lives, including intrafamily experiences (Watson, 2000).

Race and Relationship Development (Interactional)

For African American men and women, the couple relationship ideally is a comforting and trusted place, where each partner can deal with the difficult and painful topic of race—where they can share their vulnerability to race and help heal the wounds inflicted by a racist society (Boyd-Franklin & Franklin, 1998).

African American men and women are socialized differently to cope with racism. Because of the roles imposed onto Black men and women during slavery, Black women learned to rely on themselves. African American families continued to raise their daughters to be self-sufficient because of the prevailing belief that Black women can only count on themselves. On the other side of the coin, African American families have reacted to society's harsh treatment of Black males by attempting to protect their sons, discouraging them from being too aggressive and standing up for their rights with Whites.

Nancy and Charley's couple dynamics reflect the stereotype of the "super Black woman and the inferior Black man." This stereotype forms the meaning each partner gives to the other's behavior. Nancy's underlying belief that Black men cannot be counted on and Charley's underlying belief that Black women are controlling limit them in the relationship. Rather than share their racial feelings, they attempt to manage the other's behavior in order to reduce their own anxiety about not being worthy of care and of being inadequate.

Inclusion and focus on the interactional system make it possible for the therapist to consider the influence of race on relationship dynamics; this includes family organization, communication patterns, relationship expectations, and the dynamic tension that may be created because of slave legacies between the African American man and woman or because family members are at different stages of racial identity. In addition, issues related to the shortage of Black men and educational disparities between Black men and women have important implications for power dynamics in the African American couple (Boyd-Franklin & Franklin, 1998).

The Extended African American Family (Intergenerational)

African American families must be treated with consideration of the intergenerational or the extended family context. Not to do so would be to miss the significant value placed on the permanent obligation of individuals to contribute to the well-being of the extended family. Despite his not having to contribute directly to the extended family, there is an expectation that Charley will contribute to important Black social and civic causes, thereby fulfilling the obligation of the Black elite to give back. Assessing the intergenerational system helps the therapist to uncover historical racial and family intergenerational themes, and beliefs, as well as the meanings that they hold for individual and relationship functioning.

Sociocultural Contexts (Contextual)

All families have multiple sociocultural contexts of membership. Because African Americans have not been either truly accepted in society or provided with equal access to institutional resources, race is the single most important sociocultural context of membership for African Americans. Race can both constrain and enhance the way African Americans relate to one another. It is certain to affect how African Americans view life. Thus it is imperative that therapists seek an understanding of the contribution of race to individual, couple, and family functioning, as well as an understanding of the opportunities and the constraints that race presents for African Americans.

LIMITATIONS OF THE MODEL

Comprehensive or specially designed integrative models require the therapist to have knowledge about a variety of phenomena and a variety of interventions. Integrative models also require therapists to have a strong awareness of when things are not working and when to change the focus (Nichols & Schwartz,

2001). Theoretical purity simplifies therapy, whereas integration makes it a more complex process. The rigor and the certainty of one model are exchanged for possible confusion and greater demands on the therapist in an integrative approach, eliminating the specificity and the security of a pure model (Breunlin, Schwartz & Mac Kune-Karrer, 1992).

RESEARCH

The overall research findings suggest that couple and family therapy is effective. However, the vast majority of attempts to demonstrate one model's effectiveness over another in the field of couple and family therapy have yielded equivocal results. Few of the comparative research studies in couple and family therapy examined therapy process or attended to measures of the implementation of treatment. For instance, in comparing theoretical models, orientation or variables related to orientation were rarely assessed (Shadish, Ragsdale, Glaser, & Montgomery, 1995). Although Pinsof and Wynne (1995) reported integrative family–based approaches to be very effective, they concluded that it was unclear what specific difference family treatment makes within more comprehensive integrative models without component studies.

SUMMARY

Family therapy has opened its borders to include a multileveled analysis of the human system. Integrative family therapy acknowledges the multiple contexts that organize people's beliefs, behavior, and expectations. Within these multiple contexts are opportunities and constraints that affect individuals, couples, and families to a lesser or greater degree, depending on power and privilege as these pertain to sociocultural factors. Therapists would do well to consider the constraints and the opportunities for families at each of the following four levels: individual, interactional, intergenerational, and contextual. Finally, therapists are compelled to examine their own presuppositions about therapy and their own culture of origin, in order to increase their effectiveness with all families.

REFERENCES

Aponte, H. (1994). *Bread and spirit: Therapy with the poor*. New York: Norton.

Boyd-Franklin, N., & Franklin, A. J. (1998). African American couples in therapy. In M. McGoldrick (Ed.), *Revisioning family therapy: Race, culture, and gender in clinical practice* (pp. 268–281). New York: Guilford Press.

Breunlin, D. C., Schwartz, R. C., & Mac Kune-Karrer, B. (1992). *Metaframeworks: Transcending the models of family therapy*. San Francisco: Jossey-Bass.

Del Vecchio, D. (1998). Dismantling white male privilege within family therapy. In M. McGoldrick (Ed.), *Revisioning family therapy: Race, culture, and gender in clinical practice* (pp. 159–175). New York: Guilford Press.

Drewery, W., & Winslade, J. (1997). The theoretical story of narrative therapy. In G. Monk, J. Winslade, K. Crocket, & D. Epston (Eds.), *Narrative therapy in practice: The archaeology of hope* (pp.32–52). San Francisco: Jossey-Bass.

Groome, E. R. (1989). Goal setting and marital therapy. In G. Weeks (Ed.), *Treating couples: The intersystem model of the Marriage Council of Philadelphia* (pp. 22–37). New York: Brunner/ Mazel.

Hines, P. M. (1998). Climbing up the rough side of the mountain: Hope, culture, and therapy. In M. McGoldrick (Ed.), *Revisioning family therapy: Race, culture, and gender in clinical practice* (pp. 78–89). New York: Guilford Press.

Hof, L. & Treat, S. R. (1989). Marital assessment: Providing a framework for dyadic therapy. In G. R. Weeks (Ed.), *Treating couples: The intersystem model of the Marriage Council of Philadelphia* (pp. 3-21). New York: Brunner/Mazel.

Hollander-Goldfein, B. (1989). Basic principles: Structural elements of the intersystem Approach. In G. Weeks (Ed.), *Treating couples: The intersystem model of the Marriage Council of Philadelphia* (pp. 38-69). New York: Brunner/Mazel.

McDaniel, S. H., Lusterman, D., & Philpot, C. L. (2001). Introduction to integrative ecosystemic family therapy. In S. H. McDaniel, D. Lusterman, & C. Philpot (Eds.), *Casebook for integrating family therapy: An ecosystemic approach* (pp. 3–17). Washington, DC: American Psychological Association.

McGoldrick, M., Watson, M. F., & Benton, W. (1999). Siblings through the life cycle. In B. Carter & M. McGoldrick (Eds.), *The expanded family life cycle: Individual, family, and social perspectives* (3rd ed., pp. 153–68). Boston: Allyn & Bacon.

McKenzie, W., & Monk, G. (1997). Learning and teaching narrative ideas. In G. Monk, J. Winslade, K. Crocket & D. Epston (Eds.), *Narrative therapy in practice: The archaeology of hope* (pp. 82–117). San Francisco: Jossey-Bass.

Nichols, M. P. & Schwartz, R. C. (2001). *Family therapy: Concepts and methods* (5th ed.). Boston: Allyn & Bacon.

Pinsof, W. M., & Wynne, L. C. (1995). The efficacy of marital and family therapy: An empirical overview, conclusions, and recommendations. *Journal of Marital and Family Therapy, 21,* 585–610.

Shadish, W. R., Ragsdale, K., Glaser, R. R., & Montgomery, L. M. (1995). The efficacy and effectiveness of marital and family therapy: A perspective from meta-analysis. *Journal of Marital and Family Therapy, 21,* 345–359.

Walsh, F. (1998). Beliefs, spirituality, and transcendence: Keys to family resilience. In M. McGoldrick (Ed.), *Revisioning family therapy: Race, culture, and gender in clinical practice* (pp. 62–77). New York: Guilford Press.

Watson, M. F. (1998). African American sibling relationships. In M. McGoldrick (Ed.), *Revisioning family therapy: Race, culture, and gender in clinical practice* (pp. 282–294). New York: Guilford Press.

Watson, M. F. (2000). Treatment as it is influenced by issues specific to African American families. In I. D. Glick, E. M. Berman, J. F. Clarkin, & D. S. Rait (Eds.), *Marital and family therapy* (4th ed., pp. 361–371). Washington, DC: American Psychiatric Press.

Weeks, G. R. (1989). An intersystem approach to treatment. In G. R. Weeks (Ed.), *Treating couples: The intersystem model of the Marriage Council of Philadelphia* (pp. 317–340). New York: Brunner/Mazel.

Weeks, G. R., & Treat, S. (1992). *Couples in treatment: Techniques and approaches for effective practice.* New York: Brunner/Mazel.

Weeks, G. R., & Treat, S. (2001). *Couples in treatment: Techniques and approaches for effective practice* (2nd ed.). Philadelphia: Brunner-Routledge.

11

Narrative Therapy and the Practice of Advocacy

Emphasis on Affirming Difference When Working With Diverse Clients

Kevin J. Fitzsimmons, MSW
Larry M. Zucker, MSW

INTRODUCTION

Since the dawn of the social work profession, there have been those who have dreamed of building a unique and respected body of knowledge concerning helpful service to suffering persons. At the same time, there is an equally impressive history of the profession's attempt to make social and political advocacy central to the work. Clinical social workers have often failed at holding this tension between service and advocacy and have been overtaken by beliefs and practices that are more consistent with psychology and psychiatry. Practices have been adopted by social work that decontextualize and depoliticize human suffering and thus betray its unique commitment to see the person-in-context. Narrative therapy is a clinical approach that restores this commitment. "For many narrative therapists, doing therapy is just one aspect of a life committed to the pursuit of social justice" (Nichols & Schwartz, 2001, p. 393).

Specifically, narrative therapy rests on the belief that people make meaning of their lives through stories. These stories organize experience and serve as a means to interpret what of experience is worth noting and what is not. In every culture, certain preferred stories frequently have tremendous influence on how individuals interpret their experience. The conversations called *therapy* are opportunities to examine the assumptions and the effects of these stories and to decide whether or not the stories are ones that a person wants to live by. If this examination results in the individual deciding to take a stand against the influence of certain stories and for that of other stories that hold preferred values and beliefs, the therapy focuses on the commitment to these alternative stories.

In this re-storying process, the taken-for-granted nature of certain ideas and values imbedded in prevailing cultural stories becomes exposable, and thus the ideas and values become examinable. In other words, their status as truths is scrutinized. Therefore, the ideas by which clients evaluate themselves as normal, or not, often become noticeable in narrative therapy, as imbedded in a culturally preferred story of how people ought to live. The story itself is then perceived as preferred but not true.

This example regarding normalcy highlights another distinctive aspect of a narrative therapy. Narrative theorists perceive most psychotherapies as trans-mitters of ideas of normalcy and of the culturally dominant stories that carry them. This is done unthinkingly, once therapists make claims to neutrality. Consequently, narrative therapists, who believe that claims to neutrality are unsupportable, take pains to collaborate with clients in ways that can account for or, at least, address the lack of neutrality in the therapeutic setting. In short, narrative therapists believe that, in order for therapy to be other than the re-production of unexamined cultural beliefs and values, it must render the taken-for-granted examinable.

Many of the taken-for-granted values and beliefs that narrative practices aim to address are imbedded in the structure of the chapters of this text, including this one. While the structure of the chapter has been chosen with the well-intended idea of easily making comparisons from one approach to the next, complying with the expectations of this structure, without voicing concerns about it, would be a misrepresentation of the distinctions that set narrative therapy apart from other approaches.

THE CONCEPT OF THE PERSON AND THE HUMAN EXPERIENCE

Narrative therapists hold that all concepts of persons are socially constructed phenomena. What persons "are" is no more or less than a given *story* about who they are, a story created collectively through a particular use of language, shared by a given group of people. Generally, cultures prefer stories about humans that are in accord with the beliefs and the values that dominate that culture. A historical view of how a culture's stories about its members shift and evolve over time reveals that the stories comprise not discovered truths about human nature and essence but rather a reflection of currently prevailing discourses or "grand narratives" (Cushman, 1995; Parry & Doan, 1994). For instance, what constitutes a deep, meaningful, or true self in one culture is meaningless or even offensive in another. Similarly, prevailing United States culture celebrates an individualism that, in other times and places, might be seen as a pathological lack of regard for others.

Thus, to a narrative therapist, clients are saddled with whatever "concept of the person" their therapist is privileged to hold. *Privileged* here refers to the fact that the authority to narrate stories of identity is never evenly distributed. In contemporary United States culture, particularly the "culture" of psychotherapy, the mental health practitioner, a.k.a. psychotherapist, a.k.a. clinical social worker, holds the privilege of telling stories about the others' so-called natures. This does not imply that the position is worthy of the privilege or even respected by many; it simply means that the position has gained the right to have a voice in saying what, in concept, persons are. That this right is taken for granted is apparent in the heading of this section. It assumes that all paradigms have the right to have concepts of persons that must be both understood and subscribed to in order to comprehend the practices of the paradigm. Narrative therapists claim no such concept of the person or the human experience; they perceive such a concept to be the manifestation of privilege to impose upon the client's experience meanings consistent with the therapist's beliefs, but not accurately reflecting the client's understanding of his or her own identity or lived experience. Eschewing this taken-for-granted privilege, narrative practitioners attempt to elicit the client's ideas and values to guide the conversations called therapy. Bringing forth the client's ideas about humans and their experiences, rather than imposing the ideas of the therapist, allows conversations to center around the thinking and the valuing of the client. To those unaccustomed to creating therapeutic encounters that are not guided by *a priori* biopsychosocial maps, it may be initially difficult to imagine that clients' own accounts could guide the conversation. Yet narrative therapy attempts just that: the creation of a helpful encounter that is organized not around what therapists know and believe, but around the knowledge, the skills, the experiences, the beliefs, and the intentions of their clients and families, people, and shared lived histories.

HISTORICAL PERSPECTIVE

The history of narrative therapy is a short one. In the 1980s Michael White, a social worker from Adelaide, Australia, began writing of his ideas about therapy in *Family Process* (White, 1986) and in his own journal, the *Dulwich Centre Newsletter* (White, 1988). His first book, coauthored with David Epston, *Narrative Means to Therapeutic Ends* (1990), received an enthusiastic response from family therapists who had begun to question the oppressive nature of systemic practices. From the publication of this first textual explanation of narrative therapy until the present, narrative therapy has grown in popularity, to the point of being acclaimed as the approach "that now dominates family therapy" (Nichols & Schwartz, 2001, p. 187).

The intellectual history is more complex. Dismayed by traditional approaches to treatment encountered in his first social work positions in inpatient settings, White began to investigate the thinking of the French social critic Michel Foucault. Noting that knowledge is power, but doubting the validity of claims to absolute truth in the social sciences, Foucault (1965) argued that the holders of knowledge were not discovering the truth but deciding what it was. When this knowledge was then used to support institutional practices, patients were exposed to the exertion of power that was called treatment. White also became interested in the thinking of anthropologists who were interested in understanding how people from different cultures made meaning of their lives. He collaborated with David Epston, a social worker in New Zealand, who had been influenced by the anthropological use of the narrative metaphor, and wrote "The Story Corner" for the *Australian and New Zealand Journal of Family Therapy.* Both became interested in the work of Jerome Bruner (1986), who brought the narrative metaphor to sociology by positing that people interpreted their experiences through coherent stories that were constitutive of their lives. From literary theory, White adapted the notion of deconstructing texts and applied it to the therapeutic endeavor. He notes that he is using the term "deconstruction in a way that may not be in accord with its strict Derridian sense . . . " (White, 1991, p. 27). (He prefaces this comment with the admission that he is liberally borrowing Jacques Derrida's (1978) central idea that the meaning of a written text is not just in the text itself but in the social and political context of its production.) White goes on to say,

> According to my rather loose definition, deconstruction has to do with the procedures that subvert taken-for-granted realities and practices: those so-called truths that are split off from the conditions and the context of their production; those disembodied ways of speaking that hide their biases and prejudices; and those familiar practices of self and of relationship that are subjugating of person's lives. (1991, p. 27)

In the search to provide ethical and effective treatment, White questioned the authority of institutionalized practices that emphasized the deficits of those they treated. He noted how cultural stories carried values and served as the interpretive tool through which one made meaning of life. He then developed a way of working that exposed this process and offered the opportunity to challenge the authority of the stories themselves.

KEY THEORETICAL CONSTRUCTS

The key construct that informs the narrative therapy perspective is that clinical interactions do not occur outside of the culture and are therefore subject to the prevailing values, beliefs, ideologies, injustices, and structures. Culture is not one monolithic force but a rich and complex set of forces that is operating in all of our lives all of the time. To realize that therapy is part of, and not apart from, cultural expression is to realize, for example, that a therapy that defines health in terms of individuation risks imposing a "Western" value, or a therapy promoting affective expression might be imposing a "female" value. Similarly, a therapy that emphasizes generational boundaries might favor nuclear over transgenerational family structures, and a therapy that helps someone "come out" as a gay person might be marginalizing of bisexuality, and so forth. In other words, well-meaning clinical practices can be the transmitters of preferences that might not honor those of the client. Despite the intention to be helpful, clinicians' practices may have the effect of marginalizing the client, because they imply that the practitioner is privy to the knowledge of a right or a healthy way to be and the client is not. The client's ideas then are forced to the margins and out of the conversation called therapy.

From this point of view, to assume that social work services are delivered from some privileged location, apart from the politics of marginalization, is to run the tangible risk of reproducing these politics. For the individual social worker or a social work agency that is committed to accounting for these unintended marginalizing effects, a set of practices must be enacted to avoid becoming complicit with the reproduction of the status quo. Narrative therapy attempts such a practice of accountability.

This emphasis on accountability requires that practices be aligned with the political commitments of the social worker. For instance, if one professes the importance of providing services that are empowering, but then proceeds to do so without accounting for the potentially disempowering nature of the services, such efforts may have unintended effects. More specifically, if social work services are provided to a member of a marginalized group, but the services emphasize the social worker's (not the client's) wisdom, knowledge, and expertise, then the social worker could be said to be further marginalizing the client.

Perhaps it is this fear of the unintended marginalizing effects of professional knowledge that most distinguishes narrative therapy. In the Shore family, for example, one might be tempted to bring to an encounter with Rena much information that "the field" has gathered through years of practice, research, and publication. The field "knows" a lot about adoption and its effects. The field "knows" a lot about mental illness and its symptoms. The field "knows" a lot about functional and dysfunctional family systems, effective and ineffective parenting styles, and so on. To the narrative therapist, this professional "knowledge" is thought of simply as a way to story a person's experience. The therapist, therefore, is free to bring forth an account of Rena's lived experience *from her*, along with *her* knowledge and skill as it pertains to achieving *her* dreams and overcoming that which she experiences as restraining her.

Narrative therapists prefer "stories" to "explanations" or "diagnoses" for two reasons. First, they are interested in the politics of stories. They are interested in knowing whose values they reflect and who is included and excluded from authorship. Second, because narrative therapists perceive stories as political, not scientific, they are not interested in the "truth" of a story but in the "effect" of a story: What difference does it make in the life of a person to experience himself or herself *within* a given story? What makes a given story authentic is not the science behind it, but the experience of it being held by a community of others who share similar values and purposes. Were Rena's therapist overly concerned with what she knows from her training about the effects of adoption, she might, for instance, draw Rena into an account of herself as having a deep and unconscious sense of betrayal that she will have to contend with throughout her life. Yet it's quite possible that a future conversation with Rena could bring forth a different story. For example, the history of Rena's attempts to search for her birth mother and her dream of singing for her birth mother some day could become part of a conversation that would gradually evolve into a story of bravery and resilience, rather than one of betrayal and loss. Alhough both stories that flow from the experience of adoption could be "true," the story of "Rena the Brave" could end up as more authentic and useful than that of "Rena the Betrayed." Thus, from a narrative perspective, it is not enough to provide service, however well intended; the deliverer of the services must be accountable for its effects.

Deconstruction, both in concept and in practice, promotes accountability that the narrative worker requires. Deconstruction has its origins in literary theory (Derrida, 1978) and refers to the practice of "unpacking" a text to situate its meanings in the context of its production. A therapist (listening deconstructively) is alert to the political nature of *all* stories, knowing that the text of any given story of human experience has embedded in it the assumptions of its authors. The ability to deconstruct stories and practices allows that the beliefs, the prejudices, and the biases that accompany these stories and practices become noticeable. Once noticed, one has the opportunity to go along with them or not. In other words, deconstruction allows a practitioner to examine the often-unnoticed politics of clinical practices that are usually thought of simply as benevolent. In this spirit, a narrative therapist would be alert to any unexamined assumptions he might be carrying. For example, the assumption that adoption creates an interior sense of betrayal could lead to looking for this experience to be replicated in Rena's history (and likely finding it, because life is infinitely rich with experiences) and encouraging her to focus on this aspect of her life. It might be "true" that Rena has had this string of experiences, but that does not mean that emphasizing them will be good for her.

According to Michael White (1991), the term *deconstruction* "has to do with procedures that subvert taken-for-granted realities and practices: those so-called truths that are split off from the conditions and the context of their production" (p. 27). He sees deconstruction as a perspective from which to interact with one's work and with persons called clients. From this perspective, one listens deconstructively. According to instructors of narrative therapy Freedman and Combs (1996),

> Through this listening, we seek to open space for aspects of people's life narratives that haven't yet been storied. Our social constructionist bias leads us to interact with people in ways that invite them to relate to their life narratives not as passively received facts, but as actively constructed stories. We hope they will experience their stories as something they have a hand in shaping, rather than as something that has already shaped them. (p. 46)

ASSESSMENT

Narrative therapists do not "assess" in the traditional sense. Rather, a first meeting, like subsequent meetings, is an opportunity to host a collaborative conversation, in which the clients and the therapist together make sense of the experience that brought the client to therapy. These conversations are shaped by carefully developed intentions and methods that help clients describe the hopes and the dreams they have for their lives and to distinguish the forces that facilitate these dreams from those that restrain them.

In his early writing, Michael White (1986) focused on the conceptual leap from positive to negative explanation. In a theory of positive explanation, something is the way it is *for knowable reasons.* The therapist seeks to understand the reasons by asking questions or applying various instruments intended to create a working hypothesis of "why" clients are having the problems that they're having. The interviewer gathers data that are pursued according to preordained explanatory frameworks and then arranged in a way that confirms these same frameworks. In a theory of negative explanation, something is the way it is *because it is not yet some other way.* Guided by this theory, the therapist is interested in what *restrains* things from being otherwise, not in what causes them to be as initially presented. If one were to insist on distinguishing assessment as a stage, first, one invites a deconstructive conversation in which the restraining forces are rendered visible and, next, invites "re-authoring" conversations, where the client's version of lived experience, both problematic and preferred, emerges. In reality, these two types of conversations happen more or less simultaneously. To further understand assessment from a narrative therapy perspective, it is necessary to make a second conceptual leap, from structuralist to non-structuralist thought (White, 2001).

Structuralist thought posits a structure to human experience, including both interpersonal and internal experience. The conceptualizations of "permeable generational boundaries" or "weak ego" are examples of this thinking. In structuralist therapies, assessment consists of making an expert (if tentative) hypothesis explaining behavior by linking it to "causes" residing in the family system or the conceptualized interior of the client. In the non-structuralist therapy (of which narrative therapy is but one example), the restraint is thought to reside not in the alleged structure of the person or the system but in the various stories within which a person experiences her or his life. To a narrative therapist, stories don't *describe* lives, they *constitute* them. So in addition to beginning to identify how a given story constitutes a problematic experience of living, "assessment" must also include revisualizing the dream that a person has for his or her own life and beginning a story that could rewrite it.

Narrative therapists are less interested in the truth status of a given account than in its effects. An account is problematic not because of its "wrongness" but because of its "thinness" (Geertz, 1983). A thin account doesn't capture, to the satisfaction of those it concerns, lived experience. Any given account leaves important aspects of the life described outside of its margins. An account "thickens" when it manages to include previously excluded bits of life in a manner that both explains and influences that life in ways the person prefers. By definition, the account of the Shores' experience offered in the text is thin, because we have no way of asking them to evaluate its effects on their lives. Although this account seems to be a good example of the clinical description that is typical in our field, it highlights what it highlights and obscures all else. Narrative therapists might treat that description the same way they would that of a referring source: It's *someone's* account, but it's rather like an unauthorized biography. Without the Shores' help, an authorized biography is impossible. A narrative therapist would approach assessment as the first opportunity to begin to bring forth an account that the Shores find both true and helpful.

The narrative therapist starts by assuming that the story the Shores are using to make sense of their own experience isn't rich enough to produce outcomes they might prefer. Narrative therapists presume that there are always alternative stories; the process of therapy is a search for these stories. The search for such preferred stories begins with the therapist seeking bits of experience that are important to the clients but are not sufficiently included in their current understanding of themselves and their circumstances. These discrepancies between story and lived experience, referred to as *unique outcomes* (White, 1988, 1991), are the building blocks of the preferred stories that we seek to elicit. In the examples that follow, the therapist "listens" for signs of prevailing discourse embedded in the summary in the same way she would be listening in a conversation with a client. When she encounters such discourse, she questions the Shores about the effects of the discourse, what forces in the culture support it, and what other ways of storying the same experience might exist.

For example, the therapist might notice that adopted Rena Shore is described as full of latent talents and abilities, yet presents herself through distinctly self-blaming discourses. Rena accuses herself of being hooked on crises, intentionally sabotaging her progress by dropping out of school. She describes herself as reenacting her birth mother's life by replicating that woman's choices. She blames herself for intentionally bringing forth her own rejection so that she can enjoy playing the victim, implicitly blaming herself for both the behavior and the need that underlies it. What difference might it make to Rena if her assessor was alert to how a psychological discourse can enter the popular lexicon and embed itself so thoroughly that its truth status is taken for granted?

THE THERAPEUTIC PROCESS

Narrative therapists are committed to listen to people's accounts of their problems and lives as stories. This seemingly innocuous focus appears distinct only when contrasted with standard approaches to therapeutic listening, in which the therapist is trained to hear diagnostically and theoretically. Although this process is often thought to be a necessary precursor to effective treatment, narrative therapists think of it as a story that can have the effect of recruiting clients into a deficit-based, theoretical relationship to themselves. For example, to join Rena in her self-blaming discourses is to participate in reifying them. Take, for example, the popular notion of self-sabotage that emerges as Rena's story from the written description in the beginning of this book. Rena didn't invent this notion, yet she accepts it as self-description. Who invented it? Who popularized it? Perhaps it is a thinned-down derivative of psychological discourse concerning unconscious, self-destructive motivations. Does Rena have a say in whose discourse percolates through to her self-talk? Likely not. She says, *"Just look at my life . . . It is the only way I know how to live. When things are going well, I can't stand it."* The therapist could then ask, *"Why do you think you're uncomfortable when things are going well?"* But this question accepts the assumptions embedded in her statement, risks drawing her further into a deficit identity, and encourages her to further conform her experience to a theory of self-sabotage. We would be on our way to becoming coauthors, or at least publicists, of what narrative therapists call a problem-saturated story. If, instead, we ask, *"You mentioned resuming your search for your birth mother and feeling ready to think again about the painful side of that part of your history. Do you think you're doing this to upset yourself because things are going well, or do you think there might be other reasons?"* This question is not intended to elicit data or confirm a hypothesis that is forming in the therapist's mind. Rather, it is meant to challenge a taken-for-granted discourse and invite Rena's fresh reflection on her own experience, hoping to find meaningful discrepancy between her experience and the problem-saturated story. These discrepancies, or unique outcomes, will be woven together into an alternate story that comes nearer to her lived experience and thus be more helpful than a problem-saturated account. Problem-saturated stories are not merely mental constructs but are widely circulated, popular in the field and in the culture at large, and thus hard to oppose or to see around. Similarly, for the alternate stories to have lasting effects, they, too, must be more than mental constructs, achieving a modicum of popularity in the local world of the client.

The previous example typifies the choices a narrative therapist makes. Which story will dominate in the unfolding therapy: the story of self-sabotage or a yet-to-be-told story of Rena's readiness to explore her adoption history? Were the story of self-sabotage allowed to dominate, there exists a very real risk of silencing Rena's ability to make meaning of her life apart from it. Even when she is trying to live a life that copes with it, this story continues to wed her to a problem-saturated identity.

Narrative therapy proposes that problems are separate from people and emphasizes this distinction in its language. This careful and intentional use of language is called *externalization*. Far more than a linguistic trick, externalization brings forth *the relationship* between a person and a problem, avoiding language that locates problems *in* people. It includes the therapist's belief in her clients' innate resourcefulness, seeing them as possessing the tools to wrestle with human dilemmas, rather than as damaged or incomplete human beings. Imagine, for example, that Rena started talking about feeling depressed. A narrative therapist might use an externalizing form of language that treats depression as a yet-to-be-richly-described force in Rena's life and Rena as a yet-to-be-consulted expert on its effects: *"Rena, how did depression enter your life? How does it have you seeing yourself? What do you think depression wants for you?"* In this simple example, treating depression as a noun allows a conversation that describes Rena's *relationship* to depression and guards against treating it as an adjective that in any way defines who she allegedly *is*.

To illustrate how deconstructive and re-authoring conversations seek to help loosen the grip of pre-existing discourse, imagine some conversations that might help Rena separate her identity from prevailing ideas about the effects of adoption. Rena speaks of experiences of "rejection" or "being left out in the cold." By inviting conversation about these feelings, a narrative therapist helps Rena tease out parts of her experience that may not conform to prevailing ideas that adoption is fundamentally abandonment and leaves a permanent mark. In search of her local knowledge, experienced-gained knowledge that is overlooked (Geertz, 1983), a therapist might introduce a series of questions intended to elicit her expertise on the actual effects of rejection in her life. These questions attempt to help Rena create alternate stories of her experience, instead of replications of problem-saturated, pre-existing narratives.

- When these rejections occur, how do they shape how you see yourself? Do they only negatively affect your picture of yourself? How do you respond to these rejections?
- In what ways have these "out in the cold" moments been touching your life? On what sorts of occasions do they show up?
- When these "out in the cold" feelings show up, what sort of future picture do they try to talk you into? Do you always believe that picture?
- Does rejection ever make you relate to others in ways that don't suit you?
- What sorts of events in your life would rejection want you to keep track of? What events would it rather have you forget?

Such questioning is guided by the belief that Rena's freedom to make meaning is best served by inviting her to articulate the effects of problems on her life. The meaning of experiences of rejection are not already there, fitting generalized meanings that might be associated with adoption. Meaning is negotiable, malleable, and transformable. Such questions do not avoid the possibility that being adopted is significant in Rena's life, or that she might sometimes behave problematically, but they invite collaboration with her to bring forth her knowledge rather than the therapist's or "the field's" knowledge. This intention is a crucial distinction. The therapy conversations center on Rena as expert. She is acknowledged as the authority of her experiences. The therapist's expertise is in constructing a line of inquiry that facilitates disentanglement from pre-existing narratives and discourses.

As the expert, Rena can be questioned about occurrences when she has succeeded against rejection, when the tables have been turned, so to speak. This curiosity can serve as an invitation to explore times when the problem did not have its usual dominating effects.

- Have there been times when you did not allow rejection to take over?
- What led to your not letting it take over?
- Tell me of the times you have stayed with your better judgment, even when the "out in the cold" feeling was insisting you go against it?
- How have you been able to take a stand against rejection? How has it affected your relationships?

These questions focus on Rena's knowledge of a preferred way of living and how to bring it about. Gradually, a story emerges that would not have been possible within the initial discourse. Imagine a conversation starting with one of the previous questions:

Therapist: Have there been times when you did not do what rejection wanted you to do?

Rena: I think so.

Therapist: Can you think of a time?

Rena: When I was with my friend Sue and started having those feelings, but I didn't leave.

Therapist: Rejection wanted you to leave, but you stayed?

Rena: Yeah, before, I'd leave and then feel angry at Sue for rejecting me.

Therapist: And staying was better?

Rena: Yeah.

Therapist: What was better about it?

Rena: Usually, when I leave, first I'm angry at the person, but then I think I end up angry at myself. It's almost like I start to think Sue's right to reject me, like I'm not worth it.

Therapist: So you didn't give in to what rejection wanted you to do or give in to what it wanted you to think about your worth to her?

Rena: Yeah.

Therapist: Does that make room for different sorts of thoughts about yourself?

Rena: Maybe a little.

Therapist: What sort?

Rena: Maybe I'm not such a bad person after all?

The therapist opens a line of questioning to elicit a possible unique outcome, a bit of a story that contradicts the problem-saturated account, being careful to let Rena decide whether it is meaningful. If it is, together, they start to build a story that contradicts the problem-saturated account of her preference for pushing friends away.

Once an emerging alternative story of worth is established, clinical conversations attempt to thicken its plot by eliciting the aspects of Rena's experience that give it a history, a social and political context, a supporting cast of people and relationships, a detailed means of operating, and, above all, a future. Developing and circulating this alternative narrative, this counter-plot, also becomes a focus in the therapy. That is, therapeutic conversations center on the need to actively manifest the story in one's life and to know what relationships, circumstances, ideas, and values support it. For Rena, the plot thickening could be encouraged by questions like the following:

- If I interviewed people from your past about your ability to stand against rejection and hang on to a sense of your own worth, who would be least surprised to hear that rejection hasn't completely won out?

Here the therapist manifests the belief that the starting point for building the alternative story lies in the client's history. Rather than thinking of therapy as a means for rebuilding worth, the therapist thinks of it as a place to *reclaim* a lost or hidden history of Rena's experience of worth.

- If I asked these people what it was about you that enabled you to stand against rejection, what sorts of abilities or qualities would they say made this possible?

The therapist is attempting to thicken the part of story that relates to character. Who is Rena in the eyes of people who witness her struggle for worth?

- If I asked these same people to tell me some stories from your shared past, stories that exemplify these abilities or qualities, what events do you think they might recall?

Here the therapist is plotting the *meanings* associated with reclaiming worth against the *events* that make up a life. Any narrative must choose which of a near-infinite number of events to include. The story of rejection would focus on different events than would the story of worth.

- Who in your present life would "get" what we're talking about here, your ability to hang on to a sense of worth in the face of rejection? Is there anyone who doesn't get it yet but might be on the verge of getting it? How could you bring that person up to date on these developments in your life?

The therapist's intention now is community building: Who "belongs" to this telling of Rena's life? Who *could* belong? The therapist wants to explore the possibility that the client's struggle may already exist in a community of concern.

- Do you think you're alone in fighting for worth, or do you know others who are engaged in a similar struggle? Have you ever been moved by their struggle? Have others ever been moved by yours?

Again, the community-building intention of the questions is apparent. The client is invited to view the problem as one that others also must face; these others can be inspiring to and inspired by the client.

- What difference might it make to your future if this sense of worth continues to grow and rejection's power to call the shots slowly fades?

Finally, the therapist is inviting a glimpse of the future within an emerging story.

A series of such questions builds upon the unique outcome that emerges when Rena is interviewed deconstructively about her responses to rejection—a story of worth whose plot begins to thicken sufficiently to give rejection some competition. An additional series of questions would invite Rena to include her thoughts about the larger social context (class, race, gender, and culture), yet would emphasize the narrative belief that problems are situated in contexts, not in psyches. Rena, for instance, might have ideas about how prevailing gender politics have become entwined with the ideas of rejection and the struggle for worth.

- Rena, having experienced the "out in the cold" feeling as a young woman, I'm wondering if you think a young man would experience it similarly?
- If not, why do think there would be a difference? What is your stance toward this difference?
- Do you think young women and men face different challenges in their efforts to feel worthy?
- Do these gender-specified ideas strengthen the problem we have been talking about?
- If you were to become strengthened against the unwanted effects of the problem, how would you respond to these gender-specified ideas?
- Who and what would support you in this effort?

These last questions stem from a narrative therapist's aim to situate the conversation in the widest possible framework, moving it out of the confinement of the conceptualized interior spaces that preoccupy so much of traditional therapy.

APPLICATION TO DIVERSITY

The description of the previous process should make it clear that narrative therapists perceive clients as knowledgeable about the effects of membership in cultures on the margins of dominant culture. Sensitivity to this reality is demonstrated by the practice of bringing forth client expertise in the preferred story of the client's life. This sensitivity is manifested in the commitment to practices that continually seek out and prefer client expertise to that of the therapist.

Celia Falicov (1988) makes the argument for a multidimensional approach to cultural sensitivity. She notes that the universalist response asserts that human beings are fundamentally more the same than they are different, making it detrimental to focus on that difference. The particularist approach asserts that each human being is unique and distinct, a culture unto himself or herself, and, therefore, to focus on cultural difference obscures the uniqueness of a client. Falicov dismisses both of these approaches because they silence the very real differences that have too long been ignored in the world of therapy. She argues for a comprehensive definition of culture as

> those sets of world views and adaptive behaviors derived from simulta-
> neous membership in a variety of contexts, such as ecological setting (ru-
> ral, urban, suburban), religious background, nationality, ethnicity, social
> class, gender-related experiences, minority status, occupation, political lean-
> ings, migratory patterns and stage of acculturation, or values derived from
> belonging to the same generation, partaking of a single historical moment,
> or particular ideologies. Thus, cultural differences result from simultaneous
> contextual inclusion (that is, participation and identification) in different
> types of groups. . . . it is necessary for therapists to be aware of the family's
> membership in all relevant contexts simultaneously. (Falicov, 1988, p. 336)

Narrative therapists believe that this comprehensive view of culture brings a thicker context into conversation than does the idea of ethnic focus alone. Furthermore, narrative therapy posits that the bias one is attempting to ac-count for by simply increasing sensitivity to diversity exists in the practices themselves. That is, when the practices of a paradigm stem from key constructs that advance ideas about human nature that are claimed to be universally ap-plicable, the bias is in the claim. Failure to directly address biased practices, and merely offer ways to adapt them, leaves the political nature of the practices themselves unaddressed.

Narrative therapy attempts to address the biases of the therapist by pro-moting the ideas of the client while exposing the therapist's ideas for examina-tion. These practices are adhered to for all clients, not just those of a particular race, ethnicity, gender, class, and so on. This does not, however, make narra-tive therapy susceptible to Falicov's wise critique of universalist ideas that ren-der differences invisible. On the contrary, narrativists are extremely interested in making visible the distinctions. They do so by restraining generalist dis-courses, no matter how well meaning or sensitive. Narrativists prefer to dem-onstrate their sensitivity to client expertise in all its complexity and richness, focusing on all accounts of people's lives as stories. These stories exist in cul-tures with dominant narratives, values, ideas, and beliefs that often have del-eterious effects on those who are not wholly represented by them. The effect, then, of such grand narratives is to marginalize those who are not represented by them. To account for this marginalization, narrative therapy is obligated to bring forth and affirm differences between the accounts of clients based on their lived experience and those of the grand narratives to which all are sub-jected. Thus the issues related to difference in race, ethnicity, gender, class, religion, and so on, become central to the therapy. Sensitivity to them is mani-fest in the central position they take in the therapeutic conversations. When one eschews such concepts in the first place, a therapist does not have to adapt key constructs to fit people for whom they were not originally considered. Noting the blinding effects of universal constructs, the narrative therapist seeks the aid of the client in keeping the therapist's eyes, mind, and heart open.

For example, if Rena were the adopted daughter of two monolingual Farsi-speaking Muslim parents who had immigrated to the United States as political refugees, narrative therapists would think it crucial to be curious about the effects of these circumstances.

- Rena, we have been talking about your life in this private manner and I'm wondering what our meeting would mean in the world your parents were raised in?
- Has being of a religious background different from the majority of U.S. citizens affected your experience of rejection?
- Has being the only English-speaking member of your family changed the way you relate to your parents, who have been out in the cold, without the ability to communicate effectively?
- In what ways have you and your family responded to being outsiders here in the United States that you are most proud of?
- How might these things you are proud of be useful in your struggles with rejection?

To further clarify this idea, let's also imagine that Rena was the adopted daughter of two upper-middle-class English-speaking Christian parents whose family line has been in the United States for 200 years. Given this example, narrative therapists would *still* think it crucial to be curious about the effects on Rena of *these* circumstances.

- Rena, we have been talking about your life in this private manner, and I'm wondering what our meeting like this would mean to your parents, given the era and the place in which they were raised?
- Rena, how have your feelings of being "out in the cold" been affected by coming from a family that is so well established in this culture?
- Do you have any sense of how Christian thoughts and attitudes toward adoption may have affected you and your family?
- Are there any ways in which being from what might be thought of as mainstream America affected your experience of being "out in the cold?"
- Are there some less obvious ways in which people from your family might have had their own "out in the cold" experiences?

These questions, as with those asked of Rena as a refugee, generate from the therapists listening to the client's account of her actual life. They are not shaped by specialized knowledge of her ethnicity but are sensitive to her experience. Such questions do not leave her story and its meaning to her on the margins; they make them central.

LIMITATIONS OF THE MODEL

"Limitations of the Model" typically invites the naming of various categories of persons or problems for which a given theory or practice may not be well suited. Narrative therapists cannot easily comply with this request, as it would require organizing therapy around such categories. Narrative therapy works when a therapist and a unique client are successful in creating a meaningful and useful dialogue that helps bring forth and sustain preferred identities, relationships, and outcomes. Narrative therapy is limited when, in the unique experience of a particular client, it is found unhelpful. This implies that ethical practice requires a narrative therapist to invite clients to speak of therapy's unhelpfulness or to otherwise question the therapist.

Consider a different interpretation of the task of describing the limitations of the model. Narrative therapy is extremely limited when it comes to contending with marginalizing discursive practices. White, Epston, and others have made valiant efforts to emphasize politics over the psychology of human suffering. Many therapy conversations are organized around such politics, and clients often find strength in reexamining their lives from such perspectives. People who struggle with mental illness find strength in viewing themselves as resisting compliance with operations that define health merely as productivity and self-sufficiency. People breaking from addiction are encouraged by realizing that drug and alcohol misuse is only one way of succumbing to a culture of consumption that defines living as consuming. Some of the most successful strainings at the limits of therapy involve organizations like the Vancouver Anti-Anorexia League (Madigan, 1994), where women join together in political action to take their lives back from anorexia's demands. Another impressive example is the work of the Just Therapy group in New Zealand. The agency is partly staffed and largely directly by White males, yet primarily serves women and Maori and Pacific Island peoples. To account for the differences in values and perspectives between providers and recipients, minority group caucuses have been assigned the task of monitoring services that are provided to their constituents (Tamasese & Waldegrave, 1993; Waldegrave, 1990).

The compliance of narrative therapy with established structures cannot be denied, most notably the isolating and hierarchy-reinforcing practices of one-on-one conversations between individuals with problems and those thought to be in a position to help them. In the United States most narrative therapy is offered in fee-for-service private practice, reimbursed by insurance companies requiring diagnoses, provided by therapists with back-to-back schedules that preclude community involvement. Narrative therapy is dedicated to radically different practices in such conversations, but the examples of the theory blossoming into full practice, like the previously mentioned Anti-Anorexia League, are quite rare.

RESEARCH

Research that fits within the social constructionist assumptions of narrative therapy is gradually accruing. Most traditional quantitative research is not found to be conceptually useful to narrative therapists, nor has the model been heavily researched from such perspectives. Much quantitative psychotherapy outcome research is patterned after the medical model's randomized clinical trial. In such research, *DSM* diagnoses are treated with allegedly replicable treatment models, comparing outcomes of randomly matched clients, therapists, and models. Such research methods ignore how poorly this practice reflects the real world, where people with complex dilemmas find therapists in non-randomized ways and encounter eclectic therapists and treatment approaches. Meta-analyses of the results of such studies consistently discount factors pertaining to model or method, favoring variables that cut across schools of therapy. Duncan and Miller's (2000) review of therapeutic research found that only 15% of outcome was attributable to the therapists' choice of model; 15% to the clients' hope or expectancy; 30% to the clients' perception of the therapeutic relationship; and fully 40% due to extratherapeutic factors or aspects of the client's life circumstances that aid him or her regardless of formal participation in therapy.

In a qualitative study involving ethnographic interviews of a small number of families who received narrative therapy, O'Conner, Meakes, Pickering, and Schuman (1997) found parallels to Duncan and Miller's (2000) conclusions. In exploring the clients' experience of what was helpful, they found that clients' being treated like experts on their own experience and feeling respected, listened to, acknowledged, and free from blame were the most significant variables. Although the study included a careful examination of techniques and methods, such as externalizing conversation, the relational ingredients were found more helpful than methods or techniques.

Narrative therapists often treat their clients like consultants or researchers. In a logical extension of the notion that clients are experts, narrative therapists frequently ask clients to help them in their work with other clients who are struggling with similar problems. For instance, if Rena were to make significant progress in her struggle to claim worth in relation to her history of adoption, her therapist might at some point say, *"I have a client who has just learned that she was adopted as an infant. She's feeling overwhelmed by the feeling that she wasn't 'worth keeping' by her birth mother or 'worth honesty' to her adoptive parents. Do you have any suggestions for how she might keep this recent discovery from erasing her sense of her worth in the world?"* In this manner, the client's knowledge is both respected and treated as intrinsically valuable to another person. Similarly, narrative therapists have long regarded their clients as co-researchers in search of effective therapies. Narrative therapists try to create the sort of relationship in which a client feels invited to speak up about the direction of therapy, about what is and is not helpful. Some recent research supports the idea that this variable, the client's experience of having an opportunity to guide the process, has a profound effect on outcome and satisfaction (Bischoff, McKeel, Moon, & Sprenkle, 1996; Shilts, Rambo, & Hernandez, 1997). In some cases, clients found research interviews to be more helpful than the therapy being researched (Gale, Odell, & Nagireddy, 1995). For example, when allowed to speak about the direction of therapy with researchers, clients often noted such conversations to be more helpful than the therapy itself. Because the narrative therapist attempts to bring forth client involvement, it makes available client knowledge that would otherwise be found only in follow-up research. Such research has tremendous political importance, contributes to thickening the story of what works in therapy, and particularly honors clients' voices (Hubble, Duncan, & Miller, 2002). Clients, then, can be viewed as the lead investigators of the research project called their therapy.

SUMMARY

Through the practice of narrative therapy, many social workers have been able to reinvigorate their work with the values that originally brought them into the field. In narrative practice, the tension between service and advocacy is partially resolved because therapists are better able to align themselves with clients in advocating for a world preferred by both. Narrative practices have allowed some social workers a reasonably comfortable way of working after years of struggle to practice therapy more effectively and accountably. Through narrative practice, they are less likely to engage in the individualizing and decontextualizing practice of situating human suffering primarily internally. They are more adept at inviting examination of the effects of the distribution of power at the macro or cultural level and of how those same operations of power are reproduced in the relational politics of family life. They are better at avoiding disempowering practices that place them in the role of expert in others' lives. By positioning themselves to notice and otherwise elicit their clients' skills and knowledge, they are more likely to grasp and support resources that have percolated up through the unique families and diverse communities from which their clients emerge. By abandoning any claims to objectivity and, instead, organizing therapy around the careful exploration of preferred experience, they are less likely to function as inadvertent colonizing agents by conducting therapy in ways that insist upon clients' compliance with prevailing cultural values and beliefs. On a personal note, the idea that working with people on their problems can simultaneously be working for a more just world has brought a special joy to the work we do. It has reminded us to be accountable for the privilege we hold and has helped us escape from working in hierarchically superior positions, with which we were always uncomfortable. Consequently, narrative therapy practices have allowed us to join with people in their struggles and be gifted by the joining.

REFERENCES

Bischoff, R. J., McKeel. A. J., Moon, S. M., & Sprenkle, D. H. (1996). Therapist-conducted consultation: Using clients as consultants to their own therapy. *Journal of Marital and Family Therapy*, 22(3), 359–379.

Bruner, J. (1986). *Actual minds: Possible worlds.* Cambridge, MA: Harvard University Press.

Cushman, P. (1995). *Constructing the self, constructing America: A cultural history of psychotherapy.* New York: Addison-Wesley.

Derrida, J. (1978). *Writing and difference.* Chicago: University of Chicago Press.

Duncan, B., & Miller, S. (2000). *The heroic client: Doing client-directed, outcome-informed therapy.* San Francisco: Jossey-Bass.

Falicov, C. (1988). Learning to think culturally. In H. A. Liddle, D. C. Breunlin, & R. C. Schwartz (Eds.), *Handbook of family therapy training and supervision* (pp. 335–357). New York: Guilford Press.

Foucault, M. (1965). *Madness and civilization: A history of insanity in the age of reason* (R. Howard, Trans.). New York: Random House.

Freedman, J., & Combs, G. (1996). *Narrative therapy: The social construction of preferred realities.* New York: Norton.

Gale, J. E., Odell, M., & Nagireddy, C. S. (1995). Marital therapy and self-reflexive research: Research and/as intervention. In G. H. Morris & R. J. Chenail (Eds.), *The talk of the clinic: Explorations in the analysis of medical and therapeutic discourse* (pp. 105-129). Hillsdale, NJ: Erlbaum.

Geertz, C. (1983). *Local knowledge: Further essays in interpretive anthropology.* New York: Basic Books.

Hubble, M., Duncan, B., & Miller, S. (2002). *The heart and soul of change: What works in therapy.* Washington, DC: American Psychological Association.

Madigan, S. (1994). Body politics. *Family Therapy Networker*, 18(6), 27.

Nichols, M., & Schwartz, R. (2001). *Family therapy: Concepts and methods.* Boston: Allyn & Bacon.

O'Connor, T. S., Meakes, E., Pickering, M. R., & Schuman, M. (1997). On the right track: Client experience of narrative therapy. *Contemporary Family Therapy*, 19(4), 479.

Parry, A., & Doan, E. (1994). *Story re-visions: Narrative therapy in the postmodern world.* New York: Guilford Press.

Shilts, L., Rambo, A., & Hernandez, L. (1997). Clients helping therapists find solutions to their therapy. *Contemporary Family Therapy: An International Journal*, 19(1), 117–132.

Tamasese, K., & Waldegrave, C. (1993). Cultural and gender accountability in the "Just Therapy" approach. *Journal of Feminist Family Therapy*, 5(2), 29–45.

Waldegrave, C. T. (1990). Just therapy. *Dulwich Centre Newsletter, (1)*, 5–46.

White, M. (1986). Negative explanation, restraint, and double description: A template for family therapy. *Family Process*, 25, 169–184.

White, M. (1988–1989, summer). The externalizing of the problem and the re-authoring of lives and relationships. *Dulwich Centre Newsletter* (Special ed.), 3–21.

White, M. (1991). Deconstruction and therapy. *Dulwich Centre Newsletter, (3)*, 21–40.

White, M. (2001). Folk psychology and narrative practice. *Dulwich Centre Journal, (2)*, 3–37.

White, M., & Epston, D. (1990). *Narrative means to therapeutic ends.* New York: Norton.

12

Clinical Social Work and Psychopharmacology

Emphasis on Indigenous Medicine in a Latino Community

Melinda L. Morgan, PhD
Ian A. Cook, MD

INTRODUCTION

*I*n all probability, psychotropic substances have existed as an integral part of culture since the evolution of humankind (Stein, 1998). Contemporary psychopharmacology, however, is a relatively new field that has experienced tremendous growth in the last 5 decades. When used appropriately, medication has allowed severely mentally ill persons to reside in community settings rather than in hospitals and has reduced suffering tremendously. Because of the significant increase in the use of psychotropic medication, there is an increasing need for social workers to be familiar with basic psychopharmacology. With the shift away from psychodynamic theory and long-term therapy, emphasis has increasingly been placed on quick stabilization and brief treatment, which means that pharmacotherapy may become the primary (or sole) intervention. Although social work historically endorses the *bio*psychosocial perspective, the biological component is often missing from theory, practice, and education. Social workers are often not well versed in the neurochemical processes involved in psychiatric conditions or the biological risk factors in psychosocial disorders. In order to understand the function of the total human being and the process of change across the life span, especially in light of managed care's emphasis on psychopharmacology as a treatment modality, it is important to have some understanding of the biological bases of psychiatric illness.

CONCEPT OF THE PERSON AND THE HUMAN EXPERIENCE

On one end of the spectrum, psychopharmacology may be seen as a routine linear medical intervention for people with psychiatric disorders, in which rigorous scientific methods can be applied to objectively measure the outcome of specific medications. On the other end of the spectrum, a phenomenological position views the intervention in terms of the meaning that the client assigns to the experience, including such things as help-seeking behavior, physician–client relationship, conditioning, social and cultural expectations, and past experience. A social work perspective views the experience of a pharmacological intervention within an environmental context. Social work interventions in conjunction with psychopharmacology include assisting not only the client but the family (defined by Meyer, 1990, as two or more people who are joined together by bonds of sharing and intimacy) and others in the social environment. The goal is to increase the likelihood of positive change, when (or if) the client begins to respond to psychotropic medication.

Human experience transpires within the context of biological, psychological, social, and spiritual systems. Behavior, perception, and biology are simultaneously organized at many levels, and there are reciprocal interactions among them. Some people may be genetically predisposed or have a vulnerability to mental illness; however, a subset of this population may be able to regulate their neurochemical factors by engaging in behaviors such as seeking appropriately rewarding social interactions, which in turn may better regulate the course of their psychiatric disorder. On the other hand, the inability to seek positive interaction could lead to further physiological deregulation and to an increase in symptoms.

HISTORICAL PERSPECTIVE

The history and the development of somatic treatments for psychiatric disorders are replete with serendipitous discoveries, often based on clinical observations within mental hospitals. Prior to experimentation with pharmacotherapy, many remedies that now seem primitive were used to treat psychiatric illness. For example, in 1927 Manfred Sakel introduced the "insulin shock treatment" for alleviating psychotic symptoms in people with schizophrenia (Kalinowsky, 1970). The genesis of this treatment came from the observation that patients with schizophrenia who also happened to be hypersensitive to insulin were observed to temporarily lose their psychotic symptoms (sometimes dramatically) after they went into a hypoglycemic coma. Thus researchers experimented with deliberately inducing a hypoglycemic coma to control symptoms. For a period of time, insulin coma therapy was widespread and was considered the treatment of choice for schizophrenia (Kalinowsky, 1970). Independent of Sakel's work, other researchers in 1934 observed that epilepsy and schizophrenia rarely occurred in the same patient. Also, symptoms often remitted in patients who experienced spontaneous convulsions. Von Meduna, a Hungarian psychiatrist, introduced the idea of inducing convulsive seizures in patients with schizophrenia, using intravenous injections of cardiazol (Fink, 1984). This led to dramatic changes in many patients. Subsequently, seizures were induced by electrical stimulation, rather than by intravenous injections. Electroconvulsive therapy (ECT) is still used today, although the method of delivery has been dramatically and humanely refined. Patients are given anesthesia and a muscle relaxant, which means that they are unconscious during the treatments and do not experience muscular contractions. Stringent legal caveats have also been established to inform and protect the patient.

Interest in pharmacological treatments of mental illness emerged after World War II. Before then (starting in the early 19th century), drugs such as chloral hydrate and other barbiturate compounds were used only for sedative control of aggressive behavior in state hospital settings (Deniker, 1970). However, with the introduction and the mass production of antibiotics during World War II, countless lives were saved. Accompanying the tremendous success of antibiotics was a hopeful confidence that new drugs could treat illnesses of all kinds, including mental disorders. Chlorpromazine (Thorazine), the first antipsychotic medication, was introduced within this context of optimism.

Chlorpromazine is often claimed to be psychiatry's first "wonder" drug. The drug's parent compound, phenothiazine, was synthesized in Germany in 1883, as the basis for a new synthetic blue dye (Swazey, 1974). It was also tried as an antimalarial agent. From the beginning, it was observed that these substances had a strong sedative quality, but scientists considered this to be an undesirable side effect in their general use. In the 1940s, it had been observed that persons in acute psychotic states did not seem to suffer from allergic diseases; they seemed to have decreased histamine sensitivity. This led to the experimental use of antihistamines as a means of reducing the symptoms of schizophrenia. The Federal Drug Administration (FDA) approved chlorpromazine in 1954 for the treatment of nausea and vomiting in neuropsychiatry. Eventually, chlorpromazine became widely used, despite the limitations of which we are now aware.

As with the first antipsychotic medication, there are interesting stories (see Ayd & Blackwell, 1970) behind the discovery and the development of the four other classes of psychotropic medication, which include antidepressants, psychostimulants, antianxiety medications, and mood stabilizers. The last 50 years have been committed to developing related medications. In the 1980s, a wave of new-generation drugs was introduced. Anticonvulsant drugs (such as carbamazepine and valproic acid) were used as mood stabilizers in bipolar disorder. Also, non-benzodiazepine anxiolitics were introduced, along with new-generation antidepressants and antipsychotics. The new drugs continue to be studied and refined and are often the treatment of choice for many clients. Current psychopharmacological research is focused on developing new agents with precise mechanisms of action that target specific behaviors and disorders.

KEY THEORETICAL CONSTRUCTS

The theoretical perspective on the etiology of psychiatric illness has changed tremendously in the last 5 decades, with an increasing focus on biological theories and medication management to change behavior. Although biological explanations for the cause of mental disorders are not definitive, we do know that psychotropic medications produce therapeutic benefits by altering some aspect of the neurotransmitter–receptor systems. Social workers do not have to be experts in the neurotransmission process; however, some basic knowledge of the principles of psychopharmacology provides a context for understanding brain activity and behavior. Thus, we provide a brief overview of how neurotransmitters are involved in processing and transmitting information in the nervous system.

Messages are transmitted from one nerve cell *(neuron)* to another by chemical and electrical means. An electrical impulse travels through the neuron and stops at the end of the neuron *(the terminal)*. The electrical impulse, however, cannot cross the area between two neurons *(the synapse)*. In order to cross the synapse to pass information on to the adjacent neuron *(postsynaptic neuron)*, chemicals called *neurotransmitters* are released from the neuron into the synapse. The neurotransmitters act as messengers by carrying the messages between cells. When the neurotransmitter crosses the gap, it comes into contact with the receiving neuron. On the surface of this postsynaptic neuron, there are specialized molecular structures *(receptor sites)* that can receive the neurotransmitter. The analogy of a lock and a key is an apt one here, in that the neurotransmitter, like a key, must fit in a specifically shaped receptor, the lock, in order to translate the information (or to "open the door"). Depending on the site, the neurotransmitter can either continue the electrical impulse (called an excitatory response) or block the response of the postsynaptic neuron (an inhibitory response). After the neurotransmitter has transmitted its information, by either enhancing or inhibiting, it must be deactivated. One of the ways this happens is by molecules called *reuptake pumps* sweeping the neurotransmitters back into the presynaptic neuron so that they can be stored and re-released. Many psychotropic medications work by altering this process. Some medications stimulate a similar action as the neurotransmitter. A drug with this kind of action is called an *agonist*. A second effect occurs when the medication binds to the receptor but does not send the message, thus preventing neurotransmitter molecules from attaching to the receptor. This is known as an *antagonist*. An antagonist blocks the effect of what the natural neurotransmitter would do. A third effect is that a medication may cause more neurotransmitters to be released. If neurotransmitter molecules are not allowed to be recycled into the presynaptic neuron, they spend more time in the synapse, thus increasing the possibility that some of the neurotransmitters will stimulate the postsynaptic neuron. This action is called *reuptake inhibition*. In treating psychiatric illness, medications can alter the reuptake of the neurotransmitter and change the effective levels in the synapse. Over 50 neurotransmitters have been discovered, and it is suspected that 100 or more of these substances exist. The primary neurotransmitters involved in psychological function are serotonin, norepinephrine, dopamine, acetylcholine, gamma aminobutyric acid (GABA), and glutamate.

Actions in or near the synapse are primarily focused on the exchange of signals between cells. In addition, psychotropic medications may exert effects through "second messenger" pathways that are important for intracellular signaling. Both antidepressant and mood-stabilizing medications have been reported to effect biochemical cascades within neurons that influence neuroplasticity, neurogenesis, and cell survival (Coyle & Duman, 2003). Actions on the phosphoinositol cycle (Berridge, Downes, & Hanley, 1989) and on the activity of the alpha and epsilon isoforms of phosphokinase C (PKC; Manji & Lenox 1999) have been reported with lithium and valproic acid; effects on PKC in particular may be important in regulating neurite extension. Influences on transcription factors, such as cyclic AMP response element-binding protein (CREB), may interact with effects of brain-derived nerve growth factor (BDNF; Mai, Jope, & Li, 2002; Yuan, Huong, Gutkind, Manji, & Chen, 2001), and both ECT and antidepressants have been shown to alter these factors (Duman, Malberg, Nakagawa, & D'Sa, 2000). Long-term administration of antidepressant medications can upregulate the expression of BDNF and of the tyrosine kinase TrkB (cf. Nestler et al., 2002). Other effects of psychotropic medications on second messenger systems are being actively studied. Although these second messenger systems offer rich alternative pathways that may yield a more complete understanding of the putative mechanisms of the action of current and future psychotropic medications, we believe that the research base is still in flux, and it is premature to base treatment decisions on some of these intriguing findings. Prudent clinicians will want to monitor developments in this area in the research literature in the coming years.

We will briefly describe five major groups of psychotropic medication (see Table 12.1 for definitions of many of the side effects that can result from the medications mentioned in the following sections).

Mood-Stabilizing Medications

Mood-stabilizing medications are primarily used for treating clients with bipolar disorder (commonly known as manic depressive disorder). Lithium is the oldest effective medication used to treat bipolar disorder. Lithium often takes 2 or more weeks to establish a clear therapeutic effect. After the acute phase subsides (typically, the manic phase), the client usually continues taking mood-

TABLE 12.1
Adverse Effects of Psychotropic Medication

Agranulocytosis: A rare but serious decrease in the number of white blood cells.

Anticholinergic effects (ACE): Dry mouth, constipation, urinary retention, blurred vision. These side effects are related to the suppression of the action of acetylcholine in the brain and the peripheral nervous system.

Arrhythmia: Abnormality in the regularity of the heart's rhythm.

Bradycardia: Decrease in heart rate that is below normal (usually below 60 beats per minute).

Extrapyramidal symptoms (EPS): These symptoms are related to the nerve pathways that control (stereotyped) reflex movements of the muscles that are usually associated with antipsychotic medication.

>   **Akathesia:** Extreme internal restlessness, accompanied by muscle discomfort.

>   **Dystonia:** Uncoordinated, involuntary twisting movements of the jaw, the tongue or the entire body, produced by sustained muscle spasm.

>   **Parkisonian effects:** Adverse effects that mirror Parkinson's disease symptoms, such as reduction in motor abilities and coordination, shuffling gate, drooling, muscle rigidity, and tremors.

>   **Tardive dynkinesia:** Involuntary rhythmic movements in facial muscles, fingers, hands, and trunk, including spasms of the eyelids, repeated puckering of the mouth, licking or smacking movements, and lip tremors.

Neuroleptic malignant syndrome: High fever, muscle rigidity, fluctuating levels of consciousness, and instability in the autonomic nervous system, related to taking an antipsychotic (neuroleptic) medication. Rare, but potentially fatal.

Orthostatic hypotension: A sudden drop in blood pressure when rising from a sitting or a lying position to a standing one, accompanied by dizziness, lightheadedness, weakness, and an unsteady gait. Although lasting only a few seconds, it may precipitate a fall; hence, it is of particular concern with physically frail persons.

Sedation: Reduced excitability, but not to the point of inducing sleep.

Sexual dysfunction: Change in libido (drive) and physiological function, including difficulty reaching orgasm.

Soporific/hypnotic effects: Sleep inducing.

Tachycardia: An increase in heart rate that is above normal (usually above 100 beats per minute.

---

stabilizing medication as a prophylactic agent to prevent further episodes of mania or depression. As with many medications, once the client starts to feel better, he or she may not see the need to continue taking it. Much like antibiotics, many people discontinue medication when their symptoms dissipate. Not completing a full course of the prescribed antibiotics may result in a rebound infection that could be worse than the initial illness. In order for lithium to be effective, a steady blood level of the drug must be maintained. Lithium levels must be monitored carefully because there is a fine line between therapeutic and toxic levels. A blood draw to test the lithium level is usually required once a month when starting treatment and at longer intervals once the client is in remission. The social worker may be in a position to notice signs of toxicity, or the client may complain first to the social worker about adverse effects (nausea, vomiting, diarrhea, trembling, confusion, abdominal pain). Anticonvulsants, such as carbamazepine and valproic acid, are also used to stabilize mood. In 1995, valproic acid received FDA approval for use as a mood-stabilizing medication in the treatment of mania. The anticonvulsant drugs often begin to stabilize the client's mood in as few as 2 to 5 days.

Antianxiety Drugs

There are four types of medication primarily used to treat anxiety disorders: benzodiazepines, beta-blockers, the atypical medication buspirone, and serotonin reuptake inhibitors. The benzodiazepines are quickly absorbed in the gastrointestinal tract and have a rapid clinical effect, usually within 30 minutes. The main disadvantage is that they can be physically addicting over time and therefore have a high abuse potential. If a benzodiazepine is abruptly discontinued, the client may experience withdrawal symptoms, such as convulsions, depersonalization, irritability, sweating, and nausea. Benzodiazepines should be titrated gradually, over weeks to months of time. Complete discontinuation for long-term users could take 6 to 7 months.

Beta-blockers inhibit norepinephrine receptors in the brain and the peripheral nervous system. They were originally developed to lower blood pressure in persons with hypertension, but they are also effective in treating anticipatory anxiety or performance anxiety. They lower anxiety by calming the autonomic nervous system but still leave the central nervous system intact. They are fast acting and are not addicting. They are prescribed far less often than the benzodiazepines because they have a brief effect, only a few hours, and thus are most useful if the anxiety symptoms are associated with a particular event (such as giving a speech).

Buspirone is a newer drug that appears to have an impact on serotonin receptors, which are believed to be processed in the hippocampus and the limbic areas of the brain. Buspirone is quickly absorbed and must be taken regularly to achieve and maintain its effect. Part of its attraction is that it is not addictive. It does not produce psychomotor impairment, withdrawal, or cardiac problems. Because it requires 2 weeks or more to achieve full effect, it is not useful for crisis intervention or the treatment of panic disorder. Recently, buspirone has been found to have additional therapeutic benefits, such as reducing aggression and irritability in persons with brain injuries and organic disorders. More recent data has supported the widespread practice of using selective serotonin reuptake inhibitors (SSRIs), which also have antidepressant effects. Clinical trial data support their effectiveness in generalized anxiety disorder (GAD), obsessive-compulsive disorder (OCD), social phobia, and other anxiety-spectrum disorders. Because SSRIs are generally well tolerated and do not appear to have significant abuse or addiction potential, they are commonly used to treat these problems. It often requires a week or more before clinical changes are apparent.

Psychostimulants

Psychostimulants produce states of wakefulness, mood elevation, alertness, increased initiative, and enhanced competence. They are primarily used to treat persons with attention-deficit/hyperactivity disorder (ADHD) by paradoxically enhancing the ability to maintain concentration and self-control. Psychostimulants are controlled substances with high abuse potential. In the United States, the number of children, adolescents, and adults diagnosed with ADHD has grown steadily. The social work profession is often involved with clients who have been diagnosed with ADHD in a variety of settings, including schools. Some controversy exists around the accuracy of diagnosis and the treatment of ADHD with stimulants. A number of consumer groups believe that the condition is often designated by frustrated adults who cannot manage the challenges of normal, vigorously active children. The dangers of inadequate clinical management, the general problem of child and adolescent nonadherence, fears of peer ridicule, a reluctance to accept the label of being ill, possible negative effects on physical development, and ethical issues in decision making and the rights of minors demand that the appropriateness of medication be carefully assessed. Also of concern to social workers is caregiver absence or noninvolvement with children taking these medications; thus, a strong caregiver or social worker alliance is important.

Antipsychotic (Neuroleptic) Medications

Clients respond differently to the many drugs available for treating psychotic disorders, due to variations in body chemistry, metabolism, and personal habits. Furthermore, these medications tend to control the positive symptoms of psychosis (bizarre thinking and behavior) more so than the negative symptoms (apathy, withdrawal, and poverty of thought). However, recent evidence indicates that the newer medications have an impact on negative symptoms and on the cognitive symptoms (particularly, executive functions and working memory). Most antipsychotic medications work by blocking dopamine receptors in the brain. The half-lives of all the antipsychotic drugs are relatively long (10 to 20 hours), so, in many cases, they can be taken once daily; depot medications are available that can be administered every 2 to 4 weeks. "Conventional," "typical," or first-generation antipsychotics (those developed prior to the mid 1980s) are associated with symptom improvement for over two-thirds of the people who use them. Most of the gains are made in the acute phase of the illness and over the first 6 to 8 weeks following onset of treatment. A number of adjunctive medications are used for persons with schizophrenia to treat adverse effects, to treat residual symptoms, and sometimes to enhance the efficacy of the primary antipsychotic medication. The reduction of side effects can improve the quality of life; however, some of the adjunctive treatments also have adverse effects.

The newer, "second-generation" antipsychotics were originally classified as "atypical" antipsychotics because they had different actions at dopamine receptors. They do not seem to cause the same levels of extrapyramidal effects (e.g., trembling, shuffling gait, involuntary movements) that are associated with conventional neuroleptics, but they do include adverse effects (such as weight gain). Although their precise mechanisms of action are not fully known, the newer medications tend to have a broader action on neurotransmitters, affecting serotonin, acetylcholine, and norepinephrine, in addition to subtypes of dopamine receptors. Newer, "third-generation" antipsychotic medications are becoming available and appear to have "partial agonist" effects on dopamine receptor subtypes; this may account for their effect and tolerability profiles.

Antidepressants

There are three general types of antidepressants: monoamine oxidase inhibitors (MAOs), tricyclic antidepressants (TCAs), and new-generation antidepressants, such as the selective serotonin reuptake inhibitors (SSRIs). Most clients are likely to be prescribed SSRIs or mixed-action antidepressants.

Monoamine oxidase inhibitors are medications that inhibit the action of enzymes that metabolize norepinephrine and serotonin. MAOs would typically be given as a second- or third-line treatment to relieve refractory depressions that do not respond to other drugs. They are not usually given as the first drug of choice because they have a dangerous potential for reactions with foods rich in the amino acid—derivative, tyramine, prompting a hypertensive condition that can be fatal (e.g., stroke). Tyramine is found in foods such as cheese, wine, beer, and some meats. Many over-the-counter cold remedies also contain elements that can lead to a hypertensive crisis. Because the consumer must exercise a significant amount of discipline to avoid all of these foods consistently, some people do not wish to run the risk of taking MAO inhibitors. This is a point in which the social worker can engage in problem solving by reviewing dietary habits with the client and encouraging her or him to keep a written record of foods to be avoided. One also has to exercise caution when combining the MAOs with other drugs (including the other antidepressants).

Tricyclic antidepressants have been commonly prescribed from the late 1950s through the 1980s. These drugs require approximately 2 to 6 weeks to achieve therapeutic impact. Unfortunately, the anticholinergic side effects begin with the first administration. The drugs also have an immediate sedative effect, which, though troubling to some consumers, may provide relief to a depressed person with insomnia or agitation. Decisions about discontinuing medication should be made by the client in consultation with the prescribing clinician. In almost every case, the drug's dosage should be tapered gradually, over a period of 2 to 4 weeks. An abrupt discontinuation may cause short-term but very distressing effects of anxiety, insomnia, or a rebound depression. Other possible withdrawal symptoms include cardiac arrhythmias, nausea, diarrhea, sweating, chills, and fatigue.

The SSRIs have been available in the United States since 1987. Fluoxetine

(Prozac) was the first of these. Sometimes this class of antidepressant has been called "atypical" because its drugs differ chemically from the cyclic antidepressants and the MAO inhibitors. They have become the standard medication within this drug category. SSRIs have a longer half-life and are more potent than most of the TCAs. SSRIs have reduced overdose potential and fewer adverse effects than the other antidepressants groups. In addition, SSRIs do not have to be gradually introduced to the consumer. They can be initiated at a therapeutic dose and then adjusted accordingly. The shorter half-life SSRI medications (e.g., paroxetine) are associated with a "discontinuation syndrome" when they are stopped abruptly; the headache and other flu-like symptoms abate when the client restarts the medication.

Other new antidepressants are grouped as dual reuptake inhibitors, because they block the reuptake of both serotonin and norepinephrine (e.g., venlafaxine [Effexor] or duloxetine [Cymbalta]). They are frequently used when a primarily serotonergic drug has not met with clinical success, but they are useful as first-line agents as well. Buproprion, another one of the newer drugs, does not fit neatly into any class, but it is believed to have some dopaminergic action. Other medications, such as mietazpine (Remeron) and nefazodone (Serzone), affect brain levels of serotonin and norepinephrine through other mechanisms.

Special Populations

Social workers encounter clients from a broad spectrum of cultural backgrounds. Each chapter in this book includes a section on how a treatment modality might be modified to better meet the needs of a specific population. Not only are there psychosocial variations, but there are differences in the pharmacokinetics (the absorption, the metabolism, and the excretion of medication) of psychotropic medications across ethnicity, gender, and age.

Ethnic Differences

Interethnic and interindividual variation in the enzyme activity and subsequent metabolism is significantly influenced by different genetic polymorphisms (Lin, Smith, & Ortiz, 2001). Polymorphisms are chromosomes that occur in more than one form. There is a burgeoning body of research in the area of ethnic psychopharmacology supporting differential psychopharmacokinetics across ethnicities. For instance, African Americans tend to have more side effects than Caucasians do with standard doses of lithium (Adebimpe, 1981; Lawson, 2000; Strickland, Lin, Fu, Anderson, & Zheng, 1995). For people with Asian backgrounds, it is best to start with half of the standard dose (Lin & Cheung, 1999; Pi, Gutierrez, & Gray, 2000). In Latin America, lower doses of psychiatric medication are used than in the United States, and the improvement rate is faster (Adams & Dworkin, 1984; Mendoza, Smith, Poland, Lin, & Strickland, 1991). Interestingly, recent immigrants respond differently to medications than do persons of the same background who have been in the United States for many years (Mendoza et al., 1991).

Gender Differences

Historically, pharmacokinetic differences between men and women were attributed to differences in weight and percentage of body fat; however, there are also gender differences in hormonal levels and hepatic (related to the liver) clearance of enzymes involved in medication metabolism. Cyclic fluctuation over the menstrual cycle may affect the pharmacokinetics of drugs, possibly causing women to experience fluctuation in medication effectiveness and adverse reactions. During the premenstrual phase, gastric emptying may decrease; thus, serum levels may differ over the course of the cycle (Miller, 2002). In women who retain water premenstrually, there may be a decrease in the serum levels of water-soluble drugs. Central nervous system receptor numbers or sensitivity may vary over the menstrual cycle (Robinson, 2002). Women have been found to have less basal acid secretion in the stomach than men, which may result in an increase in the absorption of bases, such as tricylic antidepressants, benzodiazepines, and phenothiozines, and decreased absorption of acids, such as barbiturates. During pregnancy and lactation, the effects of psychotropic medication may vary (see reviews by Bar-Oz, Nulman & Koren, 2000; Pinkofsky, 2000; and Stewart & Robinson, 2001, for more information).

Age Differences

Psychotropic medications can be used effectively to relieve the suffering of older persons. However, treatment of older people requires special concern because of possible drug–drug interactions due to multiple medications for chronic medical conditions such as heart disease, diabetes, and arthritis. In addition, changes in the brain due to aging may include changes in the number of receptors and subtle structural damage. These factors may lead to side effects at even comparatively low doses. Many physicians guard against adverse events by adopting a prescribing policy of "start low—go slow—but go," which means that they initiate treatment at a low dose, gradually increase it over time while monitoring for adverse effects, but continue to adjust the dose until therapeutic effects are reached. A dearth of research information exists on the use of psychotropic medications for children and adolescents. In general, lower doses are prescribed and are adjusted for each individual in light of therapeutic and adverse effects.

ASSESSMENT

A thorough assessment begins with taking a detailed medication history, including prescribed medication, over-the-counter drugs, herbal remedies, nutritional supplements, and alternative therapies. Social workers should be current with the literature and should encourage clients to communicate with their physicians. These tasks clearly involve attention to the social worker's role of consultant, counselor, advocate, educator, and researcher.

The preliminary part of assessing for a medication intervention is to evaluate which clients should have a psychiatric consultation. Depending on the placement, this may already have been decided, in that the client may have entered the mental health system through a medical intervention. Prominent neurovegetative symptoms (e.g., sleep and appetite disturbances), hallucinations, delusions, and bizarre, ritualistic, or dangerous behaviors indicate that a referral is necessary. Fatigue, changes in memory, and inability to concentrate should also be explored. Significant occupational or social deficits resulting from these symptoms warrant a referral. The presence of any significant medical illness or physical symptoms should, at the minimum, be discussed with the client's primary treating physician. Active suicidal ideation always requires a referral or a consult. If symptoms are not severe, but there is a family history of psychiatric illness, it may be a good idea to refer the client for an evaluation of possible prodromal (early) symptoms of a more serious disorder. Social workers in independent practice should refer a client for a psychiatric evaluation when little or no improvement has occurred over a significant period.

Because each member of the Shore family has one or more of the characteristics listed previously, we will consider what issues would be important to evaluate during an assessment.

Charley

Charley has already been diagnosed with bipolar disorder and been prescribed lithium. The social worker and the psychiatrist would want to explore any side effects Charley may be experiencing, the history of Charley's illness, and his perception of what he has experienced. A consultation with the physician prescribing lithium would be in order, as well as obtaining available information about the hospitalization (with Charley's signed consent for release of information). The social worker would inquire about residual mood symptoms. Is Charley thinking logically or are there some low-grade delusions or grandiosity? How much of his behavior is due to an illness that is not fully controlled, and how much of the behavior is a repertoire that has become embedded in his personality style? When Charley is assessed, many of the behaviors that have been annoying to the family, such as his inappropriate humor and his irritability, might be in the hypomanic spectrum (*hypomania* being defined as a persistently elevated, expansive, or irritable mood that falls short of a true manic episode). Sometimes people with bipolar disorder have come to label these behaviors as "just part of their personality"; in contrast, if one looks at them from a symptom-based perspective, the behaviors may be understood to be symptoms of under- or untreated hypomanic episodes. These behaviors may not be indicative of a full-blown psychotic episode, but they may have been apparent long before Charley's 49th birthday, when he was first diagnosed with bipolar disorder. Typically, a diagnosis of bipolar disorder is made in early adulthood. There may have been hypomanic behaviors, as well as subsyndromal depressive episodes, that no one noted. The symptoms may have been passed off with thoughts such as "Well, that's just Charley, not being able to hold a job." Perhaps if one assessed why he couldn't hold a job, he may have been referred for care earlier. He was inattentive and distractible, as people tend to be when they are hypomanic. There are bits and pieces of his life that one could go back to and assess whether these periods contained symptoms of a mood disorder that had gone unrecognized until he had the full-blown psychotic break. Psychosis does not typically materialize one day without a prodromal context; it usually brews for awhile. If a clinician had picked up on the fact early, Charley may have avoided hospitalization and the frank psychotic episode. We would also assess whether mood-stabilizing drugs other than lithium should be considered.

Michael

Michael has two serious medical disorders (asthma and epilepsy), in addition to other behaviors that warrant attention. He has "silly" spells and bizarre behaviors, such as touching others, making strange noises, and laughing too long or at the wrong time. It would be very important to have collateral visits with Michael's family, physicians, and teachers. Children with epilepsy sometimes have behavioral oddities that are part of poorly controlled epilepsy. We would question, during the times when Michael seemed confused and lost, whether he may have been experiencing petite mal (or *absence*) seizures. A child who is having multiple seizures could have a hard time learning and socializing. We would want to rule out complex partial epileptic seizures and examine the dose and the side effects of the anticonvulsant medication. Perhaps he is getting too little of his seizure medicine and is having breakthrough seizures, manifesting as behavioral problems. It would be important to collaborate with the physicians managing the epilepsy to find out how aggressively the epilepsy is being treated. Are they aware of Michael's behavioral symptoms? If a child is not having frank grand mal seizures, the neurologist who is managing the epilepsy might not explore in detail for the behavioral symptoms. In some ways it may be a disadvantage that Nancy has a health-care background, because the providers may make assumptions that Nancy would call to their attention concerns that they would not expect from a lay person. If Michael were having seizures, he might not have an explanation for his behavior; he might feel disoriented and then want to cover up for it by saying he was "doing it for attention."

Regarding the asthma, there are many asthma medications that are stimulating; their desired effect on the airways leads them to be a stimulant to other parts of the body, such as the brain. It would be important to assess whether Michael is on the right dose of asthma medication. As the child grows and the body weight increases, the dosage needs to be scaled accordingly. It is possible that Michael had an anoxic brain problem, in which he was underoxygenated for too long. In making a differential assessment, other diagnoses to explore would be childhood bipolar disorder, obsessive compulsive disorder (OCD), and Tourette's syndrome. Especially by making funny noises, children with OCD will do bizarre rituals and inappropriate things; they may make strange sounds and grunting vocalizations. There is considerable co-occurrence of OCD and Tourette's symptoms. Some evidence suggests that the underlying problems with neuronal circuits are related. Fortunately, when one set of symptoms has been well treated pharmacologically, symptoms due to another disorder also frequently come under control.

Rena

Rena should be assessed for depressive disorder. She stays in bed until midafternoon, rarely leaves her apartment, has dropped out of school, and has lost interest in activities. Such a severe behavioral change is of concern. Because of the neurovegetative symptoms, we would consider giving an antidepressant medication, which may well be part of what Rena needs to help with her physical symptoms. In this situation, however, it is essential to combine pharmacological treatment with psychotherapy treatment. Sometimes a medication can help with symptoms such as sleep, energy, and concentration, so that the client who would otherwise be too impaired to benefit from therapy can take advantage of the therapeutic sessions. When someone's concentration is impaired with depression, even the greatest therapy in the world may not be helpful. The client may not be able to process the therapy and to apply new insights to real-life circumstances. If the therapy depends on learning new ways to behave, from either insight or cognitive behavioral training, clients have to be able to concentrate long enough to remember what is being talked about. Rena needs to be able to make connections outside of therapy to the work that is done in therapy. If her memory, concentration, and mood are impaired, she may not be able to make the connections. She may do the homework but not be able to translate it into her real-world experiences. We would also be concerned about substance abuse. People who are not well challenged may manipulate their mental state with alcohol or other substances that can also produce sleep, energy, and concentration symptoms.

Nancy

Nancy has many different concerns. During an assessment for psychopharmacological intervention, it would be important to help her compartmentalize these issues in order to guide our decision about what type of medication, if any, would be prescribed. Along with depression, Nancy reports anxiety and panic attacks. We would need to explore with Nancy the duration and the course of the anxiety. We would ask whether the anxiety was present all the time or only when the depression is pronounced. When Nancy is engaged in something pleasurable, is the anxiety still present in the back of her mind? If the anxiety is present and intermittently erupts into worse episodes, it is more akin to a generalized anxiety disorder than to a panic disorder. Panic attacks are discrete, time-limited episodes, causing the autonomic nervous system to produce symptoms such as shortness of breath, racing heartbeat, and sweaty palms.

Because Nancy is significantly overweight, it would be important to explore her eating patterns and assess for an eating disorder. Her back pain may be exacerbated by her weight. Women who suffer from chronic pain comprise a group whose medical care historically has been inadequate (Rapkin & Morgan, 2002). Nancy may become depressed, irritable, and somatically focused because she has endured the pain for an extended length of time, with little hope for relief. If Nancy were to be treated for the likely mood disorder, she might discover that the pain is tolerable. Low doses of antidepressants are sometimes used for chronic pain and are helpful in managing chronic pain syndromes. One of the signs that Nancy was on an appropriate dose of antidepressant medication would be that her pain may be more tolerable, perhaps tolerable enough so that she actually could go back to school or hold another job.

THERAPEUTIC PROCESS

The therapeutic process during a pharmacological intervention can generally be divided into three phases: the acute phase, the continuation phase, and the prevention phase (Gitlin, 1996). The acute phase is the treatment of actively occurring symptoms. The continuation phase is aimed at preventing a relapse of the current disorder, and the prevention phase is aimed at preventing future episodes. There are several important roles the social worker takes on at each of these phases. Bentley and Walsh (2001) have identified four objectives that directly apply to the social worker–client relationship during the therapeutic process:

1. To understand the effectiveness of medication in symptom reduction;
2. To monitor adverse effects, including the medication's physical, psychological and social consequences;
3. To educate clients and families about the course of physical and psychological adjustment to medications; and
4. To communicate with physicians, pharmacists, nurses, and others about the present and potential effects of medication (p. 43).

When medication helps to alleviate psychiatric symptoms, many environmental, occupational, social, cultural, and familial changes occur. The social worker can be instrumental in providing skills to facilitate the client's adjustment to these changes. The social worker can provide education for family members and help them to understand that everything may not return quickly to the previous level of functioning. Medication may relieve symptoms, but it is important not be "lulled" into thinking that the client is "all better" when the overt symptoms have dissipated. Also, once a medication begins to have an impact, it is a critical opportunity for social work intervention to enhance further positive changes. This is also a time for caution; resolution of symptoms can prematurely provide a sense of relief to others in the family, thinking that their family member has been cured. However, when the person begins to feel better and becomes more activated, this is also a time of increased risk. For instance, when a major depression begins to lift, there is an increased risk of suicide.

Monitoring symptoms that may be warning signs of possible decompensation is an important role of the social worker. It is possible for the social worker to identify prodromal decompensation before it becomes a full catastrophe. A change of medication or a voluntary hospitalization is far preferable to waiting until the situation becomes dangerous and requires involuntary treatment. The social worker should intervene when the client still has some insight and control. It is far better for a client to agree to go into the hospital in order to get things under control than to be forced into the hospital because he or she is floridly manic or psychotic. The social worker can alert the psychiatrist to the fact that there may be some prodromal behaviors that merit further evaluation. Charley is on lithium and is in the preventive or maintenance phase of treatment. For Charley, we need to look at signs that might indicate that he is entering a hypomanic state and also signs that are indicative of a depressive decompensation. For instance, if Charley became highly involved with another plan to get rich quick, or if Charley tells the social worker that he's been having a hard time getting out of bed and getting motivated, the social worker is alerted to the possibility of a recurrence of symptoms. It would be important to meet with the psychiatrist earlier than the next regularly scheduled visit. Also, it is essential to educate the other family members about prodromal symptoms. Often, it is useful to have family members become involved in a support group that reinforces recognizing problematic behaviors. The support group also reinforces the idea that there are times when the client may need to get some extra help, and this is nothing to be ashamed of.

During the continuation and maintenance phase of treatment, the social worker will most likely be seeing the client more often than the physician sees the client. Therefore, it is essential for the social worker to be knowledgeable about medication side effects. Lithium has a good track record for keeping the mood stable, but many people report feeling cognitively dulled when taking this medication (a side effect that leads many people to discontinue lithium, even though it may be controlling the symptoms of their illness). People who consider themselves to be artistic and creative sometimes report that they fear they are losing their creative edge, although some data suggest that individuals with mood disorders are actually more productive when the illness is controlled than when it is untreated (Jamison, Gerner, & Goodwin, 1979). A mood stabilizer that is also used as an anticonvulsant, such as valproic acid or carbamazepine, may be a better choice for Charley. Members of the health-care team should know which side effects to look for. For instance, lithium may cause kidney problems, which means that it would be important to ask about frequent urination. To check for thyroid-related problems, we would want to ask about heat or cold intolerance, weight gain or loss, or change in hair texture. Sometimes people will get dehydrated and their lithium levels will go up; they may become confused, or, in an extreme reaction, they can have seizures. Lithium is a salt, and as one becomes more and more dehydrated, the lithium levels will increase because the body will retain the lithium, as well as the sodium chloride. Thus people who are on lithium and are involved in physical activity (that results in sweating) should be advised of what to look for in early signs of toxicity.

What may be an acceptable side effect when someone is in the midst of an acute episode may be different 8 months later when he or she is feeling better. For example, sexual dysfunction (e.g., delayed orgasm) may not be an issue when a client is too depressed to be in a relationship. However, once the depression lifts and the client re-engages with social life, sexual side effects could lead the client to stop taking the medication. The cost-benefit is not fixed over the course of time, and the client's perception of the tolerability of a specific side effect can change and evolve.

For example, let's say the psychiatrist has prescribed fluoxetine for Nancy. Nancy is hesitant to fill the prescription because, in the past, an antidepressant had been prescribed for her, but she had no immediate results and stopped taking the medication after 1 week. However, in talking with the psychiatrist and the social worker, she has now learned that antidepressants may take 4 to 6 weeks before they have a clear, beneficial effect on the depression. Armed with this information, Nancy takes her medicine diligently, even though there are no immediate therapeutic effects. By the end of 8 weeks, she has become less depressed and less anxious. She is taking walks four times a week and has decreased the number of cigarettes she smokes each day. She also smokes outside of the house, which is in her family's best interest (particularly for Michael, because of his asthma). Her relationship with Charlie has improved, and they have resumed a sexual relationship. Nancy, however, is having a difficult time with the sexual side effects of the medication. She is uncomfortable talking about this and once again is considering stopping the medication. She has been receiving psychotherapy from a clinical social worker and has established an effective therapeutic alliance. During a therapy session, Nancy says she feels so much better that she plans to stop taking the medication, "I'm feeling good, so why should I keep taking this medicine?" Upon exploration, Nancy also tells the social worker about the sexual side effects. With supportive, solution-focused interventions, normalization, and psychoeducation, Nancy eventually does talk to her psychiatrist. The medication is switched to an antidepressant with a sexual side effect profile that is better than the one she had been taking. Feeling empowered by this experience, Nancy also discusses with the psychiatrist at what point she will be able to stop taking medication. She learns that some medications have a discontinuation syndrome and agrees with her psychiatrist and her therapist to evaluate the effects of the new medication and to think in terms of discontinuing the medication in 6 to 8 months, if all goes well. If a decision in fact is made to discontinue the medication, Nancy is aware of the importance of working with the psychiatrist to slowly titrate off the anti-depressant drug. Helping the client to learn more about the pharmacological processes not only empowers the client, but it encourages a collaborative approach.

APPLICATION TO DIVERSITY

It is critical to understand how sociocultural factors affect help-seeking behavior and interact with Western medicine. Simultaneous or sequential use of modern medicine and indigenous medicine often coexist. If herbal folk remedies are used in conjunction with psychotropic medicine, there may be a drug interaction that potentiates or inhibits drug metabolism and activity.

The following scenario is presented to sensitize clinicians to diversity in therapeutic approaches to healing. For this section, the Shores are transformed into a Latino family living in East Los Angeles. Nancy and Charley were born and raised in Mexico. They came to Los Angeles seeking employment and improvement in the quality of their lives. Rena was born in Mexico and is actually Nancy's niece. Nancy's sister died, due to childbirth complications, and the Shores have raised Rena as part of their own family. Nancy was 4 months pregnant when she and Charley left their home and extended family in Mexico. Michael was born 5 months after moving to the United States. Both Rena and Michael are bilingual and often must translate for their parents.

Nancy has made several attempts over the last 12 years to seek help from Western doctors to heal her back and to calm her anxiety. The physicians, however, could not identify an organic pathology for her back pain. They gave her medication for her anxiety, but the medication made her very drowsy. The family was also experiencing economic hardships and could not afford ongoing treatment from Western doctors. Nancy often visits local *curanderos* (healers) for spiritual consultation and physical healing. The biomedical therapies that had been offered to her did not take into account her cultural-religious practices and beliefs. Nancy was reluctant to discuss alternative forms of care with her doctor, recognizing that some of her culture's healing practices may not be acceptable to her physician's beliefs. She often used both types of healing but did not volunteer this information to her Western doctors. She felt there was a bias against some of the healing practices common in her community. Interestingly enough, when Nancy and Charley lived in Mexico, there was a common belief that when a poor person is ill, the first choice is to go to the *curandero* (male healer) or *curandera* (female healer), whereas a rich person may first go to a doctor; however, when the rich person becomes seriously ill, he or she will seek the aid of the *curanderos*. The belief system of the native Mexican population is a complex system of rules that explains the relationship of an individual to the spiritual forces, and it is these forces that guide the prescription for the health-care treatment. The beliefs originated primarily from

Mayan and Aztec teachings that have been integrated with Spanish Catholicism (Krippner, 1995). *Curanderos* use a form of folk healing, which may include spiritual rituals, healing massage, herbal medicine, prayer, and consultation. Healers who follow this tradition usually practice within their own neighborhood, tending to relatives, friends, and neighbors. The community, as well as the healer, believes the ability to heal is given by God as a result of a divine calling.

Nancy commonly goes to a *curandera* who practices in a local *botanica* (a store that sells herbal remedies). Most all marketplaces have at least one *botanica*, and the larger marketplaces often have many. On the outside, the *botanica* appears much like the other storefront shops, with vendors selling their wares along the sidewalks and on the street corners. The *botanica* is divided into two parts. The front portion of the store has a conglomeration of goods filling all the shelves and counters. Colorful statues of various saints abound. There is a complex accumulation of candles, oils, incense, religious amulets, icons of various saints, and rows of boxes and bottles containing an assortment of herbs and other remedies. The second part of the store is a room where consultations are held. During a consultation, Nancy may often be given an herbal preparation (usually in the form of a tea). Although the botanical tradition is rooted in a long history of folk healing, modern medicine uses many of the same plant-based derivatives pharmaceutically. After waiting her turn in the chairs provided outside the back consultation room, Nancy describes her ailments. The healer lights incense and waves it around Nancy's body, proceeding to fill the room with incense. She instructs Nancy to sit in front of an altar, and she begins a cleansing ritual *(una limpia).* She uses an herbal bouquet of basil, rosemary, piru leaves, and other herbs and rubs them over Nancy's body while praying for her health. She massages Nancy's back while continuing to pray. The *curandera* tells Nancy that she is trapped in a circle of "poisoning herself." In order to heal, she must break out of the circle of poison. She also tells Nancy that she suffers from *envidia* (envy). She asks Nancy to think about who could be so envious of her that they were damaging her health. The *curandera* gives Nancy a mixture of herbs and instructs her to make a tea from the herbs and drink it daily for the next 2 weeks. After the consultation and the *limpia,* Nancy feels that the healing session had cleansed and balanced her body's energy.

When a social worker engages with the Mexican American Shore family (or any family, for that matter), resources and strengths the family uses in coping with illness can be explored. An authentic interest in understanding how the cultural background gives meaning and context to the family's health behavior will facilitate the social worker's ability to be educated and sensitized to the needs of the family. Often, allopathic and traditional approaches may be used simultaneously, without creating conflict. Each approach may complement and support a well rounded treatment plan.

A set of eight questions was developed by Kleinman (1977), a medical anthropologist, to elicit the client's understanding of a medical problem. These questions can easily be applied to psychiatric concerns. If the clinician seeks to truly understand Nancy's responses and approaches the interview in an open, nonjudgmental manner, a personal story or a narrative will emerge, rather than a list of pathologies. The following eight questions serve as a basis to develop Nancy's narrative:

1. What do you call the problem?
2. What do you think has caused the problem?
3. Why do you think it started when it did?
4. What do you think the sickness does? How does it work?
5. How severe is the sickness? Will it have a short or a long course?
6. What kind of treatment do you think you should receive? What are the most important results you hope to receive from this treatment?
7. What are the chief problems the sickness has caused?
8. What do you fear most about the sickness? (Fadiman, 1997, p. 262)

RESEARCH

Studies of the effectiveness of combined psychosocial and psychopharmacological treatments primarily have concluded that combined treatment is preferable to either treatment alone (Bentley & Walsh, 2001). Each treatment seems to contribute to the other's effectiveness. Beitman and Klerman (1991) present solid empirical research to support combining treatments. Hogarty and Ulrich (1998) reported that psychotropic medication in interaction with well-supported psychosocial treatment can reduce the relapse rate by 50 percent. In a landmark study using the antidepressant medication nefazodone, Keller (2000) randomly assigned subjects to one of three groups: a medications-only group, a psychotherapy-only group, and a combined-treatment group. The overall rate of response (both remission and satisfactory response) was 48% in both the nefazodone group and the psychotherapy group, as compared with 73% in the combined-treatment group.

LIMITATIONS OF THE MODEL

A fundamental limitation to psychopharmacology as a treatment modality is the possibility that it will be used as the sole intervention. It is vital to help educate consumers on the disadvantage of taking medication solely to anesthetize painful feelings. These feelings may serve as necessary motivators for clients to examine their problems and to develop new coping skills to address the painful issues. Gitlin (1996) has discussed how using medication as an exclusive intervention can result in a "false sense of security," in which core problems may go untreated. Clients may overly rely on the drugs, attributing problems to factors beyond their own control, and then fail to acquire adaptive behaviors. It is common knowledge that taking an antidepressant medication will not fix a bad marriage or solve a workplace communications problem by itself; it may help a client feel well enough to take steps to address discord at home or in the office, but it is not a "magic bullet" treatment.

SUMMARY

Medication, like any other intervention, must be individually tailored to each client. Just as symptoms of a disorder vary, so do improvement and benefits. Effective collaboration is influenced by a clinician's awareness of the reciprocal relationship that psychosocial treatment and medication have on each other. As the fields of both social work and medicine move into the 21st century, it is our hope that further integration will occur between the mind–body–environmental systems. In order to best serve our clients, it is vital to create and maintain a permeable boundary between the psychosocial, the cultural, and the biological disciplines.

REFERENCES

Adams, G., & Dworkin, R. (1984). Diagnosis and pharmacology issues in the care of Hispanics in the public sector. *American Journal of Psychiatry, 141*, 970–974.

Adebimpe, B. (1981). White norms in psychiatric diagnosis of Black American patients. *American Journal of Psychiatry, 138*(3), 279–285.

Ayd, F., & Blackwell, B. (1970). *Discoveries in biological psychiatry.* Oxford: Blackwell Scientific.

Bar-Oz, B., Nulman, I., & Koren, G. (2000) Anticonvulsants and breastfeeding. *Pediatric Drugs, 2*, 113–126.

Beitman, B., & Kerman, G. (Eds). (1991). *Integrating pharmacotherapy and psychotherapy.* Washington, DC: American Psychiatric Press.

Bentley, K., & Walsh, J. (2001). *The social worker and psychotropic medication* (2nd ed.). Belmont, CA: Wadsworth/Thomson Learning.

Berridge, M., Downes, C. P., & Hanley, M. R. (1989). Neural and developmental actions of lithium: A unifying hypothesis. *Cell, 59*, 411–419.

Coyle, J. T., & Duman, R .S. (2003). Finding the intracellular signaling pathways affected by mood disorder treatments. *Neuron, 38*, 157–160.

Deniker, P. (1970). Introduction of neuroleptic chemotherapy into psychiatry. In F. J. Ayd, Jr., & B. Blackwell (Eds.), *Discoveries in biological psychiatry* (pp. 155–164). Oxford: Blackwell Scientific.

Duman, R., Malberg, J., Nakagawa, S., & D'Sa, C. (2000). Neuronal plasticity and survival in mood disorders. *Biological Psychiatry, 48*, 732–739.

Fadiman, A. (1997). *The spirit catches you and you fall down.* New York: Farrar, Straus and Giroux.

Fink, M. (1984). Meduna and the origins of convulsive therapy. *American Journal of Psychiatry, 141*(9), 1034–1041.

Gitlin, M. (1996). *The psychotherapist's guide to psychopharmacology.* New York: Free Press.

Hogarty, G., & Ulrich, R. (1998). The limitations of antipsychotic medication on schizophrenia relapse and adjustment and the contributions of psychosocial treatment. *Journal of Psychiatric Research, 32*, 243–250.

Jamison, K., Gerner, R., & Goodwin, F. (1979). Patient and physician attitudes toward lithium: Relationship to compliance. *Archives of General Psychiatry, 36*(8), 866–869.

Kalinowsky, L. B. (1970). Biological psychiatric treatments preceding pharmacotherapy. In F. J. Ayd, Jr. & B. Blackwell (Eds.), *Discoveries in biological psychiatry* (pp. 59–67). Oxford: Blackwell Scientific.

Keller, M. (2000). A comparison of nefazodone, the cognitive behavioral-analysis system of psychotherapy and their combination for the treatment of chronic depression. *New England Journal of Medicine, 342*(20), 1462–1470.

Kleinman, A. (1977). Explaining the efficacy of indigenous therapies: The need for interdisciplinary research. *Cultural Medical Psychiatry, 1*(2), 133–134.

Krippner, S. (1995). A cross cultural comparison of four healing models. *Alternative Therapies, 1*(1), 21–29.

Lawson, W. B. (2000). Issues in pharmacotherapy for African Americans in ethnicity and psychopharmacology. P. Ruiz, P. (Ed), Washington, DC: American Psychiatric Press. *Review of Psychiatry Series, 19*(4). J. O. Oldham, & M. B. Riba, Series Eds.

Lin, K. M., & Cheung, F. (1999). Mental health issues for Asian Americans. *Psychiatry Services, 50*(6), 774–780.

Lin, K., Smith, M.. & Ortiz, V. (2001). Culture and psychopharmacology. *Psychiatric Clinics of North America, 24*(3), 523–538.

Mai, L., Jope, R., & Li, X. (2002). BDNF-mediated signal transduction is modulated by GSK3 beta and mood stabilizing agents. *Journal of Neurochemistry, 82,* 75–83.

Manji, H., & Lenox, R. (1999). Protein kinase C signaling in the brain: Molecular transduction of mood stabilization in the treatment of manic-depressive illness. Ziskind Somerfeld Award Paper. *Biological Psychiatry, 46,* 1328–1351.

Mendoza, R., Smith, M., Poland, R., Lin, K., & Strickland, J. (1991). Ethnic psychopharmacology: The Hispanic and Native American perspective. *Psychopharmacology Bulletin, 27,* 449–461.

Meyer, C. (1990, April). *Can social work keep up with the changing family?* [Monograph]. The fifth annual Robert J. O'Leary Memorial Lecture. Columbus: Ohio State University College of Social Work.

Miller, L. (2002). Drugs and sex: Educating yourself about treating women. *Psychopharmacology Update, 13*(3), 1–5.

Nestler, E., Gould, E., Manji, H., Bucan, M. , Duman, R., Gershenfeld, H. Hen, R., et al. (2002). Preclinical models: Status of basic research in depression. *Biological Psychiatry, 52,* 503–528.

Pi, E. H., Gutierrez, M. A., & Gray, G. E. (2000). Tardive dyskinesia: Cross-cultural perspectives. In K. M. Lin, R. E. Poland, & G. Nagasaki (Eds), *Psychopharmacology and psychobiology of ethnicity* (pp. 91–108). Washington, DC: American Psychiatric Press.

Pinkofsky, H. (2002). Effects of antipsychotics on the unborn child. *Pediatric Drugs, 2,* 83–90.

Rapkin, A., & Morgan, M. (2002). Chronic pelvic pain. In R. DiClemente & G. Wingood (Eds.), *Handbook of women's sexual and reproductive health* (pp. 217–231). New York: Plenum Press.

Robinson, G. (2002). Women and psychopharmacology. *Medscape Women's Health eJournal, 7*(1), http://www.medscape.com/viewarticle/423938

Stein, D. (1998). Philosophy of psychopharmacology. *Perspectives in Biology and Medicine, 41*(2), 200–212.

Stewart, D. & Robinson, G. (2001). Psychotropic drugs and ECT during pregnancy and lactation. In N. Stotland & D. Stewart (Eds.), *Psychological aspects of women's health* (2nd ed., pp. 67–93). Washington, DC: American Psychiatric Press.

Strickland, T., Lin, K., Fu, P., Anderson, D., & Zheng, Y. (1995). Comparison of lithium ration between African-American and Caucasian bipolar patients. *Biological Psychiatry, 37*(5), 325–330.

Swazey, J. P. (1974). *Chlorpromazine in psychiatry: A study of therapeutic innovation.* Cambridge, MA: MIT Press.

Yuan, P., Huong, L., Gutkind, J., Manji, H., & Chen, G. (2001). Valproic acid activates mitogen activated protein kinases and promotes neurite growth. *Journal of Biological Chemistry, 276,* 31674–31683.

13

Spirituality Centered Therapy

Emphasis on an African American Family in a Changing Multicultural Community

Carolyn Jacobs, PhD

INTRODUCTION

The social work profession has recently begun to acknowledge publicly, through professional associations and scholarship, that spirituality is a quality and a capacity of the social worker and of importance to practice (Canda & Furman, 1999; Joseph, 1988). Because spiritual and religious practices are crucial elements of an individual's development and cultural experience, social workers should consider creating an environment that enables clients to explore these issues.

The act of exploring clients' religious and spiritual beliefs may raise spiritual issues for the social worker, challenging the clinician's basic beliefs. Professionals must address these countertransference issues—especially as they relate to suffering and death (Cornett, 1998; Derezotes & Evans, 1995; Goldberg, 1996; Grahman, Kaiser, & Garrett, 1998; May, 1987; Morgan, 1993; O'Connor, 1993).

O'Connor and Kaplan (1986) contend that spirituality is too critical an area to be left to clergy. And indeed, nonclergy do not avoid spiritual material in clinical situations. Millison and Dudley (1992) have found that listening to talk of God, sharing one's own spirituality, and exploring the meaning of life events were approaches used as often by nonclergy as by clergy.

THE CONCEPT OF THE PERSON AND THE HUMAN EXPERIENCE

O'Murchu (1991) opens his text with the following: "Our spiritual story as a human species is at least 70,000 years old; by comparison, the formal religions have existed for a mere 4,500 years" (p. 1). I would add that our physical, social, and psychological theories are significantly younger. As a result, spiritual ways of knowing have much to offer other ways of knowing. Increased dialogue about spirituality, paradigm shifts in the sciences, and changes in the psychological and social disciplines have helped social work become open to theoretical approaches to human growth and development that include contemplative perspectives. The paradigm shifts, in particular, are rooted in the physical sciences. Albert Einstein (1950) said,

> The finest thing we can experience is mystery, the fundamental emotion at the roots of true science. Those who cannot know it, those who cannot admire it, those who are no longer capable of experiencing a sense of wonder might as well be dead. (p. 26)

From his work, it is only a short step to the perspective of quantum physicists, who see the universe as an inseparable web of vibrating energy patterns, in which no one component has a reality that is independent of the entirety and which includes the observer. Identifiable objects or elements have meaning only when they are placed in context. Indeed, ideas about interconnectedness and holistic unifying energies impact our psychological and social worldviews. When one sees a holistic paradigm, the whole is greater than the sum of the parts and the interactions and the relationships among individuals take on energy greater than that of the isolated individual. As a result of these shifts in scientific thought, the dividing line between science and spirituality, between psychology and contemplation, becomes extremely thin, and we must listen to influences from our world, our society, our clients, and from deep within ourselves (O'Murchu, 1991; Wilbur, 1984; Zukav, 1979).

HISTORICAL PERSPECTIVE

Spirituality and Social Work

Spirituality in social work relates to three dimensions of practice. The first dimension can be found in the roots of social service agencies. Historically, our agencies were founded under religious auspices; Catholic, Jewish, and Protestant agencies were created to provide for the needs of immigrants, refugees, orphans, the poor, and the homeless. In religious traditions, service to others is intrinsic to spiritual practice. Gerald May (1987) summarizes this principle as follows:

> For Jews, the Hebrew law [was] recorded in Leviticus 19:18 "You shall love your neighbor as yourself. I am the Lord." In Matthew 19:19; 22:39 and Mark 12:31 Jesus states the two commandments upon which all the law and the prophets depend: love God totally and loving one's neighbor as oneself. True happiness within the Hindu scripture consists of making others happy. This is also the base of the Buddhist Bodhisattva vow that affirms that one will not attain final liberation "until all sentient beings are saved." Thus service to others is at once a means and an end to spiritual growth that leads us to the third dimension of spirituality and social work practice. (p. 297)

A second dimension is the recognition of the spiritual needs of each person and the recognition that these needs are inextricably related to the growth and the development of the whole person. To ignore this aspect of human life is to ignore people in their wholeness. Ways to understand this importance will be developed later in the chapter.

The third dimension relates to social workers, who must face the many ways they make meaning of life's joys and sorrows in their personal lives, in the lives of clients, and in the world in which they live. As social work moves toward holistic models of practice, it cannot ignore the spiritual dimensions of human life.

African American Spirituality

The African tradition provides an example of a spiritual historical perspective. African Americans have continued to participate in religious and spiritual practices from their enslavement in America to the present. Although European religions may have taken the place of traditional African religions for some, the experience of "communities of faith" has a long history in the African American experience. The African American experience included the forced participation in oppressive religious theologies (despite the clandestine practice of their traditional religions). Eventually, the rise of the Black church became a source of resistance, strength, and resiliency to systems of political, economic, and racial oppression. Expressions of spirituality unique to the Black community have sustained the individual and the collective spirit of African Americans.

Up to emancipation, the Black church defined religious rituals and programs as sanctioned opportunities for socialization, for education, and for personal and community development. It also provided a unique leadership-training opportunity. Throughout the period of industrialization, the church provided networks of support systems for families and individuals with problems, job opportunities, and collective spiritual experiences that sustained and strengthened African Americans while they coped with systems of oppression

(Bagley & Carroll, 1995, in McCubbin, 1998). Black churches were one of the few cohesive Black institutions to emerge from slavery. African Americans developed their leadership skills in Black churches and used them to move into professions. The church also became a safe place to deal with the impact of racism (Lincoln & Mamiya, 1990). Christian and Barbarin (2001) found that church attendance contributed to the resilience of children at risk for emotional and adjustment problems. The Black church continues its historical role as a resource for African American families.

Supportive social networks, flexible relationships with the family unit, a strong sense of religiosity, widespread use of extended-family helping arrangements, the adoption of fictive kin who become as family, and strong identification with their racial group are common cultural patterns that contribute to the resiliency of many African American families (McAdoo, 1998). A strong sense of religiosity derives from the integral sense of spirituality, as rooted in the traditions of African religions. Religion permeated every aspect of African life. Religious beliefs and practices are central to existence and deeply ingrained in the very psyche of African people. The strong spiritual orientation central to Africans was maintained and became an important resource throughout the history of African Americans. This spiritual conviction, as well as the church, provided a sacred space for the expression of anguish and suffering and to experience hope and joy. Spiritual and religious experiences provide ways of making meaning out of sorrow and joy. The church, with its organized groups for women, men, and youths, has provided structures for socialization, political and economic activities, and opportunities for spiritual and religious expression.

It is crucial that social workers recognize a strong spiritual base as being integral to the history of many African American individuals and families. The multiple functions of religious institutions, historically and in the present, are important resources for hope and resilience for African Americans (Dunn & Dawes, 1999). African Americans are represented in many different faith traditions, including but not limited to Buddhist, B'hai, Muslim, Jewish, Baptist, African Methodist Episcopal, Church of God in Christ, Seventh Day Adventist, Pentecostal, Lutheran, Episcopalian, and Roman Catholic. Many who are not currently involved in a religious denomination have been raised in a religion or greatly influenced by a relative who participated in organized religions or churches, giving them an internalized sense of God or spirituality.

Poussaint and Alexander (2000) discuss post-traumatic slavery syndrome, which is a culture of oppression that has taken a tremendous toll on the minds and bodies of African Americans. They state that the persistent presence of racism, despite the significant legal, social, and political progress made during the last half of the 20th century, has created physiological risks for Black people that are virtually unknown to White Americans (Poussaint & Alexander, 2000). Today, Black churches continue to provide resources to cope with the current issues of racism and spiritual and physical health issues, in ways that provide a healing community for individuals and families (Bagley & Carroll, 1998).

KEY THEORETICAL CONSTRUCTS

Definitions of religion and spirituality abound in the literature that explores the integration of spirituality and mental health practices (Cornett, 1998; Hugen, 1998; Kilpatrick & Holland, 1990; Lewandiski & Canda, 1995). When one works at the interface between religion and spirituality in the context of social work practice, it is important to differentiate them.

Religion refers to social forms or shared beliefs and rituals. Spirituality encompasses personal experiences or themes of connectedness to others and to the universe. Distinguishing the differences allows a deeper understanding of the impact of religious and spiritual practices on the individual's psychological functions, and illuminates that person's ways of making meaning out of life's circumstances (Canada & Furman, 1999, p. 37; Joseph, 1988; Lovinger, 1984; Lukoff, Lu & Turner, 1992).

Griffith and Griffith (2002) provide definitions of spirituality and religion that are applicable to the discussions in this chapter.

> Spirituality is a commitment to choose, as the primary context for understanding and acting, one's relatedness with all that is. With this commitment, one attempts to stay focused on relationships between one's self and other people, one's physical environment, one's heritage and traditions, one's body, one's ancestors, and a Higher Power, or God. It places relationships at the center of awareness, whether they are relationships with the world or other people, or relationships with God or other nonmaterial beings. Religion represents a cultural codification of important spiritual metaphors, narratives, beliefs, rituals, social practices, and forms of community among a particular people that provides methods for attaining spirituality, most often expressed in terms of a relationship with the God of that religion. (pp.15–17)

Comprehending spirituality is essential to understanding meaning making in many cultures; spiritual issues may often bring someone into therapy (Constantine, 1999). For example, spirituality can become increasingly important at specific stages of people's lives, including births, celebrations, losses, changes in life circumstances, terminal illnesses, and deaths. Enduring a loss often creates a search for meaning. How one defines the loss determines whether or not grief will begin and how it will be experienced (Morgan, 1993). Suffering can often move people to seek meaning and comfort. It is when life events do not make sense or seem unjust that one strives to find and conform to a reality in which the contradictions of living and dying, joy and sorrow, order and chaos are reconciled.

It is important to note that indigenous healers (such as Haitian or Puerto Rican spiritualists, or Mexican *curanderos*) are important resources when working with racially and ethnically diverse clients. The use of rituals, prayer, meditation, or scripture may bring feelings of joy, comfort, and peace that one needs to accept and understand as signs of healing.

In the clinical relationship, careful attention is given to the meanings the client attaches to clinical interventions. Such meanings enable the client to reflect on experiences, develop insights, and experience transformations. Spiritually oriented therapists may intervene in ways that foster empowerment by helping clients focus on their relationship with the transcendent other, the world around them, their sense of self, and their relationships with other human beings.

ASSESSMENT

Spiritual assessment is based on a strengths perspective, using engagement, continuous collaboration, advocacy, and supportive termination to generate a holistic profile. In the strengths perspective, the social worker actively engages in a therapeutic relationship in which the client is an expert in his or her own life situation. By searching for strengths and resources rather than symptomology and problems, the focus is on not what kind of life one has had but on what kind of life one wants. It is at this juncture that spirituality emerges as a life force. Life strengths and support are not fixed, nor can they be evaluated once and then used as an ongoing standard. In the context of a strengths assessment, spirituality often emerges as a stabilizing force that helps to maintain a person's sense of balance in the wake of change, difficulty, doubt, and death. Assessment from a strengths perspective invites us to ask questions that provide definition to thematic life strengths and the values that constitute our sense of ourselves in the world.

Spiritual concerns require ongoing assessment. It is not the social worker's responsibility to solve spiritual problems or concerns but to create a secure environment to nurture and support the client's exploration (Abram, 1997; Applegate & Bonovitz, 1995). People respond to and perceive their environment according to their inner structures and levels of organization. A social worker's primary responsibility is to obtain as clear an idea of the client's inner structure as possible (Vaughn, 1988).

Life reviews can provide opportunities to resolve earlier conflicts with significant others and with God. In addition to the life review, a spiritual genealogy, which charts a client's spiritual family tree, can add to ongoing work. Genograms may explore the relational dimensions of spirituality, highlighting spiritual resources, significant relationships, and other spiritually based information that may be significant for the assessment and intervention phases of therapy (Bullis, 1996; Dunn & Dawes, 1999). This includes learning what nourishes or supports a client's spirit and being open to hearing a range of responses, such as specific religious rituals, experiences of nature, music, poetry, and relationships. Whatever the assessment tools or questions, the social worker must be fully present to the client's spiritual quest for meaning at each stage of development.

Many assessment tools have been developed to explore spiritual and religious dimensions in holistic clinical work. Spiritual and religious assessment tools must be grounded in psychological and cultural theories. Dombeck and Karl (1987) provide an assessment tool that is particularly useful because of its coherence with dynamic theories. They present a short Hasidic story that captures the assessment task:

> A student asks his teacher, "I have a question about Deuteronomy 6:6, which says, 'And these words, which I command you this day, shall be upon your heart.' Why is it said this way? Why are we not told to place them in our heart?" The teacher responds: "It is not within the power of human beings to place the divine teachings directly in their hearts. All we can do is place them on the surface of the heart so that when the heart breaks they drop in." (p. 192)

This particular assessment story fits well with the theoretical orientation of object relations. Ana-Maria Rizzuto (1979), in the *Birth of the Living God*, applies an object relations framework for understanding the complexity of religious and spiritual experiences in individual development. The story of the family into which one is born provides a beginning perspective on the development of a God representation during the life cycle. This representation, in the mind of the parents, forms the mythology about the meaning of the child in the life of the primary caregivers. Often the birth of a child calls for a religious ritual (circumcision, baptism) that physically or spiritually marks a child's relationship to God. Most children complete the oedipal cycle with at least a rudimentary God representation untouched, as they continue to revise parent and self-representations during the life cycle. If the God representation is not revised to keep pace with changes in self-representation, it soon becomes asynchronous. It may be experienced as irrelevant, or even threatening or dangerous. Each new life crisis or landmark—illness, death, promotions, falling in love, birth of children, catastrophes, wars—provides opportunities for remembering a once highly relevant or feared aspect of the God representation (Rizzuto, 1979).

God, psychologically speaking, is an illusory transitional object. God comes into existence in transitional space. Winnicott (1982) says that religion is located in that illusory intermediate area of experience that helps bridge inner and outer realities throughout life. He defines that transitional domain as the space where art, culture, and religion belong. It is the place where one's life finds the full relevance of one's objects and meaning for oneself (Rizzuto, 1979).

The God representation is an object that has never been seen and cannot be proven "real." Paradoxically, for a believer, God is a fully intimate object, the only one that, as Rizutto (1979) states, "has total knowledge of the self as perceived by the self" (p. 11). For believers, God becomes the other who, in a dialectical fashion, preserves and evokes the self, particularly at the level of its unknowableness (Winnicott, 1982). The transitional sphere is "unchallenged resting space" wherein occurs the "silent or secret communication" of the unknowable self (Winnicott, 1982). Prayer, in the Winnicottian sense, is the silent or secret communication of the self with the subjective object of God (Winnicott, 1982).

Dombeck and Karl (1987) provide several questions for a religious history of placement within a religious community, personal meanings attached to symbols, rituals, beliefs, and divine figures, and relationship to religious resources:

1. *Placement within a religious community.* These questions allow us to understand the particular belief systems and dogma that provide a context for understanding various meanings of life events and human development. What is the religious affiliation? Have there been changes in religious affiliation? When did the changes take place? What is the level of present involvement? What is the relationship with the religious or spiritual leader and the faith community? These questions focus on what is placed on the heart.
2. *Personal meanings attached to symbols, rituals, beliefs, and divine figures.* This set of questions focuses on the spiritual resources that have been internalized by the individual. What religious practices are most meaningful? When and in what ways does one feel close to the divine? What does one pray about? When? Where? What gives special strength and meaning? These questions center on what has dropped into the heart. It is that area of transitional space where the individual interacts with phenomena that can be used to organize responses and give meaning to life events.
3. *Relationship to religious resources.* These questions focus on those internal objects that are used in understanding and making meaning of one's responses. What is the relationship with God? How does God feel about you? How has that relationship changed? How is God involved in your daily life? Does God help you find solutions to your problems? Has there ever been a feeling of forgiveness? At this point in the religious history, the focus is on what heals or cripples the heart. (p. 193)

In metaphorical language, Dombeck and Karl (1987) assess what has been placed upon the heart, what has or has not dropped in when the heart breaks, and what heals or cripples the heart in times of crisis. Tracing a wide concentric circle, they start with the person's placement within a religious community, with its social, cultural, and political contexts. Exploring personal meanings provides an opportunity to gain valuable information about cherished beliefs and spiritual practices. Finally, by identifying the healing or crippling nature of a person's relation to religious and spiritual resources, we are better able to assess the impact of God representations on the individual's development and functioning. Here one explores the bond, the range of affects, the ambivalence, and important internal dialogues with God images, insight questions, and feelings.

THE THERAPEUTIC PROCESS AND APPLICATION TO DIVERSITY

The synergy between spirituality and therapy provides a backdrop for understanding the client's worldviews and meaning making during the therapeutic process. In this section, the editors have allowed me to combine the sections on the therapeutic process and the application to diversity in order to best highlight the role of spirituality in the experience of an African American family. As noted earlier, African Americans are represented in many different faiths with diverse traditions, rituals, and spiritual convictions. The African American Shore family, described as follows, is one example of how spirituality can be integrated into the social work process; it is not meant to be representative of how spirituality is manifested in all African Americans.

The middle-class Shore family described in the case study will now be transformed into an African American family living in a working-class neighborhood that was once an African American neighborhood but is now a multicultural community. Nancy comes from generations of hard-working, church-going African Americans who have labored to provide a better life for the ones coming up behind them. She was the cherished only child, only grandchild, and only niece of doting adults. Charley grew up with less psychological and economic security than Nancy. Nancy's family represented the care and security that Charley longed to have. Their values are deeply rooted in the African American worldview of care of both older persons and children. The extended family and the church community viewed the adoption of Rena as an expected continuation of a family deeply rooted in African American traditional values. The shared intergenerational family home, a gift from Nancy's Aunt Flo, resonates within the cultural context. Rena moved outside of the ancestral home, and the Shores found themselves renting to people outside of the extended family. This created an additional tension to a family with a strong sense of collective African American identity. The family members are encountering social and cultural changes in their neighborhood and their lives. The African Methodist Episcopal Church where they worship continues in its historic role of welcoming newcomers to the neighborhood and the church community. Both the economic necessity and renting to strangers create additional stress in Nancy's life. She longs for the house to continue as a family home and dreams of Rena's problems being resolved and of her returning to continue the next generation of women in the house. It is Nancy's belief that Rena has an obligation to "get over her problems" and return home. She believes that Rena's presence would provide both emotional and financial support to the family.

Michael brings the transcendent into his interview, which enables the therapist to pursue the spiritual and religious content in the issues he presents. It is important for the clinical work to allow the client to speak about those issues of importance. Michael provides information for the therapist to use in spiritually oriented therapy. His direct comments about God can guide the clinical work with this family and allow the therapist to attend to the spiritual in the context of therapy.

Michael talks about "feeling funny" and "feeling bad." He feels bad because "asthma has taken away part of my life." His theory is that God gives everyone something he or she is terrific at. He says, "I haven't found mine yet—the asthma keeps me from it. I can't be a great athlete because I can't run fast. I can't have a puppy because I would wheeze. I just want to be good at something." According to his theory, God also puts a scar on everyone. People have to overcome their scars before they can find their special thing. Michael says asthma is his scar and he is waiting to outgrow it so that he can "find himself." In the meantime, he is unhappy and lonely.

Through the years, the Shores have depended on their faith and their church community to help them make meaning out of illness, conflicts, and economic difficulties. They have found supports to help them identify new ways of coping. There have been times when there were no easy solutions, and they have felt alienated from the church community and their sense of God as a support in their lives.

Using Dombeck and Karl's (1987) assessment tool, one begins to understand the impact of relationship with the transcendent on the worldview of Michael and his family. Before applying this tool, it is helpful to understand the context of the African Methodist Episcopal Church, to which they belong. One of largest Methodist groups in the United States, this church began in the late 1700s in protest against racial discrimination. It was formally organized in 1816. The foundation of Methodism is the doctrines of the Trinity, the natural sinfulness of humankind, its fall, the need of conversion and repentance, the freedom of the will, justification by faith, sanctification and holiness, future rewards and punishments, the sufficiency of the Scriptures for salvation, and the enabling grace of God and perfection. Methodism has typically been concerned with ministry to poor and disadvantaged people, expressing its faith in compassion for the human condition (Mead, 1995).

Placement in a Religious Community

The Shore family has belonged to the African Methodist Episcopal Church for several generations. Michael was brought up in the church, and his Boy Scout troop and leaders are members of the church. He goes to Sunday school and to church services regularly. His thoughts about his scar and his sinful nature come from Sunday school teachers, who have been frustrated with Michael from the beginning of his religious education experience. His early learning difficulties meant that the usual religious education materials and teaching methods did not meet his needs. During class, he often acted out and became known as the class clown. He remembers overhearing his kindergarten Sunday school teacher talking about how impossible it was to teach him, and perhaps he did not belong in religious education. He interpreted this as meaning that, he was so bad, God did not want him to be a part of the church. Yet he continues going and trying to be good enough.

Personal Meanings Attached to Symbols, Rituals, Beliefs, and Divine Figures

Michael has a strong belief that, if he prays hard enough during the Sunday worship services, he will be healed of his scar, and his family will be united. He thinks that learning the lessons during Sunday school is essential to his healing; however, he finds the teachers difficult to understand and not responsive to his questions. He sees this difficulty as a test from God for him to overcome. His is a judging God, waiting for Michael to make a mistake. When he doesn't make a mistake, he is rewarded by buttons and badges in Sunday school and in the Boy Scouts. He wonders if God is playing a game with him. He finds that it is hard to figure out how to consistently do what will result in regular rewards. He struggles to understand what works best in developing positive relationships.

Relationship to Religious Resources

Michael has internalized the desire for a personal relationship with God. His experience is one of a judging God. Michael sees himself as failing to win approval, due to his illness and lack of worthiness. He enjoys music and often wishes he were accepted as a member of the junior choir. His acting out does not allow him to be a permanent member. He regularly goes to the altar to be prayed over. During the call to prayer, he asks for healing of his scar and blessings for his family. Michael believes that God's grace will provide the miracles for which he prays but feels that there is something so sinful in him that he is causing grace to be blocked for himself and his family. God is a regular part of his life, distant at times, not available for answers, but usually there when Michael needs Him.

What I see with Michael and his family is an ambivalent relationship with God, as experienced through the church and the world of missing or lost opportunities. I would seek ways to work with the strengths of the church and this family's long history in the congregation. With the family's permission, the minister, the Sunday school teacher, the Boy Scout leader, and other church leaders who have known and worshiped with the family would be invited with the family members to a time of reflection on their need for a supportive spiritual community during the times of family and individual crises. I would invite them to participate in a spiritual genealogy of the church and the families who have contributed to the life of the church since its beginnings. During that experience, they would listen to the spiritual stories and the collective spiritual journey of the church community. They would be open to discover the significance of how families support families that are struggling, and would remember the importance of the Black church and the community in enabling African Americans to cope with individual and family issues in the midst of racism and oppression. Over time, this reflective sharing may lead to rituals of prayer and strategies for accessing the strengths of the church community on behalf of the Shore family.

LIMITATIONS OF THE MODEL

This model is not a stand-alone paradigm, with a host of its own methods, techniques, and strategies; rather, it is a therapy that is delivered within the context of dynamic theories and may be thought of as a metaparadigm. Metaparadigms do not identify specific techniques. Instead, they provide frameworks from which techniques can be created.

RESEARCH

McRae, Thompson, and Cooper (1999) use focus groups to examine how Black churches serve as therapeutic groups, providing a source of psychological and social support to African American communities. They acknowledge the research of Benson (1996), Koenig (1997), and Payne, Bergin, and Loftus (1992) that supports the assumptions, with empirical evidence, that there is a positive relationship between religion and both physical and psychological well-being. The focus group research explored ways in which the Black Christian churches create safe and supportive environments similar to those reported by researchers studying psychotherapy groups. The authors discuss three therapeutic functions of religious practices identified in the literature on Black churches. These include a tradition of giving voice to the suffering, through music and emotional expression; providing a safe haven for "acting out" primarily through dancing, possession, shouting, and crying; and validating the Black experience, especially that of racism in the dominant culture (McRae, Thomas, & Cooper, 1999).

SUMMARY

As social workers, our relationship with the client is aptly described by Garrett's (1954) quotation from a student's paper.

> It is our goal and at the same time an art, to learn to enter into people's lives, to be helpful to them, to make no demand on them, and to be able to go out of their lives again when the time comes without hardship to them. To leave them with just that "trace of relationship" that makes their ego stronger by integrating what was positive in the relationship, to enrich them and one's self for another good human contact, and ask no more. (p. 104)

In listening for the sacred, what we seek to do is to bring our mind to stillness and to hear and see the power of the transcendent in our time together (Guenther, 1992). Concerns regarding spirituality include the clinical relationship with the spiritual, however defined or experienced by the client. The historical, ethnic, and cultural context in which one's spiritual self develops is integral to the application of this model to diverse groups. It is a sacred situation, in which the person is searching for a fuller development of the spiritual self. The focus may be exclusively on spiritual matters or may include concerns of an emotional, a physical, a familial, a financial, or a career nature, as they shape and influence the person's spiritual journey (Richards & Bergin, 1998).

REFERENCES

Abram, J. (1997). *The language of Winnicott.* Nothvale, NJ: Aronson.

Applegate, J. S., & Bonovitz, J. M. (1995). *The facilitating partnership: A Winnicottian approach for social workers and other helping professionals.* Northvale, NJ: Aronson.

Bagley, C., & Carroll, J. (1998). Healing forces in African-American families. In H. McCubbin, E. Thompson, A. Thompson, & J. Futrell (Eds.), *Resiliency in African-American families* (pp. 117–142). Thousand Oaks, CA: Sage.

Benson, H. (with Stark, M.). (1996). *Timeless healing: The power and biology of belief.* New York: Scribner.

Bullis, Ron. (1996). *Spirituality in social work practice.* Washington, DC: Taylor & Francis.

Canda, E., & Furman, L. (1999). *Spiritual diversity in social work practice: The heart of helping.* New York: Free Press.

Christian, M. D., & Barbarin, O. A. (2001, February). Cultural resources and psychological adjustment of African American children effects of spirituality and racial attribution. *Journal of Black Psychology, 27*(1), 43–63.

Constantine, M. G. (1999, October). Spiritual and religious issues in counseling racial and ethnic minority populations: An introduction to the special issue. *Journal of Multicultural Counseling and Development, 27*(4), 179–181.

Cornett, C. (1998). *The soul of psychotherapy: Recapturing the spiritual dimension in the therapeutic encounter.* New York: Simon & Schuster.

Derezotes, D. S., & Evans, K. E. (1995). Spirituality and religiosity in practice: In-depth interviews of social work practitioners. *Social Thought: Journal of Religion in the Social Services, 18*(1), 39–56.

Dombeck, M., & Karl, J. (1987). Spiritual issues in mental healthcare. *Journal of Religion and Health, 26*(3), 183–197.

Dunn, A., Balaguer, & Dawes, S. Johnson. (1999, October). Spirituality-focused genograms: Keys to uncovering spiritual resources in African American families. *Journal of Multicultural Counseling and Development, 27*(4), 240–254.

Einstein, A. (1950). *Out of my latter years.* New York: Philosophical Library.

Garrett, A. (1954). Learning through supervision. *Smith College Studies in Social Work, 24*(2), 104.

Goldberg, C. (1996). The privileged position of religion in the clinical dialogue. *Clinical Social Work Journal, 32*(3), 125–136.

Graham, M. A., Kaiser, T., & Garrett, K. J. (1998). Naming the spiritual: The hidden dimension of helping. *Social Thought: Journal of Religion in the Social Service, 18*(4), 49–62.

Griffith, J. L., & Griffith, M. E. (2002). *Encountering the sacred in psychotherapy.* New York: Guilford Press.

Guenther, M. (1992). *Holy listening: The art of spiritual direction.* Boston: Cowley Press.

Joseph, M. V. (1988). Religion and social work practice. *Social Casework, 69,* 443–452.

Kilpatrick, A. C., & Holland, T. P. (1990). Spiritual dimensions of practice. *The Clinical Supervisor, 8*(2), 125–140.

Koenig, H. G. (1997). *Is religion good for your health? The effects of religion on physical and mental health.* New York: Hawthorn Pastoral Press.

Lewandoski, C. A., & Canda, E. R. (1995). A typological model for the assessment of religious groups. *Social Thought: Journal of Religion in the Social Services, 18*(1), 17–38.

Lincoln, C. E., & Mamiya, L. (1990). *The Black church in the African American experience.* Durham, NC: Duke University Press.

Lovinger, R. J. (1984). *Working with religious issues in therapy.* New York: Aronson.

Lufoff, D., Lu, F., & Turner, R. (1992, November). Toward a more culturally sensitive DSM-IV psycho religious and psycho-spiritual problems. *Journal of Nervous and Mental Disease, 180*(11), 673–682.

May, G. (1987). *Will and spirit: A contemplative psychology.* San Francisco: Harper & Row.

McAdoo, H. Pipes (1998). African-American families: Strengths and realities. In H. McCubbin,

E. Thompson, A. Thompson, & J. Futrell (Eds.), *Resiliency in African-American families* (pp. 17–30). Thousand Oaks, CA: Sage.

McRae, M. B., Thomas, D. A., & Cooper, S. (1999, October). Black churches as therapeutic groups. *Journal of Multicultural Counseling and Development, 27*(4), 207–220.

Mead, F. S. (1995). Handbook of denominations in the United States (Rev. by Samuel S. Hill). Nashville, TN: Abingdon Press.

Millison, M., & Dudley, J. (1992). Providing spiritual support: A job for all hospice professionals. *Hospice Journal, 8*(4), 49–66.

Morgan, J. D. (1993). *Personal care in an impersonal world: A multidimensional look at bereavement.* New York: Baywood.

O'Connor, P. (1993). A clinical paradigm for exploring spiritual concerns. In K. Doka & J. Morgan (Eds.), *Death and spirituality.* New York: Baywood.

O'Connor, P., & Kaplan, M. (1986). The role of the interdisciplinary team in providing spiritual care: An attitudinal study of hospices workers. In F. S. Wald (Ed.), *Proceedings of a Colloquium: In Quest of the Spiritual Component of Care for the Terminally Ill* (pp. 51–62). New Haven, CT: Yale Univeristy School of Nursing.

O'Murchu, D., MSC (1991). *Religious life: A prophetic vision.* Notre Dame, IN: Ave Maria Press.

Payne, I., Bergin, A., & Loftus P. (1992). A review of attempts to integrate spiritual and standard psychotherapy techniques. *Journal of Psychotherapy Integration, 2*(3), 171–192.

Poussaint, A. F., MD, & Alexander, A. (2000). *Lay my burden down.* Boston: Beacon Press.

Richards, P. S., & Bergin, A. E. (1998). *A spiritual strategy for counseling and psychotherapy.* Washington, DC: American Psychological Association.

Rizzuto, A. (1979). The *birth of the living God: A psychoanalytic study.* Chicago: University of Chicago Press.

Vaughn, F. (1991). Spiritual issues in psychotherapy. *Journal of Transpersonal Psychology, 23*(2), 105–119.

Wilber, K. (1984). *Quantum question: Mystical writings of the world's great physicists.* Boston & London: New Science Library.

Winnicott, D. W. (1982). Playing *and reality.* New York: Routledge.

Zukau, F. (1979). *The dancing wu li masters: An overview of the new* physics. London: Flamingo Books.

Part III

Epilogues

Epilogue

The Shores—1-Year Follow-Up

Rachelle A. Dorfman, PhD

NANCY

During the last year, both of Nancy's parents developed cancer. Her mother's was a relatively minor skin cancer, but her father's was terminal. Shortly before he lapsed into a coma, Nancy and her father talked about her childhood. Her father was genuinely surprised about her feelings of abandonment, and he reassured her of his love. Nancy also talked with her mother, who admitted that her preoccupations with friends and career when Nancy was a little girl were caused by her own unhappiness, not by a lack of love for, or a lack of interest in, Nancy.

Nancy worries about Michael more than ever, but her panic attacks occur less frequently and with less impact. She has spent a year in individual therapy and feels that the treatment has given her permission "to stop feeling guilty for everything, to stop trying to control everyone, and to stop worrying about what people think." She no longer feels compelled to return to work or school.

CHARLEY

One year later, Charley has still not read the case study. He no longer attends the vocational rehabilitation program, but otherwise his life is much the same as it was last year. His relationship with Michael is still poor, perhaps worse. Weekly performances at the comedy club are still fun. The best news is that the family is hopeful because Charley has kept a job as a trash collector for 5 months. If he is retained beyond the 6-month probationary period, he will be virtually guaranteed the municipal union job.

RENA

Six months ago, Rena found her birth mother. Aunt Flo's employer, an attorney, was able to give Rena the name of her birth mother and the name of the state in which she lived. Rena called every woman in the state with that name—a common one, at that—until she found her birth mother. After an initial "infatuation" with her birth mother, the discovery of a half-sister close to her age, and the uncovering of the facts about her birth, Rena settled down to a job in a medical office (which she has held for 7 months). She is talking about applying to nursing school and is in an "on again, off again" relationship with a young man. Rena eventually got off the waiting list and entered therapy. She dropped out after 9 months because she did not like her therapist.

MICHAEL

The last year has been a mixed one for Michael. He has not had any asthma attacks. The summer brought a successful camp experience at a new camp, and he was invited to return as a counselor-in-training. Although he has retained a few friends from camp, they are all much younger. He speaks less often of his sadness, his differentness, and his loneliness, but he clearly remains an outcast among his peers. Michael is still a loyal Boy Scout and has been appointed the troop scribe by his scout leaders. He also attends a religious educational program and frequently coaxes the rest of the family into participating in religious rituals at home. An adolescent therapy group he entered early in the year has recently been disbanded because of a drop in membership.

EDITOR'S NOTES

When I met with the Shores exactly 1 year after I interviewed them for "The Case," I was struck by the difference in their attitudes. Although family members still had problems and were still involved with social services, they demonstrated a sense of optimism that had not been present earlier. Nancy no longer expressed the concern that, after the book was published, she would run from social worker to social worker, trying to do everything suggested. All the family members expressed anticipation about soon being able to see the finished book. They were humble about their contribution ("It wasn't anything") but, at the same time, they were proud of their participation.

Because the Shores were not my clients, I do not know what kinds of therapeutic paradigms they were exposed to during the year. I only know for certain that there was some treatment. The experience of telling their story in depth, uncluttered by clinical intervention, and of "going public" has also surely had some impact on family members and on the family as a whole. It remains to be seen how they will make use of what we have written.

Epilogue

The Shores—10-Year Follow-Up

Rachelle A. Dorfman, PhD

Almost 10 years later to the day I find myself on the sidewalk in front of the Shores' house. As I approach the house, I remember that the last time I visited, their screen door was broken. It took a bit of finesse to get it open and not have it slap me in the behind as I entered. I wondered if 10 years later it had been repaired or was still "hanging on." To my delight, I found the front door to the Shore's house more solid than I had remembered. The metaphor did not escape me.

NANCY

Nancy's demeanor remains fairly unchanged. At 54, she looks thinner but is still overweight. Her image may be the only constant in her life. For a year now, from Sunday to Friday, she has lived in a posh uptown residence with the family's benefactor, Aunt Flo. When Flo's husband, Victor, became terminally ill, Nancy stayed with the elderly couple to help out. Three weeks later, Uncle Victor was dead. Nancy remained because Flo was afraid to be alone. Nancy reasons that "Aunt Flo gave us our house, paid for Michael's college education, and has given us money over the years. This is a way to finally pay her back." On the weekend, Nancy lives with Charley, although she says it is more like a date than "living with." "We have sex. I take him to the movies, pour his medicine for the week, pay the bills, and make sure there is food in the house." She says it is a perfect arrangement. "In the beginning," Nancy explains, "I stayed with Aunt Flo for her sake. Now I am there for me. After 34 years of marriage, I just want to be away from Charley. I only make his life a living hell when I am there. We are each happier this way."

Nancy describes her new life as one enriched with theater, elegant dinners, and lively conversations with Aunt Flo. Because of her aunt's generosity, Nancy has a membership to a health club. She works out, walks 2 to 3 miles a day, and is more conscious of her diet. She has lost 31 pounds. Occasionally, the old back injury acts up, only now she regards it as a minor annoyance she must live with. No longer is it "an excuse not to do anything." Nancy says, "Flo and I take care of each other. I have a purpose, and I finally have a companion."

The money problems that plagued the family have dissipated. Charley has secure employment, and in a few years he will retire with a pension. Nancy continues to receive monthly disability checks. They also have a steady rental income from the downstairs apartment.

Anxiety attacks are just an unpleasant memory for Nancy. Her chronic depression is managed by the antidepressant Zoloft. When she is with Charley for 2 days, she takes 100 mg daily. The rest of the time she takes 25 to 50 mg daily and is considering discontinuing the medication completely when she is uptown. She admits to occasionally worrying about other people's opinions, but being in the presence of the older woman's pragmatic and stoic nature has a calming effect. She is still troubled about Michael. Although she acknowledges his accomplishments, she says that she fears that he will never be happy. Nancy suspects that he has a bipolar disorder like his father and that he may have to have a breakdown before his life improves.

Nancy has not had social work treatment in 10 years. "I stopped going to therapy because the therapist was getting too close to the 'nitty gritty.' It seemed that the social worker wanted me to leave my husband so I panicked and left the therapy instead," she explains. Ironically, Nancy attributes her improvements to "getting away from Charley." Although it is corny, she says, "repeating clichés helps a lot." Her favorites are "Take one day at a time," "What's the worst thing that can happen?" and "It will all work out."

As evidence of her new frame of mind, she divulges that as a consequence of several recent falls, her doctor has made a referral for an evaluation for multiple sclerosis. She is unfazed. She says, "If I have it, it will not be so bad at my age, and, anyway, now I have a place to go." Her concern is that some other major family crisis could occur that would compel her to give up her new life.

CHARLEY

Charley agrees that the new living arrangement is better than the old one, although his take on it is a bit different than his wife's. "We are sort of like separated—not really separated, but living apart. I could have made her stay. If I wanted to have her home, I could tell her. Her aunt is like her mother. She is the only niece."

At age 62, Charley has a very simple life. Because Nancy is content with Aunt Flo and there is more financial security, there is less arguing in the Shore house and thus less need for Charley to lie to his wife. He goes fishing, bowls, and cooks. He does the laundry for Michael and himself and watches hours of television a day. Every member of the family agrees that Charley just wants "not to be bothered."

His appearance has changed over the years. He looks noticeably older and suffers from arthritis and gout. He has a work-related back injury, and his hands tremble. He has difficulty staying on a topic. Charley is not unaware of these changes. He says, "The trouble when you are mentally disturbed is at times you start drifting. That's what I do." Indeed, he "drifts" frequently, often to memories of the "Hollywood days." Charley says that the doctor thinks his "limp" is related to his medication (Depakote and lithium). According to Nancy, he is one of the 20% who do not respond to lithium alone.

During the last 10 years, Charley has been hospitalized once—after he put a knife to his chest and told Nancy he was going to kill himself. He recalls that hospitalization fondly: "If they had a swimming pool, I would have stayed longer. It was great. Three squares a day. Eat all you want." Nancy reports that his deterioration began with that hospitalization.

A city sanitation worker for 11 years, Charley was recently transferred to a new work site and a new supervisor. He complains, "My boss was nice at first, but now she takes out her frustrations on me. She always gives me a hard time. She says I curse and I don't wring out the mop right." On the one hand, he feels he is unjustly accused; on the other hand, he admits that during his 8-hour shift, "I sleep 6 and work 2." He daydreams about being a personal trainer for "fat old ladies" who don't want to exercise. He says, "I would charge $30 a half hour. Nancy won't let me do it." Charley claims that his night work keeps him from performing at the comedy club. Nancy argues that he couldn't do it anyway because his medication ruined any timing he ever had.

Charley is satisfied with his relationship with his daughter. He says, "It is decent. Our relationship depends on the mood she is in. Rena is a moody girl." Like the rest of the family, he tries to give his son advice. "I told Michael that one girl can louse up your whole life. See other girls and don't take it so hard when this one gives you a hard time (she threatens him if he says he wants to break up). The girl is no good for him."

Charley says that Nancy doesn't know that he hit Michael about 3 months ago. "He said something to me that got on my nerves. We argued, then he started choking me. I got up and smacked him in the mouth with my closed fist. I said, 'Don't you ever pick up a hand to me again.' He said, 'I'm sorry, Dad.' I said, 'I'm sorry, too. I never want to hit you again.'"

Charley has had a great deal of counseling over the years, but he doesn't think that any of the counselors helped him. "Psychologists are okay. Psychiatrists are nuts." He didn't offer opinions on social workers. He reports that what helps him most is working, relaxing, and watching television.

RENA

Rena has been a registered nurse for 5 years. At age 29 she is attractive, vibrant, and articulate. Although satisfied with her career accomplishments and her independence, she is still on a journey of self-improvement and self-discovery.

She likes providing nursing care to patients in their own homes. "I used to have a poor work history. I'd get bored and antsy, but that has changed." She is conscientious and responsible. Her remaining "rebelliousness," however, causes occasional problems. For example, she becomes infuriated when the "system" gets in the way of caring. She has said to her boss, "What do you mean I can't see this patient because insurance won't cover it? She needs continued care. Can't you work it out?" On another occasion she said, "I will not do Medicare fraud. I will not go and see a patient every day and bother her when she has a daughter who wants to take her out but can't because my employer wants me to make unnecessary visits." She laments that she is frequently too personally involved and tries to be a "rescuer."

Home-care work has been a source of personal growth. She says, "Seeing the pain and insecurities of others and witnessing the effect that their wounds have on their perception of themselves made me realize that I am not an 'alien' creature. Working with these patients helped me feel less different." She adds that many of her youthful feelings of alienation and difference stemmed from being adopted. "No one looked like me. No one had my problems, no one acted like me."

Two years ago, Rena learned that her biological father was dead, murdered by "a friend." She has few details about what happened. She has five half-brothers on her father's side, and each child has a different mother. Her biological mother, who never married, raised a younger daughter. Rena is the only child of all the children on both sides who has graduated from high school and has gone to college. Finding relatives helped her to understand herself. For example, she discovered that practically all the males on her father's side are auto mechanics, which seems to explain her mechanical ability. Meeting one of her half-brothers, "Little Jimmy, Jr.," who is 3 days younger than Rena, was a jolting experience. Jimmy is "very troubled and in and out of jail." Rena went to visit him in jail not long ago. She says that when she saw him, she saw herself. They looked at each through a glass partition and cried. "He had the same face, the same hair, the same voice."

Locating her birth mother turned out to be less dramatic than she thought it would. She reflects, "The fact that it didn't change my life, changed my life." Mother and daughter talk to each other about once a month. Rena describes her wheelchair-bound birth mother as having many health problems and as being "lost." "My biological mother," she says, "is a 'topper'— she always tops everyone else's problems. No matter what you say, she has done it better in the negative sense. She always has it worse than anyone else. She personifies victimization and martyrdom. I have to work hard in the relationship so that I don't feel guilty. I try to keep her accountable for her own problems and not take them on as my own."

Rena no longer believes her adoption theory—that is, that being adopted caused her to get rid of people before they abandoned her. Instead she says that she fears and hates rejection no more than anyone else. She maintains that she "dumped" people in the past because of her low self-esteem, not as a result of her adoption history.

Rena asserts that her parents' living arrangement is more peaceful for all involved, but she adds that Michael feels abandoned by Nancy. "She left him with the ogre." She adds, "I care about my father, but he is disturbing because he is so pathetic. I have shame issues about him. I am angry at him, but I should not be angry because he is sick. I try to work through my anger with him, but he is incapable of helping me—which only makes me more angry." One complaint is that Charley seems unable to give her the advice she longs for. "I would do anything to make him different. I would give him my kidney if that could fix him."

In contrast, Rena's relationship with Nancy is mutually satisfying. In the past, an angry Rena would not talk to her mother for weeks. Now disagreements and quarrels are resolved in a day or less, and they are soon on the phone agreeing that the tiff was ridiculous. Rena shares her mother's concern about Michael. She says that she tries to help him, but he doesn't always want her help. They don't hang out together, but they do talk on the phone.

Rena has lost most of her ambitions to sing in public. She had a boyfriend who did not want her to perform, and she recalls that relationship as one in which she gave up parts of herself in order to retain love. This past year she has taken opera lessons and did one performance in a club. Mainly, she sings only for friends. "Singing professionally plays havoc with my work schedule and is 'not conducive to my new more yuppie lifestyle,'" she says in jest. She denies being a "yuppie," saying, "My rebellious nature still despises pretension."

For the last year and a half, she has not dated because she decided to have a "hiatus" from men. "A lot of my issues are with men because I grew up in a very matriarchal family," she says. Recently, she put the word out that she was willing to date again, and in the past 2 weeks she has been asked out by four different men.

A year after our last meeting, the journal that Rena kept was "violated and read," but she refused to say by whom. She threw that one away with others she had kept and did not write another word until 2 weeks ago, when she started a new journal with "Commitments to Myself" (see Exhibit 1). She says that at this point in her life, she is on a spiritual journey, "fine-tuning," accepting some things about herself, and trying to change some lingering problems.

"I used to look at people and almost feel subhuman by comparison. I thought that other people were perfect. The most important thing for me is not to repeat my family cycle, or, if I must repeat it, I hope that it will be in diluted form." Her goals include returning to school, because she feels that she sold herself short on her education. She has not relinquished the wish to establish a more satisfying relationship with her father because she is convinced that she can't have a healthy relationship with a man unless she comes to terms with her father. Her last counseling experiencing was 2½ years ago.

MICHAEL

"Overall," Michael says, "things are better than before because I am more aware than I was as a child. My mother sheltered me more than the average mother. Now I know how good things really are, and I understand how bad things really are, but life is more complicated now."

On the one hand, Michael squirms under all the attention he receives from family members. On the other hand, he admits that he seeks out the opinions of others because he cannot think for himself, especially in matters of the heart. Nor, he says, can he evaluate his own or his family members' behavior.

At 23, he is in the "first relationship of intensity" in his life. His girlfriend is 19. He thinks that her intelligence makes her dangerous because she shows him things from a different perspective. "My parents are more controlling than I thought they were, but I only see this when my girlfriend points it out. When my girlfriend's views differ from my family's views, I don't know who to listen to. I don't trust my own opinion. Also, I don't know if I am really experiencing love, or I am just enjoying being loved so much, being infatuated, enjoying the physical contact. I have been ruled by women most of my life. Even though they love me and care for me very much, sometimes I just want to get away." When Michael gets frustrated with all the women in his life, he fantasizes about being alone—which, he thinks, may be the only way he will find himself. He talks about running away to Wyoming, where there is a lot of space and where there are relatively few people.

Michael longs for male role models and looks for them in television and books. Until now, he says, the only role models he has had have been scout-masters, teachers, and professors. "My dad hasn't been much of a role model. He just wants to come home from work with no responsibilities and watch TV. He never grew up. He never had a direction for himself just going from job to job, never having a career." Michael has no problem with his parents' living arrangement.

Michael graduated from college with a BA in history and works as a substitute teacher as part of a program that allows people with bachelor's degrees to work in city schools. However, the job is not gratifying. He says it is just "baby-sitting." The pay is good, but there are no benefits. Michael's aspiration is to earn a graduate degree in library science. He took graduate courses at the local university and applied for admission but was told that the three Bs he earned did not meet their standards, and his application was denied.

The most satisfying job he ever had was at college, where he worked for minimum wage in the library but nevertheless felt important. He states, "I have always been around books. People come up to me in libraries and ask me for help, and I am not even a librarian. Maybe it's part of my destiny to be a librarian. One of the highest points in my life was in college when I organized a study group. I tutored four or five people. One person in the group got an A, and I got an A-minus. I tutored her, and she got a higher grade than me. I was in charge, I was special, I was in control. I like when I am in control." Michael describes college as a fantasy world, "No ugly people there, just young people, every year a new crop."

After college, Michael went to Europe for a month. "If I could do one thing, it would be to earn enough money to travel." He traveled by himself, staying for a time with Nancy's half-sister in Denmark and in cheap hotels and hostels.

In our interview, Michael broke down recalling his childhood: "I always had the feeling that the medicine I took made me behave badly and never allowed me to grow up. I never learned how to act correctly. I'm learning now. It's sad. All through high school, I never had friends, I had acquaintances. People didn't dislike me, but they didn't like me enough to hang out with me outside of school." Michael talks of "missed opportunities" for peer relationships and his desire to reconnect with one girl he knew in high school. When he fantasizes about her, he imagines himself saying, "I wish I had taken the time to get to know you. I always wanted to get to know you. I never took the opportunity and I regret it." He adds, "I feel that it was my fault that I didn't have meaningful relationships in high school." He believes that he has to recapture some of these lost opportunities before he can move on.

Michael admits, "A lot of the accomplishments I achieved in high school [see Exhibit 2] were not as they appear. I volunteered because no one else wanted to do it. Take the recycling project, for example—it was a failure. A teacher started another, more successful, recycling program after I graduated. There was only one time where I competed and won. That was in an election for patrol leader."

"I've been in counseling on and off for 12 years, and I don't feel that it has done me much good. I didn't take much of what the social worker had to offer. Then again, I do feel better when I talk to someone. I search for validity; I need someone to tell me that I am not as bad as I think I am. If I am so depressed, I go in there [the therapy session] and say I am going to kill myself, that I am bad, and the therapist says, 'Oh, you're not.' That makes me realize that I am not that bad. But it only lasts for so long, then I go back to the way I was. Some people think that I achieved a lot, but I could have achieved much more." Michael says that if he wrote his autobiography, he would call it *In Search of Me*.

EDITOR'S NOTES

The Shore family—Nancy, Charley, Rena, and Michael—has allowed us to enter the family members' private lives and to know their thoughts, feelings, and fantasies. They have displayed their weaknesses and their strengths, receiving nothing tangible for their efforts. They did it because I asked them and because they believed it would help others. They are good people, who not only care about one another but also care about people they don't even know.

For all our theorizing in this book and in volume 1 of *Paradigms of Clinical Social Work*, we could not have predicted the positive changes that they have made. They deserve to be proud, and we should be humbled in the face of their contribution. I have often wondered about the impact of this project on the Shore family. Nancy recalls that after reading volume 1, she felt responsible for everything that was wrong in the family. She says, "I read it once, put it away and never picked it up again." Did the book make a difference in her life? "No," she says, "to be honest, I don't really remember the book any more. It was so long ago." Charley showed little interest in the first book. Rena and Michael, however, did ask their mother for permission to read it, but Nancy refused. Rena had hoped that the book would give her more objectivity about her family, reaffirming or negating some of her own positions. Michael was simply curious.

At the 10-year mark, the Shore children are adults and no longer subject to the discretion of their mother regarding whether or not they will read the accounts we have written. Rena and Michael have expressed their intent to read the complete works. Nancy worries that Michael's girlfriend will read the most recent epilogue and use it to say bad things about Nancy. Michael is still intensely curious about both volumes. Rena and Nancy are especially excited about an update that shows the family's positive changes.

What have we learned from this project? We are reminded of the power of family, the ways in which members persist in their concern for each other. We are also reminded of the endurance of family issues over a decade and the impact of mental and physical illnesses on the family.

What is impressive is how the Shore family seeks its own solutions. Its members have tried nontraditional living arrangements, first with little success, when Rena lived apart from the family at age 12 in the downstairs apartment, and now with apparent success, with Nancy and Charley living apart for most of the week. We are also reminded that the things that we think will make significant differences often do not. Rena was obsessed with locating her biological mother. When she did, the new relationship made little difference in her life. Perhaps there will be a third volume and another update of the Shore family (a 15- or 20-year epilogue).[1] Then we shall know what has become of Michael, who is in the throes of his first love and an accentuated identity crisis. What will come of his deep sadness for his lost youth and his longing to revisit his childhood? I would like Michael to know that we are empathic to his suffering, his struggle with the women in his life, and his longing for a male role model. We are heartened that he was able to leave his "nest" successfully in socially sanctioned ways, first to college and later on his European jaunt. We hope he will find the courage, resources, and family blessings to do so again.

Exhibit 1. Excerpts From Rena's "Commitments to Myself"

Spirit, please provide me with the strength, courage, and discipline I may need at times of weakness to keep the following commitments to myself:

1. I will not engage in any sexual activity with a man until I am confident that we have both shared enough with each other to have been "emotionally naked."
2. I will acknowledge & have consideration for Little Rena so that our issues may be dealt with & worked through.

3. I will retain my sense of self while involved with a man by deciding what will best serve myself and following through with that behavior.

4. I will identify my triggers of hurt and anger and withhold from reacting to them until I have given myself the opportunity to determine their issue of origin & work through them accordingly. I will then respond to each trigger in an appropriate and constructive way.

5. I will consistently journal and only discuss my issues with the people in my life who are safe.

6. I will allow myself to be vulnerable with the knowledge that only love, light, and joy are intended for me.

7. I will permit myself to be imperfect. When I make a mistake, I will take responsibility for my behavior, identify how I would have liked to have handled the situation, and give myself the opportunity to correct that un-desired behavior.

8. I will take advantage of opportunities to practice my new relationship be-haviors. I will keep in mind that others may be on a different journey. I will not allow their behaviors to become my excuse for discouragement, nega-tivity & destructive behavior.

9. I will pay attention to my inner voice and keep my eyes open for warning signals. I will trust my own judgment and address these warning signals by taking appropriate action.

Please let me learn my lessons quickly and gently. Thank you, Spirit.

Exhibit 2. Excerpts From Michael's "Self-Description," Written for His College Application

I would describe myself as a smart, likable, outgoing person who can be very talkative at times, especially about issues that concern me or that I am inter-ested in, like environmental problems, history, astronomy, and religion. I am very motivated, with a great deal of passion for life and learning.

In first grade I tested as learning disabled. My disability affected my fine and gross motor coordination and attention span. I was enrolled in special education classes. Now, I feel this was my greatest obstacle, which my motiva-tion has helped me overcome. In elementary and middle school, however, I felt trapped. Teachers only expected so much from me and didn't think I could handle more challenging courses usually not assigned to those classified as learning disabled.

Since childhood, I've had severe asthma, which was extremely debilitat-ing. I was heavily medicated and the combination of drugs caused behavior problems. Numerous hospitalizations due to asthma attacks disrupted my edu-cation, as well as several personal relationships I tried to develop. During this time, my self-esteem was low. Eventually, the asthma medication was reduced, causing the behavior problems to go away and my self-esteem to improve.

When it was time to enroll in high school, I wanted to start out fresh. A lot of things changed in 10th grade. I was enrolled in regular classes in a school where no one knew me. So many opportunities were available to me, and I couldn't wait to be involved in everything.

In 10th and 11th grades I had speaking parts in drama productions. In 10th grade I was a member of the local chapter of Amnesty International. I was a member of the debate team for 3 years. Also for 3 years I worked as an aide in the main [school] office. During 12th grade I was an aide in the history department. I was also elected class representative in 10th and 12th grade. In 12th grade I ran for class president. In 10th grade I was on the swimming team, and in 12th grade I managed the field hockey team.

One thing that I am most proud of and where I feel I have made a great contribution is my work in the environment. Our environment was in trouble, and I wanted to do something about it. As a member of the [student council's] executive board in 11th grade, I chaired the environmental committee. The committee worked to raise the consciousness of all students and staff about environmental problems and we started a recycling program at the school, which I continue to run.

When I was 12, I joined the Boy Scouts. I am now a Life Scout. I need five more merit badges to become an Eagle Scout. I was elected a member of the Order of the Arrow, an honor camper organization within the scouts. I am presently at the second of three levels. In the summer of 1989 I was counselor in training at [scout camp]. This year I was elected senior patrol leader.

I made the honor roll for the first time in 10th grade, which I consider my most significant achievement. It was especially significant since I did it while enrolled in all regular courses. I really felt then that I had conquered my learning disability.

I am a member of the National Honor Society and have taken rapid and advanced placement history courses. History is one of my passions, and I am seriously considering it as my major in college. I read a lot of other topics, but when they begin to bore me, I always return to historical reading. I am especially interested in American history.

I am proud that I have overcome many obstacles in my life. I have learned that through motivation and hard work, I can accomplish anything I put my mind to, and I am rewarded by a great sense of achievement.

NOTE

1. After the first interviews (for *Paradigms of Clinical Social Work*, Vol. 1) and the recent interviews for this book, I offered my services to clarify and explain the text and to counsel if needed.

Epilogue

The Shores—15-Year Follow-Up

Rachelle A. Dorfman, PhD

Life has changed dramatically for the Shores in the 15 years since the original case study was written. The bad news is that Nancy (overweight and debilitated from a back injury for most of her adult life) has developed diabetes and still experiences back pain. The good news is that her diabetes is under control, and she says that she has learned to live with her chronic pain. Nancy has not smoked a cigarette in 9 years and claims to be no more anxious or depressed than the average person. (She takes the antidepressant Zoloft and chews the nicotine gum Nicorette.) A massive benign tumor was surgically removed from Charley's adrenal gland about 1 year ago, with apparently no ill effects. Charley no longer dreams his dreams. He explains that it doesn't pay, because every great invention he ever thought of has been invented by someone else.

Except for Rena, the Shore family still lives in the second-floor apartment of a two-story duplex. Thanks to the rental income derived from the first-floor apartment, Charley's Social Security benefits, his retirement pension, Nancy's monthly disability check, and the continuing generosity of Aunt Flo, the Shores enjoy more financial security than ever before.

The Shores' newly decorated living room, with its warm earth colors, comfortable chairs, and plump sofa, reflects the changes in the family. Michael and Charley no longer fight and bicker. Nancy doesn't worry about Michael any more. These days, Josette (a miniature poodle—the newest member of the family) is the center of attention.

Rena is grown up and married. Her husband is a sales manager in a nationally known retail company. Rena (now a registered nurse) works in the workman's compensation claims section of a large insurance company. Michael's asthma is nonexistent. Most intriguing of all—Michael is studying to be a psychotherapist!

NANCY AND CHARLEY

For the last 2 years, Nancy and Charley, age 68 and 60, relate to one another (according to Nancy) more like caregiver and care receiver than husband and wife. Charley suffers from tremors, a faltering gait, memory loss, occasional bursts of anger, forgetfulness, and apathy. Nancy wonders if these symptoms are the result of Charley's bipolar disorder, or if he could have Parkinson's disease, dementia, depression, or a combination of diagnoses. The doctor offers no definitive explanations. Because Charley's symptoms are intermittent, Nancy sometimes questions whether Charley is faking it. Charley's doctor has prescribed medications for gout, hypertension, and lower back pain, as well as Aricept for memory problems and Depakote for management of mania. Charley has not been in psychotherapy for many years, although a psychiatrist checks his medications once a month, and he sees a psychologist once every 4 months (merely to fulfill the requirements of the guidance center that provides his mental health services). Charley says that the only thing he worries about these days is whether or not Michael will find a girl.

Nancy and Charley have a routine. Charley goes to the senior center every day for lunch and a little socializing. He says that he performs his comedy act there, but Nancy's face reveals her skepticism. Charley spends most afternoons and evenings watching TV and walking Josette, their red miniature poodle. On Saturday mornings, Michael drives Nancy to Aunt Flo's uptown apartment, where she spends each weekend, returning to the Shore apartment on Monday morning.

Nancy has what she calls a "semi job." She creates needlepoint cell-phone cases, checkbook covers, and purses. At first, Nancy gave away the pretty items as gifts to friends and family. Then she tried her hand at selling them at a flea market. Finally, a friend of a friend put her in touch with a boutique owner, who now sells the needlepoint cases in her shop. Even though her craft provides little income, Nancy says it is therapeutic, giving her a reason to wake up in the morning. When Nancy is not working on needlepoint, she is meeting friends who regularly share their problems and provide emotional support to one another. The rest of her day is spent reading, watching sporting events and soap operas on TV, and going online searching for facts and statistics about favorite movies, sports teams, actors, and other celebrities. Nancy's only goal is to get through every day and see that her children are not unhappy because of the lifestyle the family lived when the children were young. Her husband, on the other hand, only wants to be a better listener.

A couple of years ago, Charley (a trash collector for the city department of sanitation), was accused of making sexually inappropriate remarks to a female coworker. He agreed to attend sensitivity training classes but was still in danger of being fired. Aunt Flo (a guardian angel to the Shore family) put Nancy and Charley in contact with an attorney, who advised Charley to voluntarily retire, thereby saving his pension. Charley took the advice and retired, and the sexual harassment suit was settled. Nancy wonders whether Charley's bad judgment comes from dementia.

RENA

Rena declined to be interviewed for the epilogue, in part because of my mistake. I had not spoken to any of the Shores since the publication of volume 2 of *Paradigms of Clinical Social Work* (about 5 years ago). I called Nancy first, and she greeted me enthusiastically and agreed to an interview. She also assured me that Charley would welcome a reunion, too. Next, I called Michael and made an appointment to meet him at a local coffee shop. Nancy gave me Rena's telephone number so that I could arrange to meet her as well. Unfortunately, Rena was out when I called, and I left a brief voice message informing her that there was to be a third volume of *Paradigms* and that I was coming to town to interview her parents and her brother. I said that I was hoping to interview her, too.

The Shores' true identity has never been revealed. By leaving a voice message, I broke confidentiality (not realizing that my message would disclose the Shores's identity and participation to anyone who listened to the voice message). In fact, Rena's husband heard the message. When I eventually talked to Rena, I found her more than a little peeved at me for disclosing the nature of our relationship on a voicemail. She was also furious with her mother for giving me her phone number in the first place. Clearly, Rena did not want her husband to know about the project at that moment and surely not in that way. He was aware of the family's participation in a textbook, but his information was sketchy at best. My carelessness, she complained, would force her to provide the details her husband would want. Months later, I received a message from Rena, via Nancy. She did not want me to contact her again. Rena said that if she wanted to be interviewed, she would call me. I have still not heard from Rena.

I do know that Rena's husband is also an adoptee who is searching for his biological mother and that the couple is under some stress. Rena is unhappy with her job and is working overtime. The couple is trying to accumulate enough money to buy a house and start a family. Nancy reports that Rena is angry and jealous of the time Nancy spends with Aunt Flo and the bond Nancy has with her tenant (a young mother who looks to Nancy for nurturing).

Nancy cannot overstate the importance of her relationship with Aunt Flo. The two women often say to each other, "Why won't Rena let us be?" They take long walks, cook, talk for hours, and watch videos together. Their closeness is intellectually and emotionally satisfying. Nancy is also Aunt Flo's only heir.

MICHAEL

Michael, a handsome young man, appears to have no signs of the asthma that plagued his childhood. Other than an inability to run, Michael has no other limitations. He carries an inhaler—just in case. His only medication is Paxil, which he takes for anxiety, occasional panic attacks, and difficulty sleeping.

Michael was engaged to marry the young woman he dated for 4 years. As Michael tells it, they broke up because his girlfriend opposed his wish to postpone the wedding date indefinitely. He wanted to remain friends; she did not. Michael admits that he would like to date again, but he is not interested in just a physical relationship, nor is he interested in a long-term committed relationship—which leaves him in a quandary about what indeed he does want.

Michael has a BA degree in history but realizes that he can't earn a living from history. He especially loves the American Revolutionary period. His expertise comes in handy in his part-time job as a tour guide showing tourists the historical areas of the city and interpreting the events of that era. Michael has an unusual pastime. Each month, he purchases a pass on the city rail system ($70 a month). During the week, the pass has restricted use. However, on the weekends, parking at the stations is free, and there is unrestricted use of the railway. Michael gets on various trains, goes to the end of the line, and returns. He reads on the train, and when the train reaches the end of the line, he gets off and explores communities he never knew existed. Although his current travel adventures are limited to the "end of the line," he hopes to travel to other countries someday—alone. Michael says, "I don't have to have to compromise with someone else when I travel."

Michael writes speeches and presents them at a local chapter of Toastmasters International. His writing also includes the challenging Japanese form of poetry called haiku. (A haiku consists of three lines—the first line has five syllables, the second line has seven, and the third line has five.) Michael wrote this haiku while we ate lunch:

> Spring is on its way.
> Today is warm and sunny.
> Soon the birds will sing.

Michael sometimes wonders where he "fits in." He has been in therapy on and off since adolescence. The last course of psychotherapy, which was psychodynamically oriented, came to a halt because his insurance would no longer pay for it. "Therapy helps," Michael says, "because no one but the counselor hears what I have to say—it's like creating a living diary." Michael's positive therapy experience helped him come to terms with his parents' relationship. In his view, his father is simple—but also complex. Michael states, "My father had his dreams squashed by my mother. He had inventions, but people always told him he was grandiose. Maybe other people told great inventors that they were grandiose, too. My mother is afraid I'll develop my father's negative characteristics, like not being grounded. Maybe it's not so bad being not grounded—

it's surely more adventuresome." Michael believes that his mother "just settled" for his father. "My father may have just settled, too. I come from genes of people so afraid of being alone that they settle for anyone. The key is to embrace independence. You know how artists suffer? Loneliness may be the way I will have to suffer in order to achieve my goals."

Michael started a new job as an income maintenance welfare worker (a city position) 2 weeks ago. His salary is nearly double what he earned as a substitute teacher, plus he has benefits that allow him to join a gym, return to therapy, and continue his education.

Michael is in a master's degree program in counseling psychology, taking one course at a time while he works. He wants to get a PhD and become a psychotherapist. The first step, he explains, would be to become a guidance counselor for adolescents and young adults. He wants to help adolescents avoid the mistakes he made—for example, working as a substitute teacher for 6 years before returning to school himself. He reflects that substitute teaching made him lazy. The impending marriage and the realization that he needed more money compelled him to return to school. He wants to help, giving back to people because people helped him. Michael would advise young people not to spend lots of time trying to find themselves or let people deter them from what they want to do. Michael says, "Family can't be objective; follow your heart." After he gets his master's degree, Michael plans to move out of parents' home— and buy a duplex—when he has enough money. He would live in one unit and rent out or have his therapy practice in the other.

JOSETTE

Nancy petted Josette while we chatted. Charley took Josette for a walk before he settled down for his own interview. Josette, according to Michael, gives everyone in the family something to do. Josette has a calming effect on the entire family. The only regret Nancy has is that she didn't get a poodle earlier. Michael had desperately wanted a puppy when he was a boy—perhaps a nonshedding poodle would have helped him be less lonely and would not have affected his asthma. Aunt Flo takes care of Josette's veterinary and grooming bills.

EDITOR'S NOTES

Students always ask whether the Shores have been affected by the *Paradigm* books. Much to my surprise, the books seem to sit on a shelf, unread. Nancy stopped reading the first time she came across an upsetting viewpoint, Charley has shown no interest, and even Michael (who wants to be a therapist) is unfamiliar with the content. I did not have the opportunity to ask Rena, although Nancy says that neither one of the children has shown much interest in the texts. The Shores are obviously functioning better than they were 15 years ago, at least in part because of the children's maturity, the financial security, the psychopharmacological interventions, and Michael's psychotherapy. Nancy and Charley have their comforting routines—although, as they enter their later years, they may have new hurdles. The children's struggles are their own. I look forward to the arrival of the next generation of Shores and discovering how the three generations will interact and solve their problems. I hope Rena will forgive my mistake and that her husband will be comfortable with the Shores' 15-year contribution to the education of clinical social workers.

Author Index

Subject Index